Informatik aktuell

Herausgeber: W. Brauer
im Auftrag der Gesellschaft für Informatik (GI)

Informatik aktuell

Herausgeber: W. Brauer
im Auftrag der Gesellschaft für Informatik (GI)

Heinrich C. Mayr Roland Wagner (Hrsg.)

Objektorientierte Methoden für Informationssysteme

Fachtagung der GI-Fachgruppe EMISA
Klagenfurt, 7.–9. Juni 1993

Springer-Verlag
Berlin Heidelberg New York
London Paris Tokyo
Hong Kong Barcelona
Budapest

Herausgeber

Heinrich C. Mayr
Universität Klagenfurt, Institut für Informatik
Universitätsstr. 65–67, A-9022 Klagenfurt

Roland Wagner
Universität Linz, Institut für Informatik
Altenbergerstr. 69, A-4040 Linz

Programmkomitee:

Prof. Dr. H. D. Ehrich, Univ. Braunschweig
Dr. E. Gamma, Schweizerische Bankgesellschaft
Prof. Dr. W. Lamersdorf, Univ. Hamburg
Prof. Dr. G. Lausen, Univ. Mannheim
Prof. Dr. P. C. Lockemann, Univ. Karlsruhe
Prof. Dr. R. Mittermeir, Univ. Klagenfurt
Prof. Dr. H. P. Mössenböck, ETH Zürich
D. I. H. Thoma, Ciba-Geigy, Basel
Prof. Dr. G. Vossen, Univ. Gießen
Prof. Dr. R. Wagner, Univ. Linz (Vorsitz)

Weitere Gutachter:

Mag. Franz Burger, Univ. Linz
D. I. Christian Gierlinger, Univ. Linz
Univ. Doz. Dr. Gerti Kappel, Univ. Linz
Dr. Roland Kaschek, Univ. Klagenfurt
Mag. Claudia Kohl, Univ. Klagenfurt
Mag. Werner Retschitzegger, Univ. Linz
D. I. Reinhard Schauer, Univ. Linz
Mag. Siegfried Schönberger, Univ. Linz

CR Subject Classification (1993): D.1.5, D.2.1, D.2.10, H.1.0, J.6

ISBN-13: 978-3-540-56775-2 e-ISBN-13: 978-3-642-78270-1
DOI: 10.1007/978-3-642-78270-1

Dieses Werk ist urheberrechtlich geschützt. Die dadurch begründeten Rechte, insbesondere die der Übersetzung, des Nachdrucks, des Vortrags, der Entnahme von Abbildungen und Tabellen, der Funksendung, der Mikroverfilmung oder der Vervielfältigung auf anderen Wegen und der Speicherung in Datenverarbeitungsanlagen, bleiben, auch bei nur auszugsweiser Verwertung, vorbehalten. Eine Vervielfältigung dieses Werkes oder von Teilen dieses Werkes ist auch im Einzelfall nur in den Grenzen der gesetzlichen Bestimmungen des Urheberrechtsgesetzes der Bundesrepublik Deutschland vom 9. September 1965 in der jeweils geltenden Fassung zulässig. Sie ist grundsätzlich vergütungspflichtig. Zuwiderhandlungen unterliegen den Strafbestimmungen des Urheberrechtsgesetzes.

© Springer-Verlag Berlin Heidelberg 1993

Satz: Reproduktionsfertige Vorlage vom Autor/Herausgeber

33/3140-543210 – Gedruckt auf säurefreiem Papier

Vorwort

Seit mehr als zehn Jahren befaßt sich die Fachgruppe EMISA (Entwicklungsmethoden für Informationssysteme und deren Anwendung) der deutschen Gesellschaft für Informatik mit Methoden und Modellen für den Entwurf und die Entwicklung von Informationssystemen. In einer langen Serie von Workshops und Fachtagungen wurde dabei stets darauf hingearbeitet, die in diesem Bereich erforderliche formale Fundierung und Präzision mit der für die betriebliche Praxis notwendigen Praktikabilität zu verbinden.

Dies gilt auch für die Fachtagung "Objektorientierte Methoden für Informationssysteme", deren Beiträge im vorliegenden Band zusammengefaßt sind. Es ging uns darum, das heute in aller Munde propagierte Paradigma der Objektorientierung zu durchleuchten und insbesondere den Stand objektorientierter Methoden für Entwurf und Entwicklung von Informationssystemen im deutschsprachigen Raum festzustellen. Dies sollte wiederum aus der pragmatischen Verwendungssicht einerseits und aus grundlagenorientierter theoretischer Sicht andererseits erfolgen.

Wie die Reaktion auf unseren Call for Papers zeigte, gibt es im deutschsprachigen Raum ein breites Spektrum von Aktivitäten und Erfahrungen. Aus den eingereichten Beiträgen wurde für die Tagung auf der Basis von Beurteilungen durch jeweils drei Gutachter etwa ein Drittel ausgewählt. Ein Schwerpunkt liegt dabei auf Berichten über Erfahrungen und Anwendungen, in denen durchaus auch - wie wir es erwartet hatten - kritische Anmerkungen zu finden sind. Einen weiteren Schwerpunkt bilden Konzept-Weiterentwicklungen sowie Ansätze für spezifische Problemstellungen.

Inhalt und Qualität der hier veröffentlichten Beiträge veranlassen uns zur Überzeugung, daß die Fachgruppe EMISA mit der Fachtagung und dem vorliegenden Tagungsband einen wichtigen Beitrag zur Fortentwicklung und zum Einsatz objektorientierter Methoden im Bereich des Entwurfs und der Entwicklung von Informationssystemen leistet.

Wir danken allen, die zur Vorbereitung und Durchführung der Tagung beigetragen haben, insbesondere natürlich den Autoren der Beiträge und den Begutachtern.

Klagenfurt und Linz im März 1993

Heinrich C. Mayr, Roland Wagner

Inhalt

Eingeladene Vorträge

Methodik

Erfahrungen und Anwendungen

Methoden und Werkzeuge

Spezielle Konzepte

Objekt-Orientierung und CIM

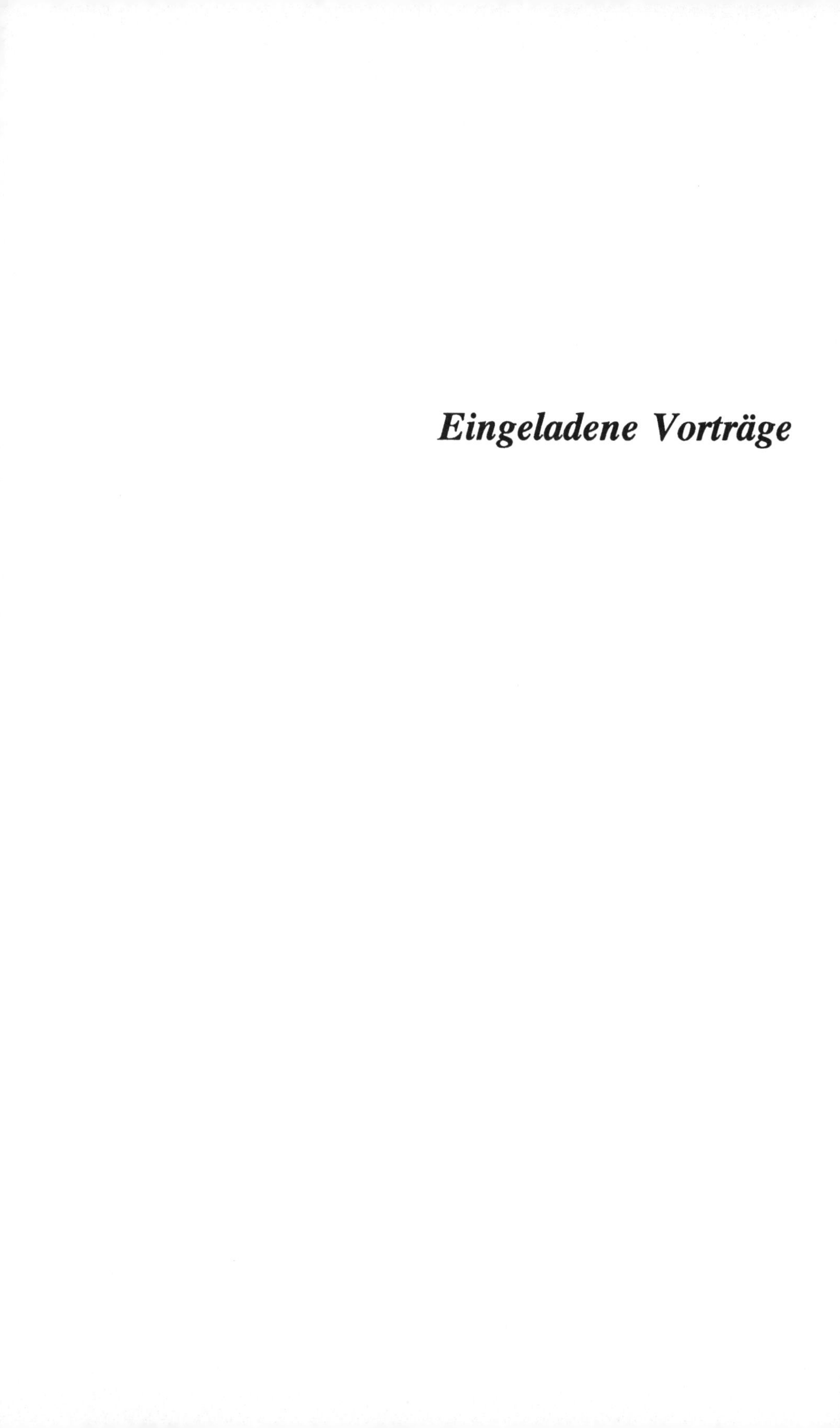

Eingeladene Vorträge

Object Orientation and Conceptual Modeling

Stefano Spaccapietra
Ecole Polytechnique Fédérale (EPFL)
Laboratoire Bases de données - DI
Ch 1015 Lausanne *spaccapietra@elma.epfl.ch*

Christine Parent, Marcos Sunye, Kokou Yétongnon
Université de Bourgogne, Département Informatique, B.P. 138,
21004 Dijon Cedex, France *badine@satie.u-bourgogne.fr*

1. Introduction

The object oriented (OO) approach is very popular nowadays. It has proved to be a powerful and practical programming paradigm for the development of large and complex software systems, including database management systems (DBMS). Among its many benefits are significant improvements in modularity, reusability, flexibility, and extensibility. The database community has already taken advantage of the OO approach and produced a number of OO DBMSs, much faster than in the case of the previous generation of relational systems.

Quite naturally, there has been a trend to export the OO paradigm from system programming to database modeling. There are several good reasons for this. The most obvious one is to avoid a new impedence mismatch problem, i.e. the DBMS reasoning with the OO paradigm and the user reasoning with another one. This is the reason why so many users up to now have been trained in relational database modeling. The second good reason is that OO concepts are much closer to the human mental model of the real world than the relational ones. It is therefore sound to promote OO modeling with respect to modeling paradigms of traditional DBMSs. A third reason is that many existing database design methods were already based on some variant of the entity-relationship (ER) approach, which makes it easy to move to more up to date technology by replacing entities with objects. OO design methods have thus been marketed even faster than OO DBMSs. One more aspect which deserves to be emphasized is that modern applications in data intensive fields must deal with highly structured and interrelated information objects. Examples may be found in many domains, including computer aided design/computer aided manufacturing (CAD/CAM), office automation, computer integrated manufacturing (CIM), robotics, geographic systems. These applications have the same complexity as large software systems, and therefore, OO technology has naturally been advocated as a key to their efficient design and implementation.

Unfortunately, OO technology applied to information systems has not, so far, completely fulfilled these expectations. When moving a technology from one domain to another one, existing concepts have most often to be reshaped to cope with the new environment, and new concepts have to be added to achieve full power with respect to the new goals. As an example of the former, as user's profile changes from system programmers to application designers and end users, some OO features may place an additional burden on end users. Data encapsulation of objects, for instance, is a highly desirable feature for efficient design management at the implementation level. It allows to decompose the design process and let each designer independently develop his/her part. Database practice, on the contrary, is based on the principle of open access to information to everybody. Therefore, encapsulation needs to be partly traded off for easy access to attributes, so that general purpose query languages (SQL-like or others) may be implemented.

As far as database and information system modeling are concerned, the primary concern is on the descriptive power of the data model. While system programming primarily aims at efficiency, database designers focus on accuracy of representation: elaborating a description of the reality of interest which captures as much as possible of the semantics of data, independently of any implementation consideration, and which is as close as possible to user's perception. This activity is called conceptual design. Its result serves as input specifications for further steps concerning logical design (the elaboration of a corresponding representation of data and performance related specifications oriented towards implementation on some specific DBMS) and physical design (dealing with storage structures and efficiency of file access mechanisms). As discussed hereinafter, the OO paradigm needs additional concepts to achieve full representational power (namely, to acquire adequate concepts for conceptual representation of associations among objects). This paper is precisely devoted to bridging the gap between the OO paradigm and its successful usage for the development of database applications.

We first contrast the features of object orientation with the requirements of conceptual modeling of data structures (objects and associations). This will point onto some deficiencies as: inadequate representation of associations, lack of proper support for generic data manipulations, lack of concepts for the description of the global application behavior. Extending the OO paradigm beyond these limits results in what is nowadays known as an object+relationship (OR) modeling approach. OR models intend to combine the advantages of OO models with those provided by traditional research in database modeling: semantic data models, for the description of data structures, and Petri net-like approaches for the description of the behavior of an information system. Second, we discuss data manipulation languages (DML), which complement the data model to provide for full and consistent capabilities for user-DBMS interactions. The discussion will be in terms of algebraic query languages, which focus on the operations needed for the manipulation of objects and associations.

The remainder of the paper is organized as follows. In the next section we examine the requirements of conceptual modeling of applications and analyze the OO approach from the data modeling perspective. In section 3 we discuss the issues relevant for the definition of data manipulation languages for defining, accessing, and managing complex objects databases. Section 4 concludes the paper.

2. Conceptual application modeling

As stated above, the major concern in conceptual modeling of application objects is to create representations which are close to reality, and independent from implementation issues. Conceptual modeling is thus made understandable by users (they need not to know about peculiarities of DBMS systems). This makes easier to check that the resulting design meets users requirements. It also improves the chances of a correct design, by separating representational issues from implementation issues. Finally, it allows to change the implementation without having to modify the conceptual schema.

Section 2.1 discusses requirements of database applications for conceptual modeling of both static (data structures) and dynamic (behavioral) aspects. The extent to which traditional data models fulfil these requirements is briefly surveyed in section 2.2. A similar evaluation for OO models is the subject of section 2.3. The last section, 2.4, introduces the characteristics of an OR model which is intended to improve over OO models towards fully supporting application requirements.

2.1. Applications modeling requirements

Database applications are characterized by their need to represent, relate and manipulate objects with complex information structures. The first step in the representation process is the identification of the objects of interest, which determines what is usually called the universe of discourse. This identification process is non deterministic: its result depends on the point of view of the designer, i.e. on the semantics the designer attaches to phenomena (s)he observes. The next step is typically based on the classification abstraction: objects considered to some extent as similar are collected into classes. Classes are described by object types. Attributes represent the static properties attached to objects in a class. The attribute structure composing an object type can be described by a tree whose root is the object type, whose branches are of variable and unrestricted length, and whose nodes represent the components of the object type. Such objects are usually called **complex objects**, to contrast them with the simple flat objects supported by the relational approach (the tuples). Each object has a unique object identity (oid), and a composite value. The object value is composed from the atomic values attached to the leaves of the tree, according to the structure of the set of attributes attached to its object type. The object identity is system defined (not visible to users) and allows to denote objects independently from their value. From the manipulation point of view, it is essential that objects may be manipulated as a whole logical unit, irrespectively of their complexity, and accessed through any of their components. An example of complex object type is given below (figure 1).

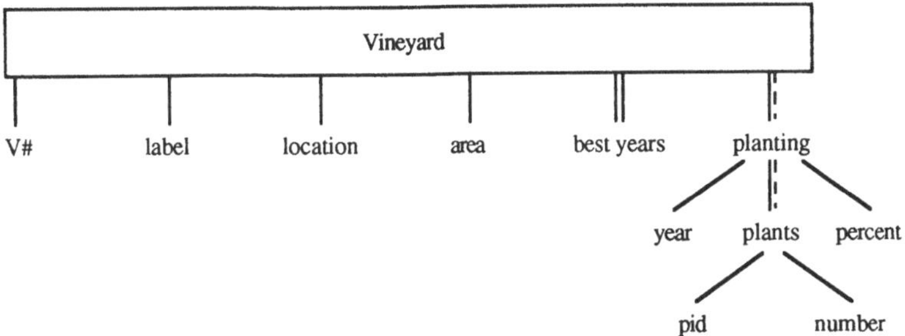

Figure 1: a complex object type

The diagram uses the following graphical notations: a single straight line denotes a monovalued attribute or role, a double line (one straight, one dotted) denotes a multivalued mandatory attribute or role, a double dotted line denotes a multivalued optional attribute or role. V, O and W are role names.
The Vineyard object type includes a set of attributes to describe its label, the location of the vineyard, and the size of the area planted. It also includes a multivalued attribute "best years" to record good harvest years for each vineyard. Whenever a vineyard is planted, in total or in part, the data base records the year of the planting, the percentage of the vineyard that is planted and the plants (the plant brand identification and the number of plants planted). These informations together form a complex multivalued attribute "planting". This attribute is multivalued, as the same vineyard may undergo different plantations over different years.

As the same objects are shared by different applications, they may be perceived by these applications in different ways. Facilities for allowing multiple perceptions of objects are therefore essential to avoid modeling conflicts. This includes the possibility for each application to attach its specific set of properties to an object, while the database keeps the knowledge that the object is unique despite its different representations. Most important is the ability to support different representational structures for the same phenomena: this will allow a designer to represent something as an object, while for another designerthe same thing is to be represented as an attribute of some other object. Similarly for the choice between object (or attribute) and relationship, for those model which provide a relatioship concept. Equally important is the ability to define different classification schemes, i.e. different object types and associations in between.

For example, let us consider a database for the management of a garage. From the receptionist's point of view, cars may be perceived as single objects, grouped in a class described by the Recep-Car object type, with properties including the description of the engine and body of the car (see figure 2). From the mechanic's point of view, engines and bodies may be perceived as independent objects and described as such in Engine and Body object types. Despite their difference, both points of view are modeling the same reality. The extent to which a modeling approach supports multiple points of view defines the degree of freedom, for an application, to define its own perception of the database without having to comply with the perceptions of other applications sharing the same database.

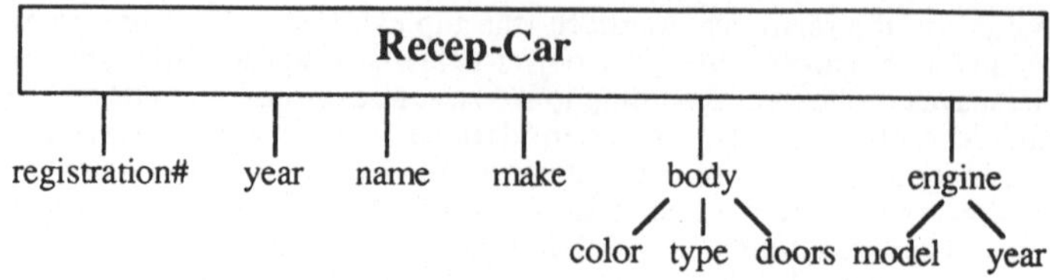

Figure 2: the car object type, as seen by the receptionist

Supporting multiple perceptions on complex objects is but the first step in representational power. Objects do not live in isolation; they are related to, and interact with, other objects. For instance, if the above garage management application is to deal also with car owners as customers, the database will include a Customer object type, whose objects will be associated to car objects to express the ownership association. Research on semantic data models has shown that there are several kinds of associations which are candidate for inclusion in a data model. They range from generic associations, whose semantics is known only to the application, not to the DBMS, to associations having a specific predefined semantics: the component (part-of) association, the generalization (is-a) association, etc [Brodie 84]. The above car ownership association is an example of the generic type. Existing data models differ in the support of association types, as they differ in the support of complex objects.

Objects, properties and associations characterize the capability of a data model to describe data structures. With respect to dynamic modeling, application requirements command capabilities to describe rules governing the behavior of objects as well as rules governing the behavior of applications. The former express how an object may evolve with time and what operations may be performed on it. Each object type bears such a description. The latter allows the description of interactions among objects and is typically based on the concepts of event, condition and action: for each event to which the database should react, a rule describes the pre- and post-conditions attached to the event and the corresponding actions to be performed. Object-specific operations also play an important role in supporting data manipulation requirements. However, they need to be complemented with generic query and update languages to support generic and ad-hoc manipulations.

2.2. Traditional data models

Current relational DBMS poorly respond to the above requirements. They only support flat data structures: relations, whose components are restricted to atomic value attributes (this restriction is known as the first normal form rule). An object in a relation (a tuple) is a set of atomic values. Composite attributes are not allowed: for instance, it is not possible to specify a date attribute as composed of day, month and year attributes. Multivalued attributes are not allowed: for instance, it is not possible to associate several values to a phone# attribute. The description of an object cannot be expressed as a self contained block of information, it is instead spread over several relations. A major hindrance of such a solution is that the resulting representations do not parallel the structure of the objects being modeled as perceived by users. Hence the problems users have in understanding a relational representation and in manipulating a relational database. Moreover, relational DBMS ignore associations. These have to be represented and managed by applications. Only the most recent versions of some major relational DBMS include a limited support for associations in the form of a capability to specify referential integrity constraints and have them checked by the system. As far as dynamic aspects are concerned, no specification mechanism is provided by relational DBMS. Dynamics is entirely within application programs. Inversely, relational DBMS support a variety of data manipulation languages: the relational algebra and calculus, as theoretical basis, SQL and QUEL as textual user oriented DML, and QBE as graphical language. Using DML functionalities, users may define their own view over the relations in the database schema. Multiple perceptions of the same objects are thus easily defined.

Many extensions or alternatives to the traditional relational data model have been proposed in order to: better capture the semantics of the real world and allow the representation of complex and/or composite objects. The most notable of these models are nested relational models (also known as NF2: non first normal form) and semantic data models. Nested relational models [Abiteboul 89] partially meet applications requirements by admitting relation-valued attributes: the value of an attribute in a tuple may be a set of tuples. This in essence relaxes the relational first normal form restriction. Relation-valued attributes can be accessed and/or retrieved in the same manner as relations. However, with respect to complex object management, NF2 models still have a major restriction in the fact that the structure of an object is purely hierarchical: sharing of components is not supported and no cycles are allowed in the structure of an object (a component cannot be of the same type as the composed object). Furthermore, facilities for restructuring a nested relation to define a different point of view are limited. Thus, NF2 models are not fully appropriate for representing complex objects and multiple perceptions. They also ignore dynamic aspects.

The goal of semantic data models has been to represent the semantics of the real world as closely as possible. However, the emphasis put on data description has not found an equivalent counterpart in the data manipulation area. Semantic models are therefore mainly used in the initial phase of database design to produce a conceptual representation of the future database. This initial representation is then translated into a lower level target model (e.g. relational, OO, etc) to be implemented onto a DBMS. An example of semantic data model is provided by extended ER models, which make use of the concepts of entity, relationship, attribute, generalization and constraint to closely represent the properties of real world objects and associations in between. An entity is the database representation of an object, with all its information attached: a complex object can be represented as a single entity. Relationships represent generic associations among two or more objects. Generalization is a specific association type used to specify that entities in one class (the sub-class) are also represented in another class (the super-class). For instance, a generalization link (also called an is-a link) associating a Sport-car entity type to a Car entity type specifies that each object in the former class also belongs to the latter class (i.e., each sport-car is a car). The ER approach has not developed concepts for the description of behavioral aspects. Dynamic rules may be expressed using associated constraint specification languages (usually based on first order logic), but no provision is made for specification of object specific operations. From the data manipulation perspective, a few languages have been proposed but none of them has been implemented in a commercial DBMS. As for support of multiple perceptions, this is achieved to a great extent [Spaccapietra 92], but work remains to be done, as in the NF2 case, on restructuring operations.

2.3. OO modeling

In the database area, the OO approach is the first significant attempt to define a data model which simultaneously takes into account both structural and behavioral specifications. As such, it definitely improves the state of the art in database modeling. We examine here how it matches application requirements.

From the data modeling perspective, the key features of the OO approach are: object identity, complex data structures, abstract data types and inheritance. The concept of object identity (oid) is used to associate each object with a unique identity. This oid distiguishes the object from other objects without having to rely on user defined values. This definitely improves denotational facilities available to applications. User defined identifiers provide the necessary complementary denotation mechanism, but they cannot safely be used as oids without confusing identity and data values [Khoshafian 90]. For example updating an attribute which is (part of) a key is not allowed even though it is a value attribute with a specific meaning as other value attributes.

Objects may be as complex as needed in an OO schema. OO models allow unrestricted iterative decomposition of an object into components. Moreover, they allow a component of an object to be an object itself (i.e., with its own identity) rather than a value attribute. Component objects may be of the same type as the object they are part of. Objects whose

composition includes other objects are hereinafter termed **composite objects**. Conversely, **atomic object** will denote an object whose components are all value attributes. This introduces a clear difference between OO models, supporting complex and composite objects, and closely related extended ER models, which support complex objects but do not support composite objects. Allowing composite objects is the OO mechanism to support multiple perceptions of the same object. Every object can at the same time be an object on its own and serve as a component within another object. This composition association is materialized by a reference attribute which points from the composed object to the component object. The domain of a reference attribute is the set of oids representing the objects referred to by the attribute. References are directed one-way links from a composite object to its components. For example, if the composition of a Car includes a Body and an Engine, where Car, Body and Engine are three object types, then this fact can be expressed through two reference attributes body and engine in the Car object type (see figure 3).
It should be noted that composite objects offer a limited flexibility in supporting multiple perceptions. For instance, it would not always be straigthforward to add to the Engine object type a reference to Car to describe the cars which possess this engine, while ensuring that this reference holds a value consistent with the values in the (inverse) references from Car to Engine.

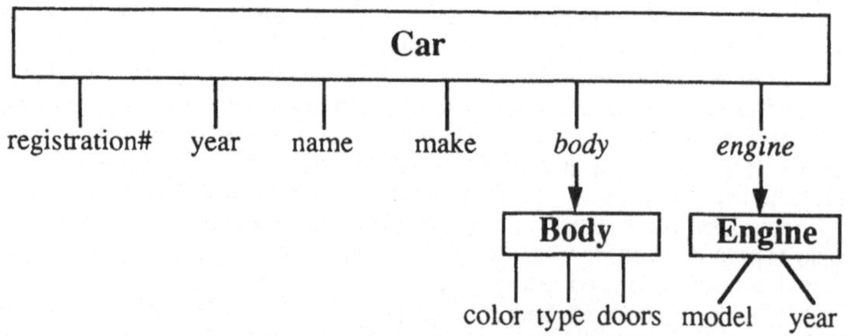

Figure 3: Car as a composite object type
(arrows with italic labels represent reference attributes)

Besides composition, OO models capabilities to express associations only include the inheritance link. An inheritance link between two object classes describes a sub-class / super-class relationship, which means that all objects of the sub-class are also objects of the super-class. It corresponds to the generalization association. Most often, the link is intended for reuse of structural (attributes) as well as behavioral (methods) definitions. The sub-type inherits these definitions from the super-type (downward inheritance). Thus, inheritance may be used as a mechanism for top-down design of a hierarchy of object types, where each design level refines the definitions (super-class) of the upper level into a set of sub-class definitions. For instance, the description of a car class can easily be established by refining the more general definition of a vehicle class. Refinement can be either in terms of adding new attributes or methods which are specific to cars and not valid for vehicles in general, or in terms of redefining existing attributes and/or methods attached to vehicle to make them more specific to cars.

Abstract data types convey the idea that the structural description of a set of objects (showing the properties they share) has to be complemented with the definition of the operations which can manipulate the objects. This allows to capture both static and dynamic aspects of objects. The definitions of the allowed operations (the methods, in OO terminology) represent the interface of the abstract data type. Essentially, this interface provides users with information on how to use the objects but not on how the objects are implemented. Furthermore, abstract data types use the concept of data encapsulation to separate implementation details from the usage of an object and to ensure that the only operations that can be performed on the objects are those specified in the interface.

While the above capabilities meet application requirements, they do not meet all of them. As the name says, OO main concern is on object description. From this point of view

OO models do provide what is needed. On the contrary, their description of associations is far too restricted. There exist only two kinds of specific associations: composition and generalization. The main concern of OO programming systems is more on reusing the code segments that are used to implement properties and methods than on achieving an accurate description of real world objects. Composition and inheritance links are essentially used to avoid redundant specifications of data structures and operations. The concept of attribute is used as a unifying abstraction both for describing object properties (value attributes) and for embodying associations between objects (reference attributes). As Albano et al. pointed out [Albano 91], the main advantage of this unification is to simplify system implementation by using the same access mechanism to manipulate both attributes and associations. This trade off between implementation efficiency and conceptual capability reduces the expressive power of the model and penalizes designers of database systems.

Creating appropriate conceptual representations can not be achieved using only the composition and inheritance associations. To illustrate this, consider the already mentioned ownership association between the object types Car and Person. Using reference attributes (composition) to express this generic association may yield many possible representations, including the following ones:

1/ a reference from Person to Car,
2/ a reference from Car to Person,
3/ cross references between Person and Car,
4/ a new Ownership object is created to include a reference to Person and another one to Car,
5/ a new Ownership object is created which is linked by cross references to both Person and Car.

Composition is a directed association. It can not properly describe, at the conceptual level, a generic association which is non directed by definition. A car is not a component of a person, and vice versa. On the other hand, composition may be used to implement the generic association. It is, indeed, when implementation aspects are considered that a choice among the above solutions can be made on the basis of performance criteria and the available information on the most frequently used access paths.

Inadequate representation is not the only drawback of using reference attributes to express generic associations. It also does not allow to express declaratively semantic information attached to the different roles in an association. Cardinality constraints (how many cars a person may own? how many owners a car may have?) are an example of information which, in the OO approach, has to be coded in the implementation of the methods which are used to manipulate the objects, and is therefore hidden from the data description point of view. Second, the representation of the association is spread over the definitions of the objects participating in it. In some of the above solutions, the definition of the Ownership association is partially specified in each of the objects Person and Car. This does not promote the definition of application objects in an independent and incremental fashion: to establish a new association among existing objects may require the modification of the definition of these objects. Finally, reference attributes are not appropriate for expressing n-ary associations or associations which have attributes.

It has already been pointed out that, besides the major hindrances of using reference attributes to express associations, the OO approach fails in meeting applications requirements on two more issues. The first one is providing for generic data manipulation languages. To this extent, the encapsulation principle has been softened to allow the development of OO SQL-like languages. The second weakness is on description of global application dynamics: how application events are monitored by the system and how they have to be taken care of with respect to the evolution of the database. A new stream of research on so-called active databases is developing OO solutions to this problem. A more traditional approach is to combine the OO paradigm with some well-known mechanism (Petri nets, for instance) which has been proved to satisfy these requirements. Enhacements to overcome the above limitations are examined in the next section.

2.4. Object relationship models

Recently, researchers have attempted to make up for the above mentioned structural limitations of object orientation in database application by including constructs for representing associations and integrity constraints in object oriented models [Rumbaugh 87, Albano 91]. Rumbaugh et al have presented an extended object oriented modeling technique which they have used to support the conceptual design and implementation of software systems. In addition to the usual features of OO models, their model supports three types of relationships which have the same meaning as their semantic data model counterparts: generalization, aggregation, and generic association. However, the model limits all relationships to binary links between object classes. Another notion that is included in their model is the cardinality concept which is used to indicate the number of objects of one class that can be related to an object of the other class. Albano et al. have also proposed mechanisms for the inclusion of relationships and integrity constraints in a strongly typed object oriented database programming language. Their extensions to the OO model are more comprehensive than the proposal in [Rumbaugh 87]. They offer capabilities for expressing n-ary relationships and relationships which have their own attributes. Their model also incorporates mechanisms for expressing a large variety of integrity constraints. For example, inclusion and disjointness constraints can be defined between object classes. Referential constraints can be specified on a class to ensure that whenever an object is inserted into a class, all the objects used as components are elements of the corresponding classes.

OO models which are extended to include the concept of generic relationships are hereinafter called object-relationship (OR) models. Another way to arrive at an OR model is turning an extended ER model into an OR model. By constrast to the proposal of Albano et al., which aims to embed relationship capabilities in a strongly typed OO programming language, this alternative proposal starts with the well-known and largely favoured by database designers, ER approach, which has specific capabilities for representing the semantics of relationships, and extends it to enable description of complex and/or composite objects. The success of the ER paradigm has many reasons: it is powerful but still simple (few concepts), its basic concepts are easily understood by users, database entities correspond to real world objects, database schemas may be illustrated with easy to read diagrams. Combining the ER paradigm with OO behavioral modeling concepts (i.e. the attachment of methods to entity and relationship types) results in complementing a tool which has been designed for conceptual modeling with features it still lacks. This might be the most profitable way to achieve the best conceptual OR model database designers are looking for.

Extended ER approaches [Elmasri 85, Parent 92] model real world objects with entity types. They use relationship types to model generic associations between two or more entities (objects). Like OO models, they provide an object identity for each entity and structural capabilities for the description of complex objects. In fact, regarding object modeling, the fundamental difference between existing extended ER approaches and the OO approach is that the ER paradigm restricts the components of an object to be attributes while the OO paradigm allows components to be objects. If objects of type B are part of objects of type A, then the ER representation will show two entity types, A and B, linked by a relationship R whose semantics will be known to the application as "B is component of A". This also holds for recursively composite objects, where a component of an object of type A is an object of the same type A. In other words, the composition association is not supported in ER and is replaced by a generic association (while OO, as stated above, does exactly the inverse).

The ER separation between objects and attributes relies on the assumption that, when a designer designates something in the real world as an object, whatever information (s)he wants to keep on this object has to be considered as a property of the object, hence represented as an attribute. The fact that another designer classifies the same reality in some other way should not inhibit the first perception. Instead of using composite objects, the OR model we favour (named ERC+ [Parent 92]) uses a more flexible mechanism to support multiple perceptions: derived entity types (also called virtual classes, or views). Similar to views in relational systems, a derived entity type represents objects which, through some derivation rule expressed in the OR data manipulation language, are built from other objects and relationships of the data base. Derived entity types model virtual objects in the sense that they do not add new objects to the database, but define a new point of view over existing information.

To illustrate how this mechanism supports multiple perceptions, let us consider again the garage example. The goal is to support both the receptionist's point of view (one object class, Recep-Car, with attributes including body and engine) and the mechanic's one (where Car, Body and Engine are object classes). The modeling process first represents by an entity type whatever is seen as an object class at least by one user. Next, relationships are defined among these entity types to represent generic and composition associations. The OR schema for the garage database will show three entity types, Car, Body, Engine, related by two relationships, Car-Body and Car-Engine. The attributes attached to each entity type are those defined by designers, except for those attributes which have been attached to a related "component" entity type. The Car entity type does not include information about the engine and body of the car (see figure 4). This information is available in the Engine and Body entity types, and may be accessed from the car entities via the relationships. The resulting structure forms the basic schema, the conceptual description of database objects. Derived entity types are added to the basic schema to represent objects which are perceived by designers differently from the structure in the basic schema. This is the case for cars as seen by the receptionist. A derived entity type, Recep-Car, is defined to merge in a single virtual entity type the information from the three basic entity types. Its schema is the one represented in figure 2. The derivation rule in this case specifies a relationship-join operation: this operation builds a derived entity type which has all the information in some existing entity type, plus the information in the entity types connected to the former through a specified relationship. The receptionist will use the derived entity type for his/her interactions with the database.
Relationships and the derivation mechanism offer more flexibility than OO composite objects. If A and B are two related object types, it is easy to define a view where A has B as component attribute and a view where B has A as component attribute. For instance, if the ownership relationship links Person and Car, relationship-join operations may build both Person-with-cars (each person with the cars (s)he owns) or Car-with-persons (each car with its owners), depending on the order of the operands. This is harder to achieve relying on composite objects, because of the inherent direction of the composition link.

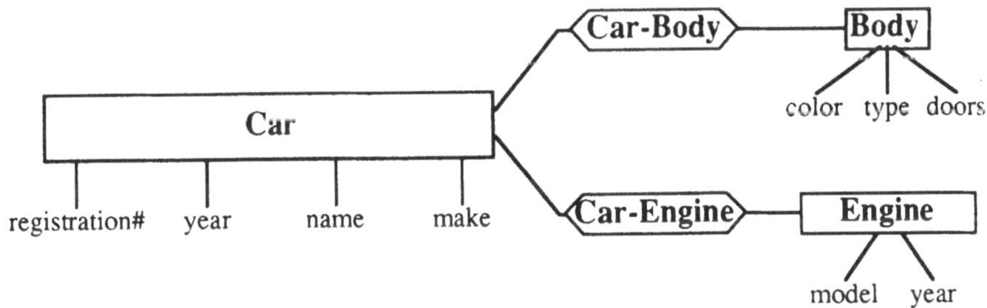

Figure 4: the garage conceptual schema described with objects and relationships
(diamond-shaped boxes represent relationship types)

The generalization association is also supported by OR models. The ERC+ model, for instance, uses it to express sub-class/super-class relationships. However, it does not associate it with an implicit inheritance mechanism. Inheritance has to be asked for explicitly as part of the database manipulation. Again, this allows for more flexibility, by letting the user specify which inheritance (downward, upward), if any, (s)he wants. Moreover, ERC+ supports another association type, called the may-be-a link, to express that objects may belong to two classes (which is called multi-instantiation), without one class being a sub-class of the other. An example of an ERC+ schema is given in figure 5.

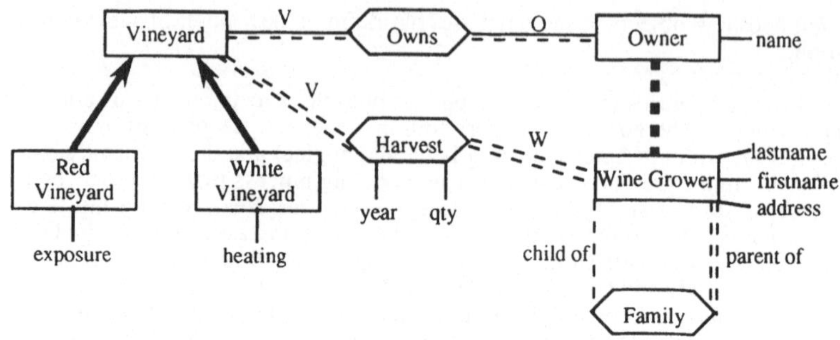

Figure 5: an ERC+ schema for a vineyard database
(not showing Vineyard attributes)

- Red Vineyard: this entity type is a sub-class of Vineyard. In addition to the attributes that it can inherit from Vineyard, it has a specific attribute to describe the exposure of each red vineyard to the sun light.
- White Vineyard: in addition to the inheritable attributes, White Vineyard includes a specific attribute "heating" to describe if there is any device in the vineyard to prevent spring frosts.
- Owner: it is an entity type used to represent vineyards owners. For each owner, its name is recorded.
- Wine Grower: for each wine grower the database stores its lastname, firstname, and address. A wine grower may also be an owner and vice versa. Thus, a may-be-a link is drawn between the entity types Owner and Wine Grower in the diagram.

The vineyard database also contains three relationship types: "Owns" which links the entity types Vineyard and Owner, "Harvest" which connects the entity type Wine Grower to Vineyard, and a cyclic relationship "Family" on the entity type Wine Grower. Note that the relationship type "Harvest" has two simple attributes to describe the year of a harvest and the quantity harvested.

3. Objects manipulation languages

Most of actual OO data models, extended ER models and OR models share the same new concepts: object identity, generalizations, objects with complex structure, composition links and/or more general relationship links between objects. This section discusses the guidelines and requirements for data manipulation languages for managing these new concepts.

One of the major principles of manipulation languages is the closure property, which requires the result of any operation to be of the same type as the operands. This allows to build expressions involving nested operators. In earlier OO models everything was either an object or a value of an object. As operators are performed on classes of objects, the result of any operation is a class of objects. In extended ER models there are several basic concepts: entity type, relationship type, attribute or value. Entity types are the main kind of objects, thus languages provide operators for manipulating them. In order to keep ER languages from being very complex, operations for manipulating relationships are typically not provided by these languages. Instead, attributes and relationships are queried through the entities to which they are bound.

Each new concept generates in the data manipulation languages either new capabilities (for instance, the crossing of reference attributes or of relationships) or modifications of the relational operators (for instance, the union of objects is based upon their oids). Those novelties are discussed hereinafter.

• Object identities (Oids)

The inclusion of oids in data models requires the addition of a new comparison operation and the modification of the usual set operations to handle objects with identities. Firstly, in order to be able to express cyclic queries involving twice the same object, a new equality operator is defined. For example, in a chess tournament one could want to verify if there is no error in the planning by asking: "Is there a player who is scheduled to play against him/her-self?"

Object based DMLs must provide two equality comparison operators:
- o1==o2 which is true when o1 and o2 denote the same object (same oid), irrespectively of their values,
- o1=o2 which is true when the values of o1 and o2 are the same.

Secondly, set operators (union, difference, intersection) of the relational model need to be modified, as their original definition is value oriented. In the relational data model, a relation cannot contain two identical tuples. In object data models, each object has a specific identity and thus two objects having the same value can coexist in the same class. Object set operators must therefore be based on the comparison of the oids and not on the comparison of values. To illustrate this, consider the following example:

- Union in the relational data model:

R1: {v1, v2, v3}
R2: {v1, v2, v4}
R1 ∪ R2 = {v1, v2, v3, v4}

- Union in data models with oids:

E1: {<o1, v1>, <o2, v2>, <o3, v3> }
E2: {<o1, v1>, <o2', v2>, <o4, v4>}
where **<oi, vi>** represents an object: **oi** is its oid and **vi** its value.
E1 ∪ E2 = {<o1, v1>, <o2, v2>, <o3, v3>, <o2', v2>, <o4, v4>}

Using comparison operations based on oids, the union operation may be performed on two classes containing objects that have the same identity but different values. What will be the values of the resulting objects in the following example?

E1: {<o1, v1>, <o3, v3>}
E2: {<o1, v2>, <o4, v4>}
E1 ∪ E2 : {<o1, f(v1,v2)>, <o3, v3>, <o4, v4>}

The objects identified by o1 above represent two different views of the same real world object. For instance, in a university database, E1 and E2 may represent a Faculty entity type and a Student entity type, respectively. o1 represents both a faculty and a student (a PhD student who teaches a course). The value corresponding to the resulting object o1 in the union of E1 and E2 is neither v1 nor v2. It is instead composed of both v1 and v2. There is no definite rule to fix how this resulting value is composed: the result depends upon the built-in rules of the data manipulation language being considered.

Lastly, with relational model, relations used as operands of set operators must have the same type (same set of attributes) to allow the comparison of their values. With object models, on the contrary, set operations are allowed to have operands with different associated types. Existing OO DMLs choose different solutions for defining the type associated with the result of a union: it can be made of either the common attributes of the operands (or the nearest common ancestor in the generalization hierarchy) [Loizou 91, Vrbsky 89] or the union of all their attributes. In ERC+ the latter solution has been adopted because it provides more descriptive information (see the discussion below about placing the result into the generalization graph).

• <u>Generalization and multi-instantiation</u>

The inclusion of the concepts of generalization and multi-instantiation in a data model generates two new aspects that must be taken into account by DMLs associated with the model: inheritance of class properties and placement of the result of a query in the generalization graph.

Inheritance applies to attributes and methods as well as to links between object classes. These links are: reference links (or composition links) in OO models and relationship, generalization and multi-instantiation links in ER models. Inheritance through generalization links is usually descending (downward from the super-class to the sub-class): each object of a sub-class is also an object of the super-class and inherits the properties associated with the objects of the super-class. But ascending inheritance can also be useful. It is a mechanism by which the properties of the sub-class object are attached to the corresponding object (having the same oid) in the super-class. For example, in the vineyard database one can wish to produce a list of all the vineyards by listing for each vineyard its properties together with the exposure attribute if it is a red vineyard, or with the heating attribute if it is a white one.

With explicit inheritance, whenever a user wants to use an attribute or a property of a super-class or a sub-class, (s)he must make an explicit reference to the name of the class to which the attribute belongs. By contrast, with implicit inheritance users can use properties of the super- or sub-class and let the system fill in the references of the corresponding classes. Most user friendly DMLs such as SQL-like and graphical languages support implicit descending inheritance. This lightens the burden of writing queries: users can quote any property of any super-class, the system will look for it upward in the generalization hierarchy.

In order to get complete DMLs (with descending and ascending inheritance), the ERC+ algebra offers descending and ascending inheritance through is-a links. May-be-a links are not oriented, thus inheritance is also possible in both directions. In order to solve the ambiguity which may arise when an entity type has several generic entity types which have properties with the same name, inheritance in the ERC+ algebra is explicit: an identity-join operator allows users to join two entity types connected by a generalization or multi-intanciation link.

The result of a query is an object class; thus it has to be placed in the generalization graph in order to express its generalization/multi-instantiation relationships with the other object classes. There are two main solutions:

1. the result of a query describes new real world objects. It is a class containing new oids, placed at the top of the hierarchy;
2. the result of a query is another point of view on real world objects which are already described (with other points of view) in the database. It is a class containing existing oids, i.e. a sub-class (or a derived class) of some existing class(es).

DMLs of the first type are called object generating languages. The properties of the new class are derived from the properties of the operands [Bancilhon 88]. In OO models, this can be acheived by defining reference attributes which point at the operand objects [Bertino 92]. DMLs of the second type are called object preserving languages. The properties of the new class are derived from the operand through the sub-class mechanism [Scholl 90, Sunye 92]. The object preserving solution generates graphs which are clearer, more easily understandable by users. ERC+ DMLs are object preserving. The result of a query, however complicated, involving one or several entity types, is an entity type which is derived from the operand entity types and whose occurrences are derived from those of the operand(s): same oids, derived values.

• <u>Complex types</u>

A large amount of research effort has been devoted to DMLs for models with complex types such as non first normal form relational models [Jaeschke 82, Roth 84] and complex objects models [Carey 88, Bancilhon 88, Zaniolo 83]. OO models and extended ER models often support, as ERC+ does, complex attributes, which are composed of other component attributes, and multivalued attributes which can have several values. A multivalued attribute may be set, multiset, list, or array-valued. An example of complex and multivalued attribute is the attribute planting in figure 1. Complex and multivalued attributes may include multivalued attributes at several levels of nesting, as the attribute plants in planting.

With complex types, the DML must provide tools for working on a value inside a set (or multiset, list ...) of values and at any depth in the complex type. Usual tools are:

1/ set operators ($\in$, $\subseteq$, =),

2/ attribute-variables at each levels of multivaluation, associated with a quantifier ($\exists$ or $\forall$),
3/ nested queries, one query for each level of multivaluation.

Nesting of queries is a commonly used solution in NF2 relational models where a multivalued attribute can take a nested relation as value [Jaeschke 82]. The operators that are used to manipulate relations are also used to work on these relation-valued attributes. By contrast, in languages with two different concepts, object (or entity) and attribute, different operators must be defined to manipulate the different concepts. For example, in the ERC+ algebra the selection operator is defined on entity types, and a new operator (the reduction) applies to a multivalued attribute of an entity type, and is used to eliminate in each occurrence of the entity type, inside the multivalued attribute, the values which do not satisfy a given predicate.

Projection is another operator which works on a complex structure. In NF2 relational models, users have to write nested projections when they want to prune a complex attribute. In models using several concepts (as ERC+), the projection operator is defined on the entity type and a dot notation allows to define the pruning of component attributes at any level.

• Relationships and reference attributes

Relationships in ER models and reference attributes in OO models are used to link objects together. The associated DML should allow users to select objects based on their links or relationships to other objects. For instance, in the vineyard database, a user may want to list all the growers which harvested "Pommard" wine in 1990. Most OO SQL-like languages allow access from one object to related objects through reference links. They often use a dot notation to move across reference and value attribute links.

An alternative solution, better suited to algebras, is to adhere to the guideline stating that each operator manipulates only its operands. Objects which are not explicitely stated as operands of an operator cannot be accessed by it. The ERC+ algebra abides by this rule. A query which involves more than one entity type must be formulated as an expression where operators which gather together into a new complex entity type several entity types linked by a relationship (relationship -join) or by an is-a or may-be-a link (identity-join), are used at first.

4. Conclusion

Many research results have documented the advantages of object oriented concepts for tackling the design of large and complex software systems. Experience gained from using OO models to design database applications has clearly stated the need to combine the key features of object orientation with concepts for representing explicit relationships among objects and for expressing the integrity constraints which are necessary to capture the semantics of database systems. We have supported in this paper the idea of an object+relationship approach to fully support database application requirements.

To achieve a full and proper definition of a modeling paradigm, data definition facilities have to be complemented with adequate data manipulation facilities. We have briefly reviewed the requirements for conceptual data manipulation languages to deal with the new advanced data modeling concepts. This is intended to suggest that an object+relationship approach is fully capable of taking care of all interactions between a user and a DBMS. It is therefore a perfect candidate to support a user interface allowing for DBMS independence, i.e. hiding to users the peculiarities of the underlying DBMS. We are currently developing such an interface [Auddino 91].

References

[Abiteboul 89] S. Abiteboul, P.C. Fischer, H. J. Scheck Eds.: *Nested Relations and Complex Objects in Databases,* Lectures Notes in Computer Science 361, Springer Verlag, 1989

[Albano 91] A. Albano, G. Ghelli, R. Orsini: *A Relationship Mechanism for a Strongly Typed Object-Oriented Database Programming Language*, 17th International Conference on Very Large Data Bases, Barcelona, September 3-6, 1991, pp. 565-575

[Auddino 91] A. Auddino & al.: *SUPER: A Comprehensive Approach to DBMS Visual User Interfaces,* IFIP WG 2.6 2nd Working Conference on Visual Database Systems, Budapest, September 30-October 3, 1991, pp. 359-374

[Bancilhon 88] F. Bancilhon & al.: *The Design and Implementation of O2, an Object-Oriented Database System*, in Advances in Object-Oriented Database Systems, K.R. Dittrich Ed., Lecture Notes in Computer Science no 334, Springer-Verlag, 1988, pp. 1-22

[Bertino 92] E. Bertino, M. Negri, G. Pelagatti, L. Sbattella: *Object Oriented Query Languages: The Notions and the Issues,* IEEE Transactions on Data and Knowledge Engineering, Vol.4, No.3, June 1992, pp. 223-237

[Brodie 84] M. Brodie, J. Mylopoulos, J. Schmidt (Eds.): *On Conceptual Modelling*, Springer-Verlag, 1984

[Carey 88] M. Carey, D. DeWitt, S. Vandenberg: *A Data Model and Query Language for EXODUS* , ACM-SIGMOD International Conference on Management of Data, Chicago, June 1-3, 1988, pp. 413-423

[Elmasri 85] R. Elmasri, J. Weeldreyer, A. Hevner: *The category concept : an extension to the entity-relationship model*, Data & Knowledge Engineering, Vol. 1, n° 1, June 1985, pp. 75-116

[Jaeschke 82] G. Jaeschke: *Remarks on the Algebra of the Non First Normal Form Relations,* ACM SIGMOD International Conference on Management of Data, Los Angeles, March 1982

[Khoshafian 90] S. Khoshafian, R. Abnous: *Object Orientation - Concepts, Languages, Databases, User Interfaces*, John Wiley & Sons, 1990

[Loizou 91] G. Loizou, P. Pouyioutas: *A Query Algebra for an Extended Object-Oriented Database Model,* International Symposium of Database System for Advanced Applications, Tokyo, April 1991

[Parent 92] C. Parent, S. Spaccapietra: *ERC+: an object based entity-relationship approach,* in Conceptual Modelling, Databases and CASE: An Integrated View of Information Systems Development, P.Loucopoulos, R.Zicari Eds., John Wiley, 1992

[Rumbaugh 87] J. Rumbaugh: *Relations as Semantic Constructs in an Object-Oriented Language*, OOPSLA Conference, Orlando, October 4-8, 1987, pp.466-481

[Roth 84] M. Roth, H. Korth, A. Silberschatz:*Theory of Non First Normal Form Relational Databases,* TR-84-36 Department of Computer Science, University of Texas at Austin, December 1984

[Scholl 90] M.H. Scholl, H.-J. Schek: *A Relational Object Model*, 3rd International Conference on Database Theory, Paris, December 1990

[Spaccapietra 92] S. Spaccapietra, C. Parent: *Model Independent Assertions for Integration of Heterogeneous Schemas*, The VLDB Journal, Vol.1, No 1, July 1992, pp.81-126

[Sunye 92] M. Sunye: *CERQLE: un SQL entité-relationi*, 7èmes Journées Bases de Données Avancées, Trégastel, September 15-18, 1992

[Vrbsky 89] S. V. Vrbsky, J. Liu and K Smith: *An Object-Oriented Approach to producing monotonically improving approximate answers,* Technical Report No. NVY N00014 89-J-1181 Dept. of Comp Science, Univ. of Illinois, Urbana-Champaign

[Zaniolo 83] C. Zaniolo, D. Maier: *The Database Language GEM*, ACM SIGMOD International Conference on Mangement of Data, San Jose, May 1983

Anwendungsmuster der objektorientierten Programmierung

Hanspeter Mössenböck
Institut für Computersysteme
ETH Zürich
CH-8092 Zürich

Objektorientierte Programmierung ist eine Technik, die in gewissen Situationen sehr elegante Lösungen erlaubt, in anderen aber wenig nützt, ja sogar zusätzliche Komplexität verursachen kann. Dieser Aufsatz stellt die Frage nach den lohnenden Anwendungen von Klassen und versucht, Muster in Programmen zu identifizieren, die sich für eine objektorientierte Implementierung eignen.

1. Einleitung

Es wird heute viel über Objektorientierung geschrieben und gesprochen aber oft in ziemlich euphorischer und unkritischer Weise. Man bekommt leicht den Eindruck, daß es sich hier um eine Technik handelt, die der herkömmlichen Programmierung in *allen* Fällen überlegen ist. Dem ist nicht so. Objektorientierte Programmierung hat zwar zweifellos ihre Stärken, aber sie hat sie vor allem bei ganz speziellen Anwendungen.

Es ist wichtig, sich bewußt zu werden, wo die Vorteile dieser Technik liegen und in welchen Situationen sie herkömmlicher Programmierung überlegen ist. Der vorliegende Aufsatz versucht daher, einige Muster für sinnvolle Anwendungen der objektorientierten Programmierung herauszuarbeiten. Die Ausführungen sind unabhängig von einer bestimmten Programmiersprache gehalten und gelten für alle hybriden objektorientierten Sprachen.

Bevor wir uns dem eigentlichen Thema zuwenden, wollen wir klarstellen, was die wesentlichen Merkmale der objektorientierten Programmierung sind. Objektorientierte Programmierung beruht auf Datenabstraktion, Typerweiterung (oder Vererbung) und auf dynamischer Bindung von Aufträgen an Prozeduren. Datenabstraktion wiederum beruht auf Information Hiding.

Unter *Information Hiding* versteht man die Eigenschaft, Bausteine bilden zu können, die die konkrete Implementierung von Daten in ihrem Inneren verbergen und nach außen hin nur eine abstrakte Sicht der Daten abieten. Die abstrakte Sicht besteht aus einer Menge von Zugriffsprozeduren, über die man die Daten abfragen und verändern kann (Bild 1).

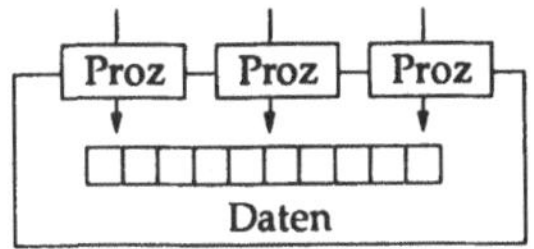

Bild 1 Baustein bestehend aus gekapselten Daten und Zugriffsprozeduren

Information Hiding ist nicht neu. Die meisten modernen Sprachen bieten diese Eigenschaft in Form von Modulen, Packages oder Ähnlichem. Wichtig ist, daß man damit Bausteine bilden kann, die zusammengehörige Daten und Operationen zu einem Ganzen vereinigen. Sie haben einen lokalen Zustand, der über die Operationen manipuliert werden kann.

Wenn man *einen* Baustein aus Daten und Operationen hat, dann ist es nur natürlich zu fordern, *mehrere* Exemplare davon anlegen zu können. Das führt zum Begriff des abstrakten Datentyps. Ein *abstrakter Datentyp* definiert einen Baustein aus Daten und Operationen und kann wie jeder andere Datentyp zur Deklaration von Variablen verwendet werden. Die so deklarierten Variablen haben alle den gleichen Aufbau und erlauben es, die gleichen Operationen auf sie anzuwenden. In der objektorientierten Terminologie nennt man abstrakte Datentypen *Klassen* und ihre Werte *Objekte*. Auch abstrakte Datentypen sind nicht neu. Man findet sie bereits in Modula-2 oder Ada.

Das wichtigste Merkmal objektorientierter Sprachen ist die *Typerweiterung* oder *Vererbung*. Sie kommt in keiner konventionellen Sprache vor und ist der eigentliche Grund für die Mächtigkeit der objektorientierten Programmierung. Typerweiterung erlaubt es, aus einem abstrakten Datentyp (z.B. für grafische Figuren) neue Typen (z.B. Rechtecke oder Kreise) abzuleiten, die denselben Aufbau und dieselben Operationen besitzen wie der Basistyp, aber noch weitere Daten und Operationen hinzufügen können. Man sagt auch, daß die erweiterten Typen vom Basistyp erben. Den Basistyp nennt man *Oberklasse* und die erweiterten Typen seine *Unterklassen* (Bild 2).

Bild 2 Rechteck und Kreis sind Unterklassen von Figur (d.h. spezielle Figurenarten)

Das Besondere an der Typerweiterung ist weniger das Erben von Code, sondern vielmehr die Tatsache, daß die erweiterten Typen mit dem Basistyp kompatibel sind. Das bedeutet, daß alle Programme, die mit Objekten des Basistyps arbeiten können, auch in der Lage sind, mit Objekten der erweiterten Typen zu arbeiten. Ein Grafikeditor, der mit allgemeinen Figuren arbeiten kann, kann ohne daß man etwas an ihm ändert auch mit Rechtecken und Kreisen arbeiten. Das macht es sehr einfach, Programme zu erweitern. Diese Art von Erweiterbarkeit ist in keiner konventionellen Sprache möglich. Man beachte, daß hier auch eine besondere Art von Wiederverwendung stattfindet. Es wird nicht ein einzelner Bibliotheksbaustein wiederverwendet, sondern das gesamte Hauptprogramm – der Grafikeditor – erweitert um verschiedene Figurenarten.

Schließlich ist noch ein letztes Merkmal nötig: die *dynamische Bindung* eines Auftrags an eine von mehreren Prozeduren, die den Auftrag ausführen können. Aufgrund der Kompatibilität zwischen Basistyp und Erweiterung kann eine Variable vom Typ *Figur* zur Laufzeit ein Objekt einer beliebigen Erweiterung enthalten. Man sagt, die Variable ist polymorph oder vielgestaltig (Bild 3).

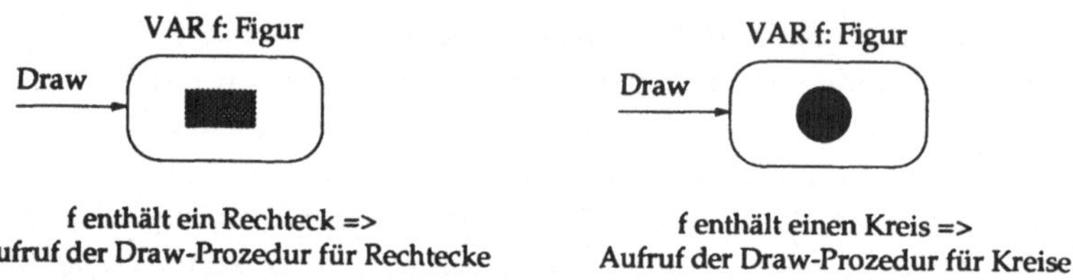

Bild 3 Die Variable *f* erhält den Auftrag *Draw* und reagiert in Abhängigkeit von ihrem Inhalt

Wenn man an die Variable einen Auftrag wie z.B. *Draw* richtet, dann hängt es davon ab, welches Objekt in ihr zur Laufzeit gespeichert ist. Ist es ein Rechteck, dann wird der Auftrag durch die *Draw*-Prozedur für Rechtecke ausgeführt, ist es ein Kreis, wird er durch die *Draw*-Prozedur für Kreise ausgeführt. Der Auftrag wird also dynamisch – das heißt erst zur Laufzeit – an eine bestimmte Prozedur gebunden, daher spricht man von dynamischer Bindung. Aufträge nennt man auch Meldungen: Man sendet dem Objekt in *f* die Meldung *Draw* und dieses reagiert durch Aufruf der entsprechenden Prozedur.

Dynamische Bindung ist ebenfalls nicht neu. Man kennt sie zum Beispiel in Modula-2 in Form von Prozedurvariablen. Wenn man eine Prozedurvariable aufruft, wird diejenige Prozedur ausgeführt, die zur Laufzeit in dieser Variablen gespeichert ist.

Objektorientiertes Programmieren ist also Programmieren mit abstrakten Datentypen unter Ausnutzung von Vererbung und dynamischer Bindung. Wir wollen uns nun ansehen, wie man diese Technik sinnvoll einsetzt.

2. Anwendungsmuster der objektorientierten Programmierung

Welche Teile eines Programms sollte man objektorientiert implementieren und welche nicht? Im Prinzip kann man natürlich alle Programme auf Objekte und Meldungen zurückführen, wie das in Smalltalk gemacht wird, wo es keine anderen Daten außer Objekten und keine anderen Operationen außer Meldungen gibt. Man *kann* also alles objektorientiert ausdrücken, aber ist das auch sinnvoll?

Meines Erachtens ist objektorientierte Programmierung eine Technik, die in gewissen Situationen sehr elegante Lösungen erlaubt, in anderen aber fast nichts bringt, ja sogar zusätzliche Komplexität verursachen kann. Die lohnenden Anwendungen von Klassen sind im wesentlichen:

- Datenabstraktion
- heterogene Datenstrukturen
- generische Bausteine
- Austauschen von Verhalten zur Laufzeit

Diese Situationen kann man als Muster auffassen, die in verschiedener Form immer wieder auftauchen. Wenn man weiß, wie man sie löst, ist das nichts anderes als wiederverwendbares Design.

Was zeichnet denn einen guten Designer aus? Doch vor allem seine Erfahrung. Er weiß, wie man gewisse Situationen löst, weil er ihnen schon Hunderte von Malen begegnet ist. Er hat von diesen Situationen abstrahiert und einen Erfahrungsschatz gebildet, der nichts anderes ist als eine Menge von Mustern, deren Lösung er kennt.

Das gilt übrigens nicht nur für den objektorientierten Entwurf, sondern auch für konventionelle Programmierung. Wir wissen zum Beispiel, daß zum Suchen in großen Datenmengen binäres Suchen oder Hashcodierung in Frage kommt. Wir wissen, daß Rekursion ein geeignetes Verfahren zum Traversieren von Graphen ist. Und genauso sollte man wissen, daß man heterogene Datenstrukturen oder generische Bausteine elegant mit Klassen implementieren kann.

Meiner Meinung nach ist die Kenntnis solcher Muster wichtiger als die Verwendung einer bestimmten Entwurfsmethode oder eines CASE-Tools. Beim Entwurf kann man fehlende Erfahrung nicht durch mechanische Tools ersetzen. Im Rest des Aufsatzes wird nun auf die oben erwähnten Muster eingegangen.

3. Klassen zur Datenabstraktion

Am häufigsten werden Klassen zur Datenabstraktion verwendet. Viele Programmierer benutzen Klassen sogar *ausschließlich* zu diesem Zweck, ohne von Vererbung und dynamischer Bindung Gebrauch zu machen. Das kann durchaus sinnvoll sein. Klassen sind tatsächlich ein ausgezeichnetes Strukturierungmittel. Sie gruppieren zusammengehörige Daten und Prozeduren und schaffen damit Ordnung in Programmen. Klassen sind auch ein gutes Abstraktionsmittel. Sie können dazu dienen, eine komplexe Datenstruktur hinter einer einfachen Schnittstelle zu verbergen.

Selbst wenn man also von Vererbung und dynamischer Bindung gar keinen Gebrauch macht, kann es sinnvoll sein, einen Datentyp als Klasse zu implementieren, einfach um ihn zu einem identifizierbaren, abgeschlossenen Baustein zu machen.

Ein Beispiel für eine sinnvolle Abstraktion ist eine Klasse für Files. Ein File ist eine komplexe Datenstruktur. Es gehören ein oder mehrere Puffer dazu, eine Position, eine Länge, Attribute, usw. Es ist sinnvoll, diese Details hinter einer einfachen Schnittstelle zu verbergen und damit eine leicht verständliche Abstraktion daraus zu machen: eine Folge von Bytes, auf die man mit Operationen wie *Read* und *Write* bequem zugreifen kann.

Datenabstraktion hat sowohl für den Benutzer als auch für den Implementierer einer Klasse Vorteile. Benutzer können eine Klasse verwenden, ohne ihre Implementierung zu kennen. Sie können sie als wiederverwendbaren Baustein in anderen Programmen einsetzen. Die Implementierung einer Klasse kann jederzeit ausgewechselt werden, ohne daß Klienten davon betroffen sind. Daneben bietet Datenabstraktion auch einen gewissen Schutz vor mutwilliger oder ungewollter Zerstörung der privaten Daten.

Natürlich könnte man Files statt als Klasse auch als Modul oder als abstrakten Datentyp implementieren. Gegenüber einem Modul hat eine Klasse aber den Vorteil, daß sie ein Datentyp ist, daß man also mehrere Variablen davon deklarieren kann. Gegenüber einem abstrakten Datentyp hat sie den Vorteil, daß man sofort sieht, welche Operationen zu ihr gehören. Bei einem abstrakten Datentyp – z.B. in Modula-2 – ist das nicht so offensichtlich, bei einer Klasse aber sehr wohl, weil ihr die Operationen syntaktisch zugeordnet sind.

Von allen Anwendungen der objektorientierten Programmierung ist Datenabstraktion diejenige, die am wenigsten Neues bringt aber auch diejenige, die am häufigsten eingesetzt werden kann. Von Vererbung und dynamischer Bindung können nur wenige Programme profitieren, von Datenabstraktion aber fast alle.

Ich glaube, daß Datenabstraktion und die damit verbundenen Strukturierungsmöglichkeiten ein wesentlicher Grund für die Popularität objektorientierter Sprachen sind. Viele Programmierer haben erst mit der objektorientierten Programmierung die Vorteile der Datenabstraktion kennengelernt. Für Modula-Programmierer ist Datenabstraktion eine längst vertraute Technik. Für Cobol- oder C-Programmierer bedeutet sie aber einen echten Fortschritt. Das ist meiner Meinung nach auch der Grund dafür, daß die einen objektorientierte Programmierung als revolutionär betrachten, während andere sie bloß als evolutionär empfinden.

Wie schon erwähnt, gibt es aber auch andere Abstraktionsmittel als Klassen, nämlich Module oder abstrakte Datentypen. Bevor man zu einer Klasse greift, sollte man sich überlegen, ob nicht ein anderes Abstraktionsmittel geeigneter ist, oder ob die Daten überhaupt komplex genug sind, daß sich Abstraktion lohnt. Bei der Wahl des richtigen Abstraktionsmittels kann man sich durch den in Bild 4 dargestellten Entscheidungsbaum leiten lassen.

Wenn die Daten und Operationen einfach sind, sollte man lieber zu einer konkreten Datenstruktur greifen. Ein Programm wird nicht einfacher, wenn man jeden Array- oder Recordtyp zu einer Klasse macht. Sind die Daten genügend komplex, sodaß sich eine Abstraktion lohnt, sollte man sich überlegen, ob es mehrere Exemplare der Daten gibt. Wenn nicht, ist ein Modul das richtige Sprachmittel. Existieren die Daten in mehreren Exemplaren, ist die nächste Frage, ob die Daten erweiterbar sein müssen bzw. ob es mehrere Varianten davon gibt. Wenn nicht, reicht ein abstrakter Datentyp und nur in den anderen Fällen ist eine Klasse gerechtfertigt.

Beispiele für Module sind Terminal, Mouse, Cursor oder die Symboltabelle eines Compilers. Hier existieren die Daten nur in einem einzigen Exemplar. Ein Modul ist daher ausreichend. Beispiele für abstrakte Datentypen sind Stack, Queue, Window oder Text. Von diesen Daten benötigt man meist mehrere Exemplare, sie müssen aber in der Regel nicht erweiterbar sein. Daher ist ein abstrakter Datentyp das Richtige. Beispiele für Klassen sind schließlich eine grafische Figur, ein Benutzerschnittstellenelement oder ein Simulationsobjekt. Von diesen Daten gibt es mehrere Exemplare und auch mehrere Varianten. Sie müssen also erweiterbar sein und hier ist die Klasse das richtige Sprachmittel.

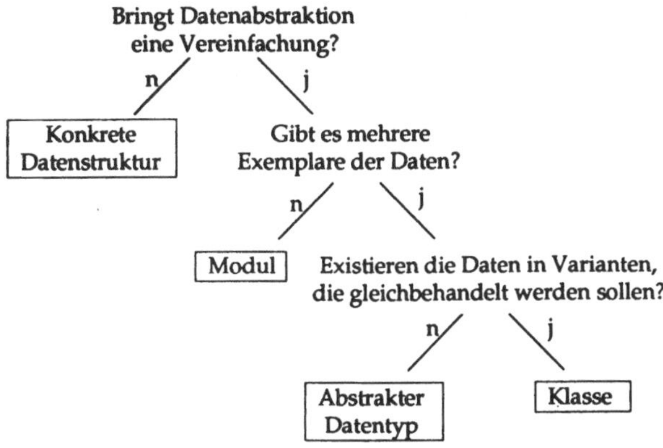

Bild 4 Wahl des richtigen Datenabstraktionsmittels

Datenabstraktion sollte nicht um jeden Preis betrieben werden. Sie ist nämlich nicht gratis. Mit einer Klasse führt man einen neuen Begriff ein und neue Operationen, deren Syntax und Semantik man erlernen muß. Eine Klasse erweitert eine Sprache um ein neues Element und je größer die Sprache wird, desto schwerer ist sie zu beherrschen. Datenabstraktion ist nur dann sinnvoll, wenn die Komplexität, die man durch sie beseitigt,wesentlich größer ist als die neue Komplexität, die man mit ihr einführt.

4. Klassen zur Implementierung heterogener Datenstrukturen

Während Datenabstraktion das *häufigste* Anwendungsmuster von Klassen ist, ist die Bearbeitung heterogener Datenstrukturen das *nützlichste* Muster, also dasjenige, bei dem die objektorientierte Programmierung der herkömmlichen Programmierung am deutlichsten überlegen ist.

Eine heterogene Datenstruktur besteht aus Objekten mit unterschiedlichem Typ und daher auch mit unterschiedlicher Größe und unterschiedlichen Eigenschaften. Solche Datenstrukturen werden oft über Zeiger verkettet (Bild 5).

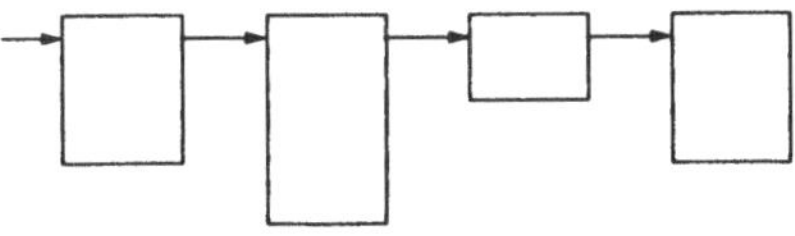

Bild 5 Heterogene Datenstruktur

Situationen dieser Art sind häufig anzutreffen. Ihre typischen Merkmale sind:

- Objekte treten in Varianten auf. In einem Grafikeditor gibt es zum Beispiel vierschiedene Arten von Figuren: Linien, Rechtecke, Kreise, usw.

- Man möchte auf alle Varianten die gleichen Operationen anwenden, ohne zwischen ihnen unterscheiden zu müssen. Man will zum Beispiel auf eine Figur die Operation *Draw* anwenden, ohne sich darum kümmern zu müssen, ob diese Figur ein Rechteck oder ein Kreis ist.
- Es soll möglich sein, später neue Varianten hinzuzufügen, ohne bestehende Programme ändern zu müssen. Zu einem Grafikeditor möchte man vielleicht später einmal Spline-Kurven hinzufügen. Der bestehende Editor soll dabei unangetastet bleiben.

Wann immer man in einem Programm Situationen dieser Art antrifft, sollte man zu Klassen greifen. Ein Beispiel einer solchen Situation ist ein Texteditor, der in der Lage ist, neben Text auch beliebige andere Objekte wie Bilder, Formeln oder Tabellen zu verarbeitet. Ein Editor dieser Art wurde im Oberon-System implementiert [Szyperski92]. Bild 6 zeigt ein Fenster dieses Editors.

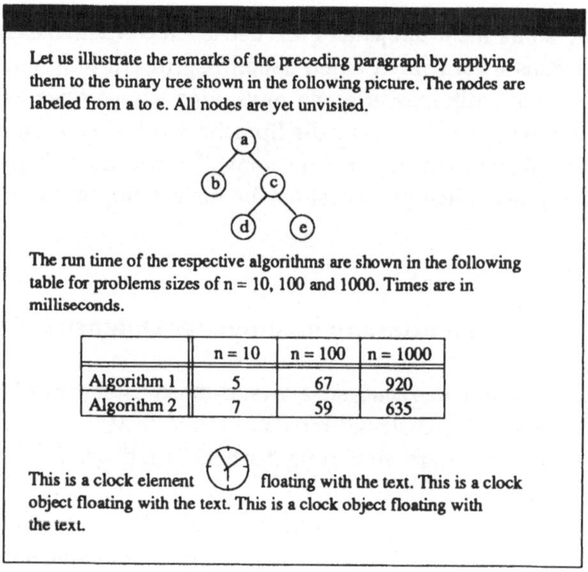

Let us illustrate the remarks of the preceding paragraph by applying them to the binary tree shown in the following picture. The nodes are labeled from a to e. All nodes are yet unvisited.

a
b c
d e

The run time of the respective algorithms are shown in the following table for problems sizes of n = 10, 100 and 1000. Times are in milliseconds.

	n = 10	n = 100	n = 1000
Algorithm 1	5	67	920
Algorithm 2	7	59	635

This is a clock element floating with the text. This is a clock object floating with the text. This is a clock object floating with the text.

Bild 6 Text mit beliebigen mitfließenden Objekten (Grafik, Tabelle, Uhr, ...)

Der Text enthält eine Grafik, eine Tabelle und eine Uhr. Diese Objekte werden vom Editor wie große Zeichen behandelt, die beim Editieren im Text mitfließen. Es handelt sich aber nicht einfach um Bitmaps, die bloß angezeigt werden können, sondern sie sind in gewisser Hinsicht aktiv und reagieren auf Mausklicks. Die Grafik kann man zum Beispiel direkt an der Stelle editieren, an der man sie sieht. Die Tabelle kann man ebenfalls anklicken und editieren und auch die Uhr ist aktiv: der Sekundenzeiger bewegt sich, und die Uhr zeigt immer die richtige Zeit an.

Wir haben hier die oben beschriebene Situation: Es gibt verschiedene Varianten von Objekten: Bilder, Tabellen, Formeln, eine Uhr, etc. Die Objekte müssen in einer Datenstruktur gehalten werden, die wegen der verschiedenen Varianten heterogen ist. Der Editor muß auf alle diese Objekte die gleichen Operationen anwenden: er muß sie am Bildschirm darstellen, er muß Mausklicks an sie weiterleiten und er muß sie abspeichern und einlesen können. Schließlich soll es möglich sein, jederzeit neue Objekte– z.B. Hypertext-Objekte – zu implementieren, die dann vom Editor so wie die bereits vorhandenen Objekte behandelt werden können.

Diese Merkmale deuten darauf hin, daß wir zur Implementierung der Objekte Klassen verwenden sollten. Bevor wir auf diese Implementierung näher eingehen, sehen wir uns an, wie man solche Situationen in konventionellen Sprachen wie Pascal oder Modula-2 behandeln würde.

Konventionelle Implementierung heterogener Datenstrukturen

In Modula-2 würde man die verschiedenen Objekt-Varianten in einem sogenannten Varianten-Record zusammenfassen, wobei die einzelnen Varianten im Speicher überlagert werden. Man kann auf diese Weise eine Datenstruktur bilden, bei der jeder Knoten eine der Varianten des Records ist. Damit ist es möglich, heterogene Datenstrukturen zu implementieren (Bild 7).

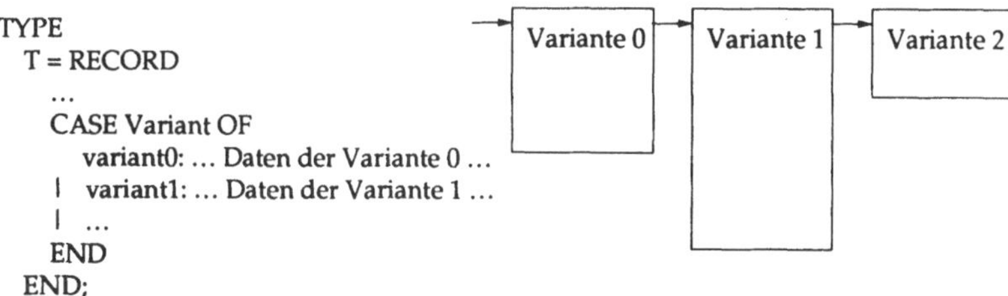

Bild 7 Varianten-Record zur Implementierung heterogener Datenstrukturen in Modula-2

Was ist der Nachteil dieser Lösung? Zunächst einmal muß man, wenn man so einen Knoten im Programm verarbeiten will, mit einer Fallunterscheidung feststellen, welche Variante vorliegt. Ist es die Variante 0 dann erfolgt Verarbeitung A, ist es die Variante 1, dann erfolgt Verarbeitung B, usw. Diese Fallunterscheidungen blähen den Code auf und machen ihn unübersichtlich.

Der scherwiegendere Nachteil ist aber, daß Erweiterungen aufwendig sind. Will man später eine neue Variante hinzufügen, muß man erstens den Datentyp ändern (was dazu führen kann, daß Klientenmodule invalidiert werden) und zweitens an allen Stellen, an denen Variablen dieses Typs verarbeitet werden, eine neue Fallunterscheidung einbauen, die berücksichtigt, daß die Variable jetzt in einer neuen Variante vorliegen kann. Das führt nicht nur zu großem Änderungsaufwand, sondern macht es auch nötig, in den Code bestehender Programme einzugreifen. Im Beispiel des Texteditors heißt das: nur weil jemand Hypertext-Objekte haben will, muß man den Code des Editors ändern. Das will man nicht.

Objektorientierte Implementierung heterogener Datenstrukturen

Bei der objektorientierten Implementierung werden diese Nachteile vermieden. Wie geht man vor? Betrachten wir dazu nochmals den Write-Editor. Der Trick besteht darin, daß der Editor nicht zwischen den verschiedenen Objektarten unterscheidet. Er weiß gar nicht, daß es Grafiken, Tabellen und Uhren gibt, sondern betrachtet alle diese Objekte als schwarze Kästen, von denen er nur die Breite und die Höhe kennt und mit denen er eine kleine Anzahl wohldefinierter Operationen ausführen kann. Er kann sie zum Beispiel auffordern, sich auf dem Bildschirm darzustellen, sich auf eine Datei abzuspeichern und wieder einzulesen und auf Mausklicks zu reagieren. Unter der Voraussetzung, daß alle Objekte diese Operationen ausführen können – jedes auf seine Weise – braucht der Editor sie nicht zu unterscheiden. Er kann einem Objekt einfach eine Display-Meldung schicken und die dynamische Bindung sorgt von selbst dafür, daß sie von der entsprechenden Objektart richtig interpretiert wird.

Wie sieht das konkret aus? Wir brauchen einen Typ, der das Aussehen und das Verhalten aller Objekte definiert. Diesen Typ nennen wir *Element*(Bild 8). Er ist der Basistyp aller zukünftigen Element-Erweiterungen und enthält als Daten nur die Breite und Höhe des Elements. Als Operationen enthält er *Display* zum Darstellen des Elements auf dem Bildschirm, *HandleMouse* zum Reagieren auf Mausklicks, *Copy* zum Kopieren und *Load* und *Store* zum Einlesen und Abspeichern des Elements.

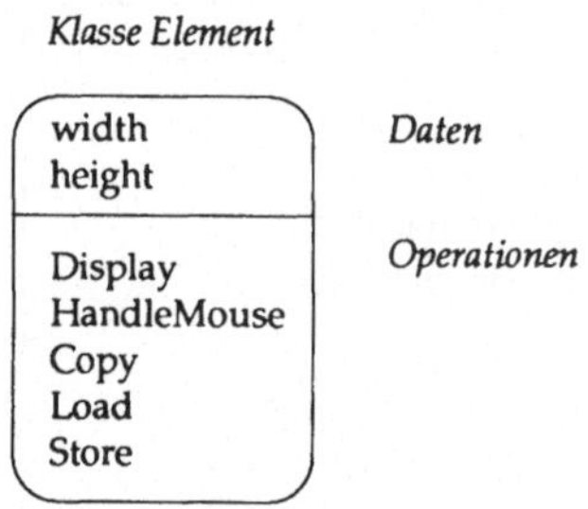

Bild 8 Abstrakte Klasse *Element* als Basistyp aller Elementarten

Natürlich können diese Operationen hier noch nicht implementiert werden, denn *Display* muß für Grafikelemente anders aussehen als für Tabellenelemente. Die Implementierung bleibt hier also leer. Wichtig ist aber, daß die Schnittstelle der Operationen festgelegt wird, also ihr Name und ihre Parameterliste. Eine Klasse, bei der die Implementierung der Operationen leer bleibt, nennt man *abstrakte Klasse*. Sie dient lediglich dazu, eine bestimmte Schnittstelle zu definieren.

Die konkreten Elementarten werden nun als Unterklassen von Element implementiert (Bild 9). Sie erben die Daten und Operationen und können weitere hinzufügen. Ein Grafikelement hat z.B. ebenfalls eine Breite und eine Höhe und zusätzlich noch eine Liste von Figuren, aus denen die Grafik besteht. Die geerbten Operationen müssen alle überschrieben d.h. neu definiert werden. Dadurch ersetzen sie in dieser Klasse die gleichnamigen geerbten Operationen. Bei Tabellenelementen machen wir es genauso. Neben einer Breite und einer Höhe haben diese Elemente eine Anzahl von Zeilen und Spalten und eine Menge von Werten, die in der Tabelle dargestellt werden. Auch hier werden alle geerbten Operationen überschrieben.

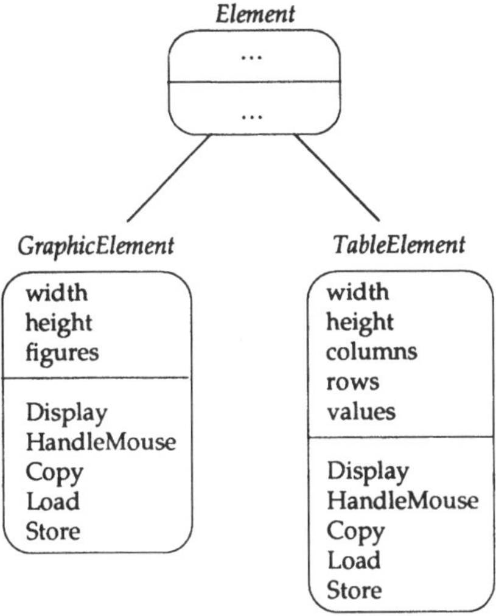

Bild 9 *GraphicElement* und *TableElement* als Unterklassen von *Element*

Wie werden die Elemente in den Text integriert? Die Datenstruktur des Texts besteht aus lauter kleinen Stücken, die *Pieces* genannt werden, und entweder reinen Text enthalten oder eben ein Element. Da es verschiedene Elementarten gibt – Zeichnungen, Tabellen oder Uhren – ist diese Liste heterogen (Bild 10).

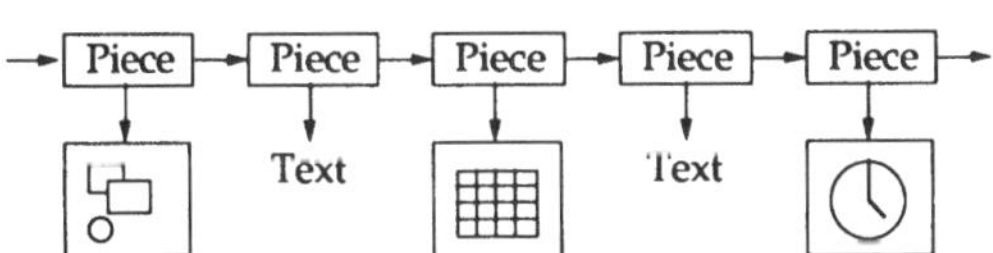

Bild 10 Datenstruktur für Texte bestehend aus Stücken, die reinen Text oder ein Element darstellen

Wenn der Editor einen Fensterinhalt neu aufbauen will, schickt er jedesmal, wenn er auf ein Piece stößt, das ein Element enthält, diesem eine *Display*-Meldung im Vertrauen darauf, daß das Element selbst weiß, wie es diese Meldung zu interpretieren hat. Der Editor muß zwischen den Varianten nicht unterscheiden, und wenn später Hypertext-Elemente hinzukommen, braucht er davon gar nichts zu wissen. Er schickt ihnen wie allen anderen eine Display-Meldung und kann dadurch plötzlich auch Hypertext-Elemente behandeln, ohne daß man etwas an seinem Code ändern mußte, ja man muß ihn nicht einmal neu übersetzen.

Einige Betriebssysteme wie zum Beispiel Oberon [Wirth92] bieten die Möglichkeit, eine Erweiterung wie diese zu einem *laufenden* Programm hinzuzuladen. Man kann den Editor in einer Grundversion starten, die noch keine konkreten Elemente kennt. Das ergibt kurze Ladezeiten und ein einfaches Programm. Wenn man während des Editierens den Wunsch verspürt, eine Grafik oder eine Tabelle in den Text einzufügen, lädt man den Code der entsprechenden Klasse dynamisch dazu. Benutzer müssen so nicht immer die gesamte Funktionalität des Editors mit sich herumschleppen, sondern laden sie erst bei Bedarf, wobei auch Erweiterungen geladen werden können, die vom Implementierer des Kernsystems gar nicht vorgesehen waren. Die dynamische Erweiterbarkeit ist eine wichtige Anforderung an objektorientierte Systeme. Ein Programm kann erst dann als wirklich erweiterbar bezeichnet werden, wenn man es *jederzeit* erweitern kann, also auch während es läuft, und wenn es *jedermann* erweitern kann, nicht nur sein Autor, der den Quellcode besitzt.

Tabelle 1 zeigt einige weitere Beispiele für Systeme, in denen heterogene Datenstrukturen eine Rolle spielen. Allen diesen Systemen ist gemeinsam, daß Objekte in Varianten auftreten, die nicht unterschieden werden sollen,und daß man neue Objekte hinzufügen möchte, ohne das Grundsystem zu ändern.

Systeme	vorkommende Objekt-Varianten	Operationen
Benutzeroberflächen	Fenster, Ikonen, Menüs, ...	zeichnen, verschieben, anklicken, ...
Dialogfenster	Buttons, Texte, Rollbalken, ...	zeichnen, verschieben, anklicken, ...
Betriebssysteme	Files, Directories, Pipes, ...	lesen, schreiben, ...
Spiele	Jäger, Gejagte, Hindernisse, ...	zeichnen, bewegen, kollidieren, ...
Simulationen	Autos, Personen, Ampeln, ...	aktivieren, verzögern, ...

Tabelle 1 Systeme mit heterogenen Datenstrukturen

5. Klassen zur Implementierung generischer Bausteine

Ein weiteres Anwendungsmuster von Klassen ist die Implementierung generischer Bausteine, d.h. solcher Bausteine, die mit verschiedenen Arten von Daten arbeiten können.

Betrachten wir ein Beispiel. Nehmen wir an, wir hätten einen Baustein zur Speicherung einer Namenmenge mittels Operationen wie *Include* und *Exclude*. Der Baustein ist spezifisch für Namen ausgelegt. Man kann in ihm zum Beispiel keine geometrischen Punkte speichern. Wenn man das will, braucht man einen zweiten Baustein, der völlig analog aufgebaut, aber auf Punkte ausgerichtet ist. In herkömmlichen Sprachen wie Modula-2 ist es nicht möglich, Bausteine zu implementieren, in denen sowohl Namen als auch Punkte und andere Objekte verwaltet werden können.

Mit Klassen kann man dieses Problem lösen, indem man einen allgemeinen Baustein implementiert, der nicht direkt mit Namen oder Punkten arbeitet, sondern mit Objekten einer abstrakten Klasse *Object*, von der Namen und Punkte abgeleitet sind (Bild 11). Da der Baustein mit *Object* arbeiten kann, kann er auch mit Namen und Punkten arbeiten, die ja von *Object* abgeleitet und daher kompatibel sind.

Diese Situation ist ähnlich wie bei heterogenen Datenstrukturen, mit dem Unterschied, daß die Datenstruktur hier homogen ist. Der Baustein enthält *nur* Namen oder *nur* Punkte. Die Homogenität kann freilich nicht durch den Compiler erzwungen werden, aber man kann sie, wenn man will, zur Laufzeit mit Hilfe von Laufzeittypprüfungen sicherstellen. In Sprachen, die ein spezielles Generizitätskonstrukt anbieten, kann man die Homogenität der Datenmenge zur Übersetzungszeit sicherstellen. Das ist mit Klassen alleine nicht möglich, aber immerhin kann man auf diese Weise überhaupt generische Bausteine herstellen.

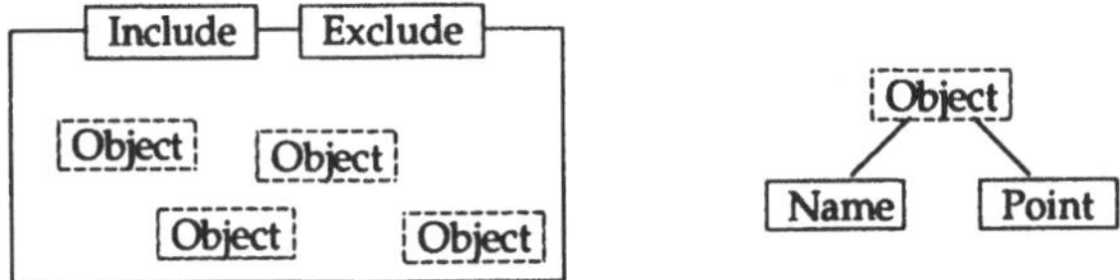

Bild 11 Generische Menge von Objekten. Sie kann mit allen Objekten arbeiten, die von *Object* abgeleitet sind.

6. Klassen zur Implementierung von austauschbarem Verhalten

Das letzte Muster, das wir betrachten, ist das Austauschen eines bestimmten Programmverhaltens zur Laufzeit. Das soll ebenfalls an einem Beispiel erklärt werden.

Nehmen wir an, wir hätten einen Grafikeditor, der in einem Fenster irgendwelche Figuren darstellt. Dazu benutzt er Zeichenprimitiva wie *DisplayRectangle* oder *DisplayCircle*. Irgendwann möchte man die Zeichnung auch ausdrucken. Das Ausdrucken ist aber nichts anderes als das Zeichnen der Grafik auf einem anderen Medium, nämlich auf dem Drucker. Der Ablauf des Zeichnen ist derselbe wie bei der Bildschirmausgabe, nur daß nun statt *DisplayRectangle PrintRectangle* verwendet wird und statt *DisplayCircle PrintCircle*(Bild 12).

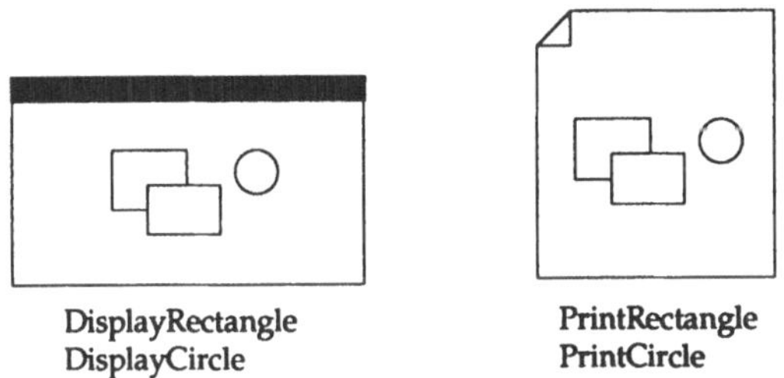

Bild 12 Ausgabe einer Grafik auf dem Bildschirm und auf dem Drucker

Man möchte also in beiden Fällen den gleichen Ausgabealgorithmus verwenden. Er soll sich aber das eine Mal so verhalten, daß er auf den Bildschirm ausgibt, das andere Mal so, daß er auf dem Drucker ausgibt. Man will sein Verhalten austauschen können. Woraus besteht dieses Verhalten? Es besteht aus den eigentlichen Zeichenoperationen für Rechtecke und Kreise.

Die Vorgehensweise ist nun die, daß man das auszutauschende Verhalten als Operationen einer abstrakten Klasse – nennen wir sie *Port* – definiert. Die Operationen dieser Klasse kann man noch nicht implementieren, sondern sie geben nur die gewünschte Schnittstelle vor. Aus der abstrakten Klasse *Port* kann man dann konkrete Klassen *ScreenPort* und *PrinterPort* ableiten (Bild 13), in denen die geerbten Operationen überschrieben werden, sodaß sie einmal auf den Bildschirm, das andere Mal auf den Drucker ausgeben.

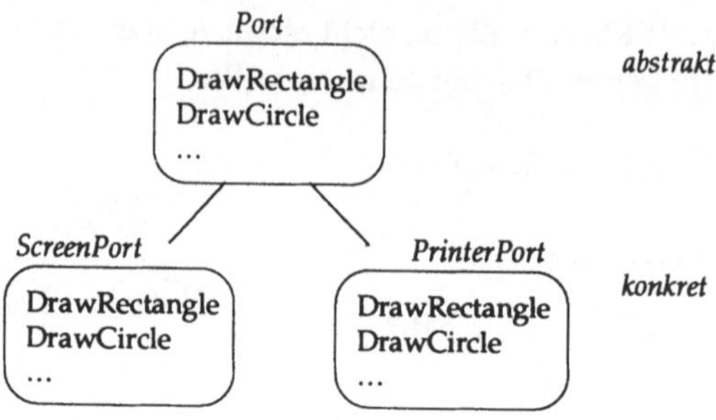

Bild 13 *ScreenPort* und *PrinterPort* als Unterklassen einer abstrakten Klasse *Port*

Den Editor implementiert man nun so, daß er mit Variablen der abstrakten Klasse *Port* arbeitet, also z.B. *port.DrawCircle*. Wenn man der *port*-Variablen zur Laufzeit ein Objekt der Klasse *ScreenPort* zuweist, werden durch die dynamische Bindung alle Ausgabeoperationen auf die *ScreenPort*-Operationen umgeleitet und die Ausgabe erfolgt auf dem Bildschirm. Wenn man der *port*-Variablen ein Objekt der Klasse *PrinterPort* zuweist, erfolgen alle Ausgaben auf dem Drucker.

Der Editor braucht überhaupt nicht mehr zwischen Bildschirm und Drucker zu unterscheiden. Er gibt einfach auf einem abstrakten Port aus, der einmal der Bildschirm und einmal der Drucker sein kann. Auf diese Weise bekommt man das Drucken umsonst. Ja man kann sogar später einmal eine neue Klasse *PostScriptPort* implementieren und ein Objekt davon der Variablen *port* zuweisen, dann wird als Ausgabe eine PostScript-Datei erzeugt.

Auch dieses Muster – das Austauschen von Verhalten – basiert wie die beiden vorhin geschilderten Muster auf der Tatsache, daß ein Objekt – hier ein Port – in verschiedenen Varianten existiert, die man nicht unterscheiden möchte. Trotzdem ist dieses Muster von den vorher genannten verschieden, weil es sich hier weder um eine heterogene Datenstruktur handelt, noch um einen generischen Baustein.

7. Wann sind Klassen sinnvoll

Klassen werden oft nicht richtig eingesetzt. Viele Leute machen den Fehler, zu viele Klassen zu bilden, auch in Situationen, wo sie gar nichts nützen, sondern sogar eher schaden. Es ist keineswegs so, daß jedes Programm besser wird, wenn man es objektorientiert implementiert. Klassen sind nur dann sinnvoll, wenn folgende Voraussetzungen erfüllt sind:

1. Wenn die Daten genügend komplex sind, sodaß sich eine Kapselung lohnt. Es hat zum Beispiel keinen Sinn, eine Klasse für die Geschwindigkeit von Fahrzeugen einzuführen. Diese Daten sind zu wenig komplex. Eine Geschwindigkeit läßt sich viel einfacher durch eine gewöhnliche Zahl ausdrücken. Eine Klasse *File* ist hingegen sinnvoll, denn sie verbirgt für Klienten unwichtige Details und macht den Umgang mit Dateien einfacher.

2. Wenn es genügend sinnvolle Operationen mit den Daten gibt. Wenn einem als Operationen nur das Setzen und Ablesen einzelner Datenfelder einfällt, ist eine Klasse meist fehl am Platz. Für eine Klasse *Speed* gibt es keine interessanten Operationen. Man kann einen Wert setzen und wieder ablesen; vielleicht kann man Geschwindigkeiten noch addieren aber das kann man mit normalen Zahlen auch. Der Aufruf einer Prozedur *Add* ist nicht einfacher als die Standard-operation +, eher im Gegenteil. Eine Klasse *File* hingegen besitzt viele sinnvolle Operationen: öffnen, schließen, lesen usw.

3. Wenn die Daten in Varianten existieren, die man nicht unterscheiden möchte, insbesondere wenn neue Varianten denkbar sind. Das ist vielleicht sogar die wichtigste Voraussetzung. Viele der nützlichsten Anwendungen der objekt-orientierten Programmierung beruhen auf heterogenen Datenstrukturen oder auf einem anderen der oben genannten Muster. Hier zahlen sich Klassen aus. Diese Situationen kann man ohne Klassen nur unbefriedigend lösen.

8. Zusammenfassung

In diesem Beitrag wurde die Frage nach den lohnenden Anwendungen der objekt-orientierten Programmierung gestellt. Einige dieser Anwendungen wurden als wiederverwendbare Muster herausgearbeitet und mit Beispielen untermauert. Klassen eignen sich besonders zur Datenabstraktion, zur Implementierung heterogener Datenstrukturen, für generische Bausteine und um Verhalten von Programmen zur Laufzeit auszutauschen.

Während Datenabstraktion das am häufigsten anwendbare Muster ist (aber auch das am wenigsten spektakuläre), sind die anderen drei Muster diejenigen, bei denen objektorientierte Programmierung im Vergleich mit herkömmlichen Techniken am meisten bringt. Bei diesen drei Mustern wird die Vererbung und die dynamische Bindung intensiv benutzt und auch benötigt. Daher sollte man hier zu Klassen greifen.

Klassen sind ein mächtiges Sprachkonstrukt. Man muß sie aber gezielt einsetzen. Sie sind nur *ein* Werkzeug neben vielen anderen. Es gehört zum Können jedes Handwerkers und erst recht jedes Ingenieurs für jede Aufgabe das richtige Werkzeug zu wählen. Daher sollte man diejenigen Situationen kennen, in denen Klassen Vorteile bringen und sie dann und nur dann einsetzen.

Literatur

[Szyperski92] Szyperski, C.A.: Write-ing Applications. Proceedings of the TOOLS'92 conference, Dortmund, 1992.

[Wirth92] Wirth N., Gutknecht J.: Project Oberon. Addison-Wesley, 1992.

Search and Retrieval in Object-Oriented Information Systems

Erich Neuhold, Karl Aberer, Wolfgang Klas, Adelheit Stein, Ulrich Thiel

German National Center for Computer Science, Integrated Publication and Information Systems Institute (GMD-IPSI)
Dolivostr. 15, 6100 Darmstadt, Germany
e-mail: {neuhold, aberer, klas, stein, thiel}@darmstadt.gmd.de

1 Introduction

Retrieving data that satisfies a complex information need is often an exploratory and incremental process. In addition, the handling of multimedia information places an additional cognitive workload on the human user. A guiding principle of system design is that the system should adapt to the needs of the human user, and not vice versa [cf. Norman & Draper 1986]. This means that the user with his strong and even more with his weak points has to be the central parameter in the interface design process. An ideal system would be one which presented the user a familiar environment, which minimizes the learning of the formal details of the system in order to work effectively with it. Therefore, the design of the information system must respond to the need for user assistance by incorporating components which address the following problems users of information systems have to face:

Finding a useful retrieval strategy: Information-seeking processes are not determined by an exactly predefined task structure, but by individual strategies and tactics of users to which the system should adapt. Taking this assumption into account, we use "case-based" dialogue plans to guide the user through the retrieval process.

Flexible dialogue control: The user must have the opportunity to alter the dialogue steps proposed by the system and by this way control the dialogue flexibly. The system should provide the user appropriate means for withdrawing dialogue steps, going back in the dialogue history, changing the retrieval strategy, etc. In addition, subdialogues have to be permitted for requesting more context information on the current state. This may result in very complex dialogue structures which should be made transparent to the user in order to avoid disorientation.

Clarification of information needs: The user should be able to access a database without knowing the particular terminology or conventions used during the compilation of the database. The system should support the user in viewing the concepts under consideration from different perspectives during the query formulation phases and the data inspection phases of the dialogue.

Visualization of information spaces: Human perceptual processes operate in a highly parallel fashion. The presentation of information in forms which are to be serially consumed by the user (such as lengthy texts) should be combined with visualizations that provide survey information at a glance (such as graphics, pictures).

Relevance assessment of retrieved items: In complex information systems, which are used for document retrieval or knowledge base access, the problem of relevance assessment arises. The system should employ interactive presentation forms which exhibit the cues that are required for this purpose.

In this paper, we outline a system architecture which is intended to meet these requirements, and show how an object-oriented DBMS, which is capable to cope with multimedia data, can support this approach. Throughout the paper, we will illustrate our ideas with examples from recent prototypes that have been developed at GMD-IPSI. In particular, we will refer to the features of **MERIT** (**M**ultimedia **E**xtensions of **R**etrieval **I**nteraction **T**ools), a knowledge-based retrieval interface [cf. Stein, Thiel & Tißen 1992], and **VODAK,** an object-oriented DBMS suitable for multimedia data. MERIT offers access to a subset of the CORDIS databases with data about European research programs, projects, and consortia in the field of information technology[1]. The system features graphical presentations of retrieval results, employs interactive maps for geographical data, and provides scanned-in documents, e.g. photos of contact persons. The database management system functionality of VODAK is extended such that it treats multimedia data, like text, audio, or video, as an integral part of the databases. Furthermore VODAK is an extendible database management system which allows to integrate information from heterogeneous and distributed resources.

The paper is organized as follows: We start with an overview of a user-centered system architecture which is intended to tackle the problems mentioned above. Next, an outline of the object-oriented DBMS VODAK is given. In the subsequent sections, we discuss some aspects of the user-centered approach in detail, starting, just as in a MERIT dialogue session, with the user's determination of the information seeking strategy that is to be supported by the system. We then outline the system's components, which provide strategical and terminological assistance to the user. Next, some interactive presentation forms for retrieved data are discussed with respect to their effects on the user's relevance assessment. The paper concludes with short accounts of related and future work.

2 A System Architecture Supporting Search and Retrieval in Multimedia Databases

In order to achieve context sensitive and flexible dialogues the *Graphical Interface* (see figure 1) is augmented by dialogue and presentation components. The *Dialogue Manager* is able to support a global dialogue strategy as well as to maintain the conversational flow of information. The *Presentation Manager* generates the presentation of information and information structures to the user in a form which can most effectively be processed by the user's cognitive and perceptual capabilities. The *Database Interface* translates the user's requests into a formal query to the underlying database.

The *Dialogue Manager* operates on an internal representation of the dialogue. Thus, it is possible to handle the direct manipulative inputs of the user in a context-sensitive way. Retrieving information from an information system can be seen as an iterative process. A complex information need can be formulated in multiple ways, e.g. with a few, but complex queries in contrast to a step by step query formulation.

The user's actions (e.g. mouse clicks, menu selections) will not only send messages to the graphical surface objects which then execute methods, but will effect transformations of the

1. MERIT runs on SUN color workstations (SPARC stations) and is written in CommonLISP. As its graphical interface, MERIT uses HyperNeWS, a NeWS-based graphics environment developed at the Turing Institute in Glasgow. Its dynamic and static knowledge bases are based on CLOS, the object-oriented extension of CommonLISP, and on CRL, a part of Knowledge Craft. It accesses a subset of the CORDIS databases which are offered online by ECHO, the official host organization of the Commission of the European Community (CEC).

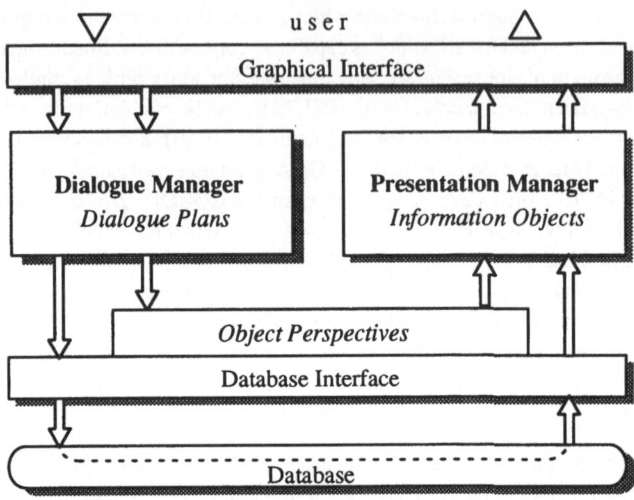

Figure 1: User-centered architecture

internal representation of the dialogue. This representation is to be maintained by the dialogue manager employing a conversational model [cf. Sitter & Stein 1992, Stein & Thiel 1993] of the interaction to keep track of the ongoing dialogue. Interpreting the interaction in terms of a conversational model allows the system to realize its reactions as instances of generic dialogue acts like Inform, Offer, Request. In general, a dialogue act performed by the system will result in the visualization of new graphical dialogue objects on the screen.

A case-based approach to user guidance [cf. Tißen 1991, Stein, Thiel & Tißen 1992, Belkin et al. 1993] allows the system to adopt a dialogue strategy which is adequate to achieve the user's dialogue goals. The strategy is determined by a sequence of steps in a dialogue plan. Steps are represented as frames which contain slots for preconditions, actions and side-effects (like plan operators in traditional approaches to plan representation, extended by input-/output descriptions and perspectives). A perspective consists of the main concept, relevant query and presentation attributes, and navigation paths to related concepts.

The main function of the *Presentation Manager* is the automatic generation of system reactions using generic presentation forms. This component provides the display of retrieved results obtained from the database. While these data form the propositional content of the system's contributions, the Presentation Manager also selects the graphical means to express the purpose (illocution) of a dialogue act, e.g. to inform, explain, comment. For the generation of dialogue contributions that do not involve data from the database, e.g. explanations, help, context information, the dialogue manager uses its dialogue knowledge bases.

The *Database Interface* translates the propositional content of the user's input into a query formulated in the query language of the underlying database. Stating restrictions in a query form sheet allows the user to specify the set of items he is interested in. In order to assist users in formulating restrictions for textual information, we also provide a facility (*Knowledge Explorer*) for semi-automatic term extension that is based on a "fuzzy association network" [cf. Kracker 1992].

The database itself can be realized in VODAK [cf. Duchêne, Kaul & Turau 1988, Klas 1990, Turau & Rakow 1993], a behavioral object-oriented database management system. The schema of the database is expressed in VML (VODAK Modeling Language) [cf. Klas et al. 1992] and provides the conceptual model for the information system. Since VML supports metaclasses as schema objects, i.e. classes and metaclasses are first class objects themselves, one can refer to classes appearing in the schema as to any other object in the database. This is the way the VODAK data dictionary is realized. The metaclass concept is also the basis for other important mechanisms. First, it allows to introduce arbitrary semantic relationships, like specialization, generalization or part-of, between classes and their corresponding objects. Second, it makes VODAK an extendible database management system as it allows to integrate schemas and databases of other database management systems. This can, for example, be used to build an object-oriented schema of the CORDIS databases.

The *query language* of VODAK, VQL [cf. Fischer & Aberer 1993], allows for a SQL-like set-oriented access to the database. In a VQL-statement arbitrary method-calls may appear and so arbitrary search strategies may be used in this way, as they may be necessary, for example, for multimedia datatypes. VODAK provides modelling primitives for representing noncontinuous multimedia data, e.g. text or graphics, as well as continuous multimedia data, e.g. audio and video. The goal is to support multimedia data in a way, that it is, like the conventional alphanumeric data, handled as an integral part of the database management system.

3 Searching Complex Objects: A Sample Domain and its Object-Oriented Representation

A typical example of mixing structured and unstructured data is the information offered by CORDIS (Community Research and Development Information Service). CORDIS provides information about the European Community (EC) Research and Technological Development (RTD) programs and related matters for organizations and individuals.[2] These data can be accessed online via a conventional full-text retrieval interface of the ECHO host.

However, in this domain the users typically do not search for documents, but for relevant *information objects*, e.g. research programs or projects which fulfill certain conditions, together with factual data, e.g. addresses, numerical data, e.g. project duration, and textual passages, e.g. a project's objectives. Given the functionality of a full-text retrieval system, the users must switch between the databases, and combine data sets retrieved from different isolated databases in order to obtain the complete information. From the users' perspective, however, it seems to be highly desirable to be able to formulate a complex query covering all relevant aspects of the information objects of interest, no matter in which particular RTD-databases the data is stored. Of course, this query formulation has to be assisted, e.g. via a form-based interface. Another prerequisite to a system capable to process such queries directly is a conceptual data model which defines the object classes of the domain of interest and their relationships.

Figure 2 provides a graphical overview of the conceptual model which serves as database schema and can be realized using VML. The conceptual model can be verbalized as follows: The EC research activities are grouped by **programs** (such as IMPACT, ESPRIT 2, etc.); each program

3. The corresponding databases are provided as CORDIS databases, e.g. *RTD-Programs, RTD-Projects, RTD-Acronyms, RTD-Comdocuments, RTD-Publications, RTD-Results, RTD-Partners* and so on.

contains a group of **projects** as *members*. Different EC **commission services** are *responsible for* different programs. Programs and projects have their contractors, *i.e. primary contractors and member contractors*, called **organizations** *located in* some **countries** and some **cities**. There are some **persons** in the role of *contact* person of program, project, or commission service. The **publications**, including **reports**, **articles**, and **conference papers**, are *issued by* organizations, programs and projects, with some person(s) as ***author(s)***. The programs, projects and publications can be classified to some ***subjects***.

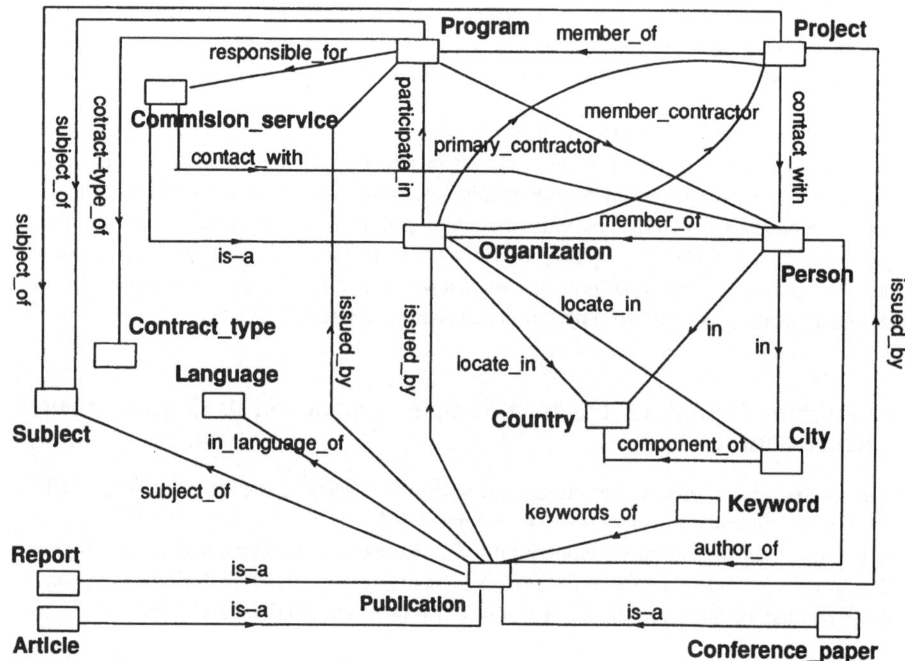

Figure 2: Conceptual Model

4 Retrieval Strategies and Flexible Dialogue Control

Information-seeking processes are characterized by the fact that information needs are not predefined distinctively, and that there is no objective underlying task-structure which strictly regulates the order of navigational steps. The information seeker may change his intentions or the thematic focus during the interaction. An intelligent system should be capable to cope with such topic shifts and changing user-strategies. At the same time it is important to facilitate the user's construction of cognitive coherence by adequate guidance. Thus, we propose to establish a dialogue control which can adapt to some extent the system's behavior to changing dialogue goals and information needs of the user. Initially the user has only vague ideas about his information need [cf. Belkin & Marchetti 1990] and how to explore the information space. For guiding the user effectively, the system relies on **dialogue plans**, which are dynamically adapted to the ongoing dialogue, and it captures the focus of the dialogue by means of **object-oriented perspectives**.

At any time the user must have the opportunity to control the dialogue flexibly in order to alter the steps of the current dialogue plan. He can do this by directly manipulating graphical objects, e.g. special dialogue-icons [for details cf. Stein, Thiel & Tißen 1992]. However, most of these graphical actions are interpreted as "communicative acts" that express dialogue goals [cf. e.g. Maybury 1990, Stein & Thiel 1993]. The formal (illocutionary) model underlying the exchange of dialogue acts in MERIT has thoroughly been discussed elsewhere [cf. Sitter & Stein 1992].

Dialogue Plans: In order to achieve a flexible and adaptive management of dialogue strategies we employ a ***Case-based Dialogue Manager,*** CADI [cf. Tißen 1991]. CADI can be seen as a special adaptation of a case-based reasoner for guiding information-seeking dialogues. The basic idea of a case-based reasoner is to use the experience from old solutions for the generation of dialogues plans. Kolodner and Simpson describe the role of experience in problem solving: *"Individual experiences act as exemplars upon which to base later decisions. Analogies to previous cases guide andfocus later decision making."* [1986, p. 99 f.] In MERIT, previous cases are used to *guide* the user through the retrieval process and to *focus* the dialogue and the presentations considering his goals. In our application, the notion of 'cases' refers to protocols of prior executions of dialogue plans, which are represented by frame-like data structures. Dialogue plans structure an information-seeking dialogue according to principles of topical coherence. They model the thematic progression and serve as a means for reducing the relevant information space.

In accordance with this approach we offer the user at the beginning of the retrieval session a selection of basic dialogue plans that can get modified during the dialogue. The library of dialogue plans can be seen as a set of prototypical cases stored in the past. In the MERIT domain of research projects, programs, and publications there are for example cases like: "Projects about tutoring systems in the current RACE program", "Overview about ESPRIT projects concerning intelligent interfaces", "Looking for university partners with project experience in text-generation". Whenever the user wants the system to memorize the current dialogue path with all its modifications, he can use the CADI system to compose and store a new plan and hereby augment the library of dialogue plans.

Object Perspectives: By dialogue goals we do not refer to any real-world goals of the information seeker, but rather to the hyperthema of the dialogue or the expected scope of information, e.g. the amount of data or the granularity of information. Nevertheless, real-world goals or interests influence the thematic scope to a large extent. Therefore we use the concept of *"object perspectives"* [cf. Tißen 1991]. An object perspective can be described as a set of assumptions and expectations associated with a specific domain object which is in the focus of the dialogue (e.g. projects), and a closely related problem-solving task (e.g. looking for project partners).

From the user's point of view a perspective describes the relevant information space in a given dialogue situation. This includes the possibilities to navigate to specific information objects within this space. The system's definition of a perspective marks the relevant information space of the database – including relations of the central information object to other objects and their attributes. It also defines a set of related perspectives. Moving to one of these perspectives maintains the local topical coherence of the dialogue. Thus, our notion of perspectives combines *semantic aspects*, the 'view' onto the represented domain-objects, with temporal or *topical aspects* (the currently selected perspective determines possible navigation paths and subsequent topics).

A hierarchy of perspectives together with a set of functions enables the system to adapt a query or presentation step directly to a new situation. For instance, the perspective concerning project information, focusing on project partners, is a sub-perspective of organizational aspects of project information. In this perspective only a small subset of database attributes is relevant to the query. If the dialogue is in a presentation state, switching from the "organizational perspective" to the more restricted "organizational-partner perspective", only the generation of a new presentation of the data, which have already been retrieved from the database, is required. This is a very simple example of a modification of a dialogue plan influencing only the amount of presented information without side effects. However, most modifications in a dialogue cause side effects to be handled by the system. For example, it may be necessary to send a new internal query to the database, or to modify the proposed subsequent dialogue steps automatically (insert, delete, or replace steps which propagate changed parameters).

The *knowledge base for perspectives* is closely related to the domain knowledge base. This implies that the perspectives have to be adapted when the conceptual domain knowledge changes. The dynamic adaptation of dialogue plans during a dialogue session is initiated by the user and controlled by modification rules. These rules use the knowledge base of object perspectives. For each executed dialogue step the dialogue manager generates a state in the *dialogue history*, representing the step with all dynamic modifications, together with the input given by the user. This explicit representation is the basis for generating a new case to increase the library of good sample cases.

Due to the close relation of object perspectives to the domain knowledge base, which is a database whose schema is described in the VODAK modeling language VML, they are preferably expressed in VML. We give the sketch of the structural part of an implementation of perspectives in VML. Each perspective is an instance of the class Perspective.

```
CLASS Perspective
  INSTTYPE
    PROPERTIES
    main-concept: Class
    zoom-in:  {Perspective};
    zoom-out: {Perspective};
              // these two properties establish the hierarchy
    shift-to: {Perspective};
              // related perspectives
    query-attributes: {Property};
    presentation-attributes: {Property};
  END
END
```

In this class definition we make use of several typical features of VML. We have defined the structural part (properties) of the type definition for the instances of the class *Perspective*. This is signalled by the keyword INSTTYPE. The properties refer to instances or set of instances of other classes. Such direct references are possible since each instance has a unique object identifier. The class definition of Perspective makes use of system-defined classes like Class and Property, which contain information about all classes and properties of a given schema. Note that each property "knows" to which class it belongs. The classes *Class* and *Property* are system-defined as they are already needed by the VODAK data dictionary.

It is clear that, in order to avoid a break in the system architecture and to avoid the introduction of complicated interfaces the other cognitive concepts, like dialogue plans, are preferably modeled within VML either. In this paper, however, we do not go into the details of this.

5 Clarification of Information Needs

5.1 Support of Query Formulation

Object perspectives [cf. e.g. Tou et al. 1982, McCoy 1986] describe subsets of the database relevant in a specific context, for the query component as well as for the presentation component. A hierarchical representation of perspectives together with a set of functions enables the system to adapt a query or presentation step directly to a new situation. For instance, the perspective concerning project information, focusing on project partners, is a sub-perspective of organizational aspects of project information. In this perspective only a small subset of database attributes are relevant to the formulation of a query.

After the case selection, the user is presented a query form [cf. e.g. McAlpine & Ingwersen 1989] listing attributes of the selected perspective (see figure 3). The user reduces the amount of relevant instances of the current concept class. This is achieved by stating *attribute restrictions*. Each line of the query form sheet represents a restriction consisting of a comparison operator selected from a menu that provides an attribute-specific choice, and a constant to which attribute values of instances in the knowledge base are to be compared. If all restrictions are fulfilled for a given instance, then this instance will belong to the set of responses.

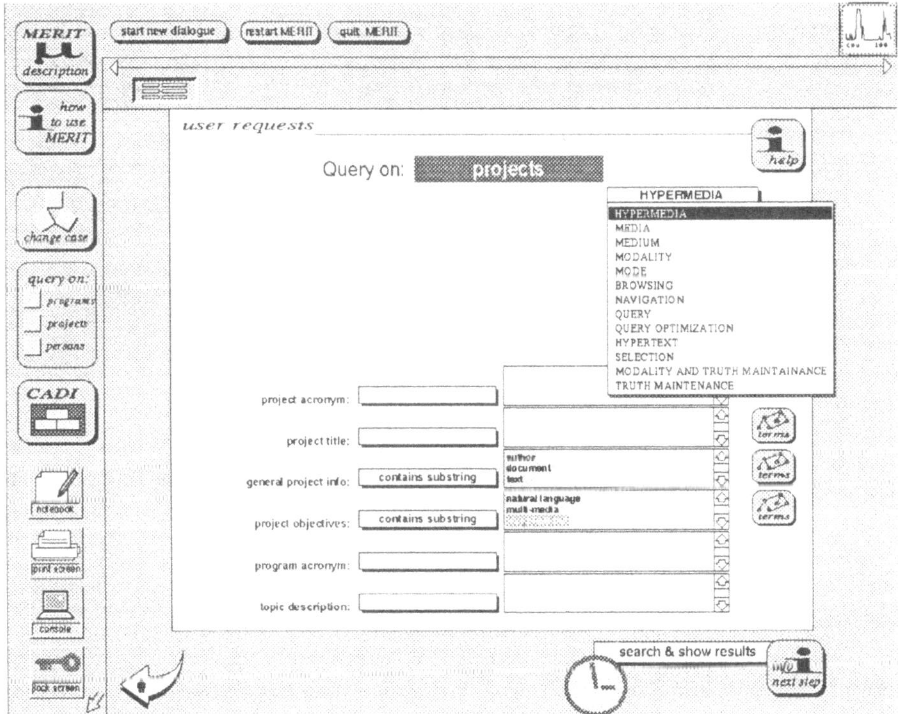

Figure 3: A sample query form

Figure 3 shows the query form for the thematic perspective of projects, i.e. it does not include organizational attributes like project partners, contact persons, location, dates, financial data, etc.

By the filled-in query all projects will be retrieved which contain the terms "*author*" or "*document*" or "*text*" in their general project information and at the same time the terms "*natural language*" or "*multi-media*" or "*hypermedia*" in their project objectives.

5.2 Support of Free Text Search

Query forms may contain multiple free text fields, for example a description of projects. The user may require that a text field of a retrieved instance must or must not contain a given search term. If search terms are given in different lines of a multiple line field they are implicitly connected by the Boolean *OR*.

Originally, the user wants to do a *content* based search, but instead he has to deal with *terms* which just are the surface representation of the content. In order to improve the recall of his query the user in general has to add several synonyms or similar concepts to each search concept. Instead of leaving the task of finding these additional search concepts to the user, we employ a module called *Knowledge Explorer* (*KX*) which has conceptual knowledge of the database domain and suggest such supplementary concepts.

This conceptual knowledge is stored as a fuzzy association network [cf. Kracker 1992]. The meaning of a concept is solely determined by its relationships to other concepts. There are four types of such relationships: A *positive association* connects concepts which are semantically similar or often used in the same context, a *negative association* is used to express some kind of opposition, a *generalization* links one concept to another which is more general in a semantic or partitive sense, and the *specialization* is the inverse of the generalization relationship (cf. figure 4).

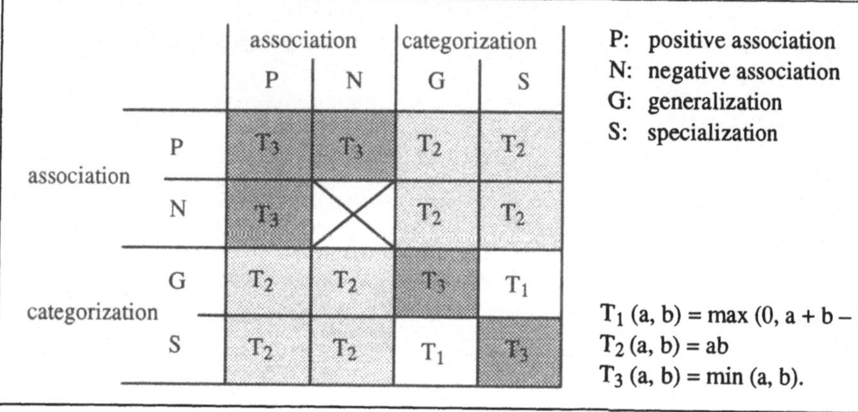

Figure 4: T-norm defining a calculus of similarity

Each pair in a relationship has a value out of [0, 1] assigned which is interpreted as the *strength* of the relationship. A positive association with a strength close to 1, for example, identifies a relation between two very similar concepts. We assume the positive association, the generalization and the specialization to be transitive relationships.

We can use the inherent transitivity of these relationships to compute relationships between two concepts even if they are not *directly* connected. There are many (in fact, an unlimited number of) T-norm functions $[0, 1] \times [0, 1] \rightarrow [0, 1]$ suitable for combining transitive relationships. They differ in the strength of the resulting relationship. Opposed to [Bezdek, Gautam & Hunag 1986], where a single T-norm function is used for all types of relationships, we employ three T-norm functions (see figure 4).[3]

The type of a derived relationship must also be specified. Again, this type is a priori determined depending on the types of the combined relationships. An extensive discussion of the inference process can be found in [Kracker 1992]. The system computes on demand for a given initial concept all relationships that are stronger than a heuristically determined cutoff value. This method is sufficient for our application described above and is fast enought for interactive use.

To give an example of how the user might get support in the domain *multimedia/ hypermedia* we again refer to figure 4. To increase the recall of that query, the user has to include additional terms in the free text field *project objectives* which he can disjunctively combine with the already specified search terms *author, document,* and *text.* Upon request, the system suggests a ranked list of semantically similar terms in a pull-down menu. Each item the user selects will be automatically inserted into the query form, e.g. *media* or *hypertext.*

6 Query Processing in VODAK

Multimedia data needs search strategies which are very different from that on conventional data. As an example we have considered free text search. Extendibility of the database primitives in VODAK allows to integrate the corresponding algorithms and data structures easily. The query language must then allow to use the new primitives without restrictions, which is obtained by allowing arbitrary method calls in query statements.

In the following we sketch how VODAK can support an extendible search strategy in the case of free text search. Assume a class is given which contains as a property a piece of text. We model the text not directly as String in the class Info but instead refer to an instance of the class Info_Text_Class which represents the text.

```
CLASS Info
  INSTTYPE
    PROPERTIES
    info_text: Info_Text_Class;
    .... (other properties)
END
```

As we want to make available a certain search algorithm on text, the class Info_Text_Class itself is an instance of a metaclass which provides these corresponding methods in its so called instance-instance-type (INSTINSTTYPE) via inheritance. In other words any instance of a class with metaclass Text_Metaclass will inherit the interface defined in the instance-instance-type of the metaclass. Note that the instances of the metaclass are classes themselves.

3. It is easy to show that $T1(a, b) \le T2(a, b) \le T3(a, b)$ holds. T1 is the most conservative function returning the smallest values. T3, on the contrary, makes the most optimistic conclusions and infers the strongest relationships. T2 assumes the arguments to be independent and treats them like independent probabilities. Depending on the types of the relationships to be combined the most suitable T-norm can be used.

```
CLASS Info_Text_Class METACLASS Text_Metaclass END

CLASS Text_Metaclass METACLASS Metaclass
  INSTINSTTYPE
    PROPERTIES
      text: BYTESTRING;
    METHODS
      search(s: STRING);
        \\ searches in text for the string s
END
```

The property text now contains the actual information. The BYTESTRING datatype is one of the new primitive datatypes provided by VODAK in order to support multimedia datatypes. Other primitive datatypes will be AUDIO and VIDEO. The method search can now be sent to any instance of a class whose metaclass is Text_Metaclass, e.g. to any instance of Info_Text_Class. We also could provide through the metaclass Text_Metaclass persistent indexing structures which can be used to speed up search.

In a VQL query we can use the method search, e.g. as in the following query:[4]

ACCESS i FROM i IN Info WHERE i.info_text->search("string").

This query returns the set of instances of Info which contain in the text represented by *info_text* the string "string".

Another feature of VQL that is important to support the interface techniques introduced earlier is the possibility of arbitrary nesting of queries and reuse of query results. Thus an iterative refinement as it can appear in the dialogue is possible.

A central part of query processing is concerned with query optimization. As we are facing in multimedia database management systems the necessity to support also search algorithms and access structures which can not be foreseen at the time the query optimizer is designed it must be extendible in the same way as the rest of the system is. This is a current focus of research in the development of the VQL query optimizer.

7 Presentation of Retrieval Results in MERIT

The mixture of textual, factual, and organizational data which is retrieved from the database as a response to a query has to be presented adequately. Our approach to the presentation of retrieval results is motivated by van Rijsbergen's logical interpretation of relevance [van Rijsbergen 1989]. Given a query Q and a set of information items D we have to determine the probability P of the fact that D entails Q: P(D ->Q). A high probability P(D ->Q) indicates that D is relevant with respect to Q.

The purpose of presenting information objects as a response to a query in a retrieval dialogue is twofold: First, to inform the user about the retrieved data, second, to convince him that the system's reaction is relevant to the query, and, as a consequence, to the user's information need. As the data are organized as a complex structure additional information must be conveyed. As

4. We use the keyword ACCESS since we allow arbitrary method calls in the query. Therefore a distinction between SELECT (no updates) and UPDATE is no longer meaningful [cf. Fischer 1992].

an example, the fact that a given part of the visualization pertains to a certain concept or search term in the query will be very useful for the user in her/his interpretation of the query result. In order to support the user's inferencing on presented data we employ cognitively motivated *presentation forms*.

For a discussion of the cognitive background of the visualization design we refer to [Kerner & Thiel 1991], in the following, however, we will concentrate on relevance assessment in regard to information presentation as a follow-up of querying a database.

7.1 Providing Survey Information

The *survey presentation form* reveals the relationships between the retrieved data items. In figure 5 the acronyms of retrieved projects are shown together with the subject index codes. These data items have been retrieved from the database in accordance to the query (cf. figure 3), and, subsequently, transformed into an object-oriented representation. This allows the user to change the contents of the visualized presentation form. He may switch to a similar graph (or a table) depicting the same project acronyms, but instead of the index terms the prime contractor companies are shown. Note that this leads to a different perspective which overlays the one originally suggested by the chosen plan.

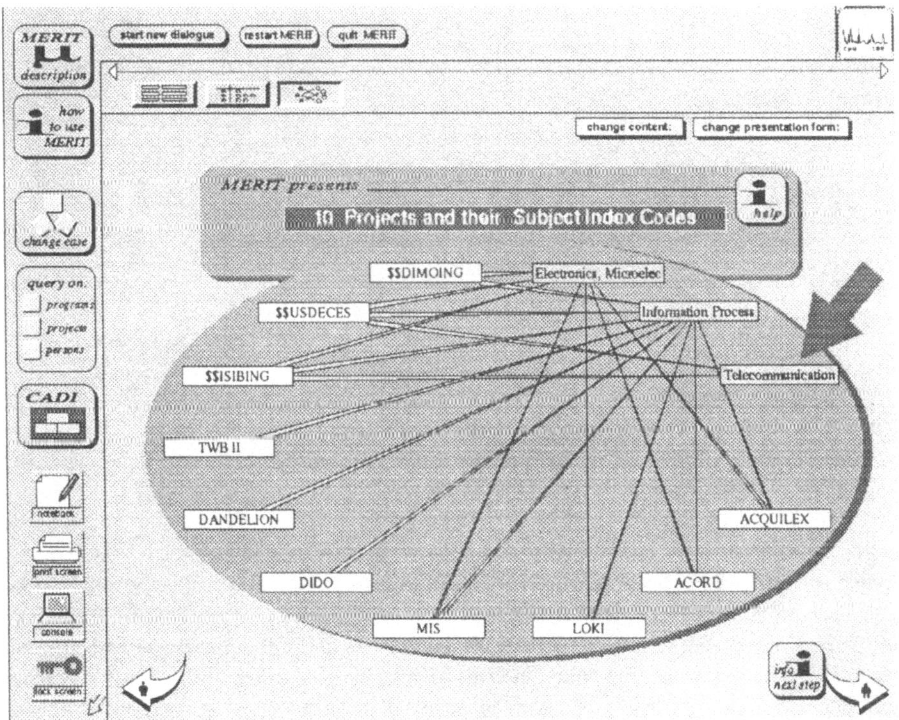

Figure 5: Survey presentation form

7.2 Presentation of Detailed Information and Additional Visual Information

If further attributes or details have to be presented, the survey presentation form fails to meet this information need. The presentation form shown in figure 6 responds to the detail-oriented information needs. In our example, the available attributes of projects like acronym, title, program, general information, objectives, prime contractor, contact person, etc. are on display. The current perspective determines which attributes are currently presented to the user. One project and its attached information items are visualized on the screen, other projects belonging to the same retrieval result are available on demand. The user selects the other projects by pressing the *next* or *previous* button.

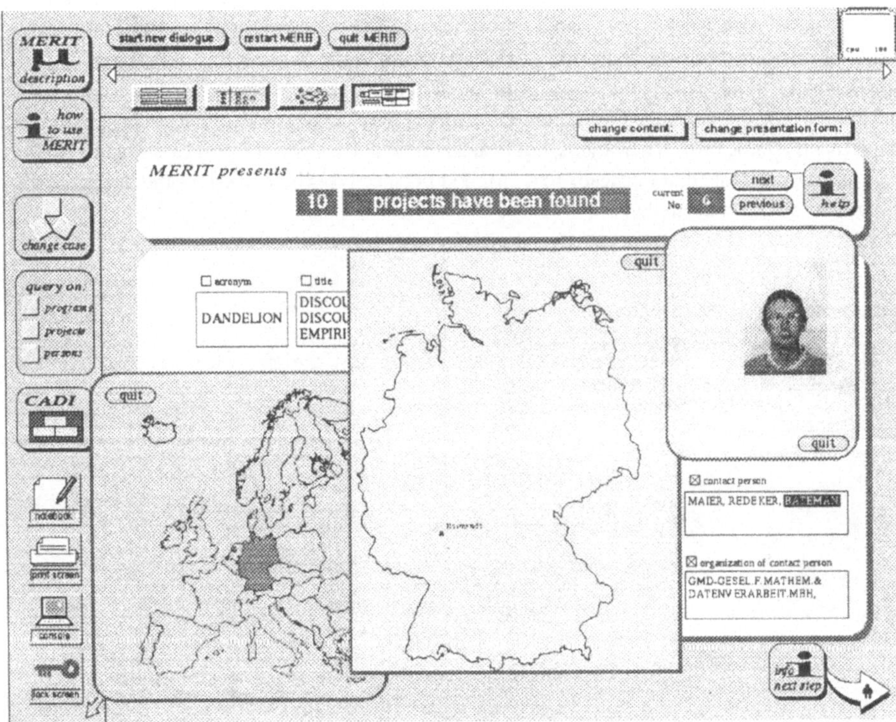

Figure 6: Maps and photo integrated into the detail presentation form

In MERIT a subset of the project data was augmented by additional scanned-in or programmed images encoded in EPS (Encapsulated PostScript). Also audio annotations can be added in order to provide further *context information*. We will illustrate this issue giving two examples: photos and maps. Contextual information supports the associations of the user. In our example, the user can click on the contact-person button in order to get additional information about the person, i.e. a photo (cf. figure 6). When the user is interested in the location of a project partner he may click on a button in order to get the geographical information. In our example he gets first a map of Europe with the country (Germany) highlighted. Then he may click on the highlighted area to get a more detailed map of Germany displaying the city of the prime contractor (Darmstadt).

7.3 Realization of the Visualization

The presentation of multimedia data stored in VODAK cannot be considered separately from the database management system. In contrast to conventional alphanumeric data, for these data special mechanisms are provided by the database management system which allow to deal with the huge amounts of data which have to be represented. Especially for continuous data these mechanisms are crucial, as only they allow to bring the right piece of data, e.g. a video frame, at the right time to the right device, e.g. a window. Also the user interaction, e.g. mouse clicks, have to be part of this process in order to support browsing and control of the presentation by the user. These issues are currently investigated in the AMOS project [for more details see Rakow et al. 1993, Aberer & Klas 1992, Klas 1992].

8 Related Work

The approach presented in this paper is interdisciplinary in nature, since it involves not only different branches of computer science, but also builds upon work in information science, psychology and linguistics.

In particular, the design of MERIT addressed problems of cooperative graphical or multimodal interfaces [cf. Hayes 1987, Neal & Shapiro 1989; Cohen et al. 1989; Allgayer et al. 1989; Arens & Hovy 1990; Moore & Swartout 1990; Feiner & McKeown 1990; Bandyopadhyay 1990; Stock 1991]. Another body of related work aims at the plan-based or task-driven automatic generation of graphics [e.g. Wahlster et al. 1991; Oei et al. 1992] and the case-based composition of video presentations [MacNeil 1991]. However, these approaches are not interactive in the sense that the end user may influence the generation process, while in MERIT the sequence of visualizations of retrieved data items results from the cooperation between user and system.

The user of MERIT engages in a *visual dialogue,* in which the interaction, although realized by graphical means, complies with conversational patterns of exchange [cf. Stein & Thiel 1992]. Similar approaches to flexible graphical interaction based on the *conversational metaphor* [cf. Hutchins 1989, Reichman 1986, 1989, Thiel 1990] treat user inputs such as mouse clicks, menu selections, etc. not as invocations of methods that can be executed without regarding the dialogue context, but instead as dialogue acts expressing a discourse goal of the user.

The object-oriented database management system VODAK will serve as a platform for the MERIT Interface system. Other object-oriented database systems supporting multimedia data like ORION [cf. Woelk, Kim & Luther 1986] as well as experiences made with hypermedia systems like *NoteCards* [cf. Halasz, Moran & Trigg 1987, Halasz 1988], *Neptune* [cf. Delisle, N. & Schwartz 1986], *Intermedia* [cf. Garret, Smith & Meyrowitz 1986, Meyrowitz 1986], and *KMS* [cf. Akscyn, McCracken & Yoder 1988] may also influence the overall design of multimedia information systems with respect to their functionality. An object-oriented database system with a visual query interface is O_2 [Bancilhon, Cluet & Delobel 1989] but which provides only a presentation component, and OQL [Lam, Chen, Ty, Qiu, & Su 1990] is an interesting approach to a graphical interface for an object-oriented query language.

9 Conclusions

MERIT supports the user by offering a selection of sample retrieval strategies (*cases*) which are modifiable to meet situative requirements. Based on a selected *case* the system adopts an appropriate *perspective* while accessing the database. Thus, irrelevant attributes of the objects of interest can be neglected. The perspective enables the system to offer situation-dependent query forms. The process of selecting search terms is assisted by a semantic component proposing additional search terms that are derived from an initially given one by associative reasoning. MERIT generates graphical presentations of retrieval results which support – in accordance to the current case – a survey or detail oriented reception of the retrieved data, thus providing visual cues for the user's relevance assessment. Additionally, the system employs interactive maps to display geographical data, and can provide scanned-in documents.

An extendible database system like VODAK is the ideal underlying database system. Due to its specific object-oriented features it allows to integrate a support for multimedia data, to integrate heterogeneous resources, and its query language is extendible for multimedia search strategies. Care has to be taken to provide a seamless interface and to exploit fully the support for presentation of multimedia data as provided by the database management system.

References

Aberer, K. & Klas, W.: *The Impact of Multimedia Data on Database Management Systems.* Technical Report TR-92-065, International Computer Science Institute (ICSI), Berkeley, CA, 1992.

Allgayer, J., Harbusch, K., Kobsa, A., Reddig, C., Reithinger, N., & Schmauks, D.: XTRA: A Natural Language Access System to Expert Systems. *Int. Journal of Man-Machine Studies, Vol. 31,* No. 2, 1989, pp. 161-195.

Arens, Y., & Hovy, E.H.: How to Describe What? Towards a Theory of Modality Utilization. In: *CogSci '90, Proc. of the 12th Annual Conference of the Cognitive Science Society in Cambridge, MA.* Hillsdale, NJ: Erlbaum, 1990, pp. 487-94.

Akscyn, R., McCracken, D.L. & Yoder, E.: A Distributed Hypertext for Sharing Knowledge in Organizations. *Communications of the ACM, 31, 7,* July 1988, pp. 820-835.

Bancilhon,F., Cluet S., Delobel C.: A Query Language for the O_2 Object-Oriented Database System. In: *Proc. of the DBPL, Salishan Lodge, Oregon* 1989.

Bezdek, J.C., Gautam, B. & Li-Ya Hunag: Transitive Closures of Fuzzy Thesauri for Information-Retrieval Systems. *Int. Journal of Man-Machine Studies, Vol. 25,* 1986, pp. 343-356.

Belkin, N., Cool, C., Stein, A. & Thiel, U.: Scripts for Information Seeking Dialogues. Paper presented at: *AAAI Spring Symposium on Case-Based Reasoning and Information Retrieval, Stanford University, CA, March 23-25, 1993.*

Belkin, N.J., & Marchetti, P.G.: Determining the Functionality and Features of an Intelligent Interface to an Information Retrieval System. In: Vidick, J.-L. (ed.): *SIGIR '90, Proc. of the 13th Int. Conference on Research and Development in Information Retrieval,* Brussels, Belgium, 1990, pp. 151-178.

Bandyopadhyay, S.: *Towards an Understanding of Coherence in Multi-Modal Discourse,* Technical Memo TM-90-01, Deutsches Forschungsinstitut für Künstliche Intelligenz, Saarbrücken, 1990.

Cohen, P. R., Dalrymple, M., Moran, D., Pereira, F., Sullivan, J., Gargan Jr., R., Schlossberg, J., & Tyler, S.: Synergistic Use of Direct Manipulation and Natural Language. In: Bice, K. and Lewis, C. (eds.): *Proc. of CHI '89, Austin, TX.* New York: ACM, 1989, pp. 227-233.

Duchêne, H., Kaul, M., & Turau, V.: VODAK Kernel Data Model. In: Dittrich, K.R. (ed.), *Advances in Object-Oriented Database Systems, Proc. of the 2nd Int. Workshop on Object-Oriented Database Systems, Bad Münster am Stein-Ebernburg, FRG.* Lecture Notes in Computer Science, No. 334. Berlin: Springer, 1988.

Delisle, N. & Schwartz, M.: Neptune: A Hypertext System for CAD Applications. In: *Proc. of ACM SIGMOD '86, Washington D.C., May 28-30.* New York: ACM, 1986, pp. 132-142.

Feiner, S.K. & McKeown, K.R.: Coordinating Text and Graphics in Explanation Generation. In: *AAAI '90, Proc. of the 8th National Conference on Artificial Intelligence, Vol. I.* Menlo Park et al.: AAAI Press / The MIT Press, 1990, pp. 442-449.

Fischer, G.: Updates in Object-Oriented Database Systems Caused by Method Calls in Queries. In: *Proc. of the 3rd ERCIM Database Research Group Workshop on Updates and Constraints Handling in Advanced Database Systems, Pisa, Italy, September 28-30, 1992.*

Fischer, G. & K.Aberer: VODAK Query Language VQL 1.0. *Internal Report GMD-IPSI, Feb. 1993.*

Garret, L.N., Smith, K.E. & Meyrowitz, N.: Intermedia: Issues, Strategies, and Tactics in the Design of a Hypermedia Document System. In: *CSCW '86, Proc. of the Conference on Computer-Supported Cooperative Work, Austin, Texas, Dec 3-5,* 1986, pp. 163-174.

Halasz, F.G., Moran, T.P & Trigg, R.H.: NoteCards in a Nutshell. In: *CHI + GI '87, Proc. of the 1987 ACM Conference of Human Factors in Computer Systems, Toronto, Ontario, Apr 5-9.* 1987, pp. 45-52.

Halasz, F.G., Reflections on NoteCards: Seven Issues for the Next Generation of Hypermedia Systems, *Communications of the ACM, Vol. 31, No. 7,* July 1988.

Hayes, P.J.: Steps towards Integrating Natural Language and Graphical Interaction for Knowledge-Based Systems. In: du Boulay, B., Hogg, D., Steels, L. (eds.): *Proc. of the ECAI '86: Advances in Artificial Intelligence – II.* Amsterdam : North-Holland, 1987, pp. 543-552.

Hutchins, E.: Metaphors for Interface Design. In: Taylor, M.M., et al. (eds.): *The Structure of Multimodal Dialogue.* Amsterdam: North-Holland, 1989, pp. 11-28.

Kerner, A., & Thiel, U.: Graphical Support for Users' Inferences within Retrieval Dialogues. In: *Proc. of the IEEE Workshop on Visual Languages, Kobe, Japan.* Washington: IEEE Computer Society Press, 1991, pp. 211-216.

Klas, W.: *A Metaclass System for Open Object-Oriented Data Models.* PhD Thesis, Technical University of Vienna, Austria, January 1990.

Klas, W.: Tailoring an Object-Oriented Database System to Integrate External Multimedia Devices. In: *Proc. of the 1992 Workshop on Heterogeneous Databases & Semantic Interoperability, Boulder, CO, Feb 10-12, 1992.*

Klas W. et al.: VML – The VODAK Model Language Version 2.2, Technical Report, GMD-IPSI, August 1992.

Kolodner, J.L. & Simpson R.L.: Problem Solving and Dynamic Memory. In: Kolodner, J.L., and Riesbeck, C.K. (eds.): *Experience, Memory, and Reasoning.* Hillsdale, NJ, 1986, pp. 99-114.

Kracker, M.: A Fuzzy Concept Network Model and Its Applications. In: *Proc. of the FUZZ-IEEE '92, San Diego, CA, March 1992,* pp. 760-768.

Lam, H., Chen, H.M., Ty, F.S., Qiu, J., & Su, S.Y.W.: A Graphical Interface for an Object-Oriented Query Language. In: *Proc. of the 14th. Int. Computer Software & Application Conf., Chicago, Ill., Oct. 31 – Nov. 2, 1990,* pp. 231-237.

MacNeil, R.: Generating Multimedia Presentations Automatically using TYRO, the Constraint, Case-Based Designer's Apprentice. In: *Proc. of the IEEE Workshop on Visual Languages, Kobe, Japan.* Washington: IEEE Computer Society Press, 1991, pp. 74-79.

Maybury, M.T.: Planning Multimedia Explanations Using Communicative Acts. In: *AAAI '91, Proc. of the 9th National Conference on Artificial Intelligence, Anaheim, CA, 1991.*

McAlpine, G. & Ingwersen, P.: Integrated Information Retrieval in a Knowledge Worker Support System. In: N.J. Belkin and van Rijsbergen, C.J. (eds.): *SIGIR '89, Proc. of the 12th Int. Conference on Research and Development in Information Retrieval.* Cambridge, MA, 1989, pp. 48-57.

McCoy, K.F.: The ROMPER System: Responding to Object-Related Misconceptions Using Perspective. In: *Proc. of the 24th. Annual Meeting of the Association for Computational Linguistics,* New York, 1986.

Meyrowitz, N: Intermedia: The Architecture and Construction of an Object-oriented Hypermedia System and Applications Framework. In: *OOPSLA '86, Proc. of the Conference on Object-oriented Programming Systems, Languages, and Applications, Portland, Oregon, Sept. 29 – Oct 2.* ACM SIGPLAN No. 21, 11. 1986.

Moore, J.D. & Swartout, J.R.: Pointing: A Way Toward Explanation Dialogue. In: *AAAI '90, Proc. of the 8th National Conference on Artificial Intelligence, Vol. I.* Menlo Park, CA: AAAI Press / The MIT Press, 1990, pp. 457-464.

Neal, J.G. & Shapiro S.C.: Intelligent Multi-Media Interface Technology. In: Sullivan, J.W. and Tyler, S.W. (eds.): *Proc. of the Workshop on Architectures for Intelligent Interfaces: Elements and Prototypes.* ACM/ Addison-Wesley, 1989, pp. 69-91.

Norman, D.A. & Draper, S.W. (eds.): *User Centered System Design. New Perspectives on Human-Computer Interaction.* Hillsdale, NJ: Erlbaum, 1986.

Oei, S., Smit, R., Schreinemakers, J., Marinos, L. & Sirks, J.: The Presentation Manager, A Method for Task-Driven Concept Presentation. In: Neumann, B. (ed): *Proc. of the ECAI '92,* Chichester et al.: John Wiley & Sons, pp. 774-775.

Rakow, T.C., Löhr, M., Moser, F. & Neuhold, E.J.: Einsatz von objektorientierten Datenbanksystemen für Multimedia-Anwendungen. To be published in: *it + ti: Special Issue on "Multimedia".* Oldenbourg, 1993 (forthcoming).

Reichman, R.: Communication Paradigms for a Window System. In: Norman, D.A. & Draper, S.W. (eds.): *User Centered System Design: New Perspectives on Human-Computer Interaction.* Hillsdale, NJ: Erlbaum, 1986, pp. 285-313.

Reichman, R.: Integrated Interfaces Based on a Theory of Context and Goal Tracking. In: Taylor, M.M., et al. (eds.): *The Structure of Multimodal Dialogue.* Amsterdam: North-Holland, 1989, pp. 209-228.

van Rijsbergen, C.J.: Towards an Information Logic. In: N.J. Belkin & C.J. van Rijsbergen (eds)*: SIGIR '89, Proc. of the 12th Int. Conference on Research and Development in Information Retrieval,* Cambridge, MA, 1989, pp. 77-86.

Sitter, S. & Stein, A.: Modeling the Illocutionary Aspects of Information-Seeking Dialogues. *Information Processing & Management, Vol. 28(2),* 1992, pp. 165-180.

Stein, A. &, and Thiel, U.: A Conversational Model of Multimodal Interaction. Paper presented at: *HCIC '93, Human Computer Interaction Consortium 1993 Winter Workshop, Atlanta/ Georgia, Jan. 23-26, 1993.*

Stein, A., Thiel, U. & Tißen, A.: Knowledge-Based Control of Visual Dialogues in Information Systems. In: *AVI '92, Proc. of the 1st Int. Workshop on Advanced Visual Interfaces, Rome, Italy, May 27-29.* Singapore: World Scientific-Press, 1992, pp. 138-155. Also available as: *Arbeitspapiere der GMD, No 662,* Sankt Augustin: GMD, July 1992.

Stock, O.: Natural Language and the Exploration of an Information Space: The ALFresco Interactive System. In: *Proc. of the IJCAI '91.* Sydney, 1991, pp. 972-978.

Thiel, U.: *Conversational Graphical Interaction with Information Systems. An Approach Based on Speechact Theory* (Dissertation, in German). Konstanz, Germany, Universität Konstanz, 1990.

Tißen, A.: A Case-Based Architecture for a Dialogue Manager for Information-Seeking Processes. In: Bookstein, A., et al. (eds.): *SIGIR '91, Proc. of the 14th Int. Conference on Research and Development in Information Retrieval,* Chicago, IL, 1991, pp. 152-161.

Tou, F., Williams, M., Fikes, R., Henderson, D.A. &, and Malone, T.: RABBIT: An Intelligent Database Assistant. In: *AAAI '82, Proc. of the National Conference on Artificial Intelligence.,* 1982, pp. 314-318.

Turau, V. & Rakow, T.C.: A Schema Partition for Multimedia Database Management Systems. In: *Arbeitspapiere der GMD, No. 729.* Sankt Augustin: GMD, 1993.

Wahlster, W., André, E., Graf, W. & Rist, T.: Designing Illustrated Texts: How Language Production is Influenced by the Graphics Generation. In: *Proc. of the 5th Conference of the European Chapter of the Association for Computational Linguistics,* 1991.

Woelk, Darrel, Kim, W. & Luther, W.: An Object-Oriented Approach to Multimedia Databases; *ACM SIGMOD Record 1986,* pp. 311-325, ACM, 1986.

Methodik

Objektorientierte Spezifikation: Konzepte und eine Notation

W. Bartsch
E. Denert

Fakultät für Informatik
Technische Universität München
Arcisstraße 21
80333 München

und

sd&m gmbh
Thomas-Dehler-Straße 18
81737 München

E-Mail: bartsch@informatik.tu-muenchen.de

1 Zur Bedeutung der Spezifikation

Die Bedeutung der Spezifikation eines Informationssystems kann gar nicht hoch genug eingeschätzt werden. Sie ist die Grundlage der weiteren Softwareentwicklung und des Projekterfolgs. Wie kommt man zu einer guten Spezifikation? Der Titel dieses Beitrags suggeriert, man müsse sie nur objektorientiert machen und ein gutes Ergebnis sei damit schon gesichert. Weit gefehlt — entscheidend ist vielmehr, daß die Designer das Anwendungsgebiet sehr gut verstehen, daß sie in der Lage sind, ein zukunftweisendes Fachkonzept und daraus eine gut strukturierte Anwendungsarchitektur zu entwickeln sowie schließlich eine detaillierte und präzise Spezifikation zu verfassen. Dazu bedarf es einer intensiven Zusammenarbeit mit den Anwendern. Die objektorientierte Methodik[1] hilft (viel besser als andere Methoden), die gewonnenen Erkenntnisse gut strukturiert auszuformulieren, aber die fachliche Durchdringung und kreative Gestaltung der Anwendung ist die entscheidende Denkarbeit der Designer.

Die Spezifikation beschreibt das Was eines Informationssystems, definiert also aus Außen- bzw. Anwendersicht die Anforderungen, denen die zu entwickelnde Software zu genügen hat. (Dafür benutzen wir das Wort Analyse nicht gern, das sich — aus dem

[1] Zur Diskussion der Begriffe "Methodik" und "Methode" siehe [Löhr93]

Amerikanischen kommend — auch bei uns eingebürgert hat; denn eine Spezifikation legt fest, was sein soll, eine Analyse liefert aber nur die Erkenntnisse über das, was ist.).

Eine Spezifikation hat die Anforderungen bezüglich dreier Bereiche zu definieren: Daten, Funktionen und Schnittstellen (zu Benutzern und anderen Systemen). Das führt dann zu der "klassischen" Dreiteilung einer Spezifikation wie in Abb. 1a. Das Grundprinzip der objektorientierten Methodik ist dagegen die innige Verbindung von Daten und Funktionen, demzufolge sich eine Trennung von Daten- und Funktionenmodell eigentlich verbietet und das eine Sicht wie in Abb. 1b nahelegt. An ihr orientieren wir uns im folgenden.

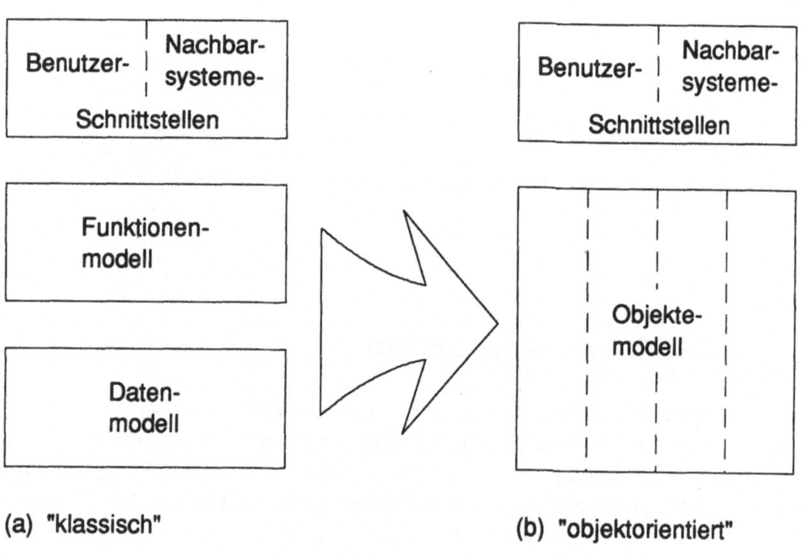

Abb. 1 Die Teile einer Spezifikation

Ein wesentlicher Inhalt einer objektorientierten Spezifikation ist also die Beschreibung der Objekte und ihres Zusammenspiels. Wie aber findet man sie? Man nähert sich der Anwendung am besten von zwei Seiten:

- Die Anforderungen resultieren letztlich aus den *Geschäftsvorfällen*, deren Bearbeitung das zu entwickelnde System unterstützen soll. Für jeden Geschäftsvorfall ist (mindestens) eine Funktion eines Objekts zu spezifizieren. Es ist dann eine der Aufgaben der Benutzerschnittstelle zu erkennen, welchen Geschäftsvorfall der Anwender bearbeiten will, und die dafür nötige Objektfunktion ausführen zu lassen (aufzurufen).

- Ein eigenständiges *Datenmodell*, etwa in Entity/Relationship-Darstellung, hat in einer echt objektorientierten Spezifikation eigentlich keine Existenzberechtigung mehr; dennoch lohnt es sich, die Spezifikationsarbeiten damit zu beginnen. Die Entitäten, die man dabei findet, bilden sehr oft Kristallisationskeime für Objekte, und das schließlich entstehende Objektebild hat viel Ähnlichkeit mit dem E/R-Diagramm. Es ist allerdings zu einfach zu glauben, man müsse an die Entitäten nur ein paar Funktionen kleben — und fertig sei das Objektemodell.

Nehmen wir an, durch Betrachtung des E/R-Datenmodells, durch die Analyse der Geschäftsvorfälle und durch andere Überlegungen seien Objekte als Einheiten von Daten und Funktion — genauer: Objekttypen (= Klassen) — gefunden und die Beziehungen zwischen ihnen etabliert worden. In einem *E/R-* sowie einem *Objekte-Bild* wird eine Übersicht der Entitäten bzw. Objekte mit ihren Beziehungen gegeben. Dann gilt es, jeden einzelnen *Objekttyp* präzise zu *spezifizieren.* Dazu verfassen wir je Objekttyp *ein Dokument* in einer Art und Weise, die wir im folgenden erläutern und motivieren wollen.

Auf eine ausführliche Diskussion der Vor- und Nachteile einer objektorientierten Methode verzichten wir hier und verweisen auf die Literatur ([Endres92], [Rumbaugh91], [Coad91], [Meyer88]).

2 Objektorientierte Konzepte in der Spezifikation

Was ist ein Objekt?

"Im allgemeinen Sprachgebrauch meint man damit etwas fest Umrissenes mit einer klaren Grenze, z.B. einen Baum, ein Buch, einen Planeten." [Denert91].

Die Objekte hingegen, denen wir bei der Spezifikation eines Informationssystems begegnen, sind *Modelle* der realen Objekte seiner Anwendung. Dabei enthält dieses Modell nur die für die Anwendung relevanten Aspekte des Objektes. Es folgen einige Ausführungen zu den Konzepten, die ein Objekt charakterisieren und für seine Spezifikation wichtig sind.

Eigenschaften

Wir beschreiben ein Objekt (genauer: dessen Modell), indem wir die *Merkmale (attributes)* und *Fähigkeiten (methods)* des Objekts beschreiben. Die Merkmale sind dabei die Größen, die man dem Objekt zuordnen kann, also zum Beispiel Gewicht, Umfang, Alter, Farbe o.ä.; Fähigkeiten sind dann die Handlungen und Aktionen, die ein Objekt ausführen kann oder die man am Objekt ausführen kann. Die Merkmale entsprechen also, technisch gesprochen, den Attributen, die Fähigkeiten den Funktionen oder "Methoden" der Objekte. Als Oberbegriff von Merkmal und Fähigkeit verwenden wir das Wort *Eigenschaft (feature).*

Fähigkeiten

Objekte haben Fähigkeiten. Mit ihren Fähigkeiten verändern sie, und nur sie die Werte ihrer Merkmale. Wir nennen dies die *Vorstellung vom aktiven Objekt* oder die *animistische*[2] *Auffassung*, denn wir verbinden mit Objekten, die man für scheinbar "tot" hält oder die gar nur ein abstrakter Begriff sind, die Vorstellung, daß sie aktiv ihre Fähigkeiten anbieten und wissen, wie sie handeln müssen, wenn eine ihrer Fähigkeiten beansprucht wird. Objekte wie *Wertpapiere* und sogar *Konten* können also mittels ihrer Fähigkeiten aktiv auf sich und ihre Umwelt einwirken.

Fähigkeiten haben (wie Prozeduren in Programmiersprachen) Ein- und Ausgaben. Die Eingaben werden verwandt, um den Ablauf einer Fähigkeit oder Ergebnisse zu beeinflussen. Ausgaben sind die Ergebnisse, die die Fähigkeit aus den Merkmalswerten ermittelt. Darüber hinaus hinterläßt das Anwenden einer Fähigkeit Spuren (nämlich Wertänderungen) in den Merkmalen des ausführenden Objekts.

Die Fähigkeiten eines Objekts können von anderen Objekten benutzt werden, um gemeinsam Aufgaben zu erledigen. Ein Objekt kann also die Fähigkeiten anderer Objekte nutzen und in eigenen Fähigkeiten verwenden.

Merkmal oder Fähigkeit?

Der Übergang von Merkmalen, also "gespeicherten Informationen", zu Fähigkeiten ist fließend. So kann man beispielsweise den *Rohertrag* aus *Verkaufspreis* und *Einkaufspreis* berechnen. Aus fachlicher Sicht sind aber alle drei Eigenschaften dieses Objekts (z.B. des Objekts *Ware*) Merkmale, und keine Fähigkeiten. Eine Fähigkeit *RohertragBerechnen()*[3] wäre ziemlich trivial und hinterließe vor allem keine Spuren in den Merkmalen der *Ware*, d.h. in einer Programmiersprache wie Pascal würde man sie als "function" (ohne Seiteneffekt) und nicht als "procedure" mit Seiteneffekt realisieren. Darüber hinaus würde diese Art der Spezifikation eine nicht erwünschte Auszeichnung des *Rohertrags* nach sich ziehen: der *Rohertrag* läßt sich zwar aus den beiden anderen Merkmalen bestimmen, aber wenn man den *Verkaufspreis* aus einem (geplanten) *Rohertrag* und dem (schon bezahlten) *Einkaufspreis* bestimmen will, benötigt man eine weitere Funktion. Im Extremfall muß man hier also drei im wesentlichen redundante Funktionen spezifizieren, ohne daß man an Verständnis oder Struktur für die Anwendung gewonnen hätte.

Daher plädieren wir dafür, alle drei Eigenschaften als Merkmale zu spezifizieren und den Zusammenhang, in dem sie stehen, als Zusicherung (*constraint*). Aus fachlicher Sicht ist das völlig ausreichend und oftmals auch viel zutreffender als die Lösung mit Funktionen (Symmetrie!); jede Eigenschaft ist als Merkmal ansprechbar, und man kann sich darauf verlassen, daß die Merkmalsbelegung konsistent ist (denn die

---

[2] von: Animismus: Glaube an die Allbelebung der Natur

[3] Das Klammerpaar deutet wie in C an, daß es sich um eine Fähigkeit handelt.

Spezifikation verpflichtet den Programmierer, dafür zu sorgen, daß die Zusicherung nie verletzt wird).

Merkmale und Typen

Der Inhalt eines Merkmals eines Objekts kann entweder ein Wert sein oder ein Verweis auf ein anderes Objekt.[4] Ist der Inhalt ein Wert, so kann man, wie in modernen Programmiersprachen üblich, von vornherein sagen, von welchem *Datentyp* dieser Wert ist. Der Datentyp ist die Menge der möglichen Werte, die das Merkmal annehmen kann. So ist der Datentyp des Merkmals *Alter* einer *Person* zum Beispiel *_Integer*[5] oder noch besser *_Lebensalter*. *_Lebensalter* ist dann möglicherweise ein[6] Untertyp *[0 .. 130]* von *_Integer*.

Analog ordnen wir allen "gleichartigen Objekten" einen *Objekttyp* zu. Gleichartig heißen zwei Objekte, wenn sie dieselben Eigenschaften haben, also dieselben Merkmale und dieselben Fähigkeiten. Dabei müssen gleichartige Objekte natürlich nicht dieselben Merkmals*werte* haben. Allerdings müssen die sich entsprechenden Merkmale denselben Typ haben.

Ohne es bislang erwähnt zu haben, haben wir Objekttypen in obigen Beispielen schon verwandt. Wir sprachen immer von den Eigenschaften einer *Person*. Es war uns aber egal, über welche Einzel-*Person* wir sprachen, denn die beschriebenen Eigenschaften galten für alle *Personen*. So hat **jede** *Person* die Merkmale *Vater* vom Typ "Verweis auf Person" oder *Alter* vom (Daten-)Typ *_Lebensalter*, und prinzipiell kann jede *Person wählen()*. Die einzelnen Personen unterscheiden sich erst durch aktuelle Belegung der Merkmale, also durch den Wert des *Alters* oder den Verweis auf den *Vater*, also eine bestimmte *Person*. Daher hätten wir korrekterweise bisher "*Person*" mit Unterstrich schreiben müssen ("*_Person*"), denn das ist der Name des Objekttyps.

Datentypen

Wir kennen in der Spezifikation einerseits die gebräuchlichen elementaren Datentypen wie *_Integer*, *_Real*, *_String*, usw.; andererseits stehen die üblichen Sprachmittel zur Verfügung, um sich neue Datentypen aus bereits definierten zu erzeugen. Diese Sprachmittel sind insbesondere die Strukturbildung (*record*), die Aufzählung (*enumeration*), die Einschränkung (*subtype*) und die erweiterte Form eines (dynamischen) Feldes (*array*). Zusätzlich kann man einem Datentyp Routinen zuordnen, die Plausibilitäten prüfen. Zum Beispiel kann man die *ISBN* als eine Datenstruktur spezifizieren, bestehend aus *Landnummer*, *Verlagsnummer*, interner *Buchnummer* und *Prüfziffer*. Eine Plausibilitätsprüfung wird dann sicherstellen, daß die

---

[4] Diese Aussage werden wir weiter unten noch präzisieren (siehe den Abschnitt *Umfassung*).

[5] Um Datentypname von Merkmalsnamen zu unterscheiden, schreiben wir vor jeden Typnamen einen Unterstrich.

[6] Wir schreiben hier "*ein Untertyp*", da es weitere Untertypen *[0 .. 130]* von *_Integer* gibt wie zum Beispiel *_Omnibusgeschwindigkeit*.

gewichtete Quersumme durch 11 teilbar ist, da es sich sonst nicht um eine gültige ISBN handelt.

Objekttypen

Objekte, d.h. Exemplare desselben Typs haben dieselben Merkmale und Fähigkeiten. Verschiedene Objekte eines Typs unterscheiden sich nur in der Belegung (den Werten) der Merkmale[7]. Die Spezifikation der Merkmale und Fähigkeiten sowie des Lebenslaufs legen wir demzufolge in der *Objekttypbeschreibung* nieder. Aus programmtechnischer Sicht kann man einen Objekttyp als abstrakten Datentyp auffassen, also als Datenstruktur (record) mit darauf operierenden Funktionen. In Ada würde man typischerweise diese Datenstruktur und die Funktionen zu einem *package* zusammenfassen.

Datentyp oder Objekttyp?

Der Übergang von Daten- zum Objekttyp ist fließend und abhängig von der Anwendung, die spezifiziert wird. Das *_Datum* ist normalerweise eine Datenstruktur, bestehend aus *Tag*, *Monat* und *Jahr*. Ist die zu spezifizierende Anwendung allerdings ein Zeitmanagementsystem, so ist vorstellbar, das man ein *Datum* als Objekt auffaßt.

Folgende Kriterien geben Hinweise auf einen Objekttyp:

- Kann man ein identifizierendes Merkmal benennen? Es sollte in der Realität vorhanden und beim Anwender in Gebrauch sein. Ein technischer Schlüssel ist hier nicht gemeint. Das identifizierende Merkmal kann auch zusammengesetzt sein; z.B. kann man ein *Buch* eindeutig identifizieren mit den Merkmalen *Landnummer*, *Verlagsnummer* und *Buchnummer*, denn das sind genau die relevanten Bestandteile der ISBN.

- Drängt es den Anwender, zu einem neu angelegten Objekt (im zu realisierenden System) weitere Informationen zu sammeln, also die restlichen Merkmale mit Werten zu versehen?

- Machen Operationen für Anlegen und Löschen eines Objekts Sinn? Oder möchte man stattdessen lieber die Informationen *eintragen?* Dann handelt es sich eher *nicht* um ein Objekt. Beispielsweise möchte man das *Alter* einer *_Person* typischerweise nicht "anlegen", sondern "eintragen"; also wird *Alter* sinnvollerweise nicht als Objekt modelliert, sondern als Merkmal einer *_Person.*

- Hat das Objekt Fähigkeiten, die über Plausibilitätsprüfungen hinausgehen?

---

[7]Es gibt Methoden, in denen zwei Objekte eines Typs unterscheidbar sind, obwohl sie in allen Merkmalswerten übereinstimmen (siehe z.B. [Meyer88]. Wir denken, man sollte in diesem Fall ein weiteres Merkmal einführen, das Objekte eines Typs eindeutig identifiziert (Schlüssel).

- Hat das Objekt einen Lebenslauf?

Diese Kriterien sind aber keine Definition für ein Objekt, sie müssen also nicht alle zwingend mit "Ja" beantwortet werden, um zu entscheiden, ob es sich um ein Objekt handelt.

Identifizieren von Objekten

Fast immer kann der Anwender zu jedem spezifizierten Objekt ein Merkmal nennen oder manchmal auch eine Merkmalskombination, mit dem sich ein Objekt eindeutig identifizieren läßt. Ein *_Wertpapier* wird eindeutig identifiziert durch die *WertpapierKennummer*, eine *_Person* durch *Vorname, Name* und *Anschrift*, ein *_PKW* durch sein *PolizeilichesKennzeichen* usw. Wir gehen noch etwas weiter, und verlangen zwingend, daß man zu jedem Objekttyp ein Merkmal oder eine Merkmalskombination angibt, deren Wert ein Exemplar eindeutig unterscheidet von jedem anderen Exemplar dieses Objekttyps.

Möglich ist auch, daß man mehrere Alternativen zur eindeutigen Identifizierung eines Objekts spezifizieren will oder muß: ein *_PKW* wird zusätzlich zum oben angegebenen Merkmal auch durch das Merkmal *FahrgestellNummer* eindeutig identifiziert, und es sind Anwendungen denkbar, in denen beide Identifikatoren notwendig sind: so muß die Polizei ein gestohlenes Auto anhand der *FahrgestellNummer* identifizieren, und Rotlichtsünder bekommen ihren Bußgeldbescheid, indem das *PolizeilicheKennzeichen* ausgewertet wird.

Zustände und Zustandsraum

Datentypen beschreiben Wertemengen. Das karthesische Produkt der Wertemengen aller Merkmale eines Objekttyps ist der *Zustandsraum* dieses Objekttyps. Jedem Objekt wird ein Punkt im Zustandsraum zugeordnet, der sich aus der Belegung der Merkmale des Objekts ergibt. Als *Zustandsvektor* bezeichnen wir demzufolge den Vektor zu einem Objekt, dessen Koordinaten gerade die Merkmalswerte des Objekts sind[8]. Jedem Objekt ist damit eindeutig ein Zustandsvektor zugeordnet. Durch jede Änderung eines Merkmalwertes ändert sich der Zustandsvektor dieses Objekts, d.h. dem Objekt wird ein neuer Punkt im Zustandsraum zugeordnet.

Umgekehrt gibt es zu jedem Punkt im Zustandsraum (also zu jedem möglichen Zustandsvektor) höchstens ein korrespondierendes Objekt zu einem festen Zeitpunkt. Das liegt daran, daß wir zwingend fordern, daß zu jedem Objekttyp ein Merkmal oder eine Merkmalskombination spezifiziert ist, die ein Objekt eindeutig identifizieren. Je zwei Exemplare eines Objekttyps müssen sich im Wert dieses Merkmals oder dieser Merkmalskombination unterscheiden.

[8]Aus diesem Grund bezeichnet man Merkmale oft als *Zustandskomponenten* des Objekts.

Die Begriffe Zustandsraum und Zustandsvektor sind wichtig zur theoretischen Fundierung der hier vorgestellten Konzepte. In der Welt des Anwenders ist dagegen der im folgenden beschriebene Begriff des Zustands wichtig:

Jedem Objekt ordnen wir implizit ein Merkmal *Zustand* zu. Der *Zustand* bestimmt sich aus den anderen Merkmalswerten, aber er ändert sich nicht zwangsläufig, wenn sich der Wert eines anderen Merkmals ändert. Ein Objekt *Person* kann zum Beispiel im Zustand *volljährig* sein, sobald der Wert des Merkmals *Alter* 18 überschritten hat. Eine Änderung des Merkmals *Körpergröße* ändert zwar den Zustandsvektor der Person, nicht jedoch den Zustand *volljährig*.

In den Zustandsraum eines Objekttyps abgebildet, entspricht der Zustand einer *Menge* von Zustandsvektoren. Gehört der Zustandsvektor eines Objekts zu solch einer Menge, dann ist das Objekt im korrespondierenden Zustand. Die Mengen, die den Zuständen eines Objekts entsprechen, müssen disjunkt sein.

Um Verwechslungen zu vermeiden, sei hier darauf hingewiesen, daß [Meyer88] nur den Zustandsvektor in unserem Sinn kennt; [Simonsmeier90] verwendet dafür in seiner deutschen Übersetzung das Wort "Zustand".

Lebenslauf

Die Zustände sowie die zustandsverändernden Fähigkeiten des Objekts kann man in einem endlichen Automaten, dem *Lebenslauf*, darstellen (Abb. 2). Die Knoten entsprechen den Ausprägungen des Zustands, die Kanten den zustandsverändernden Fähigkeiten. Darüber hinaus enthält der Lebenslauf auch die Fähigkeiten, die nur in bestimmten Zuständen des Objekts nutzbar sind, aber nicht notwendig den Zustand verändern, oder die, abhängig von einer Rückmeldung, zu verschiedenen Zuständen führen können. Zum Beispiel kann man ein *Buch* erst dann *verkaufen()*, wenn es *lieferbar* ist, und wenn man das letzte verkauft hat, dann ist es *ausverkauft*. Fähigkeiten wie *verkaufen()* zeigen sich im Graphen des Lebenslaufs als Kanten, die in den selben Zustand zurückkehren bzw. als "gespaltene Pfeile", die von einem Zustand in mehrere andere führen.

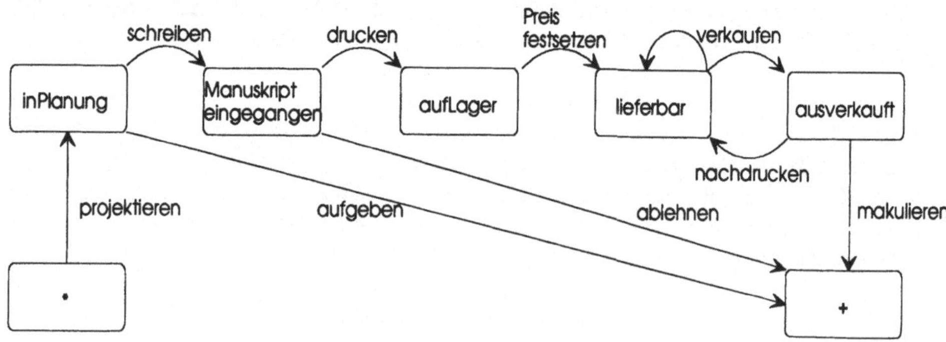

Abb. 2 Graph des Lebenslauf eines *Buches*

Beziehungen zwischen Objekten

Objekte stehen miteinander in Beziehung. Es gibt vier Arten von Beziehungen: ein Objekt *benutzt* ein anderes Objekt (genauer: es nutzt eine Fähigkeit des anderen Objekts), ein Objekt *liest* Merkmalswerte eines anderen Objekts, ein Objekt *spezialisiert* ein anderes Objekt oder ein Objekt *gehört* (zu) einem anderen bzw. das andere Objekt *umfaßt* das eine.

Nutz- und Lese-Beziehung

Die Lese-Beziehung ist ein Spezialfall der Nutz-Beziehung (*interacts-with-Relation*), denn das Lesen eines Merkmalswertes eines anderen Objekts ist in Wirklichkeit die Benutzung der (impliziten, gleichnamigen) Fähigkeit des anderen Objekts, einen Merkmalswert auszulesen. Um ganz exakt zu sein, ist ein Merkmal der Spezialfall einer Fähigkeit, nämlich die Projektion des Zustandsvektors auf eine Zustandskomponente.

Damit ein Objekt ein anderes nutzen (d.h. insbesondere dessen Merkmalswerte lesen) kann, muß man eine Beziehung in Form eines Verweises zum genutzten Objekt herstellen. Dies geschieht ebenfalls über Merkmale. So könnte eine *_Person* außer den Merkmalen *Alter* und *Zustand* auch die Merkmale *Vater* und *Mutter* haben. Die Werte dieser Merkmale sind Verweise auf (andere) *_Personen.* Um die Eigenschaften eines Objekts, auf das man einen Verweis hat, zu nutzen, verwenden wir die Punktschreibweise: das Alter der Mutter bekommt man mit *Mutter.Alter*, und mit *Vater.wählen()* kann man den Vater zum Wählen schicken. Diese Punkt-Notation kann man rekursiv anwenden, so daß beliebig lange Merkmal-Punkt-Merkmal-Folgen entstehen[9]: das Alter des Großvaters mütterlichseits ist *Mutter.Vater.Alter.* Das Verfolgen der Merkmalsverweise nennt man *Dereferenzieren.* Dereferenziert man das Merkmal *Mutter*, so "befindet man sich bei" einem Exemplar der *_Person,* nämlich der *Mutter.* Dereferenziert man *Mutter.Vater*, so befindet man sich beim Großvater. Dereferenziert man *Mutter.Vater.Alter*, so erhält man das Alter des Großvaters.

Zusätzlich zu den Merkmalen, die Daten enthalten, können auch auch verweisende Merkmale Bestandteil einer identifizierenden Merkmalskombination sein. Die Vorteile dieses Konzepts wurden ausführlich in [Ritterbach93] diskutiert.

Umfassung (Inbesitznahme)

Von ganz anderer Natur als die eben beschriebene Beziehung zu einem Objekt ist die Beziehung zu einem Datentyp. Während auf ein Exemplar eines Objekttyps (also ein

[9]Selbstverständlich müssen alle "inneren Merkmale" der Punktnotation, also alle Merkmale, die *vor* einem Punkt stehen, Verweise auf ein anderes Objekt sein.

Objekt) beliebig viele Verweise zeigen können, und somit der Wert eines Merkmals dieses Objekts praktisch öffentlich zugänglich ist, existiert das Exemplar eines Datentyps nur im Zusammenhang mit dem Objekttyp. So kann sinnvollerweise jedes Objekt eine Beziehung aufnehmen zum Exemplar (zum Objekt) "Meyer" des Typs *_Person*. Doch was soll eine Beziehung sein zum Exemplar "18" des Datentyps *_Integer?* Und wenn mehrere Objekte eine Beziehung zur "18" aufnehmen, was bedeutet das dann?

Man kann sich diese Art der Beziehung folgendermaßen vorstellen: Ein Objekt (z.B. *_Person*) kann eine "Beziehung" zu einem Exemplar eines Datentyps (z.B. *_Integer* "18") aufnehmen über ein Merkmal (z.B. *Alter)*, indem das entsprechende Exemplar kopiert wird und dann vom Objekt in Besitz genommen. Diese Kopie des Datentypexemplars gehört daraufhin dem Objekt (das Objekt *umfaßt* das Exemplar) und nur über das umfassende Objekt kann man Bezug nehmen auf das kopierte Datentypexemplar (hier "18"). Innerhalb des Systems kann es also eine ganze Reihe von identischen Datentypexemplaren geben, die dadurch unterscheidbar sind, daß sie von verschiedenen Objekten umfaßt werden.

Diese Art der Beziehung kann man ausdehnen auf Objekttypen: ein Objekttyp kann einen anderen in Besitz nehmen und umfassen, d.h. nur über den umfassenden Objekttyp kann Bezug genommen werden auf Eigenschaften des umfaßten Objekttyps. So umfaßt beispielsweise ein *_Auftrag* seine *_Auftragspositionen*. Diese Beziehung nennt man auch oft *Aggregation* oder *Objekterweiterung*.

Schließlich wollen wir auch die letzte Typkombination eines Merkmals zulassen, nämlich den *Datentypverweis*.

In Spezifikationen kommen die beschriebenen Beziehungen unterschiedlich häufig vor:

Beziehungsarten	**Datentyp**	**Objekttyp**
Umfassung	sehr häufig	manchmal
Verweis	selten	häufig

Spezialisierung (Vererbung)

in der Spezifikationsphase (und nicht nur da) erlebt man immer wieder, daß man einen Sachverhalt mehrfach aufschreiben bzw. die entsprechenden Textstellen kopieren müßte. Das passiert meist bei Objekten, die sich ähnlich sind oder sogar eine "gemeinsame Abstammung" haben, also Spezialisierungen eines gemeinsamen Vorfahren sind. Dieser Vorfahr ist fast immer ein Objekt, das in der Welt des Anwenders bereits existiert. So handeln Banken mit Aktien und Renten oder allgemeiner mit Wertpapieren.

Um solche Redundanzen zu vermeiden, nutzen wir das Konzept der *Vererbung (is-a-Relation)*. Wir notieren also alle gemeinsamen Eigenschaften von Renten und Aktien bei dem Objekttyp *_Wertpapier*. Beispiele für solche Eigenschaften sind das Merkmal *WertpapierKennummer* oder die Fähigkeit *ErtragBerechnen()*. Da sowohl *_Aktien* als auch *_Renten* die Eigenschaften des *_Wertpapiers* erben, besitzen sie die Merkmale und Fähigkeiten, die beim *_Wertpapier* spezifiziert wurden, wie "eigene", d.h. man kann normalerweise von außen nicht erkennen, ob eine Eigenschaft bei diesem Objekttyp oder bei einem Vorfahr spezifiziert wurde.

Somit ist die hier definierte Spezialisierungsbeziehung eine Beziehung auf Beschreibungsebene bzw. Objekttypebene, auch wenn wir weiter oben von einer Objektbeziehung sprachen.

Vorgeschriebene Eigenschaften und "dynamisches Binden"

Eine Besonderheit der Vererbung ist, daß sie Objekttypen erlaubt, Eigenschaften *vorzuschreiben* für ihre Nachfahren (*deferred* bzw. *virtual features*). Spezifiziert man zum Beispiel beim *_Wertpapier* die Fähigkeit *ErtragBerechnen()* als vorgeschrieben, so müssen sowohl die *_Renten* als auch die *_Aktien* eine Realisierung[10] dieser Fähigkeit anbieten[11]. Typischerweise ist das Vorschreiben einer Eigenschaft verbunden mit einer Umbenennung. So würde man die vorgeschriebene Fähigkeit *ErtragBerechnen()* bei der *_Aktie* als *DividendeBerechnen()* bezeichnen und bei der *_Rente* als *ZinsBerechnen()*.

Ein weiteres Konzept der Vererbung im Zusammenhang mit vorgeschriebenen Fähigkeiten ist das *dynamische Binden*, also die Bestimmung des Daten- oder Objekttyps erst zur Laufzeit des Systems. Dynamisches Binden ist also eigentlich ein programmtechnisches Konstrukt, doch es läßt sich auch in der Spezifikation gut nutzen, wie dieses Beispiel zeigt: Ein Objekt *_Depot* könnte die Fähigkeit *EinlagenBewerten()* haben, deren Spezifikation folgende Zeilen enthalten könnte:

> Für jedes *Wertpapier* im *Depot*
>   *Wertpapier.ErtragBerechnen(Ertrag)*
>   *Summe = Summe + Ertrag*

Die vorgeschriebene Fähigkeit *ErtragBerechnen()* muß also (zur Laufzeit) erkennen, ob das Wertpapier eine *_Rente* oder eine *_Aktie* ist und dementsprechend den *ZinsBerechnen()* oder die *DividendeBerechnen()*.

---

[10] "Realisierung" nicht im Sinne eines Programms, sondern im Sinne einer Beschreibung des Effekts der Fähigkeit, s.u.

[11] Die Realisierung der Fähigkeit wurde also *aufgeschoben*: Sie wurde nicht schon beim *_Wertpapier*, sondern erst bei der *_Rente* bzw. *_Aktie* spezifiziert. [Simonsmeier90] nennt dies deshalb *aufgeschobene Routine*.

Vererbung von Lebensläufen

ist ein schwieriges Thema. Einfach ist es, wenn ein Objekttyp keinen eigenen Lebenslauf hat: dann gilt nämlich der Lebenslauf des nächsten Vorfahren, der einen (expliziten) Lebenslauf hat. Kompliziert ist es, wenn ein Objekt einen eigenen Lebenslauf hat, aber auch ein Vorfahr. Es gibt einen sehr theoretischen Ansatz, der besagt, daß der Lebenslauf eines Nachfahren eine Verfeinerung des aktuellen Lebenslaufs sein muß. Dieser Ansatz engt häufig den sehr erwünschten kreativen Gedankenfluß des Spezifikateurs ein, da dieser versuchen muß, den Lebenslauf eines Vorfahren so zu verfeinern, daß er möglichst gut zu seinem Objekttyp paßt, anstatt den fachlichen Lebenslauf, frei von allen formalen Gesichtspunkten, so zu notieren, wie er der Wirklichkeit am ehesten entspricht.

Wir tendieren dazu, für jeden Objekttyp den fachlich korrekten Lebenslauf zu notieren. Damit gelten *gleichzeitig* dieser Lebenslauf und die Lebensläufe aller Vorfahren dieses Objekttyps. Allerdings muß nun ein Zustandsübergang in einem Vorfahr-Lebenslauf von einer Fähigkeit explizit ausgelöst werden, wobei dies typischerweise dadurch geschieht, daß man eine zustandsverändernde Fähigkeit des Vorfahren nutzt. Deshalb durchläuft auch jedes Objekt den grundlegenden Lebenslauf des *_Ding*, also des Vorfahren eines jeden Objekttyps. Dieser Lebenslauf hat die drei Zustände "*", "existiert" und "+". Alle Fähigkeiten, die ein Objekt *erzeugen*, führen es aus dem Zustand "*" in den Zustand "existiert", alle Fähigkeiten, die ein Objekt *vernichten*, führen von "existiert" zu "+".

Fähigkeiten, die Objekte eines Typs nur gemeinsam anbieten können

Es gibt Merkmale, die man nicht einem einzelnen Objekt zuordnen kann, und es gibt Fähigkeiten, die nur die Gesamtheit der Objekte eines Objekttyps leisten können. Diese Eigenschaften heißen *Typmerkmale* beziehungsweise *Typfähigkeiten*. Ein Typmerkmal ist zum Beispiel die aktuelle oder auch die maximale Anzahl von Objekten eines Typs, eine Typfähigkeit ist die Fähigkeit, die Objekte nach einem Merkmalswert zu sortieren.

Die Typmerkmale kann man nicht in den Zustandsraum abbilden, da es sich um Daten *über* den Zustandsraum und nicht *innerhalb* des Zustandsraums handelt. Somit muß es eine übergeordnete Einrichtung geben, die diese Merkmale verwaltet und die Typfähigkeiten anbietet. Wir stellen uns zu jedem Objekttyp einen *Verwalter* vor, der diese Aufgabe übernimmt.

Um eine *Typeigenschaft*, also eine Eigenschaft des Typverwalters anzusprechen, verwenden wir wiederum die Punktnotation, wobei diese jetzt an einer Stelle statt eines Merkmalsnamens einen Objekt*typ*namen enthält. So wird zum Beispiel die aktuelle Anzahl der *_Konto*'s mit *_Konto.Anzahl* bezeichnet, und es könnte die Typfähigkeit *_Konto.sortieren()* geben.

3 Eine Notation für Objekttypen

In diesem Abschnitt stellen wir eine Notation zur Spezifikation von Objekttypen vor. Es wird gezeigt, wie die eben beschriebenen Konstrukte in einer Sprache formuliert werden können. Diese Sprache entstand zum Großteil in laufenden Projekten und wurde vielen Änderungen und Ergänzungen unterworfen, doch der jetzige Wortschatz ist recht stabil. Die zugrundegelegte Semantik erfüllt nicht die Kriterien, die man an eine Programmiersprache stellt, und soll es auch nicht können. Trotzdem wollen wir diese Semantik möglichst exakt festzulegen und zugleich formalen Ballast vermeiden. Die folgende Notation soll dem Spezifikateur helfen, einen komplexen Sachverhalt strukturiert und übersichtlich zu formulieren und ihn nicht in das enge Korsett einer zu formalen Syntax zwängen.

Abb. 3 zeigt ein typisches Beispiel[12] einer Objekttypbeschreibung. Um in der Diskussion auf einzelne Abschnitte bezugnehmen zu können, wurden viele Zeilen vorne mit einer Nummer versehen; sie sind kein Bestandteil der Objekttypbeschreibung.

01	JEDE	**_Buchung**		
02	IST_EIN	**_Vertrag**		
03		Die ^**_Buchung** verbindet eine Reise (also das Katalogangebot) mit einem Teilnehmer und mindestens drei Reservierungen einer Leistung. Diese drei Leistungen nennt man das *Touristische Tripel.* [...]		
04	HAT	***[Buchungs]Nummer***	:	**_BuchungsNr**
05	HAT	***zugrundegelegtesAngebot***	--->	**_ReiseAngebot**
06	HAT	***Reiseort***	--->	**_Ort**
	HAT	***Reisezeit***	--->	**_Zeitraum**
07	HAT	***Teilnehmer***	::	**_Teilnehmer**
08	*??*	*Gehören Teilnehmer nicht besser zur Reservierung ??*		
09	*!!*	*Nein, denn man muß ihnen z.B. die Reiseunterlagen schicken oder wissen, wer gebucht hat !!*		
10	HAT	***Reservierung***	::	**_Reservierung**
11	PRUEFEN	Eine ^**_Reise** umfaßt mindestens drei ^**_Reservierungen**.		
12	HAT	***Preis***	o:	**_DM-Betrag**
	PRUEFEN	*^Preis* = Summe aller *^Reservierung.Preis* Der *^Preis* ist nicht mehr optional ab Zustand *^abgeschlossen*.		

[12] Dieses Beispiel ist hier nicht vollständig wiedergegeben und daher nicht konsistent. Es ist der Ausschnitt aus einer parallel zu diesem Papier entstehenden Arbeit, die einen Teil des touristischen Buchungssystems aus [Denert91] konsistent spezifiziert.

13 FINDEN_MIT *BuchungsNummer*
Teilnehmer + Reisezeit

14 LEBENSLAUF

*	anlegen	inBearbeitung
inBearbeitung	freigeben	freigegeben
inBearbeitung	freigeben	inBearbeitung
freigegeben	UnterlagenProduzieren	abgeschlossen
abgeschlossen	<<ändernde Fähigkeit >>	wiederaufgenommen
wiederaufgenommen	freigeben	wiederfreigegeben
wiederfreigegeben	UnterlagenProduzieren	abgeschlossen
inBearbeitung	stornieren	+
freigegeben	stornieren	+
abgeschlossen	stornieren	+
wiederaufgenommen	stornieren	+
wiederfreigegeben	stornieren	+

15 -- *Beachte, daß ^UnterlagenProduzieren() abhängig vom ^Zustand bereits produzierte Unterlagen berücksichtigen muß!*
--

16 ENTSTEHT_DURCH ***anlegen***
17 AENDERT *AbwickelndeAgentur*
StartOrt
Reisezeit
Teilnehmer
18 EFFEKT *_Buchung.NummerVergeben(BuchungsNummer)*
^*Buchungstag* = Systemdatum
19 ENDE(ok,inBearbeitung)

20 ERLISCHT_DURCH ***stornieren***
EFFEKT alle Reservierungen rückgängig machen (Anbieter benachrichtigen)
alle bereits produzierten Unterlagen einziehen und dem Altpapier zuführen
ENDE(ok,+)

21 KANN_MAN ***freigeben***
22 BRAUCHT *Sachbearbeiter* : **_Mitarbeiter**
23 ANNAHME *^Sachbearbeiter.ArbeitsStelle = ^AbwickelndeAgentur*
-- *Die Buchung darf nur von Sachbearbeitern der abwickelnden Agentur freigegeben werden.* --
EFFEKT Die für die **^_Buchung** reservierten Leistungen werden auf Konsistenz geprüft, und zwar bezüglich folgender Fragen:

- Ist für alle *^Reservierungen* ^Reservierung.bestätigt?
  sonst ENDE(ReservierungNichtBestätigt,inBearbeitung)

- Passen Flüge und Hotels zeitlich und räumlich zusammen, d.h. liegt zu jedem Zeitpunkt das Hotel, zu dem die gerade reservierten Zimmer gehören, in dem Gebiet, in das zuletzt geflogen wurde?
  sonst ENDE(FlugHotelInVerschGebieten,inBearbeitung)
  [...]
  da jetzt die Buchung konsistent ist, ENDE(ok,freigegeben)

```
   --        -------------------------------------------------------------------- --

24 DER       _Buchung.Verwalter
25 HAT       letzteVergebeneNummer          :    _BuchungsNr
26 KANN      [Buchungs]NummerVergeben
27 LIEFERT   Nummer                         :    _BuchungsNr
   EFFEKT    ...

   --        -------------------------------------------------------------------- --

28 DER       _Zeitraum
   BESTEHT_AUS von                          :    _Datum
             bis                            :    _Datum
29 PRUEFEN   von <= bis
```

Abb. 3 Beispiel für eine OT-Spezifikation

Auf den ersten Blick mag diese Notation zumindest gewöhnungsbedürftig sein. Doch sie entspricht (und entspringt) unserem obersten Prinzip, nämlich der Verwendung einer möglichst klaren und guten Sprache in der Spezifikation, dem Ringen um eindeutige und präzise Formulierungen. Nicht der Leser soll sich quälen, den Text zu verstehen, sondern der Autor muß sich ganz besonders anstrengen, den Text leicht verständlich zu gestalten.

Das Wort "JEDE"

Die Objekttypbeschreibung beginnt mit dem Wort "JEDE[R/S]" [01][13] und der Benennung des Objekttyps sowie der Einordnung in die Vererbungshierarchie [02]. Um zum Ausdruck zu bringen, daß die hier beschriebenen Eigenschaften (Merkmale, Fähigkeiten, Lebenslauf) für **alle** Objekte eines Typs gelten, beginnt die Beschreibung mit einem der Schlüsselwort "JEDE/JEDER/JEDES": *Jedes* Objekt *hat* das Merkmal oder *kann* diese Fähigkeit anbieten.

Auch im Zusammenhang mit der Vererbungsbeziehung ist uns das Wort "jedes" sehr wichtig. Es mag zum Beispiel folgendes gelten: die *_Person* "Meyer" *ist ein* Mitglied

[13] Mit einer Nummer in eckigen Klammern nehmen wir Bezug zur entsprechenden Zeile in Abb. 3.

des Vereins zur Pflege der objektorientierten Sprache. Deswegen ist aber sicherlich nicht *jede _Person* dort Mitglied. Bei der Spezialisierung gilt hingegen, daß *jedes* Objekt eines Objekttyps auch Objekt eines jeden Vorfahr-Objekttyps ist.

Lehrbuchhafte Beschreibung des Objekttyps

Es folgt eine ausführliche *fachliche* Beschreibung des Objekts [03]. Sie soll etwa wie ein entsprechendes Kapitel eines Lehrbuchs des Anwendungsgebiets aufgebaut sein, so daß die Sammlung der Beschreibungsabschnitte der Objekttypen dem Leser helfen, zum Experten der Anwendung zu werden.

Spezifikation der Merkmale

Anschließend werden die Merkmale spezifiziert, die jedes Objekt dieses Objekttyps *hat* [04-12]. Eine Merkmalsspezifikation besteht aus bis zu fünf Teilen:

Die erste Zeile [04] enthält den Merkmalsnamen, die Art der Beziehung und den Objekt- bzw. Datentyp des Merkmals. An Beziehungsarten unterscheiden wir die Inbesitznahme und den Verweis und drücken sie durch einen Doppelpunkt bzw. durch einen Pfeil aus, unabhängig davon, ob auf einen Datentyp oder einen Objekttyp Bezug genommen wird. So sind in dieser Spezifikation *_Ort* [06] und *_BuchungsNr* [04] Datentypen und *_ReiseAngebot* [05] und *_Reservierung* [10] Objekttypen, auf die in jeweils verschiedener Art Bezug genommen wird. Auf *_Ort* und *_ReiseAngebot* wird verwiesen, d.h. auch andere Objekte (auch eines anderen Objekttyps) können zu ihnen unmittelbare Beziehungen aufbauen. Die *_BuchungsNr* und die *_Reservierungen* hingegen werden umfaßt und die Exemplare, die eine *_Buchung* in Besitz genommen hat, sind nur über diese *_Buchung* erreichbar (Abb. 4).

Mit der Beziehungsart kann man, wie man in [07], [10] und [12] sieht, auch Kardinalitäten ausdrücken: der zweifache Doppelpunkt in [12] heißt, daß eine *_Buchung* nicht nur eine, sondern mehrere (genau: mindestens eine) *Reservierungen* umfaßt. Ein "o" in der Angabe der Beziehungsart in [12] steht für "optional", so daß die Umfassung von keinem, einem oder mehreren Objekt- bzw. Datentypen mit "o::" spezifiziert werden kann. Die Kardinalitätsangaben bei Verweisen schlagen sich in der Anzahl der Pfeilspitzen bzw. einem "o" im Schaft nieder, so daß zum Beispiel die Notation für einen Verweis auf kein, ein oder mehrere Objekt- bzw. Datentypen "--o>>" wäre.

Abb. 4 zeigt an einen winzigen Ausschnitt des Objekttypbildes, wie man diese Beziehungsarten auch graphisch darstellen kann.

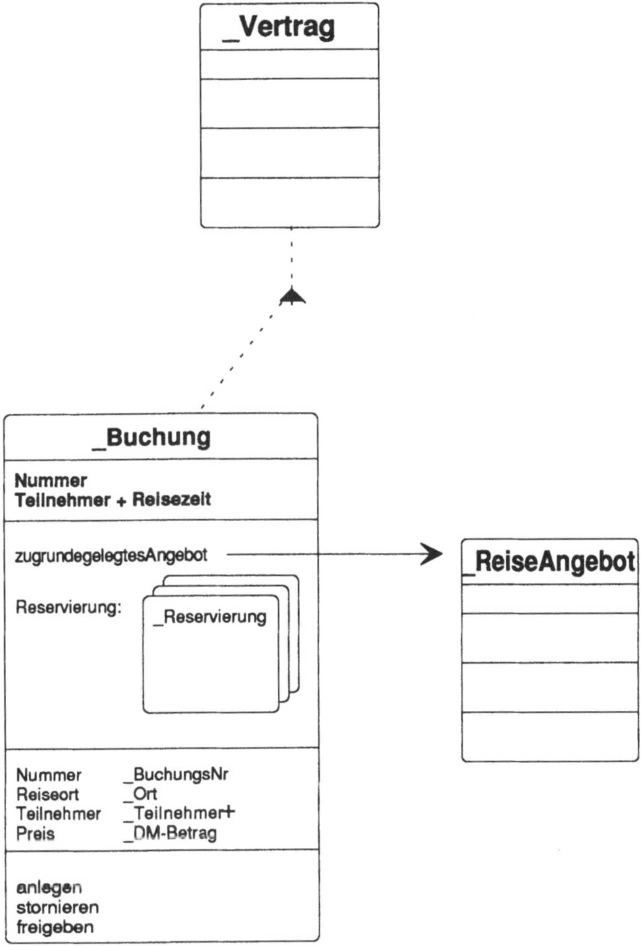

Abb. 4 Ein Ausschnitt des Objekttypbildes

Der vierte Teil einer Merkmalsspezifikation ist die optionale Beschreibung. Diese ist deswegen optional, weil sie oft überflüssig ist, wenn nur der Merkmalsname sorgfältig gewählt wurde. So wäre eine typische Beschreibung für das Merkmal *Reisezeit:* "Zeitraum, in dem die Reise stattfindet bzw. stattfinden soll". Diese Beschreibung enthält keine zusätzlichen Informationen, sondern bläht die Spezifikation auf und ermüdet den Autor, sollte dieser gezwungen sein, zum Merkmal eine Beschreibung zu finden, genauso wie den Leser. Erfahrungsgemäß leidet durch diese Ablenkung auch die Qualität des Merkmalsnamen.

Schließlich kann man zu einem Merkmal Zusicherungen oder Plausibilitätsprüfungen spezifizieren [**11**], die nicht den Merkmalstyp betreffen (siehe [**29**]), sondern das

Zusammenwirken des Merkmals mit anderen (vergleiche den Abschnitt *Merkmale oder Fähigkeiten*).

Querschnittskonzepte für Dokumente

An dieser Stelle wollen wir auf drei Konstrukte hinweisen, die in obigem Beispiel zur Spezifikation von Merkmalen benutzt wurden, aber nicht nur hier, sondern an *jeder* Stelle der Objekttypbeschreibung verwendet werden können.

Zum einen ist es das *Caret* "^", mit dem die Namen von Merkmalen, Fähigkeiten, Daten- und Objekttypen und Zuständen markiert werden dürfen und sollen ([**03**] oder [**11**]). Unsere Werkzeuge erkennen sie dann auch in frei formatierten Texten (wie Beschreibungen) und können zum Beispiel überprüfen, ob die Namen gültig sind, also ob zum Beispiel die Dereferenzierung der Punktnotation möglich ist.

Zum anderen sind es *Kommentare*, die, abhängig von der Kommentarart, in doppelte "-", "?" oder "!" eingeschlossen sind ([**08**], [**09**] oder [**15**]). Ein mit "--" markierter Kommentar ist ein herkömmlicher Kommentar, wie er von Programmiersprachen her bekannt ist. Vor allem in formalen Abschnitten wie dem Lebenslauf notiert man hier weitere, meist kurze Erläuterungen und Verdeutlichungen.

Beim Spezifizieren entstehen oft Fragen, die man nicht sofort klären kann, oder offene Enden, zu denen man noch einen Gedanken notieren will. Dazu dienen die Kommentararten "Fragen" und "Antworten". Gerade in den Fragen und Antworten schlägt sich der Entwicklungsprozeß des Dokuments deutlich nieder, und der spätere Leser wird möglicherweise dieselben anfänglichen Miß- und "Nichtverständnisse" haben wie ursprünglich der Autor. Daher sind diese Fragen, markiert mit "??", sehr nützlich für ein besseres Verständnis des Objekttyps, zumindest sobald sie beantwortet sind, und anhand ihrer kann man oft nachvollziehen, warum genau diese Formulierung und keine andere gewählt wurde. Daher löschen wir die beantworteten Fragen nicht, sondern notieren, eingeschlossen in "!!", die zugehörigen Antworten. Selbstverständlich darf es bei Abschluß des Dokuments (z.B. in Form der Abnahme der Systemspezifikation) keine offenen Fragen mehr geben; Werkzeuge prüfen dies auf syntaktischer Ebene.

Das dritte Querschnittskonzept sind die *optionale Namensteile*, die man an umfassenden eckigen Klammern erkennt, wie Zeile [**04**] zeigt. Ein Merkmal namens *Nummer* ist sicherlich nicht sehr aussagekräftig und daher *kein* gut gewählter Name, denn es wird in sehr vielen Objekttypen vorkommen. Wesentlich besser ist zum Beispiel der Name *BuchungsNummer*, also die Ergänzung des Merkmalnamens um den Objekttypnamen. Bezieht man sich aber von einem anderen Objekttyp auf dieses Merkmal, so erhält man in der Punktnotation sehr leicht einen Namen wie *MeineBuchung.BuchungsNummer*, der ärgerlich lang ist und nicht besonders schön klingt. Durch die Spezifikation *[Buchungs]Nummer* sind in unserer Notation sowohl *MeineBuchung.BuchungsNummer* als auch *MeineBuchung.Nummer* gültige Bezeichner für das Merkmal.

Diese drei Querschnittskonzepte — Markieren, um einer maschinellen Prüfung zugänglich zu machen, die verschiedenen Kommentararten sowie die optionalen Namensteile — sind nicht nur in Objekttypbeschreibungen zulässig, sondern in jedem unserer Dokumente.

Identifizierung von Objekten

Abgeschlossen wird die Spezifikation der Merkmale durch eine Aufzählung der Merkmale bzw. Merkmalskombinationen, die ein Objekt eindeutig identifizieren, also in deren Wert(en) sich je zwei Objekte dieses Objekttyps unterscheiden [**13**]. Implizit wird durch jede Zeile dieser Aufzählung eine Fähigkeit *finden_mit()* spezifiziert, die als Eingabe gerade diese Merkmalskombination hat und höchstens ein Objekt dieses Objekttyps findet.

Spezifikation des Lebenslaufs

Dieser endliche Automat wird in einer Tabelle beschrieben mit den drei Spalten Ausgangszustand, verändernde Fähigkeit und Folgezustand [**14**]. Zwei Zustände hat jeder Lebenslauf, nämlich "präexistent" und "postexistent", also die Zustände des Objekts vor Entstehen bzw. nach Beseitigung. In Anlehnung an die gebräuchlichen Symbole für Geburt und Tod bezeichnen wir sie mit "*" und "+".

Ausgezeichnete zustandsändernde Fähigkeiten

Die Fähigkeiten, die ein Objekt erschaffen, also aus dem Zustand "+" führen, und diejenigen, die das Objekt wieder vernichten, also nach "+" führen, spezifizieren wir nicht wie normale Fähigkeiten, sondern in speziellen Abschnitten "ENTSTEHT_DURCH" [**16**] und "ERLISCHT_DURCH" [**20**].

Nach der *animistischen Auffassung* ist nur das einzelne Objekt in der Lage, sich in den Zustand "+" überzuführen; es begeht also "Selbstmord", d.h. jede vernichtende Fähigkeit ist eine "normale" Objektfähigkeit. Im Gegensatz dazu muß jede erzeugende Fähigkeit eine Typfähigkeit sein, da es ja noch kein Objekt gibt, dem man den Auftrag "schaffe dich" gibt. Man kann nur den Typverwalter beauftragen, ein neues Objekt zur Verfügung zu stellen. An dieser Stelle wollen wir aber eine notationelle Ausnahme zulassen. Statt im einfachsten Fall die Zeilen

```
JEDES               _Objekt

ENTSTEHT_DURCH      anlegen
LIEFERT             Objekt --->     _Objekt
```

zu spezifizieren, so daß man ein neues *_Objekt* nur durch

```
VAR NeuesObjekt : _Objekt
^_Objekt.anlegen(NeuesObjekt)
```

erzeugen kann, ziehen wir folgende Spezifikation vor:

JEDES _Objekt
ENTSTEHT_DURCH anlegen

Der Aufruf lautet nun einfach *NeuesObjekt.anlegen()*, d.h. man richtet die Aufforderung, sich anzulegen, direkt an das neu anzulegende Objekt. Diese methodisch abweichende Notation haben wir nur aus pragmatischen Gründen eingeführt.

Wie bei der *Vererbung von Lebensläufen* bereits angedeutet, bewirken die Fähigkeiten, die im Abschnitt "ENTSTEHT_DURCH" spezifiziert werden, **implizit** immer einen Zustandsübergang von "*" nach "existiert" im geerbten Lebenslauf des Vorfahren *_Ding*, d.h. dieser Übergang muß nicht mehr explizit spezifiziert werden. Analog muß der Zustandsübergang von "existiert" nach "+", den jede vernichtende Fähigkeit auslöst, nicht notiert werden.

Spezifikation von Fähigkeiten

bestehen aus bis zu sechs Unterabschnitten. Eingeleitet durch KANN, KANN_MAN oder KANN_SICH wird die Fähigkeit benannt[14] [21]. Zwar spiegelt sich das animistische Prinzip im "*kann_sich*" am deutlichsten wider, doch daraus resultierende Formulierungen wie "*kann_sich freigeben()*" klingen zumindest ungewöhnlich.

Es folgen drei Kapitel, in denen die Eingabeparameter (BRAUCHT) und die Ausgabeparameter (LIEFERT) spezifiziert werden ([22] oder [27]). Eine Besonderheit sind die Eingabeparameter, die von der Fähigkeit direkt in das (meist gleichnamige) Merkmal kopiert werden. Zur Schreiberleichterung haben wir daher den Abschnitt AENDERT eingeführt [17], in dem diejenigen Merkmale in Form von Eingabeparametern aufgeführt werden, die von der Fähigkeit nur mit einem neuen Wert belegt werden. Besonders typisch ist diese Art der Belegung für erzeugende Fähigkeiten.

Unsere Fähigkeiten liefern nur über Ausgabeparameter Resultate zurück mit einer Ausnahme: Implizit liefert jede Fähigkeit eine *Rückmeldung*, die eine Aussage darüber macht, wie die Fähigkeit beendet wurde ("ok" oder "nicht ok" sowie weitere Informationen) und wie gegebenenfalls der Nachfolgezustand im Lebenslauf heißt (insbesondere dann, wenn eine Fähigkeit in mehreren Folgezuständen landen kann, siehe *freigeben()*). Dies wird im *Effekt* der Fähigkeit mittels der Anweisung ENDE(*Rückmeldung*, *Folgezustand*) spezifiziert [19].

Der nun folgende Abschnitt ANNAHME [23] enthält die Vorbedingungen der Fähigkeit, also Zusicherungen, die erfüllt sein müssen, bevor die Fähigkeit überhaupt ausgeführt werden kann. Dieser Abschnitt erleichtert die Spezifikation des eigentliche Fähigkeitsrumpfes erheblich, da er einen Großteil von Fallunterscheidungen vorwegnimmt und so den *Effekt* von Ballast befreit.

[14] Ausnahmen sind die erzeugenden und vernichtenden Fähigkeiten, die durch ENTSTEHT_DURCH [16] beziehungsweise ERLISCHT_DURCH [20] eingeleitet werden (s.o.).

Dieser Effekt nämlich soll möglichst klar machen, wie die Fähigkeit abläuft und welche Spuren ihre Nutzung im System hinterläßt [18]. Wir haben für die Spezifikation des Effekts *keine* fest vorgeschriebene Syntax, denn der Entwickler soll frei sein in der Wahl des am besten geeigneten Sprachmittels. Oft, aber sicherlich nicht immer mögen Pseudocode-Konstrukte angemessen sein, aber auch Entscheidungstabellen, Formeln o.ä., eventuell ergänzt um Beispiele, können den Sachverhalt klar ausdrücken, und oft ist ein gut formulierter freier Text die beste Beschreibung.

Der Typverwalter

Um exemplarübergreifende Merkmale, also die Typmerkmale, zu pflegen und um Typfähigkeiten anbieten zu können, benötigt man eine übergeordnete Einrichtung. Dies ist bei uns der *Typverwalter* [24]. Zu jedem Objekttyp stellen wir uns einen Typverwalter vor, dem wir die Typeigenschaften zuordnen. Die Notation der Merkmale [25] und Fähigkeiten [26] ist identisch zur Notation der "normalen" Eigenschaften. Als Typeigenschaft erkennt man sie ausschließlich daran, daß sie im Dokument nach der Zeile "DER <_Objekttyp>.Verwalter" [24] stehen.

Darüber hinaus gibt es zwei Ausnahmen von Typfähigkeiten, die anders spezifiziert werden: zum einen sind dies alle objekterzeugenden Fähigkeiten [16], zum anderen sind es alle *"finden_mit"*-Fähigkeiten, die implizit nur durch Angabe der Eingabeparameter definiert sind [13].

Spezifikation von Datentypen

Mit der eben beschriebenen Spezifikation der Typeigenschaft wird der Teil des Dokuments abgeschlossen, der den Objekttyp beschreibt. Im Anschluß daran, d.h. im selben Dokument, werden dann die Datentypen spezifiziert, die fachlich zu diesem Objekttyp passen [28]. Denn um eine Dokumenten(typ)inflation zu vermeiden und um alle fachlichen Informationen möglichst dicht zusammenzuhalten, werden Datentypen nicht in eigenen Dokumenten wie "Datentypbeschreibungen" spezifiziert. Bei dem Objekttyp *_Ding*, der ja ganz oben in der Spezialisierungshierarchie steht, sammeln wir die Datentypen, die zwar benutzerdefiniert sind, aber doch so allgemein, daß sie sinnvollerweise nicht einem bestimmten Objekttyp zugeordnet werden können (wie zum Beispiel *_GeldBetrag*). Dahin gehört der hier exemplarisch spezifizierte *_Zeitraum* eigentlich auch, und nicht in die Objekttypspezifikation *_Buchung*.

Datentypdefinitionen sind naturgemäß Konstrukte einer Spezifikation, die schon nahe an der Realisierung sind. Daher sind sie den Werkzeugen besonders zugänglich. Wir können aus ihnen einerseits Datenbankdefinitionen und andererseits Datenstrukturdefinitionen für eine Vielzahl von Programmiersprachen erzeugen. Da diese nicht mehr manuell programmiert werden müssen, ist eine Quelle zahlreicher Programmierfehler bereits weitgehend ausgeschaltet und Änderungen am Datentyp müssen nur noch an einer Stelle vorgenommen werden. Dies verringert den Änderungsaufwand wesentlich, falls ein Fehler in der Typdefinition erst sehr spät auffallen sollte oder sich (beispielsweise durch eine Gesetzes- oder Normungsänderung) ein Datentyp der Anwendung ändert.

4 Ausblick

Eine Objekttypbeschreibung in der vorliegenden Notation läßt sich zu erheblichen Teilen maschinell auswerten. Wir haben Werkzeuge zur Prüfung der Konsistenz der Spezifikation und setzen sie bereits in der Praxis ein. Zusätzlich läßt sich vieles aus einer Spezifikation dieser Art hinüberretten in die Realisierung und die Testphase. So haben wir auch schon Werkzeuge, die aus den Typdefinitionen für verschiedene Zielsprachen zum Beispiel Codestücke (meist in Form von Copystrecken) generieren, zur Datenbankdefinition oder als Datenstruktur im Programm. Diese Werkzeuge müssen noch vervollständigt werden. Denkbar sind auch Werkzeuge, die kontrollieren, wie die Spezifikation umgesetzt wurde, also ob es zum Beispiel zu jeder Fähigkeit eine Operation gibt.

Zur Zeit definieren wir eine Spracherweiterung, um Benutzerschnittstellen angemessen spezifizieren zu können. Diese soll insbesondere graphische Oberflächen berücksichtigen und maschinell auswertbar sein. Eine methodische Basis zur Spezifikation dieser Dialoge werden die Interaktionsdiagramme aus [Denert91] sein. Wir hoffen, einen großen Teil der Programmierung der Benutzeroberfläche einem Generator überlassen zu können, um so einerseits ein einheitliches "Look and Feel" der Oberfläche zu erreichen und um andererseits den Programmierer zu entlasten von mühseliger "Bit- und Pixelpfriemelei", die gerade bei der Programmierung graphischer Oberflächen einen Großteil der Arbeit ausmacht.

Anschließend werden wir soweit als möglich der Notation ein theoretisches Fundament geben, indem wir eine formale Semantik definieren.

In den nächsten Monaten entstehen verschiedene Fallstudien, die in dieser Notation spezifiziert sind und zum Teil auch realisiert werden in verschiedenen (herkömmlichen und objektorientierten) Sprachen.

Nicht zuletzt soll auch das Metamodell [Hesse92] in dieser Notation niedergelegt werden, wir werden den Einsatz von Hypertextwerkzeugen prüfen, Untersuchungen zum Prototyping anstellen, weitere Dokumentsichten[15] definieren, und manches mehr.

---

[15] Je nach Leserkreis bereiten wir ein Dokument wie eine Objekttypbeschreibung anders auf, um dem Leser möglichst weit entgegenzukommen. Diese Dokumentenaufbereitung nennen wir *Dokumentsicht;* sie umfaßt wesentlich mehr als nur "*pretty printing*" und ist wesentlicher Bestandteil des *Dokumentenorientierten Arbeitens* [Denert93].

Dank

Die hier beschriebenen Konzepte entwickelten sich im Laufe der letzten Jahre aus mehreren Projekten bei sd&m. Die vorgestellte Notation wurde in Zusammenarbeit mit Siemens Nixdorf, KORDOBA, erarbeitet, und wir danken insbesondere N. Höbel für seine kritischen Kommentare und wertvollen Anregungen. Vieles ist uns klarer geworden in Diskussionen mit Kollegen von sd&m, die wir nicht alle nennen können. Stellvertretend seien T. Tensi, R. Fahney, G. Koller, S. Aicher und T. Belzner genannt. G. Scholz hat nicht nur viele Ideen eingebracht, sondern auch eine Werkzeugumgebung zu dieser Methode programmiert.

Literatur

[Coad91] P. Coad, E. Yourdon: *Object-Oriented Analysis*, Prentice-Hall, 1991

[Denert91] E. Denert, J. Siedersleben: *Software-Engineering*, Springer, 1991

[Denert93] E. Denert: *Dokumentenorientierte Softwareentwicklung*, erscheint im Informatik-Spektrum (1993)

[Endres92] A. Endres, J. Uhl: *Objektorientierte Software-Entwicklung. Eine Herausforderung für die Projektführung*, Informatik-Spektrum 15 (1992), S. 255-263

[Hesse92] W. Hesse, G. Merbeth, R.Frölich: *Software-Entwicklung. Vorgehensmodelle, Projektführung, Produktverwaltung*, Oldenburg, 1992

[Löhr93] P. Löhr-Richter: *Methodologie - Methodik - Methode. Was steckt dahinter?*, EMISA-Forum 1, 1993

[Meyer88] B. Meyer: *Object-oriented Software Construction*, Prentice Hall, 1988

[Ritterbach93] B. Ritterbach: *Ein Schlüsselkonzept für das ER-Modell*, EMISA-Forum 1, 1993

[Rumbaugh91] J. Rumbaugh, M. Blaha, W. Premerlani, F. Eddy, W. Lorensen: *Object-Oriented Modeling and Design*, Prentice-Hall, 1991

[Simonsmeier90] W. Simonsmeier: *Objektorientierte Software-Entwicklung*, Übersetzung von *Object-oriented Software Construction* [Meyer88], Hanser, 1990

Objektorientierte Analyse und Geschäftsvorfallsmodellierung

Günther Müller-Luschnat
ALLDATA
Unternehmensberatung GmbH
Bereich Methoden & Tools
Prinzregentenplatz 7
8000 München 80

Wolfgang Hesse
Universität Marburg
FB Mathematik/Informatik
Hans-Meerwein-Str.
3550 Marburg

Norman Heydenreich
ADAC e.V.
Am Westpark 8
8000 München 70

Zusammenfassung

Die Frage, ob eine durchgängige Entwicklung von betrieblichen Anwendungssystemen nach dem objektorientierten Ansatz möglich und praktikabel ist, hängt entscheidend davon ab, wie gut dieser Ansatz für die frühen Phasen der Analyse und Modellierung geeignet ist. Ein Kernproblem ist dabei die Modellierung von Geschäftsvorfällen, d.h. komplexen, möglicherweise unterbrechbaren und viele Gegenstände betreffenden betrieblichen Abläufen. Dafür bieten sich zwei Möglichkeiten an: entweder als Operationen einer daran beteiligten Klasse oder als eigene Klasse, deren Objekte (Exemplare) die einzelnen konkreten Geschäftsvorfälle sind. Vor- und Nachteile beider Lösungen werden diskutiert und im weiteren Kontext von objektorientiertem Design und Programmierung betrachtet.

0. Einleitung

Ob sich die Entwicklung von Informationssystemen in Zukunft mehrheitlich nach einem durchgängigen objektorientierten (OO-)Ansatz vollziehen wird, hängt maßgeblich davon ab, inwieweit sich dieser Ansatz als tragfähig und praktikabel für die frühen Phasen der Analyse und Modellierung erweist. Die meisten der gegenwärtig praktizierten Verfahren folgen dem Ansatz der sogenannten "semantischen Datenmodellierung" nach dem Entity-Relationship (E/R-) Prinzip. Um von diesen zum objektorientierten Vorgehen überzugehen, sind vorrangig drei Probleme zu lösen:

1. Modellierung komplexer Klassen, Objekte und Klassen-/Objektbeziehungen wie Generalisierung/Spezialisierung, Aggregation und Nachrichtenübermittlung ("strukturelle Objektorientierung", vgl. (6))
2. Integration von Daten- und Funktionsmodellierung zu einer Methode "aus einem Guß" analog zu den bekannten Prinzipien der Datenkapselung ("verhaltensmäßige Objektorientierung")
3. Modellierung komplexer betrieblicher Vorgänge, die mehrere Klassen und Objekte betreffen und die sich häufig über längere Zeiträume erstrecken ("objektorientierte Vorgangsmodellierung")

Die Standardwerke für OO-Analyse und -Entwurf (2,3,9,10,11) haben sich ausführlich und gründlich mit den ersten beiden Problemen beschäftigt.

"Frag nicht zuerst, was das System tut: Frag, WORAN es etwas tut!"
Dieses Zitat wird von Meyer (9) als grundlegende Eigenschaft des objektorientierten Entwurfs bezeichnet. Wir stimmen der Aussage dieses Zitats zu! Wir wollen jedoch die Funktionalität (das WAS), vor allem bezogen auf das Gesamt-Anwendungssystem, nicht aus den Augen verlieren. Bisher wurde, wie wir meinen, der Methodik zur Beantwortung dieser Frage innerhalb der OOA nicht genügend Beachtung gewidmet.

Stellt man bei einem Versicherungsunternehmen der Fachabteilung die Frage: "WAS soll das System tun?", bekommt man die Antwort: Das System muß unsere Geschäftsvorfälle bearbeiten und steuern können. Die Funktionalität eines Systems, hier die Geschäftsvorfälle, stehen aus Anwendersicht im Vordergrund. Einer der wichtigsten Bestandteile der Analyse ist der Transfer von Wissen von Fachleuten zu Entwicklern. Die Sicht der Anwender, also hier die Betrachtung von Geschäftsvorfällen muß dabei einen hohen Stellenwert haben. Wie können nun diese Geschäftsvorfälle in die objektorientierte Analyse eingeordnet und dort beschrieben werden? Wie beantwortet man die Frage nach dem WAS? Wir versuchen hierfür im folgenden Antworten und Hinweise zu geben.

1. Der Geschäftsvorfall

Die Definitionen von "Geschäftsvorfall" in der Literatur sind nicht eindeutig. Bei Denert (5) finden wir:

> Ein Geschäftsvorfall ist ein Vorgang im Rahmen der Tätigkeit eines Unternehmens, gleichgültig ob von außen oder innen verursacht.

Eine weitere Definition von der ARAG Lebensversicherung (1) lautet:

> Ein Geschäftsvorfall ist eine eigenständige unternehmerische Tätigkeit, angestoßen von einem Auslöser.

Eine exakte, einheitliche Definition von "Geschäftsvorfall" gibt es nicht. Folgende Merkmale geben jedoch weitere Hinweise zum Charakter von GV's:

- Ein GV besteht aus einer Menge von Tätigkeiten, genannt Bausteine (auch zu finden: Aktionen, Geschäftsprozesse) im Unternehmen, die in einem logischen und zeitlichem Zusammenhang stehen.
- Bausteine oder Teile von Bausteinen können manuell, DV-unterstützt oder auch automatisiert durchgeführt werden. Für die Modellierung spielt dies zunächst keine Rolle.
- Geschäftsvorfälle werden rein fachlich, d.h. unabhängig von ihrer späteren DV-Realisierung beschrieben.
- Die Bearbeitung eines GV kann sich über einen längeren Zeitraum (z.B. einige Monate) erstrecken, ist aber eine logisch geschlossene Einheit mit einem bestimmten Ziel oder Ergebnis.
- Ein GV kann unterbrochen werden, um z.B.
  - Informationen von außen einzuholen (Arztbericht) oder
  - andere GV's anzustoßen, die Voraussetzung zur Erfüllung seines Ziels sind.

  Ist die Information eingeholt oder der angestoßene weitere GV beendet, so kann der GV wiederaufgenommen werden.

Mit der Beschreibungseinheit Baustein lassen sich GV's modular aufbauen, d.h. ein Baustein kann in mehreren Geschäftsvorfällen als Bestandteil vorkommen, wird aber nur an einer Stelle beschrieben. Eine Baustein kann nicht isoliert angestoßen werden. Beispiele sind erfahrungsgemäß die beste Erläuterung einer Definition, deshalb folgt hier eine Aufzählung von Geschäftsvorfällen jeweils mit der betroffenen Branche:

Versicherungssumme erhöhen	*Versicherung*
Lebensversicherung neu beantragen	*Lebensversicherung*
Konto neu anlegen	*Bank oder Sparkasse*
Mitarbeiter einstellen	*Beliebige Unternehmen*
Reise buchen	*Reisebüro*
Programm überführen von Test in Produktion	*Alle Unternehmen mit eigener DV*
Nächstes Geschäftsjahr planen	*Management jedes Unternehmens*

2. Gegenwärtige Praxis der Modellierung von Geschäftsvorfällen

Einsatzbereiche der GV-Modellierung sind

- die klassische Ablauforganisation:
  Vor allem im Finanzbereich (Banken und Versicherungen) ist der Geschäftsvorfall der Begriff für die Beschreibung des Geschäfts schlechthin. In anderen Bereichen findet man die GV's auch, allerdings oft unter anderem Namen, z.B. Vorgang oder Ablauf.

- die Strategische Informationsplanung (SIP):
  Neben einer Betrachtung der Ziele des Unternehmens sowie einer groben semantischen Datenmodellierung werden Geschäftsvorfälle als Beschreibung des Geschäfts des Unternehmens herangezogen.

- die Analyse:
  Neben einer groben semantischen Datenmodellierung werden Geschäftsvorfälle modelliert, um sich das Wissen der Sachbearbeiter so nah wie möglich an ihrer täglichen Arbeit zu sichern. Erst in einem zweiten Schritt wird dann die klassische Funktionsmodellierung und eine Verfeinerung der Datenmodellierung durchgeführt.

Die Arbeit von Sachbearbeitern besteht zum großen Teil in der Bearbeitung von Geschäftsvorfällen. GV-Modellierung heißt "Wissens-Engineering" beim Sachbearbeiter. Dieses Wissen ist oft schlecht dokumentiert, verstreut, nicht systematisch strukturiert. Es steckt in Arbeitsanweisungen, mündlich weitergegebenen Verfahrensregeln, oft auch nur in den Köpfen der Mitarbeiter. Andererseits finden wir dieses Wissen auch im Funktionsbeschreibungsteil von DV-Fachkonzepten, dort aber häufig schon sehr implementierungsorientiert mit Dateinamen und -formaten, Datenfeldbeschreibungen etc..

Modular aufgebaute, für Fach- und DV-Personal gleichzeitig verwendbare Beschreibungen von Anwendungssystemen sind eher selten. Der Bezug zum Datenmodell (falls so etwas überhaupt existiert) ist unvollständig, schwer nachzuvollziehen, oder Funktions- und Datenmodelle sind inkonsistent. Wieder- und weiterverwendbare Anwendungsdokumentationen gibt es noch kaum. Vorgänge, die sich an bestimmten Datenbeständen wiederholen (z.B. an den Verträgen verschiedener Sparten) werden immer gleich oder ähnlich beschrieben.

Als Beispiel einer (recht gut dokumentierten) Beschreibung von Geschäftsvorfällen soll folgender für das Lebensversicherungsgeschäft typischer Geschäftsvorfall diese Ausführungen erläutern (siehe Abbildung 1).

Neuantrag einer Lebensversicherung

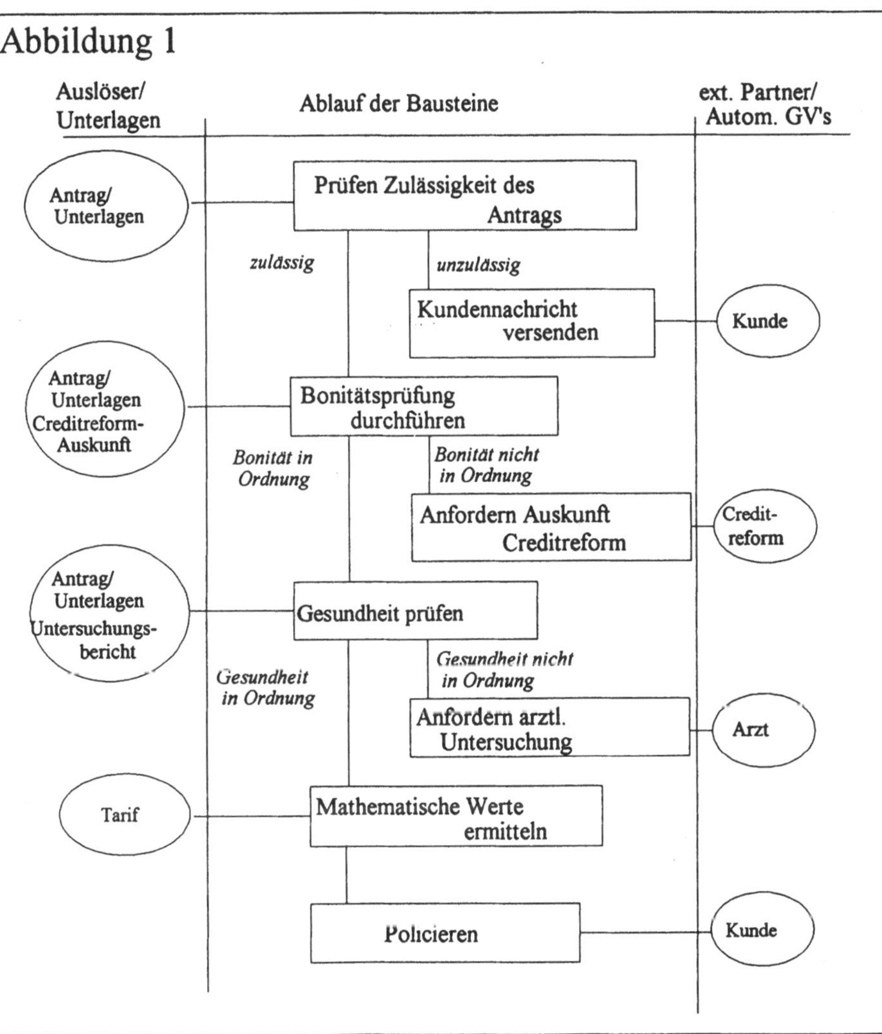

Zur Notation der graphischen Darstellung in Abbildung 1:

Dies ist eine Ablaufdarstellung, also gerichtet, von links nach rechts, von oben nach unten zu lesen. Die Rechtecke stellen die Bausteine des Geschäftsvorfalls dar. Die linke Spalte dient zur Darstellung der Auslöser und der vom Geschäftsvorfall benötigten Unterlagen. In der rechten Spalte werden die externen Partner dokumentiert, die der Geschäftsvorfall anspricht.

Dieser Geschäftsvorfall ist im Original von der ARAG (1) beschrieben worden. Es wird die dort vorgeschriebene graphische Darstellungsart verwendet, jedoch wird der GV in diesem Beispiel der Übersichtlichkeit zuliebe sehr vereinfacht dargestellt (Der echte GV besteht aus 45 Bausteinen). In diesem Geschäftsvorfall wird beschrieben, welche Tätigkeiten (Bausteine) in welcher Reihenfolge durchgeführt werden müssen, damit aus einem Antrag eines Kunden ein in Kraft getretener Vertrag einer Lebensversicherung wird. Dazu muß die Zulässigkeit eines Antrags geprüft werden, z.B. die Geschäftsfähigkeit des Kunden oder ob die Mindestsumme für eine Lebensversicherung überschritten wird. Sodann muß die Bonität des Versicherungsnehmers untersucht werden und in Zweifelsfällen evtl. eine Auskunft bei der Creditreform eingeholt werden. Diese Auskunft wird meist schriftlich eingeholt, so daß in diesem Fall der Geschäftsvorfall unterbrochen werden muß. Trifft die Antwort der Creditreform ein, so ist die Bonitätsprüfung noch einmal durchzuführen. Ein ähnliches Verfahren gilt bei der anschließenden Gesundheitsprüfung, bei der auch ein Gutachten eines Arztes eingeholt werden kann. Der Geschäftsvorfall endet mit der Ermittlung der mathematischen Werte, z.B. Beitragshöhe sowie der Policierung.

Zur objektorientierten GV-Modellierung sind uns keine Beiträge in der Literatur bekannt. In den Standardwerken zu OOA/D (2,3,4,9-12) beschränkt sich die Betrachtung der Dynamik eines Systems auf die Beschreibung der Lebenszyklen einer "normalen" Klasse (KUNDE, KONTO oder RESERVIERUNG). Am weitesten gehen noch bei der Modellierung Klassenübergreifender, das ganze System berührender Geschäftsvorfälle Ferstl/Sinz (7) mit ihren "Vorgangsobjekten".

3. Objektorientierte Geschäftsvorfallsmodellierung

3.1 Objektorientierte Modellierung von Bestandsklassen

Beim objektorientierten Entwurf (wie z.B. in 3,8,9 empfohlen) werden meist wie bei den herkömmlichen Verfahren zuerst diejenigen Informationen des Unternehmens beschrieben und strukturiert, die man zur Abwicklung und Unterstützung der betrieblichen Abläufe benötigt und verfügbar halten will (in der DV-Realisierung dann in Form von Dateien oder Datenbanken). Wir stellen uns solche Informationen als zu Bestandsobjekten gruppiert vor und fassen gleichartige Bestandsobjekte zu *Bestandsklassen* zusammen.

Definition: Eine *Bestandsklasse* ist eine Zusammenfassung gleichartiger Bestandsobjekte, d.h. von Gegenständen des betrieblichen Ablaufs, an denen Tätigkeiten, Verrichtungen oder Folgen von Zustandsänderungen vorgenommen werden.

Die Bestandsklassen sind vergleichbar mit den Entitätstypen des erweiterten Entity-Relationship-Ansatzes.

Abbildung 2 zeigt für das hier betrachtete Beispiel die Struktur der wichtigsten Bestandsklassen (Notation nach Coad/Yourdon(3), kurz beschrieben im Anhang A.1).

Die eine zentrale Klasse ist der VERTRAG, der aus genau einer Hauptversicherung (der eigentlichen Lebensversicherung) und diversen Zusatzversicherungen besteht. Sowohl Haupt- als auch Zusatzversicherungen haben ähnliche Eigenschaften, so daß es sinnvoll ist, eine Superklasse VERSICHERUNG *zu definieren. Eine Zusatzversicherung kann z.B. entweder eine BUZ (Berufsunfallzusatzversicherung) oder eine UIZV (Unfall- und Invaliditätszusatzversicherung) sein. Beispiele für Attribute von VERTRAG sind: Vertragsnummer, Juristi-*

scher-Beginn, Zahlweise, etc.. Operationen des VERTRAGs sind neben den "klassischen" DB-Operationen wie einfügen, verändern und löschen z.B. Alter-des-vertrags (Es wird mit Hilfe des aktuellen Datums sowie des juristischen-beginns das Alter in Jahren berechnet.).
Die zweite zentrale Klasse ist der PARTNER, der Versicherungsnehmer eines Vertrages oder durch eine Versicherung versichert ist.

Abbildung 2

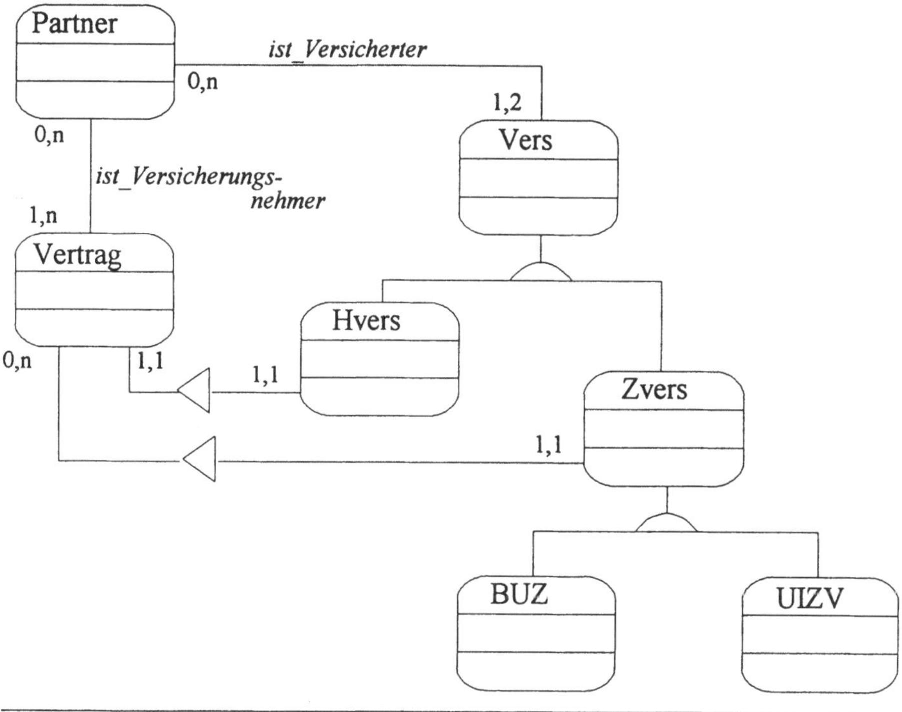

Die grundlegenden Beschreibungsmerkmale des objektorientierten Entwurfs sind die Klassen mit ihren Attributen und Operationen. Wir gehen davon aus, daß diese Grundelemente für die GV-Modellierung benutzt werden. Daher ist zu fragen: Wie lassen sich die Geschäftsvorfälle in die Klassenstruktur einordnen?

3.2 Objektorientierte Behandlung von Geschäftsvorfällen: Regel 1

Intuitiv besteht die Antwort zu obiger Frage aus folgender Regel:

Regel 1: Ordne den Geschäftsvorfall als Operation der zugehörigen Bestandsklasse zu.

Analog zur Zuordnung von Attributen zu Entitätstypen bei der Entity-Relationship-Modellierung werden die Geschäftsvorfälle, da sie dynamischen, also eher funktionalen Charakter besitzen, als Operationen der zugehörigen Bestandsklassen definiert.

Was bedeutet hier "zugehörige" Bestandsklasse? Betrachten wir die Geschäftsvorfälle, so hat die Durchführung eines Geschäftsvorfalls das Ziel der Erzeugung, Veränderung oder Löschung eines Exemplars einer zentralen, "zugehörigen" Bestandsklasse. Mit folgenden Beispielen soll dies erläutert werden:

i) *Der "Neuantrag einer Lebensversicherung" führt im positiven Fall zum Vertragsabschluß, also zur Erzeugung eines Exemplars von VERTRAG (natürlich ebenfalls zur Erzeugung von Exemplaren von HVERS, ZVERS, die von VERTRAG über Aggregation abhängig sind.). Ordne also hier gemäß Regel 1 "Neuantrag einer Lebensversicherung" als Operation der "zugehörigen" Klasse VERTRAG zu!*

ii) *Die "Kontoeröffnung" hat das Ziel der Erzeugung eines Exemplars der Klasse KONTO.*

iii) *Die "Jahresplanung" einer Organisationseinheit eines Unternehmens (dies kann eine Hauptabteilung, eine Abteilung oder ein Referat sein) hat das Ziel die Planungsdaten dieser Einheit zu verändern. Also ordne "Jahresplanung" als Operation der Klasse ORGANISATIONSEINHEIT zu.*

In dieser, der zugehörigen Bestandsklasse zugeordneten Operation wird mindestens die Steuerung des GV beschrieben. Die einzelnen funktionalen Teile des GV, die Bausteine, können Operationen der Klasse selbst sein. Im allgemeinen werden jedoch zur Durchführung eines Geschäftsvorfalls die Attribute und Operationen vieler anderer Klassen benötigt.

Abbildung 3 zeigt eine grobe Beschreibung der Klasse VERTRAG (angenäherte EIFFEL-Syntax, siehe kurze Beschreibung der Syntax im Anhang A.1).

Abbildung 3

```
class VERTRAG export
    vertragsnummer, juristischer_beginn,
    zahlweise, ändvormerk, neuantrag_leben,
    unterbrechen, wiederaufnehmen

feature
    vertragsnummer:      NUMMER
    juristischer_beginn: DATUM
    zahlweise:           ZAHLWEISE_CD
    ändvormerk:          BOOLEAN

    versnehmer:          PARTNER
    versicherter:        PARTNER
    hvers:               HVERS
    zvers:               ZVERS
```

```
neuantrag_leben is
Local
    bearbeitungszustand:  TEXT
    sachbearbeiter:       MITARBEITER
    abl:                  ABLEHNBRIEF
    begr-ablehnung:       TEXT
    grund:                TEXT
do
    bearbeitungszustand:= in_Arbeit
    IF NOT neuantrag-ist-zulässig
    THEN
        abl.schreiben
            (versnehmer, begr-ablehnung)
    ELSE
        neuantrag_leben_ab_boni
    ENDIF
end  neuantrag_leben
```

```
neuantrag_leben_ab_boni is
    Local
    Credausk: AUSKUNFT_CREDREF
do
    IF NOT
      versnehmer.bonität_in_Ordnung
        Credausk.schreiben
        grund := bonität
        unterbrechen(grund)
    ELSE
        neuantrag_leben_ab_gesund
    ENDIF
end  neuantrag_leben_ab_boni

neuantrag_leben_ab_gesund is
    Local
    arztaus: ARZTAUSKUNFT
do
    IF NOT
        versicherter.gesundheitsprüfung_ok
    THEN
        arztaus.schreiben (versicherter)
        grund := gesundheit
        unterbrechen(grund)
    ELSE
        mathematische_werte
        policieren
    ENDIF
end  neuantrag_leben_ab_gesund

unterbrechen(grund:TEXT) is
do
    bearbeitungszustand := unterbrochen
-- sichere Zustand des Geschäftsvorfalls
    .
end  unterbrechen

wiederaufnehmen(grund:TEXT) is
do
    -- Stelle Zustand des GV wieder her
    IF grund = bonität
    THEN
        neuantrag_leben_ab_boni
    ENDIF
    IF grund = gesundheit
    THEN
        neuantrag_leben_ab_gesund
    ENDIF
end  wiederaufnehmen

neuantrag-ist-zulässig: BOOLEAN is
            -- GP 111
do
    IF hvers.vers-summe-zu-klein
    THEN
        Result := false
        begr-ablehnung:=
        "Versicherungssumme zu
            niedrig"
    END

    IF NOT versnehmer.geschäftsfähig
    THEN
        Result := false
        begr-ablehnung:=
        "Versicherungsnehmer ist nicht
                    geschäftsfähig"
    END
end  neuantrag-ist-zulässig

mathematische_werte is
do
...
end

policieren is
do
...
end

end -- class VERTRAG
```

3.3 Objektorientierte Behandlung von Geschäftsvorfällen: Regel 2

Die Regel 1 scheint also im ersten Ansatz die richtige Behandlung von Geschäftsvorfällen in der Objektorientierung zu gewährleisten. Dies trifft bei der Betrachtung nur eines Geschäftsvorfalls zu. Modellieren wir aber noch weitere Geschäftsvorfälle, so fallen Gemeinsamkeiten auf: Die "Erhöhung Lebensversicherungssumme" ist bei einer Lebensversicherung ein weiterer GV . Bei genauer Betrachtung stellt sich heraus, daß viele der schon vom GV "Neuantrag-_Leben" benötigten Attribute wie z.B. Sachbearbeiter oder Bearbeitungszustand auch als Attribute von "Erhöhung Lebensversicherungssumme" benötigt werden. Ja sogar einige der Operationen wie "unterbrechen" oder "wiederaufnehmen" unterscheiden sich nicht oder sind ähnlich.

Darüber hinaus kann dann festgestellt werden, daß fast alle der im System zu betrachtenden Geschäftsvorfälle diese Attribute oder Operationen benötigen. Eines der Hauptziele des objektorientierten Entwurfs ist jedoch die Vermeidung von Redundanz und die Förderung der Wiederverwendbarkeit. Das Konzept, das diese Ziele bei der Objektorientierung vornehmlich unterstützt, ist die Vererbung. Vererbung ist aber nur auf Klassen-, nicht aber auf Attributs- oder Operationsebene möglich. Dies bedeutet also: Wir benötigen so etwas wie einen generellen Geschäftsvorfall, in dem wir die Attribute und Operationen, die in allen Geschäftsvorfällen in gleicher Weise vorkommen, zentral beschreiben. Modellieren wir diesen generellen Geschäftsvorfall als Klasse, so kann er nur an seine Subklassen vererben, so daß wir gezwungen sind, folgende Regel aufzustellen:

Regel 2: Modelliere einen Geschäftsvorfall als Klasse.

Wendet man das soeben skizzierte Verallgemeinerungsprinzip konsequent an, so ist eine Superklasse GESCHÄFTSVORFALL zu erstellen, die alle Merkmale enthält, die für sämtliche GV's relevant sind, also z.B. die Attribute Bearbeiter, Eröffnungsdatum, Auslöser, etc. und die Operationen beginnen, unterbrechen, wiederaufnehmen und abschließen. Jeder einzelne Typ von GESCHÄFTSVORFALL wird zu einer selbständigen Klasse, also zum Beispiel wird der GV "Kontoneuanlage durchführen" zur Klasse KONTONEUANLAGE. Solcherart gebildete Klassen nennen wir *Vorgangsklassen*.

Definition: Eine *Vorgangsklasse* ist eine Zusammenfassung gleichartiger Objekte, der sogenannten *Vorgangsobjekte*, die aus betrieblichen Abläufen, Tätigkeiten, Verrichtungen oder Folgen von Zustandsänderungen bestehen. In der Regel beziehen sie sich auf Objekte mehrerer Bestandsklassen und können sich über längere Zeiträume (Stunden, Tage, Wochen,...) erstrecken.

Vorgangsklassen können speziell zur Modellierung von Geschäftsvorfällen herangezogen werden. Jedes Exemplar einer solchen Klasse, d.h. jedes Vorgangsobjekt entspricht in diesem Falle einem konkreten GV des genannten Typs.

Beispiel: Der Kunde Mustermann möchte ein Girokonto eröffnen. Der sich daraus ergebende Ablauf ist ein Exemplar der Klasse "Kontoneuanlage".

Diese Klasse enthält die Steuerung des speziellen Geschäftsvorfalles (auch in Form einer Operation). Sie verwendet die Operationen und Attribute von anderen Klassen oder auch der eigenen Klasse.

Für das durchgängige Beispiel ist dies in Abbildung 4 (Notation gemäß Coad/Yourdon) dargestellt:
Jeder Geschäftsvorfall wird zu einer Klasse, hier LV_SUMME_ERHÖHEN und NEUANTRAG_LEBEN. Diese Klassen erben aus der Superklasse GESCHÄFTSVORFALL die für alle einzelnen Geschäftsvorfallsklassen generell geltenden Attribute und Operationen.
Vorgangsklassen und Bestandsklassen sind vielfältig miteinander verbunden. Z.B. gibt es zwischen der Klasse NEUANTRAG_LEBEN und der Klasse VERTRAG eine 1:c-Exemplarbeziehung. Diese ist aber nicht in Abbildung 4 dargestellt, sondern der Übersichtlichkeit wegen nur die charakteristischste Beziehungsart zwischen den Vorgangsklassen und den Bestandsklassen: die Verwendung. Sowohl die Klasse NEUANTRAG_LEBEN als auch die Klasse LV_SUMME_ERHÖHEN verwenden die Attribute und Operationen von vielen Bestandsklassen wie VERTRAG, PARTNER etc..

Abbildung 4

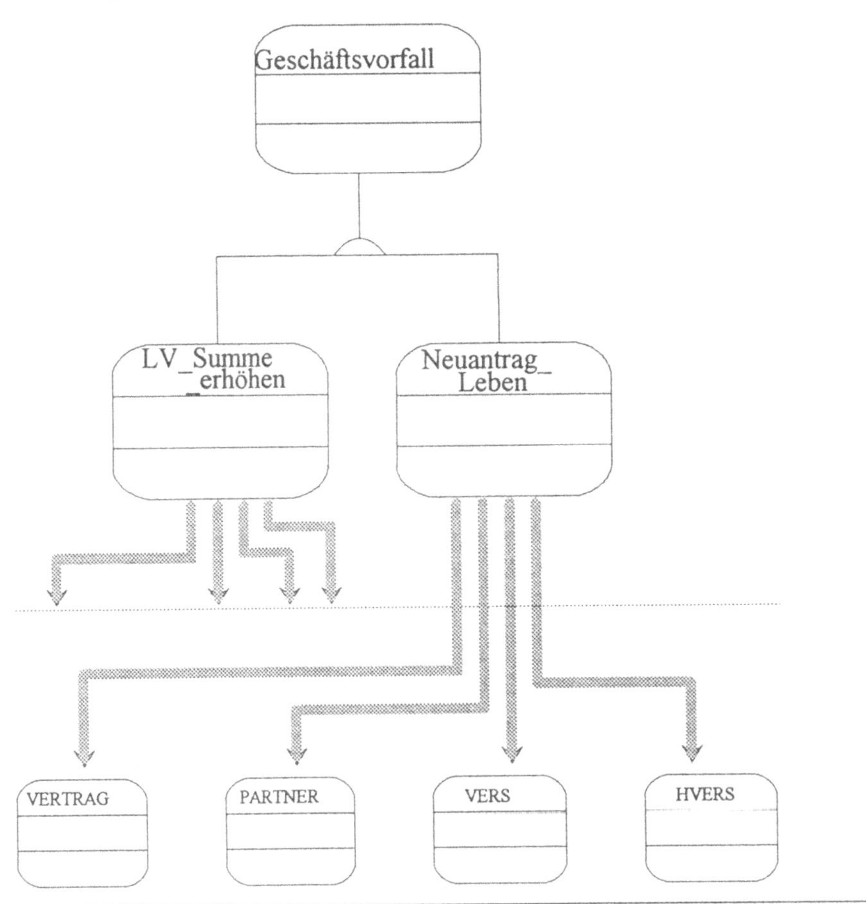

In Abbildung 5 wird sowohl die "Superklasse" GESCHÄFTSVORFALL als auch die gemäß Regel 2 entstandene Klasse NEUANTRAG_LEBEN in angenäherter EIFFEL-Syntax (siehe Anhang A.1) beschrieben. Die Operationen und Attribute, die alle Geschäftsvorfälle haben, sind in diese Klasse GESCHÄFTSVORFALL ausgelagert.

Im Fallbeispiel sind in der Klasse GESCHÄFTSVORFALL die für alle Geschäftsvorfälle geltenden Operationen beginnen, unterbrechen, wiederaufnehmen sowie beenden beschrieben. Zu beachten ist die Operation weiter_nach_wiederaufnahme. Es ist eine rein interne Operation, kann in der Klasse GESCHÄFTSVORFALL jedoch nicht detailliert beschrieben werden, da sie in jeder Subklasse aufgrund der speziellen Funktionalität der Geschäftsvorfälle gesondert erstellt werden muß. In der Klasse NEUANTRAG_LEBEN sind die allen Geschäftsvorfällen gemeinsamen Attribute und Operationen nicht mehr vorhanden, bzw. werden von der Klasse GESCHÄFTSVORFALL geerbt.

Abbildung 5

```
class GESCHÄFTSVORFALL export
    sachbearbeiter, eröffnungsdatum, auslöser,
    bearbeitungszustand, beginnen,
    unterbrechen, wiederaufnehmen, beenden

feature
    sachbearbeiter:         MITARBEITER
    eröffnungsdatum:        ZEITPUNKT
    auslöser:               EREIGNIS
    bearbeitungszustand:    TEXT
    grund:                  TEXT

    beginnen is
        do
            ...........
            bearbeitungszustand := in_arbeit
        end

    unterbrechen is
        require
            bearbeitungszustand = in_arbeit
        do
            --Sichere Zustand des GV --
            bearbeitungszustand := unterbrochen
        end

    wiederaufnehmen (grund:TEXT) is
        require
            bearbeitungszustand = unterbrochen
        do
            -- Stelle Zustand des GV wieder
                 her --
            ...........
            bearbeitungszustand := in_arbeit
            weiter_nach_wiederaufnahme(grund)
        end

    weiter_nach_wiederaufnahme
                            (grund:TEXT) is
        deferred
        end

    beenden is
        require
            bearbeitungszustand = in_arbeit
        do
            ............
            bearbeitungszustand := beendet
        end

end -- class GESCHÄFTSVORFALL
```

```
class NEUANTRAG_LEBEN export
    neuantrag_leben, sachbearbeiter,
    eröffnungsdatum, auslöser,
    bearbeitungszustand, beginnen,
    unterbrechen, wiederaufnehmen,
    beenden

inherit GESCHÄFTSVORFALL

feature
    vertrag:        VERTRAG
    abl:            ABLEHNUNGSBRIEF
    begr-ablehnung:     TEXT
    grund           TEXT

    neuantrag_leben is
        do
        beginnen
        IF NOT neuantrag_ist_zulässig
            abl.schreiben
              (vertrag.vn, begr-ablehnung)
        ELSE
            neuantrag_leben_ab_boni
        ENDIF
    end neuantrag_leben

    weiter_nach_wiederaufnahme
                            (grund:TEXT) is
        do
        IF grund = bonität
        THEN
            neuantrag_leben_ab_boni
        ELSE
        ..............
        ENDIF
        end

    neuantrag_ist_zulässig:BOOLEAN is
     do
     ..............
     end

    neuantrag_leben_ab_boni is
     do
     ..............
     end

    neuantrag_leben_ab_gesund is
     do
     ..............
     end

end --class NEUANTRAG_LEBEN
```

Die Klasse VERTRAG wird in Abb. 5 nicht mehr dargestellt. Im Gegensatz zu Abb. 3 (also gemäß Regel 1) ist diese Klasse jetzt gemäß Regel 2 wesentlich "schlanker", da eine Vielzahl der Operationen (die Geschäftsvorfälle) selbst zu Klassen geworden sind. Bei der Klasse VERTRAG sind Attribute wie vertragsnummer, juristischer_beginn, zahlweise, etc. verblieben.

Die Möglichkeit zur Verallgemeinerung ist nicht der einzige Vorteil von Regel 2, wie folgendes Beispiel aus der Lebensversicherung zeigt:

Für den Geschäftsvorfall "LV_Summe_erhöhen" kann es parallele Exemplare geben. Warum? Ein Lebensversicherungsvertrag kann mehr als einen Versicherungsnehmer (VN) haben. Jeder dieser Versicherungsnehmer hat das Recht, zunächst unabhängig vom anderen VN, einen Antrag auf Erhöhung der Lebensversicherungssumme zu stellen. Es kann vorkommen, daß dies auch zeitlich überlappend geschieht, d. h. zu einem Exemplar von LEBENSVERSICHERUNG gibt es gleichzeitig zweimal den Versuch die Lebensversicherungssumme zu erhöhen. Dies ist erlaubt, muß aber natürlich harmonisiert werden.

Zwei verschiedene Exemplare des gleichen Geschäftsvorfalls können also gleichzeitig zu einem Exemplar der zugehörigen Bestandsklasse existieren. Bei Befolgung von Regel 1 ergeben sich Schwierigkeiten, weil wir damit ja den Geschäftsvorfall als Operation der Bestandsklasse definieren. Diese Operation müßte also zweimal parallel aufgerufen werden. Regel 2 dagegen unterstützt diesen Fall, da ein Exemplar eines Geschäftsvorfalls nicht eineindeutig einem Exemplar der Bestandsklasse zugeordnet sein muß.

3.4 Diskussion von Regel 1 und Regel 2

Ist Regel 2 für alle von der Fachabteilung so bezeichneten Geschäftsvorfälle anzuwenden?

Betrachten wir als Beispiel den Geschäftsvorfall "Änderung Kundenadresse": Der Kunde schickt seine Adreßänderung an das Unternehmen. Der Sachbearbeiter erfaßt sie. Dabei kann es natürlich noch zu Fehlern kommen (falsche PLZ, etc.). Es wird aber auf jeden Fall sofort das Ende des GV, sei es positiv oder negativ, erreicht. Im negativen Fall, also wenn die Adresse nicht automatisch richtig gestellt werden kann, wird der Kunde ersucht, die Adreßänderung erneut an das Unternehmen zu melden und damit ist der GV beendet. Meldet sich der Kunde ein zweites Mal, so ist dies wieder ein neues Exemplar des Geschäftsvorfalls. Es kann in diesem Fall also nicht zu Unterbrechungen oder auch zu Parallelität kommen. Wird zusätzlich von der Fachabteilung kein Sinn darin gesehen, diesen Geschäftsvorfall zu archivieren, so gibt es keinen Grund, den GV "Änderung Kundenadresse" zu einer eigenen Klasse zu machen.

Die aufgeführten Beispiele zeigen, daß eine allgemeingültige, präzise Entscheidungshilfe, wann Regel 1 oder Regel 2 anzuwenden sind, nicht gegeben werden kann. Vielmehr gibt es Anhaltspunkte, die mehr für die Anwendung der einen oder der anderen Regel sprechen. So lernen wir aus dem letztgenannten Beispiel, daß Regel 1 vorzuziehen ist, wenn

- der Geschäftsvorfall von kurzer Dauer und im Regelfall ununterbrechbar ist,
- es nicht notwendig ist, über längere Zeiträume hinweg ("persistent") Daten über den GV zu halten,
- sich der Geschäftsvorfall genau einem Exemplar einer Bestandsklasse zuordnen läßt und zu diesem Exemplar nicht gleichzeitig mehrere gleichartige Geschäftsvorfälle existieren können,

- keine Notwendigkeit besteht, den GV in eine Vererbungshierarchie einzubauen, um Eigenschaften übergeordneter (verallgemeinernder) GV's zu übernehmen oder solche an untergeordnete (speziellere) GV's weiterzugeben.

Umgekehrt muß Regel 2 nicht für alle von der Fachabteilung so bezeichneten Geschäftsvorfälle verwendet werden. Sie sollte aber angewendet werden, wenn

- die Notwendigkeit einer persistenten Datenhaltung von Geschäftsvorfällen (z.B. bei Unterbrechung und Wiederaufnahme) gegeben ist,
- Verallgemeinerungsmöglichkeiten über Vererbung (gemeinsame Attribute und Operationen von verschiedenen GV's) genutzt werden müssen,
- die Notwendigkeit besteht, mehrere GV-Exemplare zum gleichen Objekt einer Bestandsklasse (z.B. Exemplar von VERTRAG) zu bilden.

Was haben nun Bestands- und Vorgangsklassen gemeinsam und worin unterscheiden sie sich voneinander? Beginnen wir bei der Klassenstruktur, d.h. bei der Zusammensetzung aus Attributen und Operationen: Attribute von Bestandsklassen beschreiben den Zustand oder die Struktur von Bestandsobjekten, wie z.B. einen Kontostand, den Status eines Versicherungsvertrages oder die Höhe und Zahlungsweise der Prämienzahlungen. Attribute von Vorgangsklassen dienen vorrangig der Zustandsbeschreibung der Vorgangsobjekte, d.h. der konkret in Arbeit befindlichen Geschäftsvorfälle. So lautet ein typisches Attribut einer Vorgangsklasse GESCHÄFTSVORFALL "Bearbeitungszustand" (vgl. Abb. 5). Weiter werden Attribute dazu genutzt, den Bezug zu dem vom GV betroffenen Bestandsobjekten herzustellen. Sie sind also Bezüge auf Bestandsobjekte.

Operationen von Bestandsklassen entsprechen in erster Linie den klassischen Datenbankoperationen INSERT, UPDATE und DELETE, d.h. dienen zum Anlagen, Modifizieren oder Löschen von einzelnen Bestandsobjekten. Etwas ähnliches finden wir auch bei der Superklasse GESCHÄFTSVORFALL, die die generischen Merkmale für alle Geschäftsvorfälle enthält (s. Abb. 5): Einzelne Geschäftsvorfälle können gestartet, unterbrochen, wiederaufgenommen oder beendet werden. Anders dagegen verhalten sich die Vorgangsklassen für spezifische Typen von Geschäftsvorfällen. Sie haben normalerweise eine ausgezeichnete Operation, die die Durchführungsanweisung für die Abwicklung des Geschäftsvorfalls (etwa im Sinne von Abb. 1) enthält. Im Beispiel (Abb. 5) ist dies die Operation NEUANTRAG_LEBEN. Eine derart ausgezeichnete Operation wollen wir *Hauptoperation* nennen.

4. Ausblick: Geschäftsvorfälle in OOD und OOP

Die hier vorgeschlagenen Techniken zur GV-Modellierung lassen sich nicht nur im Analyseprozeß, sondern für die gesamte Systementwicklung vorteilhaft anwenden. Das Hauptargument dafür ist grundsätzlicher Art (für eine ausführliche Diskussion siehe W.Hesse (7)): Durch die Objektorientierung wird eine durchgängige Systemstruktur gefördert. Das bedeutet, daß die Klassen, die in der objektorientierten Analyse definiert wurden, in den darauffolgenden Entwicklungsstufen (Entwurf, Programmierung) weiter existieren und dabei ausgebaut, verfeinert und den Erfordernissen einer spezifischen Implementierungsumgebung angepaßt werden. Das gilt nicht nur für Bestandsklassen wie VERTRAG oder PARTNER, sondern auch für die Klasse GESCHÄFTSVORFALL und ihre Spezialisierungen.

Ein weiterer wichtiger Gesichtspunkt, der den gesamten Lebenszyklus von Geschäftsvorfällen betrifft, ist die Möglichkeit zur Standardisierung und Weiter- bzw. Wiederverwendung. So wie heute auch bei Unternehmen mit relativ traditioneller Vorgehensweise bestimmte Funktionen wie Masken- und Fehlerbehandlung, Dialog- und Menüsteuerung, Hilfesysteme, Fehler- und Alarmbehandlung standardisiert werden, kann man auch - wie oben beschrieben - bei der Behandlung von Geschäftsvorfällen einiges standardisieren: nämlich genau die Attribute und Operationen, die wir in der generalisierten Klasse GESCHÄFTSVORFALL gebündelt haben. Wird diese Klasse in den folgenden Entwurfs- und Realisierungsphasen um die notwendigen Implementierungsdetails ergänzt, so gelangen wir zu einer allgemeinen, in vielen Anwendungssystemen wiederverwendbaren Komponente "Geschäftsvorfallssteuerung".

A.1. Kurzbeschreibung der verwendeten Notationen

i) Graphische Darstellung nach Coad/Yourdon

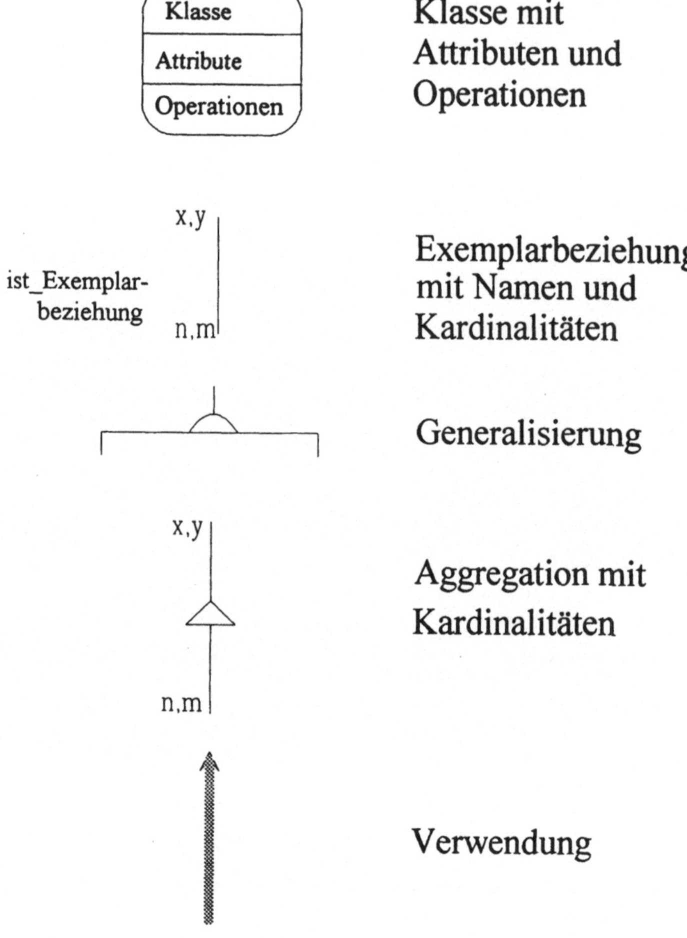

ii) EIFFEL-Syntax (angenähert)

class klassenname
....
....
end

Klausel für die Klasse und ihren Namen, die nach ihrem Be schreibungsteil mit end endet.

export merkmal (*)

Klausel zur Angabe der Merkmale (s.u.), die die Klasse exportiert, also für den Zugriff von anderen Klassen zur Verfügung stellt.

inherit klasse (*)

Die Vererbung wird in EIFFEL durch die inherit-Klausel gesteuert. Es werden die Namen der Klassen angegeben, von denen diese Klasse erbt.

feature merkmal (*)

Mit feature beginnt der Teil der Klassenbeschreibung, der die Attribute und Operationen der Klasse aufzählt und spezifiziert. Attribute als auch Operationen sind in EIFFEL features, also Merkmale.

merkmal: KLASSE

Einem Merkmal, hier ein Attribut, wird ein Typ, wiederum eine Klasse, zugeordnet.

merkmal **is**
do
end

Dies ist die Syntax für die Beschreibung einer Operation (Prozedur, Funktion) in EIFFEL. Die zu beschreibende Funktionalität der Operation wird zwischen do und end abgelegt.

deferred

Mit deferred (aufgeschoben) wird die Operation einer Superklasse bezeichnet, die zwar der Superklasse bekannt ist, aber nur in den Subklassen zu dieser Superklasse explizit implementiert ist.

local merkmal (*)

Die local-Klausel ist innerhalb der Beschreibung einer Operation möglich zur Definition von lokalen, nur für die Operation gültigen Merkmalen.

result :=

Ein Merkmal mit dem Charakter einer Operation kann gleichzeitig das Ergebnis der Operation darstellen, also ein Merkmal ist Attribut und Operation gleichzeitig. Mit der result-Klausel wird dem Merkmal als Attribut der Ergebniswert zugewiesen.

require bedingung

Die require-Klausel bestimmt eine Vorbedingung für eine Operation. Die Operation darf nur ausgeführt werden, wenn die Bedingung den Wert "wahr" annimmt.

A.2. Literatur

(1) ARAG Lebensversicherung AG: Geschäftsvorfallsmodellierung
1988

(2) G.Booch: Object-oriented Design with applications
Benjamin/Cummings 1992

(3) P.Coad, E.Yourdon: Object-Oriented Analysis
Yourdon Press 1990/91

(4) P.Coad,E.Yourdon: Object-Oriented Design
Yourdon Press 1991

(5) E.Denert: Software Engineering
Springer Verlag 1991

(6) K.R. Dittrich: Objektorientierte Datenbanksysteme
in "Das aktuelle Schlagwort", Informatik Spektrum 12
Seite-215-220 (1989)

(7) O.K.Ferstl, E.J.Sinz: "Ein Vorgehensmodell zur Objektmodellierung betrieblicher Informations-systeme im Semantischem Objektmodell (SOM)"
in Wirschaftsinformatik 6/91

(8) W.Hesse: Objektorientierte Anwendungsmodellierung - ein Weg zu einem durchgängigen Software-Entwicklungsprozeß,
in G. Kugel (Hrsg): Praxiserprobte Software-Entwicklungswerkzeuge im Überblick, Reihe Kontakt und Studium
Expert-Verlag 1992

(9) B.Meyer: Objektorientierte Software-Entwicklung
Hanser, Prentice Hall 1990

(10) Rumbaugh et al.: Object-Oriented Modeling and Design
Prentice Hall 1991

(11) S.Shlaer, S.Mellor: Object-Oriented Systems Analysis
Yourdon Press 1988

(12) S.Shlaer, S.Mellor: Object Lifecycles
Yourdon Press 1992

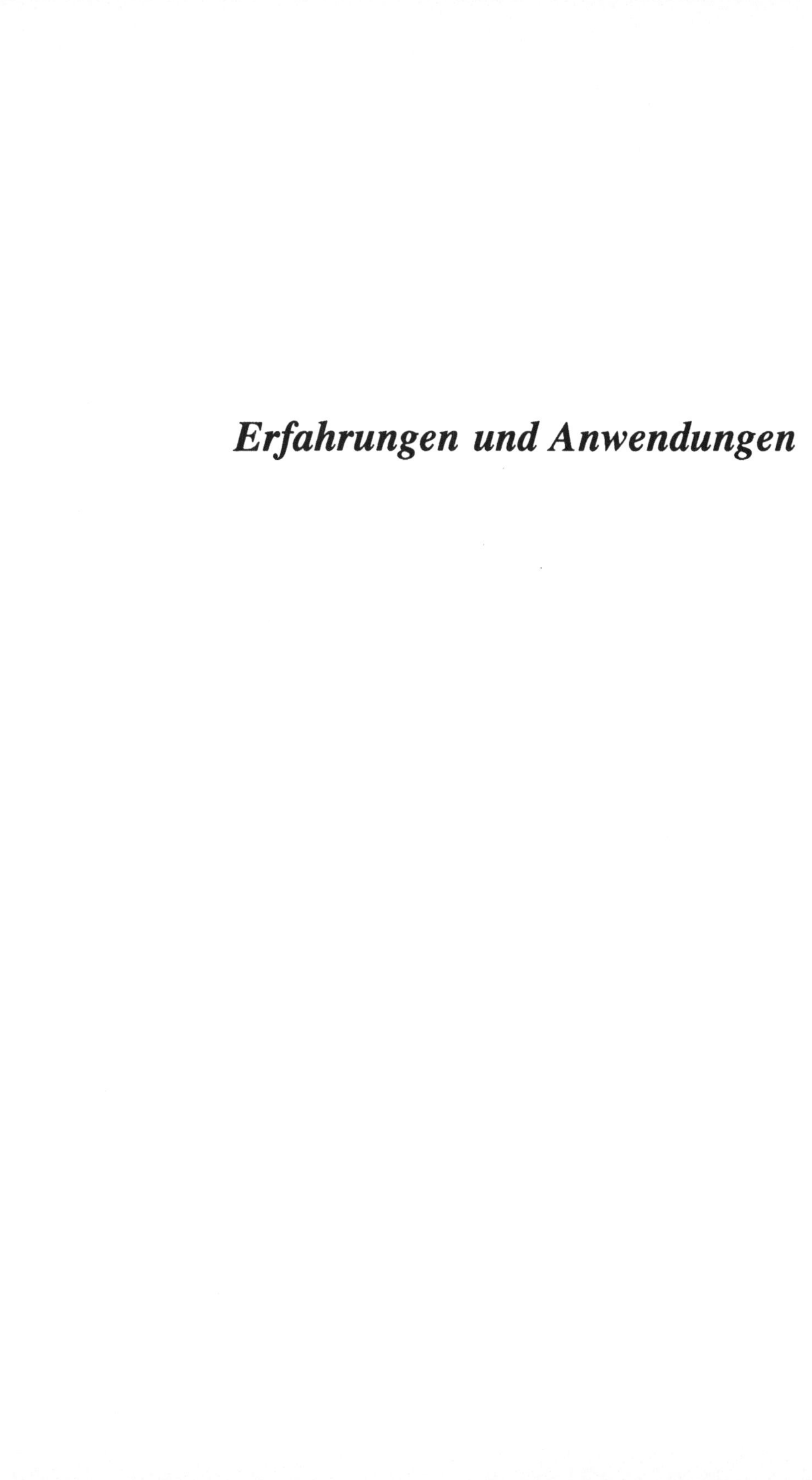

Erfahrungen und Anwendungen

Die objektorientierte Analysemethode von COAD und YOURDON: Anwendung und Bewertung am Beispiel eines Lagerverwaltungssystems unter besonderer Berücksichtigung der Wiederverwendung

P. Stahlknecht, W. Appelfeller,
Universität Osnabrück, Fachgebiet BWL/Wirtschaftsinformatik I

1 Einleitung

Seit ca. zwei Jahren werden im verstärkten Maße Analyse- und Designmethoden entwickelt, die die Konzepte objektorientierter Programmiersprachen /WIN 90/ verwenden. Keine dieser objektorientierten (oo-) Methoden hat sich bisher durchsetzen bzw. zu einer Art Standard entwickeln können. Erfahrungen mit den einzelnen Methoden sind gegenwärtig noch gering.

Gegenstand der vorliegenden Arbeit ist eine Auseinandersetzung mit der oo-Analysemethode von COAD und YOURDON /COA 91a/. Kapitel 2 zeigt am Beispiel eines fiktiven Lagers, wie diese Methode angewendet wird. Im Kapitel 3 wird dargestellt, welche grundsätzlichen Vor- und Nachteile ein oo-Vorgehen in der Analysephase besitzt. Darüber hinaus werden eine spezielle Bewertung des Vorgehens von COAD und YOURDON vorgenommen und Verbesserungsvorschläge für diese Methode gegeben. Kapitel 4 stellt die Zusammenhänge zwischen Objektorientierung und Wiederverwendung dar. Insbesondere wird aufgezeigt, wie auf Basis der Methode von COAD und YOURDON mit Hilfe eines Fragenkatalogs die Wiederverwendung einzelner Komponenten überprüft bzw. erhöht werden kann.

2 Objektorientierte Analyse (ooA) des Lagerverwaltungssystem

2.1 Anforderungen an das Lagerverwaltungssystem

Gegenstand der Betrachtung ist das Fertigwarenlager eines Produktionsbetriebs. Die Lagereinrichtung besteht aus fortlaufend numerierten Hochregalen, die in ebenfalls fortlaufend numerierten Regalzellen aufgeteilt sind. Eine Zelle kann jeweils eine Palette aufnehmen. In der Produktion bekommen die sortenrein gepackten Paletten einen Begleitschein, der die Artikelnummer und die Produktionsmenge enthält. Bei der Einlagerung, die palettenweise und ohne Berücksichtigung von Ordnungskriterien erfolgt, erhalten die Paletten einen weiteren Begleitschein, der z.B. Angaben über den Lagerort enthält. Das Lagerverwaltungssystem soll folgende Aufgaben unterstützen:

- Palettenweise Einlagerung von Fertigwaren aus dem Produktionsbereich: Erfassen der Artikelnummer und Menge, Zuordnung einer freien Regalzelle, Drucken des Palettenbegleitscheins, Bestandsabgleich und physische Einlagerung.
- Kommissionierung der von der Vertriebsabteilung bearbeiteten Kundenbestellungen: Erfassen der Kundendaten und der einzelnen Positionen der Bestellung, Überprüfung der Verfügbarkeit der Bestellpositionen, Drucken der Entnahmeliste (mit Menge und Lagerort der Artikel) und gegebenenfalls der Fehlliste, Bestandsabgleich, physische Auslagerung und Drucken des Lieferscheins.

- Auslagerung von nicht für den Verkauf vorgesehener Ware (z.B. fehlerhafte Produkte) auf Anweisung der Vertriebsabteilung: Erfassen der Artikelnummern und der entsprechenden auszulagernden Mengen, Drucken der Entnahmeliste, Bestandsabgleich und physische Auslagerung.
- Durchführung wöchentlicher, buchmäßiger Inventuren für die der Finanzbuchhaltung angeschlossenen Controlling-Gruppe: Ausgabe einer Liste mit den folgenden Daten jedes Artikels: Artikelnummer, Artikelbezeichnung und Bestand.
- Abfragen: Ausgabe freier Lagerkapazitäten und vorhandener Lagerbestände.

Anmerkung: Auf die Spezifikation der Benutzerschnittstelle wird hier verzichtet, da sie bei COAD und YOURDON erst in der Designphase vorgesehen ist /COA 91b, S. 56-71/. Die physische Ein- bzw. Auslagerung wird vom System dadurch gesteuert, daß den Staplerfahrern mit dem Palettenbegleitschein und den Entnahmelisten (jeweils mit Lagerkooordinaten) die entsprechenden Fahraufträge erteilt werden.

2.2 ooA des Lagerverwaltungssystems mit der Methode von COAD und YOURDON

2.2.1 Grundlagen

Gegenstand der oo-Analyse (ooA) ist das Verstehen des Problembereichs und die Formulierung der Systemanforderungen /COA 91a, S. 8/. COAD und YOURDON betonen dabei, daß die Analyse festlegt, "WAS" ein System zu leisten hat, jedoch nicht bestimmt, "WIE" diese Leistungen zu realisieren sind. Letzterer Aspekt ist Gegenstand des objektorientierten Designs (ooD) /COA 91b, S. 17/ (Für einen Überblick zum ooD siehe /STA 92/).

Ergebnis der objektorientierten Analyse ist eine Abbildung des Problembereichs und der Systemanforderungen in objektorientierter Form. COAD und YOURDON schlagen hierfür ein Fünf-Schichten-Modell vor. Zur Erstellung dieses Modells wird der Analyseprozess in fünf Aktivitäten aufgeteilt, deren Ergebnis durch jeweils eine Schicht des Modells dargestellt wird. Abbildung 1 zeigt das Fünf-Schichten-Modell mit den zugrundeliegenden Aktivitäten.

Aktivität	Schicht
3. Identifizieren von Subjekten	Subjekt-Schicht
1. Bestimmen von Klassen u. Objekten	Klassen-&-Objekt-Schicht
2. Identifizieren von Strukturen	Struktur-Schicht
4. Definieren von Attributen u. Instanzverbindungen	Attribut-Schicht
5. Definieren von Services u. Nachrichtenverbindungen	Service-Schicht

Abb. 1: Das Fünf-Schichten-Modell der ooA

Die einzelnen Schichten des Modells hat man sich als transparente, übereinanderliegende Folien vorzustellen, deren Detaillierungsgrad von oben nach unten zunimmt. Die Ziffern vor den Aktivitäten geben die vorgesehene Bearbeitungsfolge wieder. Zur Erstellung des Fünf-Schichten-Modells werden die einzelnen Aktivitäten mit zunehmendem Verständnis des Problembereichs mehrfach durchgeführt. Ein Einhalten der Reihenfolge erfolgt höchstens beim ersten Durchlauf.

2.2.2 Bestimmen von Klassen und Objekten

Theorie

Objekte stellen Abstraktionen von Elementen (von "Irgendetwas") aus dem Problembereich dar, die die Fähigkeiten des Systems reflektieren. Sie bestehen aus Attributen und den darauf exklusiv anwendbaren Services. Eine Klasse ist eine Beschreibung eines oder mehrerer Objekte mit gleichen Attributen und Services (Methoden) /COA 91a, S. 53/.

Nach Gesprächen mit Fachleuten, Unterlagenstudium und ähnlichen Aktivitäten werden zur Identifizierung möglicher Klassenkandidaten folgende Fragen gestellt:

1. Zu welchen Dingen und Ereignissen muß das System Informationen, die unter Umständen über einen längeren Zeitraum relevant sind, bereithalten?
2. Mit welchen anderen Systemen steht das betrachtete System in Verbindung?
3. Mit welchen Vorrichtungen und Geräten muß das System kommunizieren?
4. Welche Personen spielen im betrachteten System eine Rolle?
5. Welchen organisatorischen Einheiten gehören die Personen des Systems an?

Die potentiellen Klassen werden anhand nachstehender Hinweise überprüft:

- Können einer Klasse keine problemrelevanten Attribute (vgl. Abschnitt 2.2.5) oder Methoden (vgl. Abschnitt 2.2.6) zugeordnet werden, ist sie für das Modell ohne Nutzen.
- Bei Klassen mit einem einzigen Attribut muß zur Vereinfachung des Modells nach anderen Klassen zur Aufnahme dieses Attributs gesucht werden.
- Klassen, die nur eine einzige Instanz besitzen, sind meistens ein Indiz für unentdeckte Verallgemeinerungen.
- Klassen, die die Realisierung des Systems beschreiben (z.B. Speichermedien, Terminals), sind in der Analyse außer acht zu lassen.

Für die Notation der ersten Schicht werden zwei Symbole eingeführt, und zwar

a) das Klassensymbol für sogenannte abstrakte Klassen, die selber keine Objekte (Instanzen) besitzen, und
b) das Klasse-&-Objekte Symbol für sogenannte konkrete Klassen, von denen Instanzen erzeugt werden können (vgl. Abb. 2).

Im Text sind mit Klassen, falls nicht genauer beschrieben, sowohl konkrete als auch abstrakte Klassen gemeint. Die Namen der Klassen werden in den oberen Abschnitt der Symbole eingetragen.

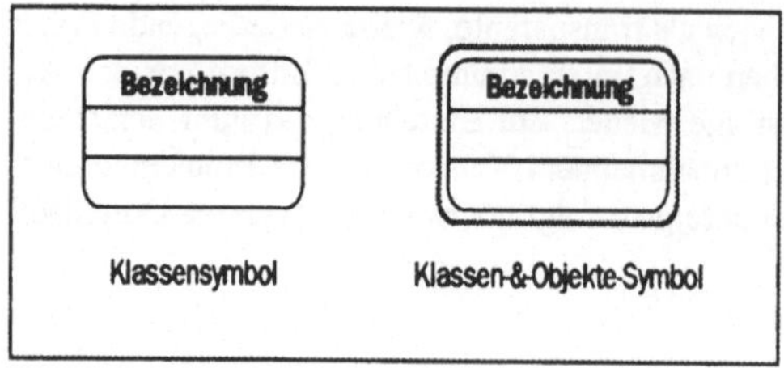

Abb. 2: Symbole für Klassen

Anwendung

Abbildung 3 zeigt das komplette Fünf-Schichten-Modell für das Lagerverwaltungssystem. Auf die getrennte Abbildung der fünf Schichten ist aus Platzgründen verzichtet worden. Die Ableitung der Klassen erfolgte durch die Anwendung des oben angegebenen Fragenkatalogs.

Zu Frage 1 (Dinge/Ereignisse, über die das System Informationen bereithalten muß):
- *Artikel, Lieferschein, Fehlliste, Artikelposition, Entnahmeliste, Palettenbegleitschein-_Produktion, Kundendaten.*
- *Inventur, Kommissionierung, Auslagerung, Einlagerung, Bestellung.*

Zu Frage 2 (in Verbindung stehende Systeme):
- *Fibu/Controlling, Vertrieb, Produktion.*

Zu Frage 3 (Vorrichtungen und Geräte, mit denen das System kommuniziert):
- *Regal, Regalzelle, Palette.*

Zu Frage 4 (Personen, die im System eine bestimmte Rolle spielen):
- Personen spielen im betrachteten System nur eine untergeordnete Rolle. Anstelle der bei Frage 2 aufgeführten Abteilungen hätten alternativ auch Mitarbeiter der Abteilungen angegeben werden können. Da die Darstellung der Schnittstelle zu anderen Systemen als wichtiger erachtet worden ist, wurde auf diese Alternative verzichtet. Kunden spielen im System nur eine passive Rolle. Lediglich die Daten der Kunden werden als Attribut einiger Klassen benötigt. Deshalb ist zu Frage 1 eine Klasse *Kundendaten* aufgenommen worden.

Zu Frage 5 (organisatorische Einheiten):
- Je nach Blickwinkel können die zu Frage 2 aufgeführten Klassen auch an dieser Stelle zugeordnet werden.

Bei genauer Betrachtung der einzelnen Klassen fällt auf, daß nicht alle einer Überprüfung der oben aufgeführten Hinweise standhalten. Warum diese Klassen trotzdem aufgenommen worden sind, wird in Abschnitt 3.2 diskutiert.

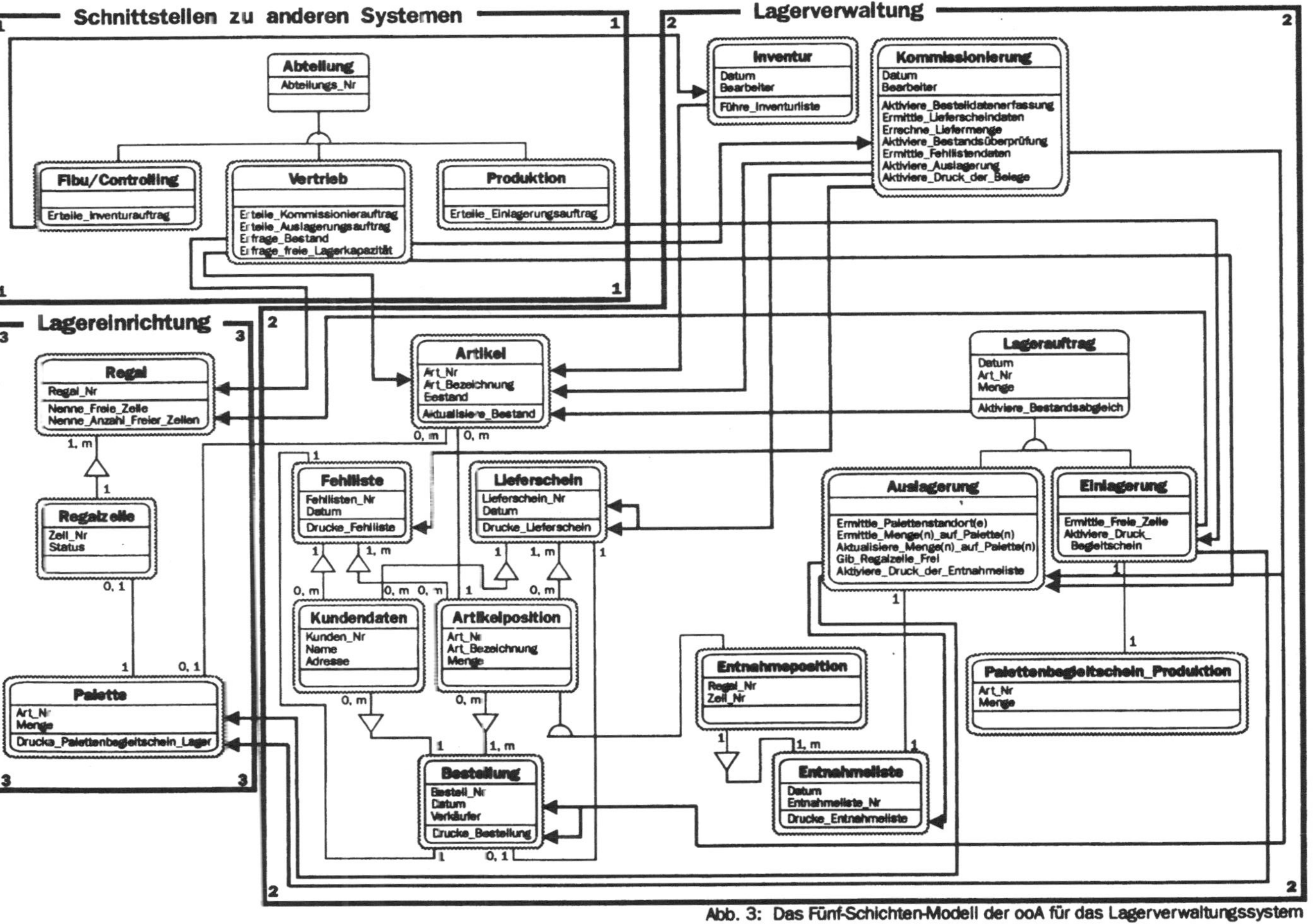

Abb. 3: Das Fünf-Schichten-Modell der ooA für das Lagerverwaltungssystem

2.2.3 Identifizieren von Strukturen

Theorie

In der ooA werden zur Bewältigung der Komplexität des Problembereichs zwei Arten von Strukturen verwendet. Die Verallgemeinerungs/Spezialisierungs-Struktur (Gen/Spec-Struktur) drückt die Verwandtschaft bestimmter Klassen des Problembereichs aus. Die Ganz/Teil-Struktur gibt an, wie sich eine Klasse aus mehreren einzelnen Bestandteilen zusammensetzt /COA 91a, S. 79/.

Abbildung 3 enthält mehrere Beispiele für die Notation. Durch Halbkreis und Geraden verbundene Klassen stehen in einer Gen/Spec-Beziehung. Beispiel: Lagerauftrag und Ein- /Auslagerung. Durch Dreieck und Geraden verbundene Klassen stehen in einer Ganz/Teil-Beziehung. Beispiel: Regal und Regalzelle. Die Zahlen bei der Ganz/Teil-Beziehung geben an, aus wievielen Teilen ein Ganzes besteht (ein Regal besteht aus einer bis m Regalzellen) bzw. zu wievielen Ganzen ein Teil gehört (eine Regalzelle gehört zu genau einem Regal).

Zur Ableitung von Gen/Spec-Strukturen sollte jede Klasse als Verallgemeinerung bzw. als Ganzes angesehen werden. Für mögliche Spezialisierungen bzw. Teile sind folgende Fragen zu stellen:

- Sind sie Teil des Problembereichs bzw. der Systemanforderungen?
- Genügen sie den in Abschnitt 2.2.2 angegebenen Hinweisen zur Überprüfung von Klassen?

Im zweiten Schritt wird jede Klasse als Spezialisierung bzw. Teil interpretiert. Anschließend werden die oben aufgeführten Fragen für potentielle Verallgemeinerungen und für Ganze gestellt.

Anwendung

Für das Lagersystem sind folgende Gen/Spec- und Ganz/Teil-Strukturen relevant (vgl. Abb. 3):

- *Fibu/Controlling*, *Vertrieb* und *Produktion* sind spezielle *Abteilungen*.
- *Auslagerung* und *Einlagerung* sind spezielle *Lageraufträge*.
- Eine *Entnahmeposition* ist eine spezielle *Artikelposition*.
- Ein *Regal* besteht aus mehreren *Regalzellen*.
- *Lieferschein*, *Fehlliste* und *Bestellung* enthalten einen Satz *Kundendaten* und ggf. mehrere *Artikelpositionen*.
- Eine *Entnahmeliste* enthält ggf. mehrere *Entnahmepositionen*.

2.2.4 Identifizieren von Subjekten

Theorie

Subjekte teilen die Klassen eines Systems in Gruppen logisch zusammengehörender Klassen auf. Somit ist ein Subjekt ein Mechanismus, um einen Leser (Analytiker, Fachmann, Manager, Kunde) durch ein großes Modell zu führen. Ferner sind Subjekte hilfreich, um größere Projekte in einzelne Arbeitsabschnitte zu zerlegen /COA 91a, S. 106/. Zwischen den Subjekten sollten möglichst wenige Beziehungen bestehen.

Eine mögliche Notation für Subjekte ist das Einrahmen der zu dem Subjekt gehörenden Klassen.

Anwendung

Für das System läßt sich folgende Einteilung in Subjekte vornehmen (vgl. Abb. 3):

- Das Subjekt 1 *(Schnittstellen)* enthält die Klassen zur Modellierung von benachbarten Abteilungen.
- Das Subjekt 2 *(Lagerverwaltung)* enthält die Klassen, die für die eigentliche Lagerverwaltung bzw. für die Abläufe im Lager zuständig sind.
- Das Subjekt 3 *(Lagereinrichtung)* enthält die Klassen, die den Aufbau des Lagers beschreiben.

2.2.5 Definieren von Attributen und Instanzverbindungen

Theorie

Ein Attribut ist ein Datum, für das jedes Objekt einer Klasse einen eigenen Wert annimmt. Attribute detaillieren die in Form von Klassen und deren Beziehungen vorliegenden Abstraktionen des Problembereichs /COA 91a, S.119/.

Objekte der realen Welt lassen sich durch eine Vielzahl von Attributen beschreiben. COAD und YOURDON geben folgende Strategie an, mit der die problemrelevanten Attribute herausgefiltert werden können:

- Identifizieren der Attribute:
  Zunächst wird eine Liste mit möglichen Attributen aufgestellt. Aus Sicht des Objekts wird der Frage nachgegangen, welches Wissen es zur Erfüllung der ihm zugedachten Aufgaben tatsächlich haben muß. Daraufhin werden unnötige Attribute gestrichen.

- Positionieren der Attribute:
  In Vererbungsstrukturen sind Attribute, soweit sie für die Verallgemeinerungen gelten, so hoch wie möglich einzufügen.

- Überprüfen jedes einzelnen Attributs:
  Ein Attribut sollte für jede Instanz einen sinnvollen Wert haben. Ist dies nicht der Fall, kann ein Hinweis auf eine nicht erkannte Vererbungsstruktur vorliegen. Für Klassen, die nur über ein Attribut verfügen, sollte nach möglichen Vereinfachungen gesucht werden.

Die Attribute einer Klasse werden in das mittlere Feld des Klassensymbols eingetragen.

Zur Erfüllung der Aufgaben, für die ein Objekt (Instanz) zuständig ist, reichen die in den Attributen abgelegten Informationen häufig nicht aus. Es kann notwendig werden, auf Informationen von Objekten zuzugreifen, zu deren Klassen keine der in Abschnitt 2.2.3 beschriebenen

Beziehungen bestehen. Eine solche Relation wird durch eine Instanzverbindung verdeutlicht. Instanzverbindungen modellieren Assoziationen /COA 91a, S. 126/. Die Notation ähnelt der Notation der Ganz/Teil-Struktur. Lediglich das Dreieck entfällt.

Anwendung

Abbildung 3 enthält die für das System relevanten Attribute und Instanzverbindungen. Die Notwendigkeit der eingetragenen Attribute und Instanzverbindungen kann durch einen Vergleich mit den in 2.1 aufgeführten Anforderungen schnell überprüft werden.

Exemplarisch soll die Instanzverbindung zwischen den Klassen *Palette* und *Regal* erklärt werden. Eine *Palette* ist zu einem bestimmten Zeitpunkt keiner oder einer *Regalzelle* zugewiesen. Eine *Regalzelle* enthält zu einem bestimmten Zeitpunkt keine oder eine *Palette*. Notwendig ist diese Verbindung, um den Lagerort eines Artikels bzw. einer Palette, die ihn enthält, bestimmen zu können.

2.2.6 Definieren von Services und Nachrichtenverbindungen

Theorie

Services (Methoden) beschreiben in algorithmischer Form bestimmte Verhaltensweisen, über die ein Objekt verfügen muß, um den ihm zugedachten Teil der Systemanforderungen umsetzen zu können. Ferner werden über Methoden die Attributwerte eines Objekts manipuliert /COA 91a, S.143-144/.

COAD und YOURDON empfehlen für die Service-Schicht folgende Strategie:

- Identifizieren von Objektzuständen:
  Ein Objektzustand ist durch eine Menge von Attributwerten bestimmt. In einigen Fällen reagieren Objekte auf Methodenaufrufe in Abhängigkeit von bestimmten Zuständen unterschiedlich. Diese Zustände müssen identifiziert und in einem Objektzustandsdiagramm dokumentiert werden.

- Identifizieren der erforderlichen Methoden:
  Die Methoden können zwei Kategorien zugeordnet werden: Algorithmisch einfache Methoden, wie das Erzeugen von Instanzen oder Setzen und Lesen von Attributwerten. Algorithmisch komplexe Methoden, die zur Berechnung bestimmter Ergebnisse auf die eigenen bzw. auf fremde Attributwerte zugreifen oder die Überwachung und Steuerung von externen Geräten übernehmen.

- Identifizieren von Nachrichtenverbindungen:
  Nachrichtenverbindungen sind erforderlich, wenn ein Objekt zur Erfüllung seiner Aufgaben auf die Dienste anderer Objekte zugreifen muß.

- Spezifizieren der Methoden:
  Die Algorithmen der Methoden werden in einer Funktionskarte spezifiziert, die den Ablauf des Algorithmus in einer dem Programmablaufplan ähnlichen Weise beschreibt.

Die Methoden werden in den unteren Abschnitt des Klassensymbols eingetragen. Dabei wird auf einen Eintrag der algorithmisch einfachen Methoden verzichtet. Die Darstellung der Nachrichtenverbindungen erfolgt mit einem Pfeil, der vom aufrufenden Objekt ausgeht.

Die Darstellung der Klassen eines Systems wird ergänzt durch sogenannte Klassenspezifikationen, die detaillierte Attributbeschreibungen (Zweck, Wertebereich etc.), Angaben über die Kommunikation mit externen Geräten (Drucker, Bildschirm etc.), Objektzustandsdiagramm, Funktionskarten und ergänzende Informationen zusammenfassen.

Anwendung

Objektzustände sind lediglich für die Klasse *Regalzelle* relevant. In Abhängigkeit des Attributs *Status* (belegt/nicht belegt) erfolgt die Abarbeitung der Methoden *Nenne_Freie_Zelle* und *Nenne_Anzahl_Freier_Zellen* der Klasse *Regal* unterschiedlich. Aufgrund der Einfachheit ist in diesem Fall auf ein Objektzustandsdiagramm verzichtet worden.

Abbildung 3 enthält die für die einzelnen Klassen erforderlichen Methoden sowie die benötigten Nachrichtenverbindungen. Aus Übersichtlichkeitsgründen wurden die Nachrichtenverbindungen, die die Erzeugung von Instanzen darstellen, in die Abbildung nicht mit aufgenommen.

Beispiel: Die Klasse *Vertrieb* besitzt die Methoden *Erteile_Komissionierauftrag*, *Erteile_Auslagerungsauftrag*, *Erfrage_Freie_Lagerkapazität* und *Erfrage_Bestand*. Zur Durchführung dieser Methoden greift sie auf (zum Teil algorithmisch einfache) Methoden der Klassen *Kommissionierung*, *Auslagerung*, *Regal* und *Artikel* zurück. Dementsprechen bestehen Nachrichtenverbindungen zwischen diesen Klassen und der Klasse *Vertrieb*.

3 Bewertung der ooA und der Methode von COAD und YOURDON

Zur Bewertung der ooA wird in zwei Schritten vorgegangen. Zunächst wird dargestellt, welche Vor- und Nachteile ein oo-Vorgehen in der Analysephase unabhängig von einer bestimmten Methode hat. Im zweiten Schritt werden dann eine Bewertung der Methode von COAD und YOURDON vorgenommen und mögliche Verbesserungen vorgeschlagen. Eine klare Abgrenzung zwischen grundsätzlicher und methodenspezifischer Bewertung ist dabei nicht immer möglich.

3.1 Grundsätzliche Bewertung der ooA

Der Hauptunterschied der ooA zu anderen Methoden wie etwa Structured Analysis (SA) /DEM 78/ oder der funktionalen Dekomposition /WIR 71/ besteht darin, daß Funktionen und Daten eines Systems gemeinsam betrachtet werden. Die Verschmelzung von Daten und Funktionen (Methoden) führt zum Objekt- bzw. zum Klassenbegriff und damit zu den Bausteinen der Systemarchitektur. Die Übereinstimmung von Klassen und abstrakten Datentypen gewährleistet automatisch den Einsatz von Datenabstraktion, funktionaler Abstraktion und Information Hiding /NAG 90/, /PAR 72/. Ein weiteres Prinzip zum Beherrschen von Komplexität wird durch das mit den Vererbungsbeziehungen realisierte Vorgehen nach dem Prinzip von Analogie und Abweichung ergänzt.

Die Wahl von Objekten bzw. Klassen als Grundlage der Systemarchitektur bedingt eine Reihe weiterer Vorteile.

Objekte bzw. Klassen sind die am wenigsten flüchtigen Komponenten eines Systems /COA 91a, S. 145/. Ein Lagerverwaltungssystem wird immer Klassen wie *Artikel*, *Lieferschein*, *Einlagerung*, *Auslagerung* etc. enthalten. Die einzelnen Attribute und Methoden dieser Klassen werden in Abhängigkeit von den Anforderungen an das System variieren. Davon bleibt die Systemarchitektur aber unberührt, denn die grundlegenden Klassen und ihre Beziehungen ändern sich nicht oder nur wenig. Diese Sachverhalte begünstigen die Erweiterbarkeit und Wiederverwendbarkeit der Analyseergebnisse.

Die Ableitung der Klassen bzw. Objekte ist, soweit es sich um physische Objekte des Problembereichs (Regal, Regalzelle, Palette, Artikel, Fehlliste, Entnahmeliste etc.) handelt, recht einfach. Bei den verarbeitungsbetonten Klassen wie *Inventur*, *Kommissionierung*, *Ein- Auslagerung* und *Abfrage* erfordert der Ableitungsprozeß größere Anstrengungen. Gleichwohl läßt sich die viel propagierte Behauptung, daß die Objektorientierung eine natürliche Abbildung des Problembereichs erlaubt (vgl. z.B. /KRE 90, S. 224/), durchaus bestätigen. Die Zusammenarbeit mit Problembereichsexperten zur Analyse des Lagersystems dürfte auf Basis der abgeleiteten Objekte recht einfach sein. Die Experten sehen ihren Arbeitsbereich direkt abgebildet.

Die Modellierung des Systems auf Basis von Klassen und Objekten erlaubt die Übernahme der Analyseergebnisse in das Design /COA 91b/. Dadurch wird mit der Analyse bereits ein Teil der softwaretechnischen Lösung des Systems erarbeitet, und es findet kein Strukturbruch beim Übergang von der Analyse zum Design statt. Im betrachteten Fall des Lagerverwaltungssystems können viele der Analyseklassen ohne Änderung oder mit kleinen designspezifischen Erweiterungen in das Design übernommen werden.

Als nicht unwesentlicher Nachteil der ooA hat sich die schlechte Nachvollziehbarkeit von fachlichen Abläufen des Problembereichs erwiesen. So werden z.B. beim Kommissioniervorgang, ausgelöst durch die Methode *Erteile_Kommissionierauftrag* der Klasse *Vertrieb*, Methoden bei ungefähr der Hälfte aller Klassen des Systems ausgelöst. Diese Kette von Methodenaufrufen ist aufgrund der dezentralen Systemarchitektur, insbesondere in ihrem zeitlichen Ablauf, nur mit Mühe nachzuvollziehen.

3.2 Bewertung der Methode von COAD und YOURDON

3.2.1 Bewertung des Fünf-Schichten-Modells und seiner Notation

Das Fünf-Schichten-Modell stellt sowohl statische (Schicht 1-4) als auch dynamische Aspekte (Schicht 5) von Systemen dar. Damit werden die wesentlichen Informationen an einer Stelle zentral zusammengefaßt und nicht wie bei anderen Methoden (vgl. /SHL 92/) auf mehrere Diagramme verteilt. Diese komprimierte Darstellung begünstigt zusammen mit dem überschaubaren Symbolvorrat die Verständlichkeit der Analyseergebnisse.

Für die Ganz/Teil-Beziehung wäre es sinnvoll, optionale Teilklassen in besonderer Weise zu kennzeichnen. Einfacherweise könnte man das Dreieck auf der Verbindungsstrecke zu optionalen Klassen schraffiert zeichnen. Ein Beispiel für eine optionale Teilklasse ist ein Gegenstand, der nur bei Sonderausstattungen in ein Produkt eingeht.

Die Subjekte eines Systems gruppieren logisch zusammengehörende Klassen. Bei der Einrahmung dieser Klassen erscheint es sinnvoll, den Subjektnamen in den Rahmen einzufügen, um dem Leser den Gruppierungsgrund sofort sichtbar zu machen (vgl. Abb. 3). Die Notation von COAD und YOURDON sieht diesen Eintrag nicht vor.

Bei sehr großen oo-Systemen sollte eine weitere Subjektebene zugelassen werden, die logisch zusammengehörende Subjekte gruppiert. Diese Erweiterung könnte das schrittweise Einarbeiten in ein Modell erleichtern. Bei konventionellen Systemen werden in der Regel ebenfalls mehr als zwei Abstraktionsebenen benutzt (vgl. z.B. /NAG 90, Kapitel 4/).

Bei Nachrichtenverbindungen empfiehlt es sich, den Unterschied zwischen Aufrufen von algorithmisch einfachen und algorithmisch komplexen Methoden deutlich zu machen. Dies kann z.B. dadurch geschehen, daß beim Aufruf algorithmisch einfacher/komplexer Methoden der Nachrichtenpfeil am Attribut-/Methodenabschnitt des Klassensymbols endet (vgl. Abb. 3). Auf diese Weise kann der Leser den Zweck der Nachrichtenverbindung sofort eingruppieren.

Anmerkung: Durch keinen der Änderungvorschläge wird der Symbolvorrat der Notation erweitert. Somit bleibt eine schnelle Einarbeitung weiterhin möglich.

Das Arbeiten mit dem Modell muß unbedingt durch ein Tool unterstützt werden, das u.a. folgende Funktionen zur Verfügung stellt:

- Beliebiges Ein- und Ausblenden der einzelnen Schichten des Modells;
- Einblenden der Instanzverbindungen einer einzelnen Klasse;
- Einblenden der Kette von Nachrichtenverbindungen, die durch den Aufruf einer Methode ausgelöst wird;
- Ablegen von detaillierten Informationen in Dokumentationstemplates, die mit den Klassen in direkter Verbindung stehen;
- Einblenden von attribut- bzw. methodenbezogenen Informationen aus dem Dokumentationstemplate einer Klasse.

3.2.2 Bewertung der Aktivitäten und Regeln der Methode

Insgesamt ist das beschriebene Vorgehen praktikabel und gut erlernbar. Die mehrfache Bearbeitungsmöglichkeit der einzelnen Schichten ermöglicht ein inkrementelles Vorgehen, dem in der oo-Entwicklung eine besonders hohe Bedeutung zukommt.

Der zur Ableitung der Klassen angegebene Fragenkatalog liefert, wie das Beispiel des Lagerverwaltungssystems bestätigt, instruktive Hinweise zum Auffinden der Klassen eines Systems. Ergänzend sei zur Ableitung von Klassen empfohlen, bei oo-Entwicklungen nicht zuerst nach den Funktionen des Systems zu fragen, sondern die Frage zu stellen, "Woran" das System Aktivitäten vornimmt /MEY 90, S. 54 /.

Die Regeln zur Überprüfung von potentiellen Klassen (vgl. Abschnitt 2.2.2) sind nur mit Einschränkungen anzuwenden. Im System sind mehrere Klassen aufgenommen worden, die keine eigenen Methoden oder Attribute enthalten. Hierzu gehören z.B. die Klassen *Abteilung*, *Fibu/Controlling*, *Vertrieb* und *Produktion*. Das Verzichten auf diese Klassen hätte das Fehlen der Schnittstellen des Systems und damit die Vernachlässigung einer wichtigen Komponente des Problembereichs zur Folge gehabt.

Die Klasse *Regalzelle* besitzt zwar keine Methoden, gibt aber über die Ganz/Teil-Verbindung zur Klasse *Regal* den Aufbau des Lagers besser wieder als bei einer direkten Zuordnung der Klasse *Regal* in Form eines Attributs. Ähnlich kann für die Klassen *Kundendaten*, *Artikelposition* und *Entnahmeposition* argumentiert werden. Aufgrund dieser Erfahrungen ergibt sich folgende Empfehlung: Um den Problembereich vollständig und transparent zu beschreiben, sollten ggf. auch Klassen aufgenommen werden, die den Anforderungen der Checkliste aus Abschnitt 2.2.2 nicht in allen Punkten genügen.

Die Zerlegung eines Systems in Subjekte erfolgt im dritten Schritt. Auch wenn kein streng sequentielles Vorgehen beabsichtigt ist, hat die Erfahrung gezeigt, daß ein Ableiten von Subjekten erst nach der Bestimmung der wichtigsten Klassen möglich ist. Dies ist insofern ein Nachteil, als daß eine Arbeitsteilung zu Beginn nicht festgelegt werden kann. Ein weiteres Problem in diesem Zusammenhang ist die Unabhängigkeit der einzelnen Subjekte. Wie das erstellte Modell zeigt, stehen einige Klassen unterschiedlicher Subjekte über Instanz- und Nachrichtenverbindungen in Beziehung. Eine Modellbildung mit völlig unabhängigen Subjekten erwies sich im betrachteten Fall als nicht möglich.

3.3 Resümee

Wegen ihrer zentralen Bedeutung für die Wiederverwendbarkeit und die Erweiterbarkeit dürfen die Stabilität der Systemarchitektur und der ohne Strukturbruch durchführbare Schritt zum ooD als die wichtigsten Vorteile der ooA angesehen werden. Der Methode von COAD und YOURDON kann insgesamt bescheinigt werden, daß sie wichtige Hinweise zum Ableiten des Modells gibt und eine gut überschaubare Darstellungstechnik anbietet. Um den Einsatz der Methode zu forcieren muß das erstrangige Ziel die Entwicklung eines Tools sein, das den oben beschriebenen Anforderungen genügt. Ohne ein solches Tool, das verschiedene Sichten auf das Modell ermöglicht, wird auch die Notation von COAD und YOURDON unübersichtlich.

Die beschriebenen, auf die dezentrale Architektur des Modells zurückzuführenden und grundsätzlichen Probleme der ooA können nach Meinung der Autoren durch ein Tool mit den oben beschriebenen Leistungen zwar erheblich entschärft, aber letztendlich nicht völlig beseitigt werden. Diese "Restprobleme" müssen zugunsten erweiterbarer und wiederverwendbarer Software in Kauf genommen werden. Sobald von der dezentralen Architektur abgewichen wird und an mehreren Stellen hierachische, ablauforientierte Konstruktionen eingebracht werden, ist das System für die Erfüllung einer oder mehrerer spezieller Aufgaben ausgelegt. Damit wird die Wiederverwendbarkeit und Erweiterbarkeit aber negativ beeinflußt. Benötigt werden Komponenten, die weitgehend unabhängig von einer speziellen Anwendung in einem bestimmten Problembereich von Bedeutung sind.

4 Wiederverwendung im objektorientierten Softwareentwicklungsprozeß

4.1 Grundlagen der Wiederverwendung

ENDRES bezeichnet mit Wiederverwendung einen Softwareentwicklungsprozeß, der nicht am Punkt Null beginnt, sondern vorhandene Software in die Entwicklung neuer Produkte mit einbezieht /END 88, S. 86/. In Abgrenzung zur Wiederverwendung ist die Wiederverwendbarkeit ein Maß für die Leichtigkeit, mit der früher abgeleitete Komponenten in neuen Situationen eingesetzt werden können /PRI 87, S. 7/.

Bei der Wiederwendung werden im wesentlichen die Bausteintechnik und die Schablonentechnik unterschieden /END 88, S. 88/. Mit der Schablonentechnik wird kein vollständiges und lauffähiges Programm bereitgestellt, sondern nur das Gerippe oder Muster eines Programms. Hier wird vorausgesetzt, daß die Ablauflogik von Anwendung zu Anwendung erhalten bleibt und lediglich Variablen-, Feld- oder Dateinamen sowie halbfertige Anweisungen ergänzt werden müssen. Mit der Bausteintechnik werden Teile so entwickelt, daß aus ihnen Programme nach dem Baukastenprinzip zusammengesetzt werden können. Die Bausteine werden auch Komponenten oder Module genannt; COX spricht in Anlehnung an den Hardwarebereich von Software-ICs /COX 91, S. 74/.

4.2 Objektorientierung und Wiederverwendung

Vergleicht man die Methoden der Wiederverwendung mit den Begriffen der Objektorientierung, so wird schnell ersichtlich, daß im oo-Softwareentwicklungsprozeß die Klassen mögliche Bausteine repräsentieren. Ferner lassen sich aber auch Merkmale der Schablonentechnik wiederfinden. Dies ist z.B. bei abstrakten (vgl. Abschnitt 2.2.2) und insbesondere bei aufgeschobenen Klassen /MEY 90, S. 252/ der Fall. Diese Klassen stellen Schablonen für ihre Nachkommen dar, durch die sie vervollständigt und zu lauffähigen Programmteilen weiter entwikkelt werden. Die Vervollständigung kann eine Ergänzung von Attributen und Methoden, eine Redefinition von Methoden oder auch eine erstmalige Definition von aufgeschobenen Methoden beinhalten. Das Umsetzen einer solchen Anpassung bzw. Vervollständigung wird durch das Vererbungsprinzip möglich, dem damit im Hinblick auf die Wiederverwendbarkeit eine zentrale Rolle zukommt.

MEYER beschreibt in seinem Grundlagenwerk /MEY 90, Kap. 2-4/ sehr deutlich, warum Klassen die an Bausteine gestellten Eigenschaften /END 88, S. 90/ wie Modularität, Geheimnisprinzip, innere Festigkeit etc. besonders gut erfüllen und die oo-Softwareentwicklung somit zur Wiederverwendbarkeit einen wesentlichen Beitrag leistet. LEWIS u.a. haben in einem großen Projekt die Erfahrung gemacht, daß bei einem oo-Ansatz die Produktivität durch Softwarewiederverwendung stärker gesteigert werden kann als bei einem konventionellem Ansatz /LEW 92, S. 41/.

Eine einzelne Klasse ist dabei nicht der primäre Gegenstand der Wiederverwendung. Von Interesse ist vielmehr eine Mengen von konkreten und abstrakten Klassen, die für bestimmte Anwendungen wiederverwendet werden können. DEUTSCH nennt solche Mengen von Klassen Multiple-Class-Frameworks. Soll nur eine einzelne Klasse wiederverwendet werden, spricht er von Single-Class-Frameworks /DEU 89, S. 66/. WIRFS-BROCK und JOHNSON verwenden analog die Bezeichnung Framework und Abstract Class /WIR 90, S. 116/.

Bekannt geworden sind Frameworks durch ihre erfolgreiche Verwendung bei der Entwicklung von graphischen Benutzeroberflächen. Ihr Einsatz ist aber nicht auf dieses mehr problembereichsunabhängige Gebiet beschränkt. WIRFS-BROCK und JOHNSON behaupten, daß die meisten Frameworks problembereichsabhängig sein werden /WIR 90, S. 117/. Das Ziel ist, die Gemeinsamkeiten von verschiedenen Anwendungen eines Problembereich zu erfassen und diese im Rahmen des Designs mit Hilfe eines Frameworks abzubilden. Auf dieser Basis gibt der

Framework das grobe Design für konkrete Anwendungen vor, die dann durch Spezialisierung des Frameworks entwickelt werden können /WIR 90, S. 119/.

4.3 Ein Fragenkatalog zur Ableitung von wiederverwendbaren Klassen auf Basis der Analyseergebnisse

Im objektorientierten Softwareentwicklungsprozeß ist keine starre Abgrenzung zwischen den Phasen Analyse und Design möglich. Wie in Abschnitt 3.1 bereits angedeutet, werden im Design die in der Analysephase abgeleiteten Klassen beibehalten und um für die Realisierung notwendige Details ergänzt.

Diese Beziehungen legen es nahe, bereits im Rahmen der Analyse die Wiederverwendung zu berücksichtigen. COAD und YOURDON definieren Wiederverwendung für die Analysephase als das Einbeziehen früherer Analyseergebnisse in die aktuelle Analyse. Wegen der hohen Stabilität des Problembereichs halten sie die Analyseergebnisse für die Wiederverwendung als besonders geeignet /COA 91a, S. 11/. Leider geben sie im Rahmen ihrer ooA-Methode aber kaum Hinweise, durch welche Schritte die Wiederverwendbarkeit der Analyseergebnisse begünstigt werden kann. Da auch im oo-Softwareentwicklungsprozeß die Wiederverwendung nicht automatisch erreicht wird /JOH 88, S. 22/, ist im Rahmen der Entwicklung des Lagerverwaltungssystems ein Fragenkatalog erarbeitet worden, mit dessen Hilfe die Wiederverwendbarkeit der Klassen systematisch überprüft und erhöht werden kann. Die Fragen des Katalogs sind bereits beim Analysieren zu berücksichtigen, nach dem ersten Abschluß der Analyse nochmals zu überprüfen und schließlich beim Übergang zum Design zu stellen.

Für jede einzelne Klasse sind folgende Fragen zu stellen:

1. Gibt es eine Menge von Attributen und/oder Methoden, die in einem allgemeineren Zusammenhang verwendbar ist und als Oberklasse ausgegliedert werden kann?

2. Gibt es eine Menge von Attributen und/oder Methoden, die eine selbständige Klasse modelliert und im Rahmen einer Ganz/Teil-Beziehung als Teilklasse ausgegliedert werden kann?

3. Gibt es speziellere Klassen, deren Unterscheidung für andere Systeme relevant sein kann?

4. Gibt es andere Klassen, durch deren Hinzunahme der abgebildete Ausschnitt des Problembereichs vollständiger modelliert werden kann?

Nachfolgend soll exemplarisch gezeigt werden, wie einzelne Klassen auf Basis des Katalogs abgeleitet worden sind:

- Zu Frage 1: Die Klasse *Lagerbewegung* kann mit ihren Attributen und Methoden für die Modellierung anderer Systeme leichter eingesetzt werden als die spezielleren Klassen *Auslagerung* und *Einlagerung*.

- Zu Frage 2: Die Klasse *Artikelposition* ist in mehreren Klassen im Rahmen der Ganz/Teilbeziehung enthalten. Durch ihre Ausgliederung kann sie in anderen Lagersystemen oder ähnlichen Anwendungsbereichen eingesetzt werden.

- Zu Frage 3: Hierzu gibt es in der betrachteten Anwendung kein Beispiel, deshalb wird sie in einem anderen Umfeld erklärt. Für die Verwaltung eines Fuhrparks von LKW sind sicherlich die Klassen *Fuhrpark* und *Fahrzeug* erforderlich (vgl. linke Struktur in Abb. 4). Soll diese Struktur in einem ähnlichen System, das auch PKW berücksichtigt, eingesetzt werden, so ist die in Abbildung 4 rechts eingetragene Struktur universeller einsetzbar.
  Anmerkung: Der Unterschied zu Frage 1 besteht in dem Perspektivenwechsel.

- Zu Frage 4: Für die Instanzen der Klasse *Artikel* werden mehrere Methoden benötigt, bei deren Abarbeitung nicht nur ein einzelner Artikel, sondern die Menge aller Artikel oder eine Teilmenge hiervon angesprochen werden muß. Hierzu gehören Methoden, wie das *Suchen* nach einem bestimmten Artikel oder das *Hinzufügen* eines Artikels zum Artikelstamm. Aus diesem Grund ist im Rahmen des Designs eine Klasse *Artikelmanager* aufgenommen worden, die entsprechende Methoden bereitstellt.

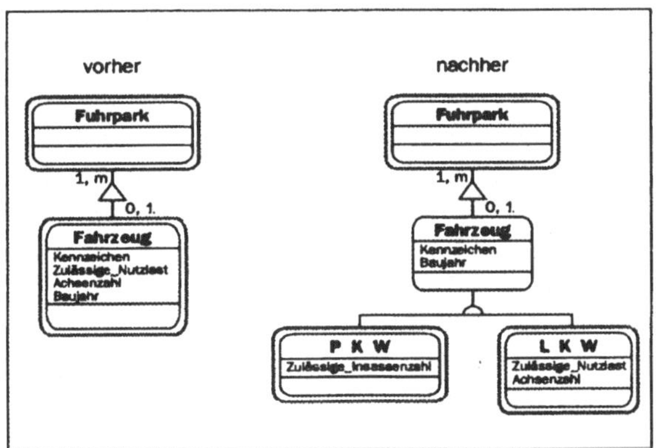

Abb. 4: Klassen zur Verwaltung eines Fuhrparks

5 Ausblick

Zu vermuten ist, daß im Softwareentwicklungsprozeß der Zukunft nicht erst im Design auf Frameworks zurückgegriffen werden wird, sondern bereits in der Analysephase der Einsatz einer Art Analyse-Framework erfolgt. Ausgehend von einem solchen Framework könnten konkrete Analysemodelle erstellt werden. Zwischen Analyse- und Design-Framework muß dann eine Teilmengenbeziehung bestehen. Der Design-Framework ergänzt die Analyseklassen um Implementierungsdetails und neue implementationstechnische Klassen. Eine solche Klasse wäre im Lagerbeispiel der *Artikelmanager*.

Das vorliegende Analysemodell des Lagerverwaltungssystems ist zwar noch kein universell einsetzbarer Analyse-Framework für Lagersysteme, es ist aber zu erwarten, daß die Ergebnisse für die Analyse eines ähnlich aufgebauten Lagers zumindest von ihrer Grobstruktur wiederverwendet werden können. Der Softwareentwicklungsprozeß müßte also nicht bei Null beginnen.

Ein weiteres kürzlich begonnenes Projekt hat die Entwicklung eines universell einsetzbaren Analyse-Frameworks für Lagersysteme zum Ziel. Abweichend von dem hier beschriebenen

Vorgehen, wird nicht versucht, auf Basis der Entwicklung eines weitgehend erdachten, einfachen Systems nach möglichen Verallgemeinerungen zu suchen, vielmehr werden anhand der Anforderungsbeschreibungen unterschiedlicher, realer Lagersysteme zunächst die Gemeinsamkeiten dieser Systeme herausgestellt. Eine Klassenmodellierung für einen Analyse-Framework erfolgt dann auf der so gewonnenen abstrakteren Basis.

Der Dank der Verfasser gilt den Herren cand. rer. pol. Frank Hohmann und cand. rer. pol. Andreas Schumm, die durch ihre Diplomarbeiten viel zum Entstehen der vorliegenden Arbeit beigetragen haben.

Literaturverzeichnis

/COA 91a/ COAD, P., YOURDON, E.: Object-Oriented Analysis. New Jersey, 1991

/COA 91b/ COAD, P., YOURDON, E.: Object-Oriented Design, New Jersey, 1991

/COX 91/ COX, B. J., NOVOBILSKY A. J.: Object-Oriented Programming An Evolutionary Approach. 2. Auflage, Massachusetts, New York, Bonn u.a., 1991

/DEM 78/ DEMARCO, T.: Structured Analysis and System Specification. Ort, 1978

/DEU 89/ DEUTSCH, L. P.: Designing Reuse and Frameworks in the Smalltalk-80 System. In: BIGGERSTAFF, T.J., PERLIS, A.J.: Software Reusability, Volume II. Massachusetts, New York, Bonn u.a., 1989, S. 57-71

/END 88/ ENDRES, A.: Software-Wiederverwendung: Ziele, Wege, Erfahrungen. In: Informatik Spektrum, 11/1988, S. 85-95

/JOH 88/ JOHNSON, R. E., FOOTE, B.: Designing Reusable Classes. In: Journal of Object-Oriented Programming, 2/1988, S. 22-35

/KRE 90/ KREUTZER, W.: Grundkonzepte und Werkzeugsysteme objektorientierter Systementwicklung. In: Wirtschaftsinformatik, 3/1990, S. 211-227

/LEW 92/ LEWIS, J. A., HENRY, S. M., KAFURA, D. G.: On the relationship between the object oriented paradigm and software reuse:an empirical investigation. In: Journal of object oriented Programming, July/August, 1992

/MEY 90/ MEYER, B.: Objektorientierte Softwareentwicklung. München, Wien, London, 1990

/NAG 90/ NAGL, M.: Softwaretechnik: Methodisches Programmieren im Großen. Berlin, Heidelberg, New York u.a., 1990

/PAR 72/ PARNAS, D.: On the criteria to be used in decomposing systems into modules. In: Communications of the ACM, 12/1972, S. 1053-1058

/PRI 87/ PRIETO-DIAZ, R., FREEMAN, P.: Classifying Software for Reusability. In: IEEE Software, 1/1987, S. 1-16

/SHL 92/ SHLAER, S., MELLOR, S. J.: Object Lifecycles-Modeling the World in States. London, Sydney, Toronto u.a., 1992

/STA 92/ STAHLKNECHT, P., APPELFELLER, W.: Objektorientiertes Design (ooD). In: Wirtschaftsinformatik, 2/1992, S. 249-252

/WIN 90/ WINBLAD, A. L., EDWARDS, S. D., KING, D. R.: Object-Oriented Software. Massachusetts, New York, u.a., 1990

/WIR 90/ WIRFS-BROCK, R. J., JOHNSON, R. E.: Surveying, Current Research in Object-Oriented Design. In: Communications of the ACM, 9/1990, S. 104-122

/WIR 71/ WIRTH, N.: Program Development by stepwise Refinement. IN: Communications of the ACM, 4/1971, S.221-227

Case Study with Object–Oriented Methods

Ch. Krakhofer
Alcatel Austria–ELIN Research Centre
Ruthnergasse 1–7
A–1210 Vienna, Austria

1. Introduction

The principal objective of software engineering is to help to produce quality software. Traditional software development methods focus either on the functional or on the data aspect as the basis for their structure. Unfortunately these methods often fail to take into account the evolutionary nature of software systems. Software quality factors like compatibility, reusability and extendibility [Meye88a] , which provide the key to system modularization, are not sufficiently considered.

Recently a new model of information structuring is creating a growing interest in the software community. This model of structuring, called Object–Oriented (OO) model, uses the concept of objects (abstractions of sets of real world things, containing both: data and the functions operating on them) to build up the system functionality. This model has already been proved to be efficient at the programming level. However, for large scale industrial use it is important to provide not only the basic technology (languages such as C++, Eiffel, Smalltalk, ...), but also a method for the application of the technology in order to benefit as soon as possible from the advantages of OO–modeling.

Currently, there are several object–oriented analysis and design methods on the market. The situation is characterized by a high momentum of development: Existing functional and data–oriented methods are extended towards OO, and existing OO–methods are enhanced in order to achieve broader applicability. However there are many critical factors for the success of methods in software projects. As a consequence many object–oriented methods are not mature enough for wide scale industrial use.

This document presents results and experiences of applying two OO methods to a common example. The evaluated methods are selected for the following reasons: to cover both analysis as well as design and to show different ways how methods fit to the object–oriented model.

Section 2 lists the requirements for the application example. They define a small PABX (Private Automatic Branch Exchange) adapted to the scope of the evaluation. The PABX example (with reduced functionality) is called the 'Small PABX'.

The first studied method was OOSA [Shla88] (outlined in section 3). The method addresses the first phase – the analysis of the problem domain – in the software development process. The method uses well known notations like entity–relationship, state transition and data flow diagrams. An overview of the method is given first. Impressions whether the listed traditional notations are capable of modelling OO–applications, can be found within the figures of the overview and pragmatically observed in the documentation of my experiences in applying the method to the Small PABX example.

Section 4 presents the second method Responsibility Driven Design [Wirf90a]. It supports not only the design phase in the software development process, but also the preceding analysis phase, because the process is initiated only with a given informal requirements specification of the problem. Responsibilities are the key concept of the method which allow to concentrate on the usage of the objects instead of their capabilities. It is possible to abstract responsibilities into contracts and to refine them into signatures. The structure of the description of the experiences is similar to that one of section 3. Finally Section 5 provides a summary of the conclusions drawn in this work.

2. Requirements Specification of Small PABX

This section gives some requirements for a PABX (Private Automatic Branch Exchange). A PABX is a machine which has the ability to switch several phones in e.g. a company. Such machines have often more features than the "normal call" (e.g. diversion, wake up, conference call, brokers call, ...). The following requirements (which are not on a very detailed level) cover some of the characteristic problems of such exchanges.

- A subset has the following specification:
  - A subset is identified by its *physical_subset_number* (0 to 19).
  - A subset is able to go *offhook* and *onhook*.
  - A subset is able to send digits 0 to 9 and d*iversion key*.
  - A subset is able to receive *ringon* and *ringoff*.
- The *switching_matrix* has the following specification:
  - A subset can be connected to another subset with message *connect (physical_subset_number_1, physical_subset_number_2)*.
  - A subset can be connected to one of five possible tones: *dial_tone*, *ring_back_tone*, *waiting_tone*, *nulltone* or *busy_tone*.
- A normal call is started by lifting the handset (*dial_tone*) and dialing a digit when the *nulltone* heard. Dialing a valid number (*ring_back_tone*) rings the called subset (*ringon*) if it is free. In case of a busy subset the *busy_tone* is heard instead of the *ring_back_tone*. If the called party goes offhook (*ringoff*), conversation can be done. Onhook of one of the subsets will finish the call. The remaining party will hear the *busy_tone*.
- There is a timeout between offhook and first digit to be dialed (*first_digit_timeout*) and a timeout between two digits (*interdigit timeout*). If a called subset does not go offhook within a specified amount of time (*diversion_timeout*) the call is automatically diverted to physical line 0.
- *Automatic call diversion* is a feature which diverts (after invocation) all incoming calls to another extension. *Automatic call diversion* is invoked after *offhook* by pressing *diversion key* and dialing the number of the subset to which calls should be diverted. Canceling *automatic call diversion* is possible by pressing the diversion key and dialing "99".

3. OOSA

The method Object–Oriented System Analysis (OOSA) was developed by S.Shlaer and S.J. Mellor of Project Technology, Inc. The following overview and the presented examples are based on [Krak91]. Detailed information concerning the method can be found in [Shla88] and [Team89].

3.1. Overview of the Method

The OOSA method can be partitioned into three distinct activities:

- find objects and relationships (information model),
- find lifecycles for objects and relationship instances (state and communication model), and
- derive processes from lifecycles (process model).

These activities were applied to the initial given requirements and described hereafter in varying degrees of detail.

The Information Model

The first thing to do is to build the information model to define the conceptual units you will be working with. The notation of the information model is based on an entity–relationship diagram with objects (entities), attributes (data of the objects) and relationships (possibility to define single inheritance and dynamic relationships) between the objects. A graphical representation of the Small PABX model is given below.

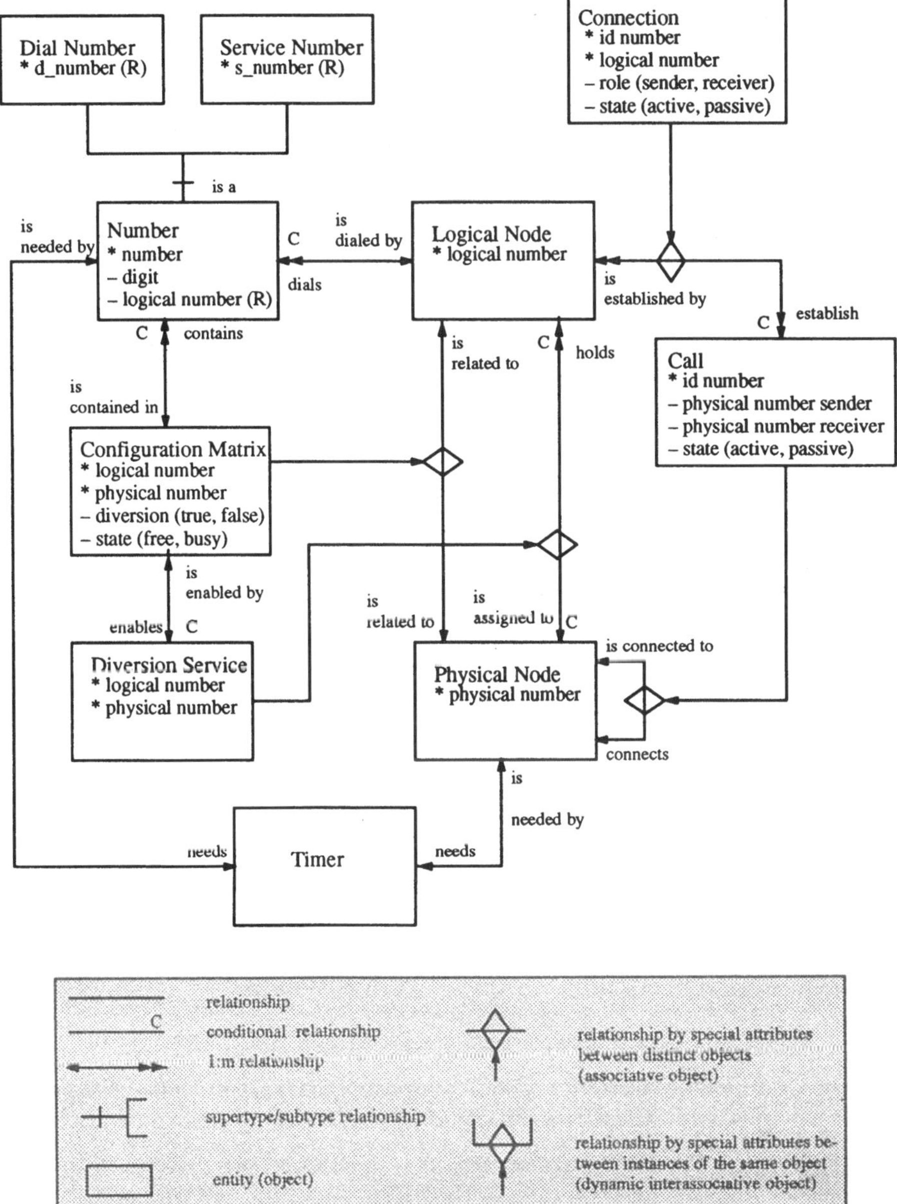

Figure 1: Information Model of the PABX

The next step after building the information model presents the definition of the life cycle aspects for all objects. This activity is outlined in the following section.

The State Model

The life cycle aspect can be formalized with the aid of state transition diagrams in terms of states, events, transitions and actions. Associated with each state is an action which occurs immediately when the state is entered (Moore notation). It is possible to specify the activation order of processes (the building blocks of actions) by using numbers before their names.

For example, the state model of the logical node is shown below. Remember, a normal call is started by lifting the handset (the offhook event occurs) and dialing a number. After dialing a valid number the ringback_tone or the busy_tone is heard. If the called partner goes offhook, conversation can start.

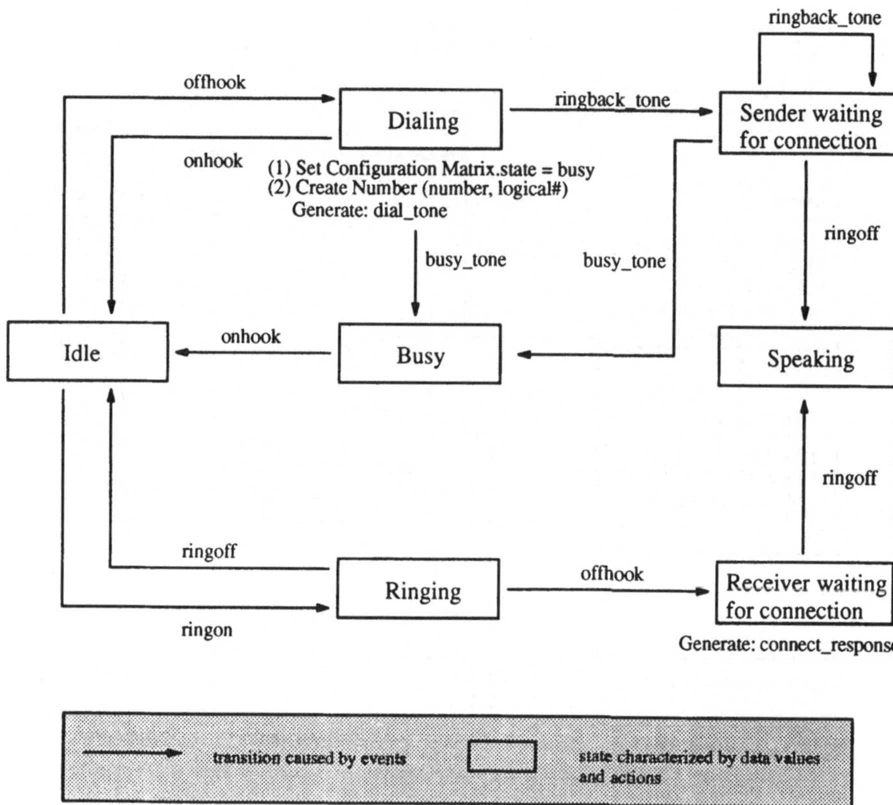

Figure 2: State Transition Diagram of Logical Node

Of course, each identified object in the information model requires its own state model. Therefore the above shown state model presents only one part of the formalized system behaviour.

The next diagram illustrates one exemplary dynamic communication taking place among objects and relationships of the Small PABX. This graphical representation of the messages between the object state models is called the *Object Communication Model*. An object communication model can be constructed to show the events that carry out the communication between state models.

In the following model are only those events mentioned which are necessary to create and delete a *Call* instance. After establishing a call between two physical nodes conversation can only be done through this kind of instance.

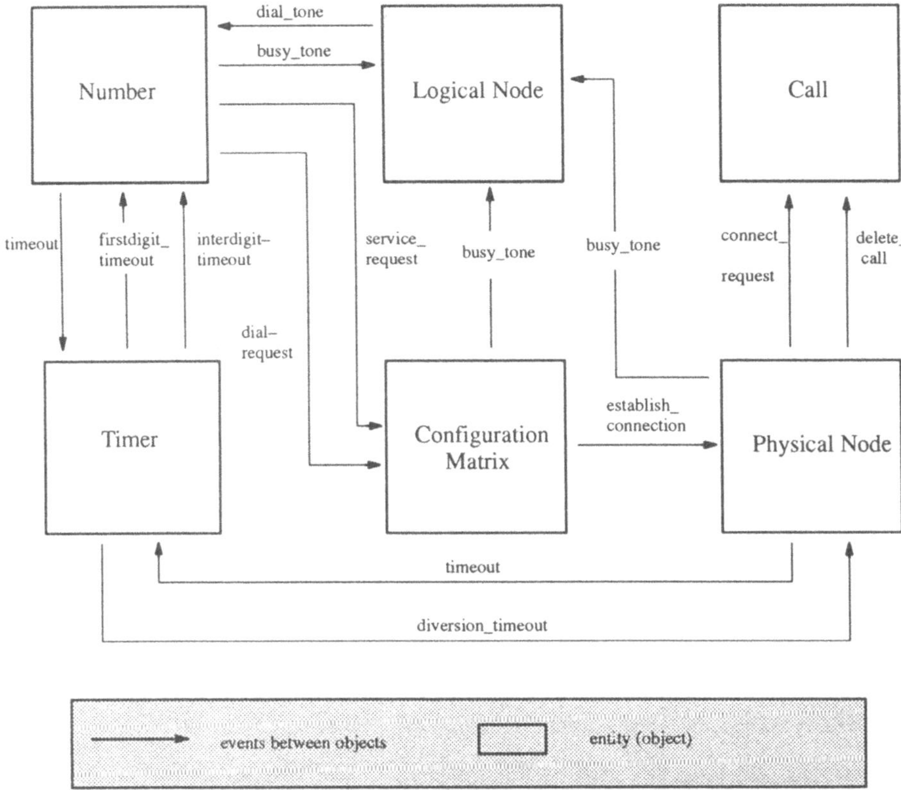

Figure 3: Object Communication Model to initiate a new call

For each event in the object communication model the containing data are listed (the symbol '#' presents an abbreviation of number).

Events	Data with Events
dial_tone	number + logical#
busy_tone	logical#
timeout	id# + (number I physical#)
firstdigit_timeout	number
interdigit_timeout	number
diversion_timeout	physical#
service_request	logical# + number
dial_request	logical# + number
establish_connection	physical1# + physical2# + logical# + number
connect_request	id# + logical# + number
delete_call	id#

Figure 4: Data related to specific Events

The last step in building the OOSA model presents the expression of already identified actions by the aid of data flow diagrams.

The Process Model

The data flow diagram (De Marco) is a graphical tool for modeling transformations and manipulations of data. Each process of an action can be expressed by a data flow diagram. But the data aspect of the initial requirements is a weak one so that these diagrams are not covered by the analysis model of the Small PABX.

3.2. Experiences with the Small PABX analysis

In this section I will outline my experiences in modeling the Small PABX. The first impression during reading the requirement specification pointed certainly to a quite simple application. But the analysis of the problem domain (Small PABX) quickly resulted in a high effort. The main reasons were surely the functional orientation of the example and that I had no previous knowledge on the application area before. Further pros and cons are described below.

Advantages

In my opinion the information model provides a good overview about the conceptual units and their properties (data and relationships). The relationship lines are annotated with verb phrases which provide an additional description. The relational model of data is well known. In order to express relations between two instances of the same object I introduced a newly defined entity, called 'dynamic interassociative object', in the information model (see Figure 1). This new entity is not in conflict with the pure Shlaer/Mellor method. Another way to express such entities may be the definition of cardinalities above relations.

The behavior aspect is expressed with the aid of state transition diagrams. The Shlaer/Mellors extension of this diagram is the listing of all processes associated with a special state so that the developer gets a good view of system functionality.

Points of Consideration

The information model addresses only the data aspect of the system. While the information model covers the attribute aspect, methods are not covered. This separation limits the scope of the application and as a consequence concepts like encapsulation or information hiding are not possible (all data can be seen by related objects).

The supertype/subtype construct expresses relationships only in terms of attributes. Furthermore its relation to state models is undefined and unclear. There are no facilities to restrict a supertype to a special subtype during runtime (for example dial number in the brokers call feature). Furthermore it is not possible to access different subtypes of one supertype (not in the sense of inheritance).

The straightforward way, which is proposed for the analysis of the problem domain, (first build the information model, then define the life cycle of each object and in the last step the data flows diagrams of each process) failed, because the definition of the analysis model is a highly iterative process. Changes in the static structure often cause a completely new modeling of the concerned state models (the reuse mechanism is not enough addressed, lack of loosely coupled components).

Another disadvantage of the information model as well as state model is the fact, that the degree of dependency between different objects is not visible (only visible in the object communication model, which is not treated very extensively in the method).

There are two ways to model different kinds of relationships in the static structure. The first one is the use of referential attributes and the other one the use of explicit constructs like correlation tables or associative objects. But one essential question for me was: in which case is it better to use referential attributes and when to use entities like correlation tables and so on. On one hand foreign keys (equal to referential attributes) are artificial and do not contribute to the proper meaning of the objects. Furthermore the assigning of referential attributes to an entity increases its complexity and in the following manner the complexity of the whole entity relationship diagram. On the other hand the use of autonomous entities to state relationships is also problematic. They contain redundant information, increase the dependence according to state models and involve often more than two entities in a specific relation (so new events must be mentioned or defined). Also the mapping of relationships, in the information model, with the state models is unclear (one question is: which objects are involved in one relationship).

In the PABX example the function aspect is a well defined one so that the behavior model becomes an important or key point in the analysis of the PABX. In modeling the behavior with the aid of state transition diagrams, I was often faced with a too detailed analysis. My impression is that state machines are not abstract enough to define the dynamic aspects of functional, tightly coupled components at analysis: Here the analyst is faced with too much and complex information about the whole system, because state transition diagrams are low level tools to model behavior aspects during the analysis phase. Furthermore, in this way the analyst concentrates most of its effort on design and implementation decisions so that it comes to a premature rush to implementation.

The OOSA method uses the concept of state transition diagrams not only to define the pure control flow, because each event contains also data. Further associated with each state is an action which is performed when the state is entered. So in my opinion the analyst is overcharged with too much information in modeling the behavior.

In the Small PABX example the data flow aspects are handled sufficiently in the state models so it was not necessary to draw also the data flow diagrams.

4. Responsibility Driven Design

The method Responsibility Driven Design was developed by R. Wirfs–Brock, Wilkerson and Wiener. The following overview and examples are based on [Krak91]. Detailed information concerning the method can be found in [Wirf90a].

4.1. Overview of the Method

The process of design can be partitioned into two distinct phases: the exploratory and the analysis phase.

The exploratory phase starts with a given requirements specification as input, identifies the classes required to model the application, determines what behaviour each class is responsible for and defines what collaborations must occur between classes to fulfill those responsibilities.

The analysis phase spends time in analyzing and improving class hierarchies, models collaborations in more detail for better encapsulation of subsystems, determines protocols, and completes the specifications of classes, subsystems and client–server contracts.

Classes

The first task in an object–oriented design is to find the classes that will compose it. The only available input presents the requirements specification of the problem domain. During the process of reading the requirements noun phrases are extracted which form the basis of candidate classes. These classes are recorded on simple index cards, one class per card, as outlined in Figure 5.

A further goal is to find as many abstract classes as possible, because they help to structure the software. An abstract class derives from a set of classes that share a useful attribute. Also if behavior is shared by several classes, the analyst should design an abstract superclass to capture that shared behavior in one place. Subclasses can then inherit that behavior.

Responsibilities

A key concept of the method is the notion of responsibilities. Responsibilities are used to define the purpose of an object and its place in the system. They include two key items: the knowledge an object maintains and the actions an object can perform.

Responsibilities can be identified by the requirements specification (extraction of all verbs) and by already identified classes. Each responsibility is assigned to the class or classes it should logically belong to. Of course, each assigned responsibility is recorded on its corresponding class card (responsibilities listed on a superclass card, need not be listed on a subclass card).

Classes can fulfill their responsibilities by performing the necessary computation themselves, or by collaborating with other classes. The next section shows how to connect classes to each other.

Collaborations

Collaborations represent request from a client to a server to fulfill a client responsibility. They are paths of communication between classes which show the flow of control and information.

During the process of examining the responsibilities associated with classes collaborations are identified by answering the following questions: With whom does this class need to collaborate to fulfill its responsibility? Who needs to make use of the responsibility defined for this class?

The output of the exploratory phase presents classes, abstract classes, responsibilities and collaborations. This information is covered in so called CRC (Class Responsibility Collaboration) cards which forms the basis for creating a good design. For completeness the purpose of a class can be written on the back of the card. In this manner the use of CRC cards is quite natural and obeys the encapsulation principle of the object–oriented approach.

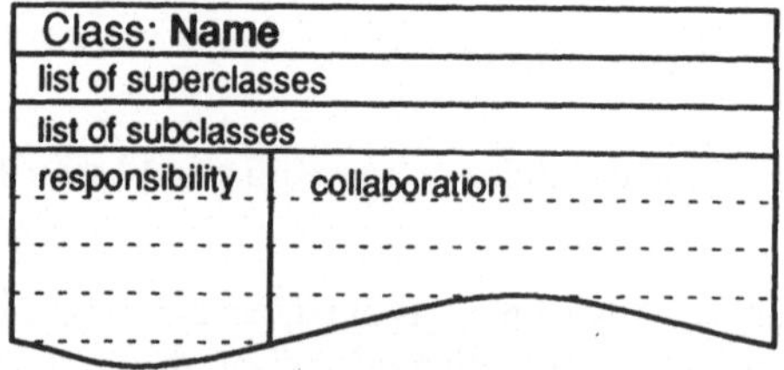

Figure 5: CRC Card

CRC cards are a good vehicle for discussion either between analysts or between analysts and clients. All the information relevant to a particular class is readily available on one card. Discussion can easily be focused on one part of the system without having to tackle the complete specification. The CRC cards representing the relevant part of the hierarchy can be discussed in isolation. They can easily be distributed amongst several analysts with only a minimum of coordination effort needed to integrate the results. CRC cards can also form the basis of the documentation of the classes. The inheritance between the classes is expressed on the CRC cards accordingly.

Contracts

Contracts are used for grouping the responsibilities of a class that are related in some manner. Furthermore, a contract defines a cohesive set of requests that a client can make of a server. A class can support one or more distinct contracts. There are also private responsibilities which are not part of any contract.

Contracts are recorded on server class cards as shown in the figure below (each contract is characterized through a unique number).

Class: **User Interface**	
1. Get the input from the user	
Know if user has responded	
Know user's response	
Provide feedback on input	

Figure 6: A Contract of the Class User Interface

In the following the concept of contracts is used for analyzing the paths of communication between objects.

Collaborations Graph

A collaborations graph contains the collaborations between classes in graphical form. The graph helps the analyst in identifying areas of unnecessary complexity, duplication, or places where encapsulation is violated. The collaborations graphs represent classes, contracts, collaborations and superclass–subclass relationships. Figure 7 shows the final collaborations graph of the class User Interface for the Small PABX. For example the functionality of contract 1 (listed within the class symbol of User Interface) is needed by the following classes: Number, Subset, Normal Call and Service Number.

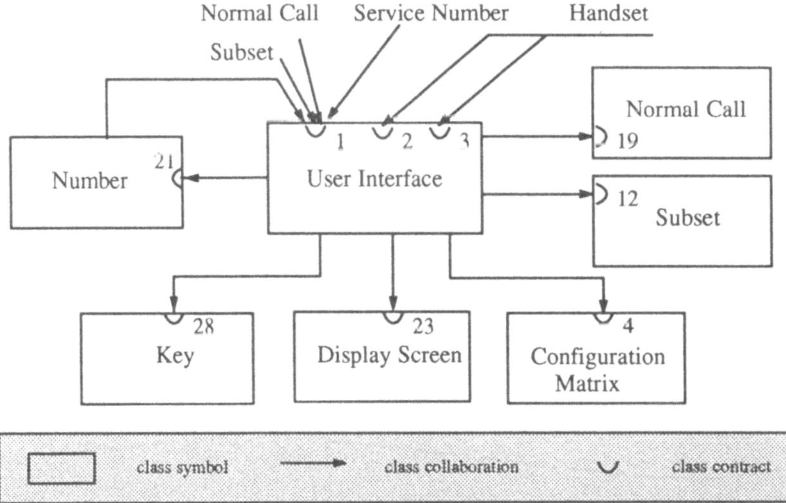

Figure 7: The Collaborations Graph of the Class User Interface

Subsystems

Subsystems are groups of classes that collaborate among themselves to support a set of contracts (unit of functionality). To identify the contracts supported by a subsystem, all classes have to be determined that provide services to clients outside the subsystem. These are the contracts supported by the subsystem. But subsystems are only conceptual entities, they do not exist during execution. They therefore cannot directly fulfill any of their contracts. Instead, subsystems delegate each contract to a class within them that actually supports the contract.

Subsystems are identified by drawing the collaborations graphs of the design. Collaborations graphs with frequent and complex collaborations between classes are candidates for new subsystems, if it is possible to name groups of strong coupled classes. The following two guidelines should be noticed in determining new subsystems:

- Classes in a subsystem should collaborate to support a small and strongly cohesive set of responsibilities.
- Classes within a subsystem should be strongly interdependent.

Furthermore, subsystems are concepts which are used to simplify the design. The application is decomposed into subsystems, and those subsystems are repeatedly decomposed until all required information and details have been modeled (like the top–down method).

Protocols

The goal of this step is to ensure that responsibilities are refined and messages are named. Responsibilities are listed of each class or subsystem, and each responsibility is turned into a set of signatures (protocol). Each responsibility will have one or several messages associated with it. Along with the message names, the types of all required arguments and the type of object returned by the method, if any, are specified.

Specifying the Design

At the end of the design process, the designer must fully describe each class, subsystem and contract. This process includes more information than captured so far on index cards. The amount of information is recorded on full sheets of paper and each class, subsystem and contract specification starts with a new page. The descriptions are ordered from the most global to the most specific. For example, the next figures give the complete class specification template of the class User Interface.

Class: User Interface (Concrete)
Superclasses: none
Subclasses: none

Hierarchy Graphs: none
Collaboration Graphs: page 4

Description: This class is responsible for reading and analyzing the user's input. According to the input a specific action is performed.

Figure 8: The Class Specification of the Class User Interface (first part)

Contracts

1. **Get the input from the user**
   Know if user has responded
   Know user's response
      uses Key (28)
   Press digit key
      uses Number (21)
   Provide feedback on input
      uses Display Screen (23)

2. **Connect interface with subset**
   Offhook by the calling partner
      uses Configuration Matrix (4)
   Offhook by the called partner
      uses Normal Call (19)

3. **Disconnect interface from subset**
   Onhook by one partner
      uses Configuration Matrix (4), Subset (12)

Private Responsibilities
   Display the stand–by message
      uses Display Screen (23)

–12–

Figure 9: The Class Specification of the Class User Interface (second part)

The final design document for the Small PABX did not contain: subsystems, contract specifications and abstract classes. The reason for having no subsystems can be found in the system architecture. The components which build up the system are strongly coupled so that the identification of subsystems was not feasible. Also the system functionality was not complex enough, consequently it was not essential to simplify the patterns of communication. On the other hand the reason for omitting the contracts specifications is quite a simple one. In my mind this kind of specifications provides no additional information compared with collaborations graphs and class specifications. In the PABX example the design document would only be larger and more complex without benefit.

In the example the responsibilities were already rather detailed so that defining the signatures would have provided no additional profit.

4.2. Experiences with the Small PABX design

In this section I outline my experiences in modeling the Small PABX. The design activity was easier to accomplish than for the analysis activity, because I already knew the application area of the PABX more closely. But I had problems in establishing distinct design decisions, for example which class is responsible for the initialization of the whole system or how to design the user interface.

As for the analysis method, I will describe here the pros and cons of the design method in more detail.

Advantages

The only required input to initiate the design process is the given informal requirements specification of the problem domain. This means that no preceding analysis phase is needed so that no gap between analysis and design can occur. The analysis phase is replaced in the design process through a preliminary design phase. It's the duty of this phase to find the classes, which build up the system, their responsibilities and their collaborations. Furthermore design decisions like system initialization, user interaction, timeouts or the deallocation of no longer needed objects are considered. Only when the preliminary design phase is completed, the detailed design phase can be initiated. Here the main activity is in designing the class interfaces (distinguish between private and public responsibilities, define the contracts of each class) and identifying qualified subsystems.

The final design document for the problem domain is implementation independent. It consists of two graphical notations (hierarchy and collaborations graphs) and of three textual notations (classes, subsystems and contracts specifications).

The collaborations graph is a powerful notation which shows the patterns of object communication. I have made the following useful experiences during drawing these graphs in:

- finding missing collaborations (has–knowledge–of, depends–upon relationship),
- identifying frequent and complex communication paths,
- identifying classes with complex behavior,
- reviewing the modeled system (responsibilities and collaborations) and
- eliminating unused contracts (to model the real interfaces).

The concept of contracts supports the structuring of the design (eliminates the incoherent set of responsibilities delivered from the preliminary design phase). They provide a good overview about the whole functionality of the system and enable the access to a restricted set of responsibilities (the interface). Also contracts help in finding missing responsibilities and other required contracts (the depend–upon relationship).

Points of Consideration

The designer is confronted with the modeling of too much information during the preliminary design phase, because there is no preceding analysis phase. Furthermore this amount of information is in no way structured (only the responsibilities are listed in the class specifications).

One of the main aspects in the PABX example is its functional orientation. The sequencing of invocations of functions is an important part of the specification. Unfortunately the first phase of the method provides no support to sequence the functions (missing behavioral model).

Classical design methods use the functions, not the data, as the basis. Responsibilities are both: data and functions. According to the object–oriented sense, classes stand for the implementation of abstract data types. This means that a class is an aggregate of named data elements and a set of operations designed to manipulate that data. In my mind responsibility driven design is like the functional–oriented approach during the preliminary design phase, because the data type aspect is not clear. After identifying the classes required to model the application, the next step is to determine what behavior the system is responsible for. So the data members of the classes are not observed and their relations to the functions are not clear. However this drawback will be handled sufficiently in the second design phase with private responsibilities and protocols.

Collaborations are paths of communication between classes which represent requests from a client to a server to fulfill a client responsibility. If a responsibility requires several collaborations, each server class name is listed directly to the right of that responsibility. Unfortunately there are no possibilities to specify the order of client requests, for example the responsibility 'Initiate call request' needs a collaboration with Handset first (must go offhook) and only then a collaboration with Line. In my opinion the problem to state conditions about the order of client requests can be easily solved. One solution is to split the client responsibility into several parts. But in doing so the component responsibilities would lose their context. Another way of stating conditions is the assignment of a sequence number to each listed server class, which determines the order of the access (or record server classes in the needed accessing sequence).

Contracts are one of the possibilities to structure the design. For this reason it is necessary to define for each responsibility (except private responsibilities) and for each cohesive set of responsibilities a superior specification – the contract. In my opinion the definition of a contract in case of a class with only one or two responsibilities is not necessary, because:

- the class complexity increases
- a new label for the contract must be defined
- a contract specification template has to be filled in

My impression is that classes which possess not more than one or two responsibilities are often meaningless. Here it is better to find a way of adding their functionality to another class.

Each contract is identified through an unique number. These numbers are assigned to the contracts in ascending order. But the design process is a very dynamical one so that the defined order can imply difficulties. For example I was often forced to change all assigned numbers, because of integrating newly defined contracts. But that is what happens in modeling large systems. Here it is a must to support the design process with a special text or graphic editor (the idea to work solely with index cards is in my opinion intolerable).

Another problem for me was the question: 'How to extend contracts inherited from a superclass ?'. For example the contract 'End of call' presents such a case. The method itself provides no help for this question (contracts may not be refined or extended). I have solved this problem by recording the same contract in both classes (Call and Normal Call), whereas the subclass Normal Call extends the contract with the functionality of timeouts.

The collaborations graph of the whole system is too complex and detailed. One reason for this lack can be found in the kind of the example (not a typical object–oriented application) and the weak data type aspect. The functionality of the system is modeled through tightly coupled components so that the identification of usable subsystems was not possible.

5. Summary

OOSA [Shla88] was the first method under study. This analysis method uses well known notations like entity–relationship (an extension with subtype/supertype relations, conditional relationships and associative objects), state transition and data flow diagrams to build OO models. Another notation is provided by the object–communication model, which illustrates the communication taking place among objects and relationships. The method also is easy to learn. It enables a short and powerful description of the problem domain. On the other hand OOSA does not take into account many object–oriented concepts (e.g. encapsulation and information hiding are neglected, no data hiding between instances) and also the terminology is confusing (objects are classes).

The analysis of the example required much effort. The reasons were the functional orientation of the example, that I had no previous knowledge on the application area before and the necessarily extensive modeling of the behavioral view (to determine the sequencing of actions) with the aid of state transition diagrams. In using these diagrams, I was often faced with a too detailed analysis: state machines are not abstract enough, it is difficult to define the dynamic aspects of functional, tightly coupled components at analysis. Furthermore an exact definition of the semantics of several basic concepts is missing (e.g. impact of using inheritance on state models, relations, etc.), so that additional problems occurred.

The second method Responsibility Driven Design [Wirf90a] can be partitioned into two distinct phases: the exploratory phase to build an initial model and the detailed analysis phase to improve the structure of class hierarchies in order to maximize code reuse. In this way the design method supports also the previous analysis phase, because the process is initiated only with a given informal requirements specification of the problem. A key concept of the method is the notion of responsibility. Responsibilities are used to define the purpose of an object, its place in the system and are a high level concept comprising both attributes and methods. Furthermore it is possible to abstract responsibilities into contracts and refine them into signatures. Objects fulfill their responsibilities in one of two ways: by performing the necessary computation themselves, or by collaborating with other objects. Collaborations identify paths of communication between classes (describe the flow of control and information according to the client–server model).

The design activity was easier to accomplish than the analysis activity, because I already knew the application area of the PABX more closely. But I had problems in establishing distinct design decisions, for example which class is responsible for the initialization of the whole system or to design the user interface. On the other hand the method enables a short, powerful and implementation independent description of the problem domain. The class interfaces are shown in a good manner (a distinction between private and public responsibilities is accomplished). The use of contracts defines a way to structure the responsibilities inside a class, but the method & template support for contracts is weak. Collaborations graphs provide a good graphical notation for improving encapsulation and understanding patterns of object communication. The method takes into account many object–oriented concepts, but the concept of responsibilities (to model both: data and functions) is rather new to the programmers scope of view.

Finally, the case study points out the old problematic of methodologies, because the question 'which aspects should be addressed at analysis/design?' cannot be clear answered (see PABX example where the analysis model is more detailed than the established design).

6. References

[Alca91] C. Destor, G. Gabriel, G. Gobillard, C. Gourraud, C. Krakhofer, R. Lewandowski, M. Mulazzani, F. Steimann, "*State of the Art Report on Object Oriented Analysis and Design Methods*", Alcatel report, TOOPIE project, D3.1, 1991.

[Krak91] C. Krakhofer, "*Evaluation of Object–Oriented Methods*", Diplomarbeit, RC/SEM Report 91–13, Nov. 1991.

[Meye88a] B. Meyer, "*Object Oriented Software Construction*", Prentice Hall, 1988.

[Shla88] S. Shlaer, S.J. Mellor, "*Object–Oriented Systems Analysis: Modeling the World in Data*", Yourdon Press Computing Series, 1988.

[Shla89a] S. Shlaer, S.J. Mellor, "*An Object–Oriented Approach to Domain Analysis*", ACM Sigsoft Software Engineering Notes, Vol. 14/5, pp. 66–77, Jul. 1989.

[Shla89b] S. Shlaer, S.J. Mellor, "*Understanding Object–Oriented Analysis*", Hotline on Object–Oriented Technology, Vol. 1/1, pp. 6–8, Nov. 1989.

[Team89] Project Technology Inc., "*Object–Oriented Analysis: State and Process Models with Teamwork*", Teamwork version of Project Technology seminar, 1989.

[Wirf89] R.J. Wirfs–Brock, B. Wilkersen, "*Object–Oriented Design: A Responsibility–Driven Approach*", OOPSLA' 89 Proceedings, special issue of SIGPLAN Notices, Vol. 24/10, acm PRESS, pp. 71–75, Oct. 1989.

[Wirf90a] R.J. Wirfs–Brock, B. Wilkersen, L. Wiener, "*Designing Object–Oriented Software*", Prentice Hall, 1990.

[Wirf90b] R.J. Wirfs–Brock, R.E. Johnson, "*Surveying Current Research in Object–Oriented Design*", Communications of the ACM, Vol. 33/9, pp. 104–124, Sep. 1990.

Erfahrungen mit OO-Entwicklung in der Lehre und deren Konsequenzen

Stefan BIFFL Thomas GRECHENIG
Institut für Softwaretechnik,
Technische Universität Wien
Resselgasse 3/2/188,
1040 Wien
Email: grechenig@eimoni.tuwien.ac.at

Abstract

Die vorliegende Arbeit beschreibt Erfahrungen mit der Einführung des objektorientierten (OO) Paradigmas in einem klassischen Software Engineering (SWE) Lehrgang. Die hier beschriebene zweisemestrige Ausbildung an der Technischen Universität Wien (TU) besteht aus einer Vorlesung mit drei Wochenstunden und einer Übung, in deren Rahmen Studenten in Teams zu fünf bis sieben Personen Dokumente und Programme entwickeln. Die Lehrveranstaltung ist verpflichtender Teil des ersten Abschnitts des Informatikstudiums und findet im zweiten Studienjahr statt. Der/die "typische" Studierende hat etwa drei Jahre Erfahrung in der Programmentwicklung mit einer prozeduralen Sprache.

Vorlesung und Übung folgen dem klassischen V-Modell des Softwarelebenszyklus. Das Endprodukt beinhaltet als Dokumente eine Anforderungsanalyse, eine funktionale Spezifikation (SADT, ER), gut kommentierten Quellcode, Black-Box-Testfälle, sowie Anwender- und Wartungshandbuch. Als OO-Entwicklungsumgebungen werden Turbo Pascal 6.0 (mit TurboVision als User Interface Tool sowie einem selbstentwickelten OO-Datenbank Tool) oder die C++ Umgebung von Borland verwendet.

Im allgemeinen verstanden die Lehrveranstaltungsteilnehmer das OO-Paradigma ganz einfach als ein neues Programmierkonzept. Sie empfanden OO weniger als grundlegend neues Entwurfskonzept, denn als geringfügige Modifikation einer prozeduralen Sprache. "Records, die Prozeduren beinhalten" ist ein typisches Zitat, das dieser ersten Einschätzung der Studierenden entspricht.

Unser Ziel, daß sich die Programmstrukturen durch die Einführung des neuen Paradigmas den bekannten Vorteilen der OO entsprechend verändern würden, wurde nicht erfüllt. Die Grundstruktur der meisten Programmsysteme entsprach der der klassischen prozeduralen bzw. strukutierten Entwürfe und Implementierungen. Die auszubildenden Software-Ingenieure und -Ingenieurinnen tendierten weiters bei der Definition der Objekte oft zu einem reinen "bottom-up" Ansatz. Ihre Objekte wurden von den Klassenbibliotheken und Beispielobjekten des Datenbank- oder Interface-Tools abgeleitet. Oft entstanden die Klassen und Objekte einfach als analoge Kopien des Übungsbeispiels, welches aus einem komplett vorspezifizierten, vorstrukturierten Programm mit vordefinierten Objekten bestand.

Aufgrund dieser Erfahrung widmen wir in diesem Studienjahr den Themen OO-Analyse und OO-Entwurf besonders große Aufmerksamkeit. Ohne eine intensive Vermittlung der OO Methoden gibt es für die Studierenden zuwenig Anstoß, die bestehenden Denk-, Entwurfs- und Programmierstrukturen zu verwerfen.

Wir haben derart empirisch etwas erfahren, was eigentlich offensichtlich sein sollte: Gute OO-Struktur entsteht weder zufällig noch durch die Verwendung von OO-Werkzeugen. Wer sich dazu entschließt, OO-Sprachen in einem Software Engineering Lehrgang zu verwenden, muß auch auf eine besonders intensive Vermittlung von Fähigkeiten zum OO-Information Engineering achten.

Keywords: Software Engineering Ausbildung, objektorientierte Entwicklung, objektorientiertes Design

1. Einleitung

Die Vermittlung von OO-Entwicklungskenntnissen ist sowohl im akademischen als auch im industriellen Bereich ein wichtiges Ziel geworden. OO-Entwicklung umfaßt bekanntlich die Konzepte von Objekt, Klasse, Methoden und Vererbung. Objekte beinhalten Datentypen und deren Operationen (Methoden). Mit diesen Mitteln soll Software erstellt werden, die einfacher als bisher zu ändern, wiederzuverwenden oder zu erweitern ist. Die Objektstruktur soll helfen, den Problembereich weitgehend natürlich abzubilden. Das Konzept der Klassenvererbung beinhaltet bereits eine implizite Möglichkeit zur Wiederverwendung.
Diese vielversprechenden Qualitäten sowie die recht einheitlichen, manchmal geradezu enthusiastischen Aussagen der internationalen SWE Gemeinschaft bewogen uns dazu, unseren Lehrplan dem OO-Entwicklungsparadigma anzupassen.
Nach einer Taxonomie typischer SWE Kurse, wie sie etwa in [LeMy87] vorgeschlagen wird, absolvieren die Informatikstudenten der TU Wien einen SWE-Lehrgang, der sowohl "Early-Life-Cycle" als auch "Later-Life-Cycle" Kurs ist. Sie müssen Dokumente zu den Phasen Anforderungsanalyse, Spezifikation, Systementwurf, Detailentwurf, Codierung, Test und Wartung erstellen. In den letzten Jahren wurden auch Dokumente zur Protokollierung, Standardisierung und Kontrolle des Projektmanagements gefordert.
Der endgültige Quellcodeumfang eines Teamprojektes von durchschnittlicher Größe enthält 15.000 bis 30.000 ausführbare Zeilen. Die Projekte beschäftigen sich im allgemeinen mit Bereichen wie Buchhaltung, Lagerverwaltung oder der Organisation kleiner Geschäfte wie etwa eines Videoverleihs.
Von 1982 bis 1986 wurde in COBOL auf einer VMS-Vax-730/750-Konfiguration programmiert. Während der folgenden drei Jahre wurde die Implementierung in Modula-2 auf PCs oder MacIntosh-Computern durchgeführt. Der Grund für diese Entscheidung war ein entsprechender Wechsel der Programmiersprache in der Lehrveranstaltung "Einführung ins Programmieren" für die Studienanfänger.
Seit 1990 werden die meisten Implementierungen in C++ oder OO-Turbo Pascal durchgeführt. Das Ziel der Lehrveranstaltung war natürlich viel weiter gesteckt als die Übung der Implementierung von kommerziellen Anwendungen in einer bestimmten, gerade aktuellen Sprache. Die Codierphase hat daher nie länger als zwei Monate gedauert. Es war stets eines der wichtigsten Lehrziele, die Fähigkeit zur Teamarbeit zu verbessern oder zumindest die Erfahrung zu vermitteln, daß effiziente Kommunikation in einer Entwicklungsgruppe höchst notwendig ist.
Wir lehrten die gängigen SWE-Methoden, die in den bekannteren SWE Lehrbüchern (wie etwa [Bell92], [Pres92], [Somm92]) vorgeschlagen werden. Im Lauf der Zeit wurden veraltete Methoden gestrichen. So etwa HIPO (Hierarchy plus Input-Process-Output) oder die Jackson Methode ([Jack83]). Eine Begründung dieser Wertung siehe z.B. in [Pomb91].
Es war immer Strategie des SWE-Kurses, einen vernünftigen Kompromiß zwischen den "state-of-the-art" Ergebnissen der Forschung und der tatsächlich aktuellen industriellen Praxis zu finden. OO ist durch die SWE Gemeinschaft in den späten 80er Jahren stark propagiert worden. OO verspricht verschiedene Möglichkeiten, Software höherer Qualität zu erreichen und kann daher als ein attraktives grundlegendes Entwurfsprinzip in der SWE Ausbildung gelten. Darunter fallen unter anderem erweiterte Kapselung, Vererbung, Lokalität, Programmkontrolle und Kommunikation mit Messages sowie die Wiederverwendung von Softwarekomponenten. 1990 schienen uns die kommerziell verfügbaren OO-Werkzeuge reif genug, um als Ausbildungsumgebung dienen zu können. OO-Programmiersprachen, OO-Benutzerschnittstellen, OO-Datenbanken und OO-Entwicklungsumgebungen hatten den größten Teil ihrer Kinderkrankheiten hinter sich und waren daher für Lehrzwecke ausreichend.

OO zu lehren gilt allgemein als schwierig. Es gibt einige Erfahrungsberichte über OO-Lehrtätigkeit: [Werth89] konzentriert sich etwa auf ein Werkzeug, das sich an der Macintosh MPW/MacApp Umgebung orientiert. [LiRi89] berichten über Erfahrungen in der Lehre von OO-Design (OOD) und Programmierung (OOP); sie konzentrieren sich dabei auf die Konzepte von Klassen, Methoden und Vererbung und lassen den Rest des Life-Cycle weg. [Beck89] beschreibt Erfahrungen in der Lehre von OO-Analyse (OOA; der Autor nennt es "OO-Thinking"), wobei er echte Karten als Analogie für Objekte verwendet und so eine Art Aussehen, Angreifbarkeit und Fühlbarkeit von Objekten bereitstellt.
Eines der Probleme in der OO-Ausbildung ist es, die Studierenden dazu zu bewegen, jene Vorstellung von globaler Programmkontrolle aufzugeben, welche bei der prozeduralen Programmierung erforderlich ist. Das Vertrauen auf die Idee von lokaler Kontrolle im Sinne der Interaktion relativ autonomer Objekte (z.B. [Beck89]) muß hergestellt werden.
Die vorliegende Arbeit beschreibt zuerst die Organisation der Software Engineering Ausbildung. Die Einführung des OO-Paradigmas in Vorlesungs- und Übungsorganisation wird vorgestellt. Weiters werden die Erfahrungen von Betreuern und Entwicklern berichtet. Im letzten Abschnitt des vorliegenden Artikels werden die Konsequenzen aus diesen Erfahrungen für die Lehr- und Übungsinhalte vorgestellt. Diese bestehen im wesentlichen in der Intensivierung der Ausbildung und Übung von OO-Analyse und OO-Design.

2. Beschreibung des Software Engineering Lehrplanes

Die Lehrveranstaltung aus "Software Engineering" dauert zwei Semester. Sie findet im zweiten Ausbildungsjahr des Informatikstudiums an der TU Wien statt und wird von etwa 450 bis 550 Personen pro Jahr besucht. Die Teilnehmer müssen im Schnitt sechs bis acht Stunden pro Woche über einen Zeitraum von acht Monaten aufwenden.
Der SWE-Kurs ist eine der wenigen Lehrveranstaltung im Lehrplan der Informatik, die sich mit Teamarbeit in Teams von mehr als vier Personen beschäftigt. Es ergeben sich damit zwei Schwerpunkte als Lehrziele für die Studierenden:

- Anwendung moderner SWE-Methoden und Werkzeuge
- Softwareentwicklung als ein Mitglied eines Teams

Die Anforderung an jedes Team lautet in etwa "Analysiert, entwerft und konstruiert ein mittelgroßes kommerziell verwendbares Softwareprodukt.".
Die Organisation von mehr als 500 Studenten in einem praktisch orientierten Kurs erfordert einiges an Logistik, sodaß ausreichend Anleitung, Kontrolle, Auswertung und Management über den Fortschritt der Projekte bereitsgestellt werden kann (siehe Bild 1).
Die Studierenden bilden Teams zu fünf bis sieben Personen. Die Ergebnisse werden teils individuell und teils als Gruppenarbeit bewertet. Zwei bis drei Teams werden jeweils von einem erfahreneren Studenten, der die SWE-Ausbildung schon abgeschlossen hat, als Tutor betreut. Jeder Tutor trifft seine Teams zumindest einmal in der Woche. Die Tutoren erklären die Methoden und Werkzeuge sowie die Anforderungen und die Organisation des Kurses. Sie lösen die "normalen" fachlichen und Alltags-Probleme innerhalb einer Arbeitsgruppe und sorgen für die Qualitätssicherung von Dokumenten. Einmal pro Woche berichten die Tutoren an die ihnen zugeordneten Assistenten des Institutes über den Projektfortschritt und fragen um Rat bei unüblichen Konflikten innerhalb ihrer Teams sowie bei Entscheidungen, die außerhalb ihres Verantwortungsbereichs liegen.
Jeder Assistent betreut vier bis fünf Tutoren (im Normalfall etwa 12 Studententeams). Er/Sie trifft die Tutoren einmal pro Woche und die Teams einmal alle drei bis vier Wochen (etwa eine Stunde pro Team). Bei diesen Treffen beurteilen die Assistenten den Teamfortschritt anhand der abgegebenen Dokumente, der detaillierten Aufzeichnungen der Tutoren sowie anhand der Vorschläge der Studierenden selbst.

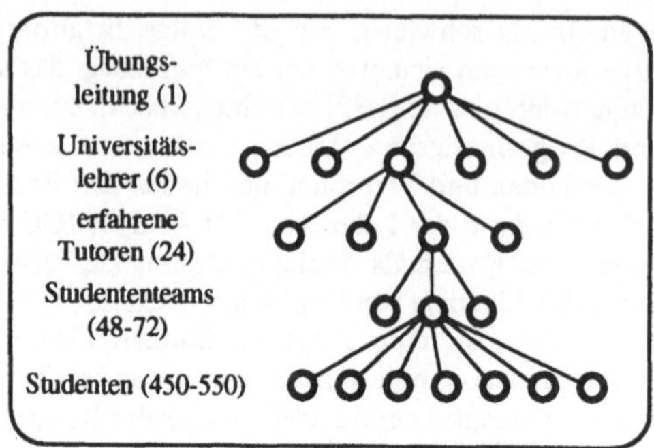

Bild 1: Die Organisationspyramide der SWE-Übung

Ein erfahrener Universitätslehrer ist für die Vorlesung zuständig, ein anderer für die Planung und Organisation der praktischen Übungen. Insgesamt wird der Arbeitsaufwand auf alle Mitglieder des Lehrpersonales am Institut gleichmäßig aufgeteilt.
Offensichtlich ist die Auswahl qualifizierter Tutoren ein besonders wesentliches Kriterium für die Qualität des gesamten Kurses. Etwa die Hälfte der Tutoren eines Jahrganges werden aufgrund der Empfehlungen ihrer Assistenten im Folgejahr wieder angestellt. Die andere Hälfte wird aus den besonders guten Absolventinnen und Absolventen des abgelaufenen Studienjahres ausgewählt.
Der Lehrplan des Kurses ist in drei Phasen unterteilt (siehe Bild 2). Am Beginn muß jeder Student u.a. seine Fähigkeit nachweisen, in einer prozeduralen Programmiersprache wie C oder Pascal programmieren zu können. Diese Vorgehensweise garantiert jenes Minimum an technischen Fähigkeiten, um den darauffolgenden Anforderungen der Übungen ensprechen zu können. Gleichzeitig wird eine Verschwendung der ohnehin raren Betriebsmittel verhindert.

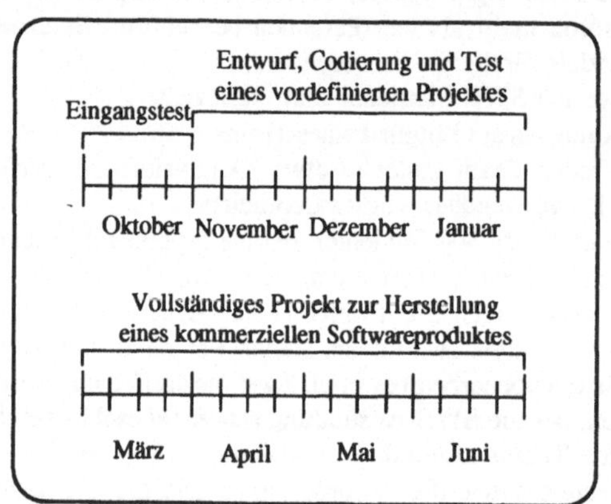

Bild 2: Der ursprüngliche Kursverlauf der SWE-Übung

Jene Studierende, die den Eingangstest bestehen, bilden Teams, die eine vorspezifizierte Anwendung (für alle Gruppen gleich) vervollständigen müssen. Die Kursteilnehmer können sich anhand dieses standardisierten Beispiels mit den Methoden und Werkzeugen für Benutzerschnittstellen, Datenbankdesign, Programmierung sowie Projektmanagement über den Zeitraum von acht Wochen vertraut machen.
Die Grundidee hinter der Vorgehensweise, allen Teams die gleiche Projektspezifikation zu geben, ist die Möglichkeit des direkten Vergleiches aller Dokumente und der Ergebnisse zwischen den Teams. Jene Gruppen, die größere Schwierigkeiten mit der geforderten Arbeit zu

einem bestimmten Meilenstein hatten, können für nachfolgende Aufgaben auf eine Musterlösung zurückgreifen. Blindes Kopieren erweist sich für die Teams wegen eines individuellen Tests am Ende des Semesters als nutzlos.
Nach der Test-Review dieser Standardanwendung erhält jedes Team die Dokumente eines anderen Teams. Die Teammitglieder müssen entscheiden, ob sie anhand dieser Unterlagen bestimmte Wartungsaufgaben am Programm durchführen können oder nicht. Zu diesem Zweck führen die Teams eine Art Akzeptanztest durch. Falls ihr Ergebnis negativ ist, müssen sie erklären und belegen, warum die Anwendung des anderen Teams zu schlecht ist, um gewartet zu werden. In diesem Fall wird ihnen eine ansprechendere Version des Programmes ausgehändigt. Falls ein Team die Arbeit der anderen Gruppe akzeptiert, verpflichtet es sich, die geforderten Änderungen und Erweiterungen in der verfügbaren Zeit durchzuführen. Die Möglichkeit, ein Projekt zurückzuweisen, wird nicht zu einfach gemacht, sondern muß auch den ursprünglichen Autoren persönlich erklärt werden. Diese Vorgehensweise bereitet die Teams darauf vor, ihr eigenes Projekt in der zweiten Hälfte des Kurses auf einer vernünftigen Qualitätsstufe herzustellen.
Dieser zweite Teil hat das Ziel, eine mittelgroße kommerzielle Anwendung für einen wirklichen Kunden oder Benutzer zu entwickeln. Das System ist als komplettes SWE-Projekt von der Anforderungsanalyse bis zur Produktpräsentation umzusetzen. In der begleitenden Vorlesung werden alle geforderten SWE-Methoden vorgestellt.
Seit vielen Jahren wurden dabei SADT und Entity-Relationship für die Phasen Analyse und Design verwendet. Dies war eine geeignete Entscheidung für den darauffolgenden Detailentwurf und die Programmierung in prozeduralen Sprachen wie COBOL, PASCAL und MODULA-2. Durch die Einführung der Objektorientierung mußte diese Entscheidung überprüft werden.

3. Die Einführung der objektorientierten Entwicklung - ein erster Versuch

Da die vorliegende Lehrveranstaltung auch weiterhin den Anforderungen des Informatik-Curriculums nach Überblick über verschiedene Techniken und Methoden des SWE entsprechen sollte, wurden die Inhalte der Vorlesung im wesentlichen beibehalten. Die Anpassung der Inhalte an aktuelle Entwicklung in Forschung und Praxis wurde ohnehin laufend gemacht. Neue, klarere oder passendere Methoden wurden aufgenommen, wobei die entsprechenden alten Methoden ersatzlos gestrichen wurde.
Analog wurde bei den Inhalten und der Struktur der Laborübungen verfahren. Neue Paradigmen wurden eingeführt, wenn gute Werkzeuge verfügbar waren. So geschehen etwa bei der Umstellung auf Mouse/Window orientierte Benutzerschnittstellen. Die Vorlesungsinhalte tangierte dies zumeist nicht. Im genannten Fall genügte eine Präsentation der ereignisgesteuerter Programmierung, die durch eine gründliche Einführung in die Schnittstellenmodule abgedeckt werden konnte. Abgesehen von einigen allgemeinen Bemerkungen über die steigende Bedeutung des Entwurfes von Benutzerschnittstellen im SWE mußte an der Vorlesung im vorliegenden Fall nichts modifiziert werden.
Bei der Einführung von OO wurde eine ähnliche Vorgehensweise verfolgt. Ein Grund dafür war die oben beschriebene Tradition. Ein anderer war unsere eigene wohl eher programmtechnische Sichtweise von OO, im Gegensatz zur informationsmodellierenden Sichtweise.
Innerhalb der eher technisch orientierten Gruppe von Software-Ingenieuren war der Erfolg der Objektorientierung wohl auf zwei Ursachen zurückzuführen: a) die konzeptionelle Klarheit auf formaler und systemtheoretischer Ebene, b) auf die verfügbaren Entwicklungsumgebungen für OO-Pascal und C++ auf der praktischen und pragmatischen Ebene. Reine OO-Sprachen wie etwa Smalltalk haben zwar ursprünglich Anfang der 80er Jahre das OO-Konzept in wissenschaftlichen Kreisen bekanntgemacht, aber bei Software-Ingenieuren nie Verbreitung erlangt (erst in letzter Zeit erfreut sich Smalltalk auch bei Praktikern großer Beliebtheit).

Die programmier- oder theorieorientierten Software-Ingenieure tendieren unbewußt zur Annahme, daß schon OO-Werkzeuge allein Objektorientierung erzwingen. Wir verfielen dieser Tendenz ebenso. Die OO-Informationsmodellierung wurde in der Vorlesung nur in unzureichendem Ausmaß abgedeckt. Heute wissen wir, daß hier die Hauptursache für die unbefriedigenden Programmstrukturen lag (siehe Teil 4).
Die Studierenden bekamen eher allgemeine Anleitung für den Entwurf von OO-Systemen (entsprechend Coad&Yourdon). Sie sollten autonome Objekte definieren, die Methoden und Daten enthalten. Daß sie ihre traditionelle Sicht von Datenstrukturen und Dateien nebst der funktionalen Zerlegung eines Problems erst auflösen mußten, wurde von uns praktisch nicht beachtet.
Die Studierenden erhielten entweder die Entwicklungsumgebung des OO-Turbo-Pascal 6.0 (mit TurboVision als Interface-Tool und ein OO-Datenbank-Tool) oder die C++-Entwicklungsumgebung von Borland. Die Teams konnten zwischen diesen zwei Umgebungen wählen.
Die SWE-Vorlesung blieb im wesentlichen wie sie war. Natürlich wurden OOA und OOD in zwei Vorlesungseinheiten vorgestellt. - Das war schlicht zuwenig.
Wir verhielten uns als sei die Objektorientierung nur eine Art neues Werkzeug, das sich selbst beschrieb durch die Verwendung guter Werkzeuge.
Das folgende Kapitel zitiert einige konkrete Erfahrungen. Diese zeigen, daß Software-Ingenieure, die in prozeduralen Programmiersprachen geübt sind, größte Schwierigkeiten haben, ein Programm in echtem OO-Stil zu schreiben. Das Resultat ist meist ein funktional strukturiertes Programm in der "Verkleidung" der OO-Notation.

4. Reaktionen der Entwickler und deren Bewertung durch die Lehrenden

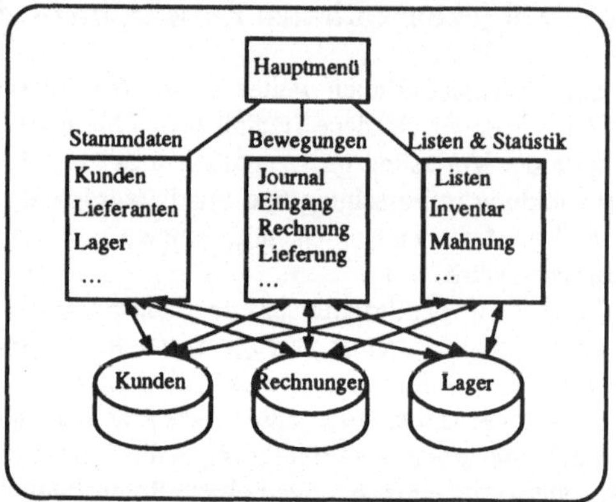

Bild 3: Typische Struktur (auf oberster Ebene)
eines traditionellen (prozeduralen) Studentenprojektes

Bild 3 zeigt eine (stark vereinfachte) Struktur der obersten Analyseebene einer typischen Geschäftsanwendung, wie sie von Studenten vor der Einführung des OO-Paradigmas entwickelt wurde. Es gibt Module für Stammdaten, für Transaktionen sowie für Listen und Statistiken. Die Module sind hierarchisch unterteilt in Untermodule, Prozeduren und Funktionen - typischerweise bis zu einer Tiefe von vier bis fünf Ebenen. Die Kontrolle im Programm erfolgt über Menühierarchie. Die funktionale Kontrollstruktur der Programmkomponenten ist mehr oder weniger äquivalent zur Struktur der Benutzerschnittstelle. Ein unabhängiger Datenbankentwurf für das gesamte System ermöglicht den Unterkomponenten des Softwaresystemes Zugriff auf die Dateien.

Die "ideale" OO-Struktur eines Programmes ist ganz anders: Daten und Funktionen, die zu einer Klasse gehören, werden in dieser Klasse definiert und verwaltet, sodaß für ein Maximum an "Information-Hiding" und Kapselung gesorgt ist. Die Objekte agieren als selbständige Einheiten, die durch Messages Daten abfragen und weiterschicken. Auch im Kontrollbereich wird das Konzept der Informationsweitergabe zwischen unabhängigen Objekten verwendet. Bild 4 zeigt eine ideale OO-Struktur dieser Art.

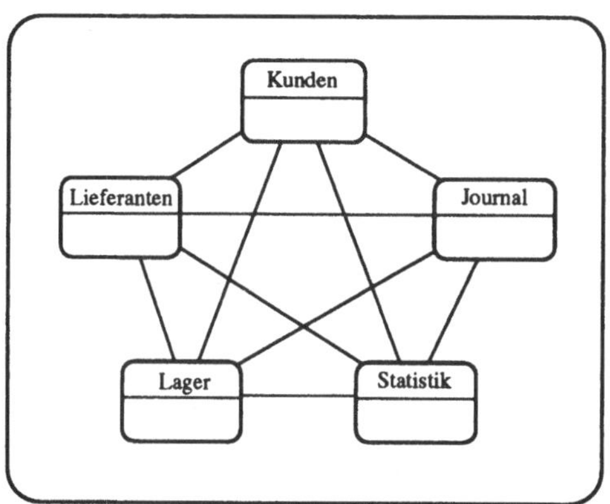

Bild 4: Eine "ideale" OO-Struktur
(auf oberster Ebene) einer Geschäftsanwendung

Bild 4 illustriert das Idealziel und die Erwartung an die Struktur der Studentenprojekte. Bild 3 symbolisiert, welches gedankliche Modell die meisten Studierenden von ihrer Anwendung hatten, bevor sie mit OO in Berührung kamen. Im folgenden werden einige Reaktionen von Studenten über ihre Erfahrungen mit OO-Struktur und OO-Werzeugen aufgezählt. Die Kommentare der Studenten sind *kursiv* geschrieben. Die Interpretationen der Betreuer folgt in normaler Schriftart:

> *"Es hat uns eine Menge Zeit gekostet, die OO-Idee und vor allem die OO-Werkzeuge zu erlernen und zu verstehen."*
>
> *"Zuviel Aufwand am Anfang; das Werkzeug ist sehr komplex. Es war nicht genug Zeit, es zu verstehen, bevor wir es verwenden mußten."*

Tatsächlich war uns bis dahin nicht klar, daß das Einarbeiten in die Datenbank und die Werkzeuge für die Benutzerschnittstelle so viel Zeit brauchen würde. Eigentlich mußten sich die Studenten mit drei Neuheiten auf einmal auseinandersetzen: 1) Mit der OO-Entwurfsidee, 2) den OO-Datenbankwerkzeugen und 3) den erweiterten Möglichkeiten beim OO-Entwurf von Benutzerschnittstellen.

> *"Objekte werden von Masken/Fenstern der Anwendung und von den Beispielen im TurboVision-Manual abgeleitet."*
>
> *"Jedes Fenster ist zumindest ein Objekt."*

Dieser Ansatz ist manchmal wirklich geeignet, aber nicht immer. Ausschließlich die Benutzersicht als Quelle für Objekte heranzuziehen, ergibt eine Programmstruktur, die vor allem an der Benutzerschnittstelle orientiert ist. Die funktionale Seite des Softwaresystemes trägt dabei zuwenig zur Gesamtstruktur bei und muß "unnatürlich" aufgeteilt werden.

> *"Es ist gar nicht so schwer; Man kann das OO-Konzept ganz leicht an das bisherige Wissen über eine prozedurale Sprache anpassen. Stell es Dir als eine Recordstruktur mit Funktionen drinnen vor."*

Das ist ein guter Ansatz, um einem prozedural geschulten Programmierer die anfängliche Furcht zu nehmen. Trotzdem spricht so nur ein OO-Anfänger , d.h. eine Person, die die ganze Idee noch nicht verstanden hat. Vererbung und Kapselung werden von dieser "billigen" Analogie nicht berührt.

"Objekte wurden durch Beispiele des Datenbank-Werkzeuges angeregt und als modifizierte Beispiele der vordefinierten Klassen und Objekte entworfen."

Teams, die verstanden haben, daß in einer kommerziellen Anwendung die Verarbeitung von Daten eine zentrale Rolle spielt, betrachteten die Datenbanken als Hauptobjekte, die beinahe alle Funktionen des Systemes zur Verfügung stellen. Die Kritik ist hier ähnlich wie die an dem ausschließlich benutzerschnittstellenorientierten Ansatz.

"Objekte wurden von dem vorgegebenen Projektbeispiel 'Bibliothek' abgeleitet. Irgendwie konnte diese vorgegebene OO-Struktur an unseren eigenen Anwendungsbereich angepaßt werden."

Dieser Effekt war tatsächlich geplant. Er hat durchaus befriedigende Ergebnisse in Bezug auf die Objektstruktur der Programme gezeigt. Trotzdem war dieser Ansatz oft

1) einfaches Kopieren, manchmal auch ohne Verständnis des Originalentwurfes, oder
2) in größeren Problemstellungen oder in grundsätzlich anderen Anwendungsbereichen nicht funktionstüchtig.

"Die Objekte kommen von"offensichtlich notwendigen" Programmteilen (z.B. Objekte 'Hauptmenü' oder 'Suche')."

Speziell in jenen Teams, die bereits vor unserem Kurs Erfahrung mit der Entwicklung von Softwaresystemen hatten, konnten wir den Effekt beobachten, daß typische Komponenten der der Benutzerschnittstelle oder der Anwendungsfunktionen als besonders "natürliche" Objekte betrachtet wurden. Diese Teams hatten einen konventionellen Entwurf im Kopf. Der Effekt war am stärksten bei jenen Studenten zu beobachten, die einen Anwendungsbereich gewählt hatten, in dem sie schon früher ein Programm entworfen und implementiert hatten.

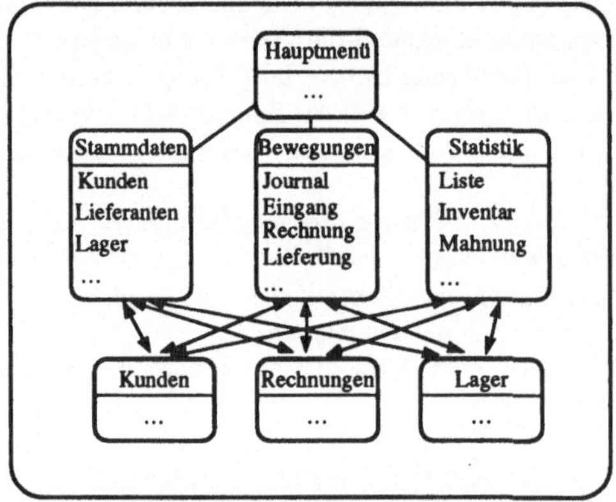

Bild 5: Eine typische OO-Struktur
(auf oberste Ebene) eines Studentenprogrammes

Bild 5 beschreibt eine typische Objektstruktur wie sie von den Teams entworfen worden ist. Die Objekte sind nicht wirklich in der Art unabhängig, daß Datenstrukturen, Datenbanken und Funktionen in sich abgeschlossen sind. Die Kohäsion der Objekte ist offensichtlich zu niedrig. Ein einfaches Objekt wie "Hauptmenü" ist auf der gleichen Ebene angesiedelt wie die Objekte "Bewegungen" oder "Stammdaten" für den Datenbankzugriff (welche vom OO-Standpunkt her ohnehin eher "zweifelhaft" sind). Die unästhetische, ineffiziente und unpassende Struktur in Bild 5 illustriert eine konzeptuelle Schwäche am Top-Level, die den Projekten auch auf unterer Ebene innewohnte.

Bild 6 zeigt einige der Schwächen. Die beiden mit 1 markierten Objekte sind aus einem vorgegebenen Programm kopiert worden. Die Bezeichnungen der Attribute sind zwar zum Teil unverständlich, Wahl und Struktur der Objekte ist jedoch sinnvoll. Die mit 2 markierten Objekte haben jeweils das gleiche Attribut und die gleiche Methode. Hier fehlt offensichtlich das Konzept eines gemeinsamen Vorgängerobjektes. Das mit 3 markierte Objekt hat ein einzelnes Attribut und eine einzige Methode. Da dieses Objekt keine Vorgänger hat und daher weder ererbte Attribute noch Methoden haben kann, muß für eine sinnvolle Verwendung des Inhaltes des Attributes das Prinzip des 'Information Hiding' durchbrochen werden: Mit der Methode *SetDatum* kann das Datum zwar gesetzt, jedoch nicht wieder gelesen werden. Offenbar wurde hier (wie auch bei den Objekten 2) das Prinzip "*Ein Objekt ist ein Record plus Prozeduren*" angewendet. Das mit 4 markierte Objekt hat überhaupt keine Attribute, sondern besteht ausschließlich aus Methoden. Der dafür zuständige Programmierer meinte dazu, daß er bisher immer Prozduren verwendet hätte und nach der Umstellung auf OO-Notation eben einige Prozeduren in Form eines Objektes zusammenfassen mußte.

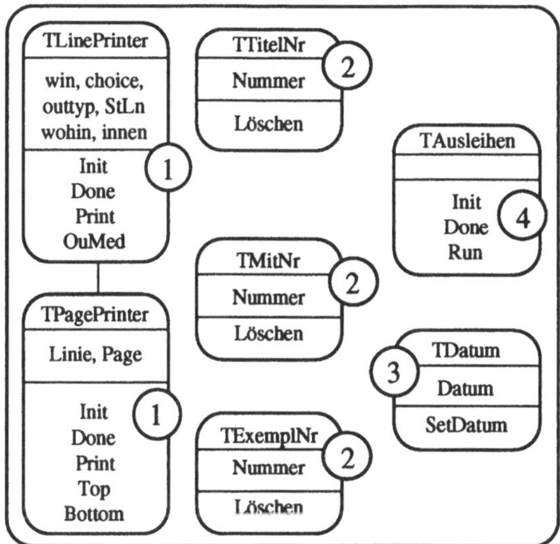

Bild 6: Ausschnitt aus dem OOP-Modell eines realen Studentenprojektes

Dies ist nur ein konkretes Beispiel unter vielen, das die Zitate von vorhin belegt. Zusammenfassend haben wir gelernt, daß es ein grundsätzlicher Fehler war, die Studenten nicht ganz intensiv auf OO-Analyse und OO-Entwurf vorzubereiten. Die Lehrveranstaltungsteilnehmer brauchen genügend Zeit, um die OOA- und OOD-Ideen zu verstehen. Sie müssen zwei Dinge auf einmal lernen: SWE als Team einerseits und OO-Entwicklung andererseits. Aufgrund der zu knappen Zeit für ein wirkliches Umdenken haben sie nach dem ersten festen Halt gegriffen, der sich ihnen geboten hat. Das war entweder das Interface-Tool oder das Datenbank-Tool oder das vorgegebene Beispielprogramm oder das bisherige Denkmodell. Es wurden letztlich eher konventionelle funktionale/modulare/prozedurale Programmsysteme entworfen.
Letztlich erhielten wir, was wir verdienten: wir haben die Information-Engineering Aspekte von OO zuwenig ernst genommen. An den Studierenden ist es nicht gelegen: Die zogen nach dem einen Jahr SWE zu mehr als zwei Drittel OO-Struktur und OOP dem prozeduralen Ansatz vor.

5. Konsequenzen und Schlußfolgerungen aus dem ersten Versuch

In dieser Arbeit haben wir einige Erfahrungen mit der Einführung von Objektorientierung in einem typischen SWE-Lehrgang aufgezeigt. Letztendlich erkannten wir, daß wir einen sehr unbewußten Ansatz verfolgt haben. Allerdings werden unsere Fehler von vielen akademischen und industriellen Ausbildungsprogrammen wiederholt: Die üblichen Materialien, Methoden und Vorgehensweisen im Software-Life-Cycle werden beibehalten. Eigentlich wurde nur eine prozedural orientierte Programmierumgebung gegen eine OO-Umgebung mit OO-Datenbank und OO-Interface ausgetauscht. Es werden konventionelle Methoden für Analyse, Spezifikation und Entwurf gelehrt, wobei OOA und OOD als eine weitere, im vorliegenden Fall geeignete Methode vorgestellt wird.

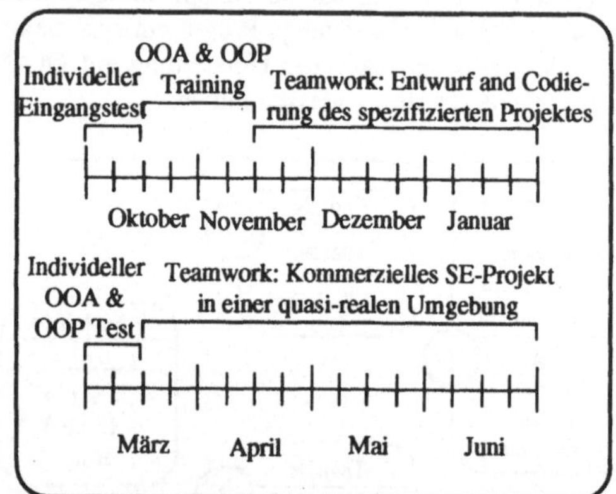

Bild 7: Der angepaßte Kursverlauf der SWE-Übung

Als Ergebnis unserer Erfahrungen wird der Zeitplan für dieses Jahr geändert. Wir konzentrieren uns auf das Vermitteln von OOA in einer sehr frühen Phase (siehe Bild 7). OOA und OOD werden anhand von mehreren Beispielen aus verschiedenen Domänen vorgestellt. Die traditionellen Methoden werden auch erwähnt, aber nicht im Detail diskutiert. Zur gleichen Zeit werden die neuen Programmierwerkzeuge eingeführt.

Erfahrungsgemäß probieren Informatiker gerne neue Werkzeuge aus. Durch das spezielle Training in OOA und den ungezwungenen Zugang zu OOP werden die beiden "Enden" der OO-Entwicklung (OOA als problemorientierte Sicht und OOP als Sicht der Implementierung) intensiv behandelt. Die notwendige Zeit für das OOA-Training wird durch die weniger intensive Vermittlung der traditionellen Spezifikations- und Entwurfsmethoden gewonnen.

OOD wird geringerem Ausmaß gelehrt. Einige Konzepte und Ideen werden zusammen mit einem Beispiel vorgestellt. Wir sehen OOD vor allem als einen Prozeß zur Verfeinerung und Anpassung von OOA-Spezifikationen. Diese Annahme gilt ja u.a. als eine der besonderen Vorteile des OO-Paradigmas (siehe [CoYo91a], [CoYo91b]).

Unsere Schlußfolgerung: Es besteht die Tendenz, bei der Einführung der Objektorientierung die Aspekte des Information Engineerings zu unterschätzen. Dies gilt unserer Erfahrung nicht nur für den Bereich der akademischen Lehre, sondern auch für den industriellen Entwickler. Auch dort beginnt die Umstellung auf OO derzeit mit dem Erlernen der neuen Werkzeuge und endet auch gleich wieder damit.

Literatur

[Alab88] *Transformation of Data Flow Analysis Models to Object Oriented Design*, Alabiso B., Proc. of the Conf. on OOPSLA '88: 335-353, Sept. 1988

[Barb92] *Object-oriented analysis of systems through their dynamical aspects*, Barbier F., Journal of Object-oriented programming, p.45-51, May 1992

[Beck89] *A Laboratory For Teaching Object-Oriented Thinking*, Beck K., Proceedings of the OOPSLA '89, Oct. 1-6 1989, p. 1-6.

[Bell92] *Software Engineering - A Programming Approach*, Bell D., Morrey I., Pugh J., 2nd ed., Prentice Hall International, 1992

[Bilo92] *Book Review - Object-Oriented Software Engineering*, Bilow S.C., Journal of Object-oriented Programming, p.85-87, Juni 1992

[Blai92] *The impact of distribution on support for object-oriented software development*, Blair G.S., Lea R., SE Journal, p.130-138, März 1992

[Cham92] *A comparative study of object-oriented analysis methods*, Champeaux D. de, Faure P., Journal of Object-oriented programming, March/April 1992, p.21-33

[Chid91] *Towards a metrics suite for Object Oriented Design*, Chidamber S.R., Kemerer C.F., ACM Sigplan Notices, OOPSLA '91, p. 197-211., 1991

[Coad92] *Object-Oriented Patterns*, Coad P., Comm. of the ACM, Vol. 35, No. 9, p.152-159, 1992

[Cole92] *Introducing Objectcharts or How to Use Statecharts in Object-Oriented Design*, Coleman D., Hayes F., Bear S., IEEE TSE, Vol. 18, No.1, p.9-18, 1992

[Cox 90] *There Is a Silver Bullet*, Cox B.J., Byte, Oct. 1990, p.209-218

[CoYo91a] *Object Oriented Analysis*, 2nd ed., Coad P., Yourdon E., Yourdon Press, 1991

[CoYo91b] *Object Oriented Design*, Coad P., Yourdon E., Yourdon Press, 1991

[DeNa90] PANEL: *OOP in the Real World*, DeNatale R., Irby C., LaLonde J., Leathers B., Phillips R., ECOOP/OOPSLA '90, Oct. 21-25, 1990, p.299-302

[Dunt90] *New Objects For Old Structures*, Duntemann J., Marinacci C., Byte, April 1990, p.261-266

[Gibs90] *Objects - Born and Bred*, Gibson E., Byte, Oct. 1990, p.245-254

[Hare87] *State Charts: A Visual Formalism for Complex Systems*, Harel David, Science of Computer Programming, Vol. 8, No. 3, pp. 231-274, June 1987

[Haye91] *Coherent Models for Object-Oriented Analysis*, Hayes F., Coleman D., ACM Sigplan Notices, OOPSLA '91, p.171-183, 1991

[Heit90] *Hierarchical Object-Oriented Design for development of large technical and realtime software*, Heitz M., HOOD, CISI Ingenierie, Direction Midi Pyreness, 1990

[Hend90] *Object-Oriented Systems Life Cycle*, Henders-Sellers B., Edwards J.M., Communications of the ACM, Sept. 1990, vol. 33, no. 9, p. 142-159

[Hodg92] *A proposed object-oriented development methodology*, Hodge L.R., Mock M.T., SE Journal, March 1992, p.119-129

[Jack83] *System Design*, Jackson M., Prentice Hall, 1983

[Leav91] *Introduction to Literature on OO-Design, Programming, and Languages*, Leavens G.T., OOPS Messenger 2(4):40-53, ACM Press, Oct 1991

[LeMy87] *Components of Typical Undergraduate Software Engineering Courses: Results from a Survey*, Leventhal L., Mynatt B., IEEE TSE SE-13(11): 1193-1198, 1987

[Lewa92] *Finite State Machines and Object Orientation*, Lewandowski R., Mulazzani M., Proc. of the 7th Joint Conf of OCG and NJSZT, Oct. 1992

[LiHo89] *Assuring goodstyle for object-oriented programming*, Liebherr K.J., Holland I.M., IEEE Software, Sept 1989, pp. 38-48., September 1989

[LiRi89] *Contributions to Teaching Object-Oriented Design and Programming*, Lieberherr K., Riel A., Proceedings of the OOPSLA '89, Oct. 1-6 1989, p. 11-22.

[Loy 90] *A Comparison of Object-Oriented and Structured Development methods*, Loy P.H., Software Engineering Notes 15(1): 44-48, Jan 1990

[Ners92] *Applying Object-Oriented Analysis and Design*, Nerson J., Comm. of the ACM, Vol. 35, No. 9, p.63-74, 1992

[Pomb91] *Adjusting our sails - objectives for Software Engineering Education*, Pomberger G., IFIP Working Group on Software Engineering, Zürich 1991

[Pres92] *Software Engineering - A Practitioner's Approach*, Pressman R. S., 3rd ed., McGraw-Hill International Editions, New York 1992

[Rajl92] *Two object-based decomposition methodologies: a case study*, Rajlich V., Silva J., SE Journal, Jan. 1992, p.35-42

[Smit92] *A framework for testing object-oriented programs*, Smith M.D., Robson D.J., Journal of Object-oriented Programming, Juni 1992,p.45-53

[Stah92] *Das aktuelle Schlagwort - Objektorientiertes Design (ooD)*, Stahlknecht P., Appelfeller W., Wirtschaftsinformatik, Jahrgang 34, Heft 2, April 1992, p.249-252

[Stew91] *Object projects: what can go wrong*, Steward M.K., Hot Line on object-oriented technology vol.2, no. 6, April 1991

[Somm92] *Software Engineering*, 4th ed., Sommerville I., Addison Wesley, 1992

[Wass91a] *From OO-Analysis to OO-Design*, Wasserman A.I., JOOP 4(5), p. 46-50, Sept 1991

[Wass91b] *The spiral model for object software development*, Wassermann A.I., Pircher P.A., Hot Line on Object-Oriented technology Vol.2, no. 3 p.8-12, Jan 1991

[Wegn90] *Concepts and Paradigms of Object Oriented Programming*, Wegner P., OOPS Messenger Vol. 1/1, Aug. 1990

[Wert89] *Teaching Object-oriented Programming Using the Macintosh MPW/MacApp Environment*, Werth L., Werth J., Lectures Notes in Computer Science (1989) vol.376, p.141-155.

[Wils90] *Class Diagrams: A Tool for Design, Documentation, and Teaching*, Wilson D.A., JOOP 2(5):38-44, 1990

[Wirf90] *Surveying Current Research in OO-Design*, Wirfs-Brock R.J., Johnson R.E., CACM 33(9):104-124, Sept. 1990

[Wolc92] *Encapsulation, delegation and inheritance in object-oriented languages*, Wolczko M., SE Journal, March 1992, p.95-101, 1992

Grenzen objekt-orientierter Analysemethoden am Beispiel einer Fallstudie mit OMT

Roland Kaschek, Claudia Kohl, Heinrich C. Mayr

Institut für Informatik
Universität Klagenfurt
Universitätsstraße 65
A-9020 Klagenfurt
e-mail: <name>@ifi.uni-klu.ac.at

Abstract

Methoden der objekt-orientierten Analyse sind en vogue, Erfahrungsberichte dagegen noch selten. Das Risiko, eine solche Methode auf ein umfangreiches betriebliches Projekt anzuwenden, ist dementsprechend hoch. Die vorliegende Arbeit versucht, hier einen Beitrag durch eine nähere Betrachtung des OOA-Anteils der Object Modeling Technique OMT [Ru91] zu leisten. Es werden die von OMT verwendeten Modellierungsbegriffe kritisch gewürdigt und Stärken und Schwächen, die wir beim Entwurf einer Beispielsanwendung bemerkten, aufgezeigt.

1. Einleitung

Der wachsende Einsatz objekt-orientierter Konzepte beim logischen Entwurf und bei der Systemrealisierung macht auf der konzeptuellen Ebene den Übergang von der reinen Datenmodellierung hin zum gesamtheitlichen objekt-orientierten Entwurf erforderlich. Zusätzlich zu semantischen Datenmodellen werden also semantische Modelle benötigt, die es gestatten, Dynamik-Aspekte des betrachteten Umweltausschnittes (universe of discurse, UoD), d.h. Aktivitäten, deren Auswirkungen und Randbedingungen zu beschreiben. Derartige Modelle gehören zum Instrumentarium der sogenannten objektorientieren Analyse (OOA), wobei sich hierunter - analog zur Methodenvielfalt im Bereich der ER-Modelle als Hauptvertreter der klassischen semantischen Datenmodelle - mittlerweile eine Reihe recht ähnlicher, in Begriffswahl und hauptsächlich Darstellungskonventionen (also Notationen) umso verschiedenere Ansätze verbergen (vergleiche dazu [FK92, p.29] und [Ru91, p.273]).

Im Zusammenhang mit der Vorbereitung eines vom Institut für Informatik der Universität Klagenfurt seit Mai 1992 dreimal veranstalteten (COMETT-geförderten) einwöchigen Hochschulkurses "Object-Orientation in Software and Database Engineering" hatten wir die Aufgabe, eine dieser Methoden auszuwählen und im Detail zu prüfen. Es galt, sie als Grundlage praktischer Übungen zum Themenkreis "Semantische Modellierung und objekt-orientierter konzeptueller Entwurf" aufzubereiten, wobei der Frontalunterricht auf einer methodenunabhängigen Basis gestaltet wurde.

Aufgrund der Ausrichtung des Kurses auf Teilnehmer aus der betrieblichen Praxis lag es nahe, nur solche Methoden in die engere Wahl zu ziehen, für die es hinreichend veröffentlichtes, leicht zugängliches Material und gegebenenfalls sogar Werkzeuge gibt. Da letztere, wenn überhaupt vorhanden, erst in den Kinderschuhen steckten und wohl auch heute noch stecken (vergleiche dazu etwa die Anmerkungen in [Br92, p.375] zu OMTool), bildeten sie letztendlich doch kein Entscheidungskriterium, sodaß aufgrund der dazu veröffentlichten umfassenden Bücher die OOA-Ansätze von Coad und Yourdon [CY91], Shlaer und Mellor [SM92] sowie Rumbaugh et al. [Ru91] zur Auswahl standen. Die Entscheidung fiel schließlich für den OOA-Anteil des letztgenannten Ansatzes (d.h. der Object Modeling Technique OMT), wobei hauptsächlich die Konzepte der dynamischen Modellierung und die mit wenigen Ausnahmen als natürlich empfundenen Darstellungskonzepte den Ausschlag gaben.

Die vorliegende Arbeit handelt von den Erfahrungen, die wir bei näherer Betrachtung dieser Methode und insbesondere bei ihrer Anwendung auf das erarbeitete Übungsbeispiel gewannen. Dabei gehen wir davon aus, daß diese Erkenntnisse aufgrund der engen Verwandtschaft der Methoden untereinander weitgehend auf die anderen Ansätze übertragen werden können.

Nach einer kurzen Darstellung unseres Verständnisses vom Wesen des konzeptuellen Entwurfs in Abschnitt 2 geben wir in Abschnitt 3 einen komprimierten kommentierten Überblick über die wesentlichen Konzepte des OOA-Anteils von OMT. In Abschnitt 4 behandeln wir knapp das Anwendungsbeispiel, um dann in Abschnitt 5 unsere Erfahrungen bei der objektorientierten Analyse mit OMT zu schildern. In Abschnitt 6 schließlich berichten wir kurz vom Übergang auf die logische Ebene im Sinne einer Implementierung der Anwendung unter Verwendung des objekt-orientierten Datenbanksystems O_2 [De91].

Wir danken Herrn Dipl.-Ing. Klaus Kienzl für dic anregenden Diskussionsbeiträge beim Entwurf des Anwendungsbeispiels.

2. Konzeptueller Entwurf und objekt-orientierte Analyse

Um Mißverständnissen vorzubeugen, die sich durch die paradoxerweise gerade im Bereich der semantischen Modellierung uneinheitliche Begriffsbildung ergeben könnten, werden im folgenden die wichtigsten von uns verwendeten Begriffe aus dem Bereich des konzeptuellen Entwurfs eingeführt. Wir stützen uns dabei hauptsächlich auf [BCN92] und [MDL87] ab.

Ziel des *konzeptuellen Entwurfs* ist es, ausgehend von Anforderungsspezifikationen über ein gegebenes UoD zu einem *konzeptuellen Schema*, d.h. einer "high-level description" [BCN92] des für das UoD geplanten Informationssystems zu kommen. Dabei muß man sich nicht, wie von manchen Autoren behauptet, auf diejenigen Aspekte beschränken, die mittels eines rechnergestützten Informationssystems realisiert werden sollen, vielmehr kann das gesamte UoD Gegenstand der Beschreibung sein, vergleiche z.B. die Stichworte Organisations-/ und Unternehmensmodellierung [Rup92] und Objektsystembeschreibung [FS91].

"High-level" bedeutet dabei, daß es sich um eine abstrakte Beschreibung handelt, die von irgendwelchen gegebenenfalls zur späteren Realisierung eingesetzten oder einsetzbaren Oberflächen (Datenbanksoftware, Implementierungssprachen usw.) unabhängig ist. Für diese Beschreibung wird vielmehr ein *konzeptuelles Modell* verwendet, d.h. ein System aufeinander abgestimmter, eindeutiger Begriffe. Spätestens seit [Ch76] hat es sich eingebürgert, die Bedeutung der Begriffe eines konzeptuellen Modells natürlichsprachlich zu erklären, als bekannt vorauszusetzen oder zu rekonstruieren [WO80], d.h. mit einer *a priori* Semantik zu unterlegen. In diesem Fall spricht man daher auch von einem *semantischen Modell.* Die Anwendung eines semantischen Modells, d.h. *semantische Modellierung* war - zumindest explizit - in der Vergangenheit vorwiegend Gegenstand des konzeptuellen Datenbank-Entwurfs, wobei man sich hier mit wenigen Ausnahmen auf semantische Modelle beschränkte, die ausschließlich Begriffe zur Beschreibung statischer UoD-Zusammenhänge enthielten. Dementsprechend handelte es sich um sogenannte *semantische Datenmodelle*, unter denen sich die ER-Derivate und -Extensionen durchgesetzt haben.

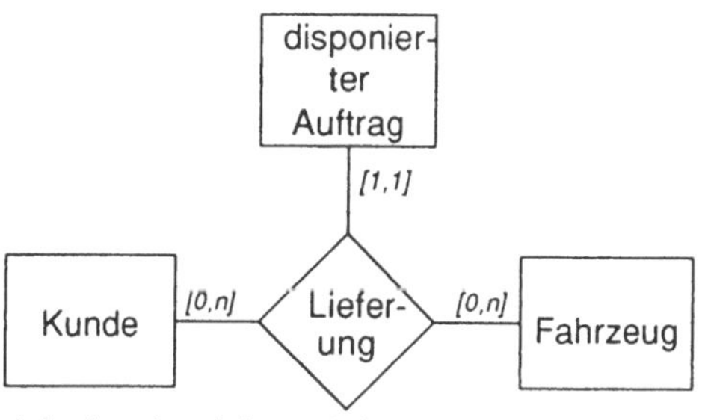

Jeder disponierte Auftrag geht in genau eine Lieferbeziehung ein, Kunden und Fahrzeuge können in beliebig viele eingehen.

Abb. 2.1: Kardinalitäten in einer Relationship mit Valenz 3.

ER-Modelle enthalten bekanntlich (vergleiche [BCN92, p.31 f]) die Grundbegriffe *Entity* und *Relationship*. Entities sind Klassen von Gegenständen eines UoD, Relationships sind Klassen von Beziehungen zwischen Gegenständen von mindestens zwei Entities. Jede elementare Eigenschaft, die einem Entity oder einer Relationship eines UoD zugeordnet ist, nennen wir *Merkmal*, die Zuordnungsvorschrift selbst nennen wir *Charakteristik*.

Mit Hilfe von *Kardinalitäten* (vergleiche [BCN92, p.23] und Abb. 2.1) spezifizieren wir Relationships und Charakteristiken. Ist ein Gegenstand e Exemplar eines Entities E (d.h. in E enthalten), so wird e durch Merkmalsausprägungen zu den jeweiligen Merkmalen von E charakterisiert. Jede Merkmalsausprägung ist Element einer mit dem Merkmal assoziierten *Domain*. Unter der *Valenz* einer Relationship R verstehen wir die Anzahl der an R beteiligten Entities.

Semantische Modelle lassen sich auch zur Beschreibung dynamischer Aspekte, allgemein des *Verhaltens*, von und in UoD's formulieren und beim konzeptuellen Entwurf einsetzen. Genau dies findet bei der objekt-orientierten Analyse statt: Sie benutzt semantische Modelle für die Beschreibung statischer und dynamischer UoD-Aspekte, wobei diese Modelle in dem Sinne objekt-orientiert sind, als sie die üblichen Konzepte der Objekt-Orientierung (komplexe Objekte, Identität, Kapselung usw.) unterstützen. Objekt-orientierte Analyse ist also objekt-orientierter konzeptueller Entwurf.

Abschließend sei noch darauf hingewiesen, daß insbesondere im Bereich der Unternehmensmodellierung und Wirtschaftsinformatik statt des Begriffs Schema häufig der Begriff Modell (z.B. das 'Datenmodell eines Unternehmens'), für den Begriff des Modells selbst dagegen derjenige des *Metamodells* verwendet wird.

3. Objekt-orientierte Analyse in OMT

3.1 Modellierungsbegriffe für statische Gegebenheiten: Objektmodell

OMT ist eine objekt-orientierte Entwurfsmethode, die mit dem Anspruch durchgängiger Einsetzbarkeit von der Informationsbedarfsanalyse bis zum Realisierungsentwurf antritt. Sie wurde in ihren ersten Ansätzen in [LSR87] präsentiert und in einem 1991 erschienenen, verhältnismäßig systematischen Buch [Ru91] umfassend dokumentiert.

Das grundsätzliche, von OMT unterstützte Vorgehen besteht in der Durchführung der beiden Schritte Analyse und Design, wobei diese natürlich weiter untergliedert werden (siehe Abb. 3.1). Da wir uns in dieser Arbeit auf die objekt-orientierte Analyse beschränken, wird auf die Design-Phase im folgenden nicht weiter eingegangen. Die Analysephase besteht im wesentlichen darin, durch die Sammlung sogenannter "Problem Statements" ein natürlichsprachliches Modell der Bedürfnisse und Probleme der Anwendungssituation zu erhalten und dieses durch weitere Tätigkeiten der Informationsbedarfs-Sammlung und -analyse in ein konzeptuelles Schema der geplanten Anwendung zu überführen (vergleiche [Ru91] p.260 f.). Dieses kann als Grundlage einer Machbarkeitsstudie dienen und soll die Implementierung vorbereiten.

Auf der konzeptuellen Ebene kennt OMT die beiden grundlegenden Modellierungsbegriffe *Objekt* und *Link* ([Ru91, p.21,27]). Objekt bezeichnet dabei ein Konzept, ein Ding oder eine Abstraktion mit unverwechselbarer, nicht mit seinen Merkmalsausprägungen korrelierender Identität. In [BPR88] werden Objekte in Abgrenzung zur im ER-Bereich [Ch76] üblichen Begriffsbestimmung als etwas definiert, *was existiert und eine Identität hat.*

Links sind Beziehungen zwischen Objekten.

Gleichartige Objekte werden zu *Objektklassen* und gleichartige Links zu *Assoziationen* zusammengefaßt. Objekten und Links können Merkmale im Sinne von Abschnitt 2 zugeordnet werden, wobei diese als *Attribut* bezeichnet werden, wenn es sich um Werte (im Sinne von

Exemplaren von Datentypen) handelt bzw. *Operationen*, wenn es sich um funktionale Eigenschaften handelt. Mit Werten und Funktionen werden also die vom Betrachter als wesentlich erachteten Eigenschaften des Systems wiedergegeben, wobei OMT keine klare Unterscheidung zwischen Merkmal und Merkmalszuordnung im Sinne von Charakteristiken vornimmt. Das mag darin begründet sein, daß in einer früheren Version [LSR87] offenbar ein algebraischer Ansatz mitverfolgt wurde: Den dortigen Klassenbegriff kann man interpretieren als ein Paar aus einer Signatur und einer Menge darüber gebildeten Algebren (wobei letztere mit den Objekten zu identifizieren sind). Die Merkmale einzelner Objekte entsprechen dann den Belegungen von Merkmalsvariablen, d.h. letztere können mit den in Abschnitt 2 genannten Charakteristiken verglichen werden. Die Operationen entsprechen den zur Signatur passenden Operatoren.

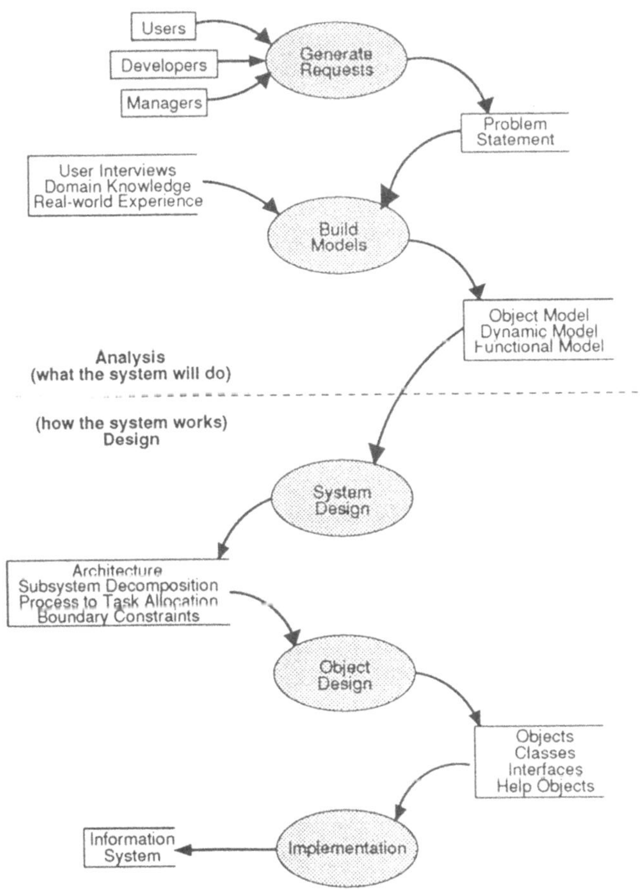

Abb. 3.1: OMT als Datenflußdiagramm

Bei diesem Ansatz hat man allerdings Schwierigkeiten, die Bedeutung der Mehrfach-Instantiierungen von Variablen bzw. Operatornamen zu erklären; in vergleichbaren Ansätzen behilft man sich hier mit der Einführung von Set, List - und ähnlichen Konstruktionen (siehe etwa [De91, p.35]). Die notwendigen mathematischen Grundlagen zu einer eingehenden Analyse solcher Fragestellungen sind etwa in [EGL89] zu finden.

Besondere Arten von OMT-Assoziationen sind die bekannten Abstraktionen *Aggregation* (hier part_of-Aggregation) und *Generalisation*. Für die Spezifikation von Beziehungseigenschaften kennt OMT im wesentlichen folgende Begriffe: *Multiplicity*, *Qualification* und *Ordering*.

Multiplicity entspricht in etwa dem in der ER-Modellierung häufig verwendeten Begriff der Kardinalitäten. Im Fall von Assoziationen der Valenz 2 erreicht das von OMT vorgeschlagene Darstellungskonzept eine gewisse Reduktion von Redundanz gegenüber anderen Ansätzen im Sinne einer geringeren Zahl anzuschreibender Zeichen (siehe dazu Abb. 3.2). Die in [BPR88, p.416 f.] gegebene Definition, die in [Ru91, p.30] im wesentlichen übernommen wird, ist allerdings nur auf Beziehungen mit der Valenz 2 anwendbar. In [LSR87, p.195] werden überhaupt nur solche Assoziationen zugelassen. Um im Falle von Valenzen größer 2, die nach [Ru91] jetzt zulässig sind, Spezifizierungen zu ermöglichen, wird in [Ru91, p.71] der Weg beschritten, Assoziationen als Tables im Sinne des Relationenmodells aufzufassen, mit wie üblich den Objektidentifikationen der beteiligten Objekte als Fremdschlüssel. Für diese Tables sollen dann Schlüsselkandidaten bestimmt werden. Dieses Vorgehen erreicht allerdings nicht die Mächtigkeit der Kardinalitäten. Die Ansicht der Autoren von OMT ([Ru91, p.159]), daß sich die meisten Assoziationen mit einer Valenz größer 2 verlustfrei in solche der Valenz 2 zerlegen lassen, teilen wir nicht, wie auch die OMT-Erfahrung, daß Valenzen größer 3 in der Praxis nicht auftreten. Zwar kann man natürlich jede derartige Assoziation formal in ein System von Assoziationen mit Valenz 2 umwandeln, indem man die betreffende Assoziation selbst als Objekt modelliert, allerdings geht dadurch semantische Information über den besonderen Zusammenhang verloren. Die Beschreibung relativer Kardinalitäten innerhalb einer Assoziation höherer Valenz ist bei dieser Umformung nur noch durch eine komplexe Integritätsbedingung über ein System von Assoziationen möglich.

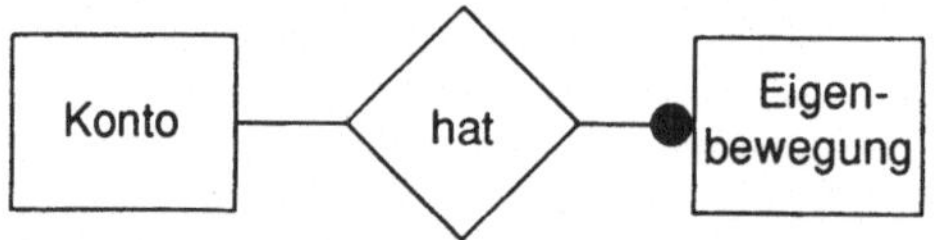

Jede Eigenbewegung ist genau einem Konto zugeordnet; ein Konto kann keine, eine oder mehrere Eigenbewegungen haben.

Abb. 3.2: Multiplicity

Die Verwendung von Multiplicities zur Spezifikation von Aggregationen legt den Schluß nahe, daß diese für OMT eigentlich eine Menge von Assoziationen der Valenz 2 sind. Dies wird in [Ru91, p.37] ausdrücklich bestätigt und ist natürlich eine irreführende und unnötige semantische Schwäche: Unabhängig von der Art der betrachteten Assoziation sollte eine formal saubere Behandlung höherer Valenz möglich sein.

Qualification ist ein Konzept, mit dem die Multiplicity von Beziehungen eingeschränkt werden kann. Eine klare Definition wird aber in den uns zugänglichen OMT-Arbeiten nicht gegeben, obwohl es in [BPR88, p.418] als eine der wesentlichen Neuerungen von OMT herausgestellt wird.

Mit Hilfe des *Ordering* kann man die multiplen Seiten von Assoziationen als geordnete Mengen spezifizieren. Analog zum klassischen ER-Modell kennt OMT Rollen, analog zum klassischen ER-Modell werden diese nicht weiter behandelt.

Bemerkenswert ist ferner, daß OMT zwar Mehrfachvererbungen zuläßt, aber keine Konzepte zur Behandlung dabei auftretender Konflikte anbietet. Statt dessen rät OMT dazu, diese Konflikte zu vermeiden und gegebenenfalls die Semantik der Implementationssprache zu beachten.

3.2 Modellierungsbegriffe für dynamische Aspekte: Dynamikmodell und Funktionsmodell

Betrachtet man das UoD als dynamisches System, so erkennt man darin Instanzen, d.h. aktive Dinge, die untereinander Strömungsgrößen austauschen und diese gegebenenfalls verändern. Diese Instanzen wirken zur Erreichung gemeinsamer Ziele zusammen und sie tun dies ausschließlich durch den Austausch und durch die Bearbeitung von Strömungsgrößen. Es liegt nahe, die Instanzen mit den Objekten und die Strömungsgrößen mit den Parametern zu identifizieren, die beim *"message passing"* auftreten. Da die Reaktion einer Instanz auf eine Strömungsgröße von ihrem Zustand abhängen kann, erfordert die Beschreibung der dynamischen Aspekte des UoD die Beantwortung folgender Fragen:

1. Welche Zustände und Zustandsübergänge treten bei den Instanzen, d.h. Objekten, auf und wodurch werden diese Übergänge bewirkt?

2. Welchen Transformationen werden die Strömungsgrößen durch die Instanzen unterworfen?

Die hier erkennbare und von OMT tatsächlich verfolgte Dreiteilung eines Schemas des UoD in ein Statik-, ein Dynamik- und ein Funktionsschema (bei OMT jeweils Modell genannt) wurde beim Entwurf von Informationssystemen schon früher verwendet ([Ce83], siehe auch Abb. 3.3). Auch in der Theorie der relationalen Datenbanken wurde die Notwendigkeit der Spezifikation dynamischer Eigenschaften von Tupeln, Tabellen und Datenbanken bereits festgehalten, siehe etwa [Pa89].

Geht man davon aus, daß die statischen Aspekte von UoD's durch das Objektmodell abgedeckt werden, so bleiben die Begriffe zu beschreiben, mit denen OMT die beiden vorgenannten Fragestellungen hinsichtlich Dynamik und Funktionalität angeht.

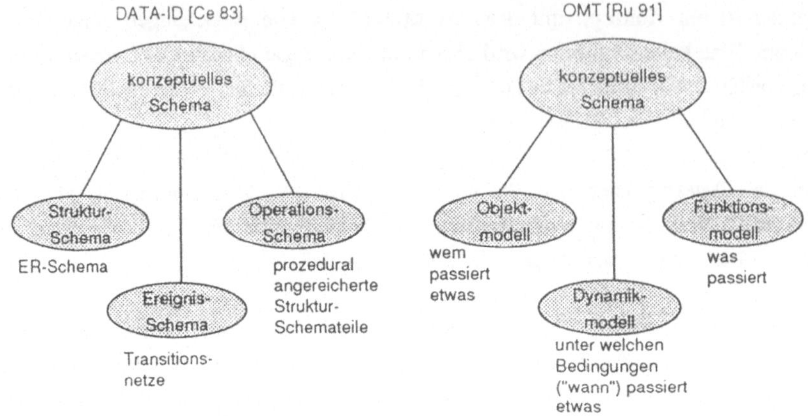

Abb. 3.3: Vergleich der Teilschemata von OMT und DATA-ID

Für die Beschreibung der Zustände von Objekten eines UoD und ihrer Übergänge verwendet OMT endliche Automaten mit Ein- und Ausgabe. Dies ist insofern naheliegend, als die Verwendung solcher Automaten in der formalen Beschreibung von Informationssystemen eine lange Tradition hat (z.B. [LM78], [LB82]) und diese ausreichend mächtig sowie flexibel einsetzbar sind. Beispiele für derartige Automaten finden sich in Abb. 5.2. Für die Beschreibung der Funktionalität, d.h. der von Objekten ausgeführten Operationen mit ihren Auswirkungen auf die Strömungsgrößen, verwendet OMT Datenflußdiagramme.

Bemerkenswert ist hier zunächst nur, daß entsprechende Notationen und Teilmodelle im Gegensatz zu [SM89] ursprünglich in [LSR87] und [BPR88] nicht vorgeschlagen wurden. Ferner ist zu bemerken, daß der Ansatz von OMT nicht zwingend ist. Beispielsweise verwendet [KS91] "high-level"-Petrinetze um einerseits Objekt-Lebenszyklen und andererseits die Operationen der Objekte zu spezifizieren. Auch andere Methoden, wie etwa die algebraische Spezifikation, sind geeignet, die Funktionalität der Objekte festzulegen. [HC91] kritisieren an Datenfluß-Diagrammen die implementierungsnahe Vorwegnahme von Prozeßabfolgen und schlagen deshalb eine realisierungsunabhängige Spezifikation mittels pre und post conditions vor.

Die Menge der Automaten-Schemata für eine konkrete Anwendung konstituiert nach [Ru91, p.261] in OMT das *Dynamikmodell*, die Menge der Datenflußdiagramme das *Funktionsmodell* (siehe auch Abb. 3.1), wobei man gemäß Abschnitt 2 hier eigentlich von *Dynamik-* und *Funktionsschema* sprechen sollte.

3.3 Analyse-Methodik

Für die Erstellung eines Objektschemas für ein gegebenes UoD schlägt OMT das erstmals in [Ab83] (vergleiche dazu [Gr91, p.196]) verwendete Verfahren vor, nämlich die Problembeschreibung und die Benutzeranforderungen (Problem Statement, siehe Abb. 3.1) einer syntaktischen und semantischen Analyse zu unterziehen. Kandidaten für Objekte sind danach die Subjekte von Anforderungssätzen, Kandidaten für Merkmale sind über Hilfs- und Modalverben verbundene Substantiva, Kandidaten für Methoden transitive Verben (siehe dazu auch [Fe92]). Die so identifizierten Kandidaten sind auf ihre Tauglichkeit zu testen. OMT empfiehlt u.a., hierbei zunächst nicht auf Objektbeziehungen zu achten, sondern auf aussagekräftige Namen Wert zu legen, die mit der Natur des betreffenden Objektes im UoD korrespondieren. Für die Entfernung untauglicher Klassen wird die Eliminierung derjenigen empfohlen, die mit dem Problem nichts zu tun haben oder deren Instanzen nicht eindeutig bestimmt sind. Bei der Bestimmung von Merkmalen rät OMT, weil es ja den Begriff der Assoziation vorsieht, von der Verwendung objektwertiger Merkmale ab und folgt damit der von ER-Modellen vorgegebenen Linie. Ebenfalls abgeraten wird von der Modellierung abgeleiteter Merkmale, eine den Autoren nicht einsichtige Selbstbeschränkung (vergleiche [Ru91, p.152f]).

Ein durch Identifikation und Tauglichkeitsprüfung erarbeitetes initiales Objektschema wird dann systematisch durch Verwendung von Abstraktionsbegriffen, d.h. Identifikation von Integrations- und Generalisationsbeziehungen vereinfacht, durch Klassenzusammenlegungen gegebenenfalls modifiziert und konkretisiert.

Für die Erstellung des Dynamikschemas geht OMT von sogenannten *Szenarien* aus, womit Ereignisfolgen gemeint sind, die während einer bestimmten Systemaktivität auftreten. Unter *Ereignis* wird hierbei *"Something that happens at a point in time"* ([Ru91, p.85]) verstanden. Ein Beispiel für ein derartiges Szenario findet sich in Abb. 3.4a Szenarien werden in sogenannte *"event traces"* überführt, die die Abfolgen parametrisierter Handlungen von Objekten visualisieren (siehe Abb. 3.4b). Die einzelnen Elemente dieser traces werden dann umgesetzt in Zustandsübergänge der Zustandsautomaten der beteiligten Objekte, d.h. die Zustände selbst ergeben sich implizit als die Start- und Zielpunkte solcher Übergänge. Hier entsteht das Problem der Identifikation gleicher Zustände aus verschiedenen event traces und natürlich auch der Frage der Vollständigkeit. Hierzu werden von OMT keine Verfahrensvorschläge angeboten.

Die Mikrobank fragt das Konto: Bist Du gelöscht?
Das Konto antwortet: nein
Die Mikrobank teilt der Klasse Geschäftsfall mit, daß eine neue Instanz zu erzeugen ist.
Die Klasse erzeugt eine Instanz. Diese teilt dem Konto mit, daß sie zu buchen ist.
Das Konto bucht den Geschäftsfall und teilt ihm mit:gebucht.
Der Geschäftsfall meldet Mikrobank:fertig.

Abb. 3.4a Beispiel eines Szenarios

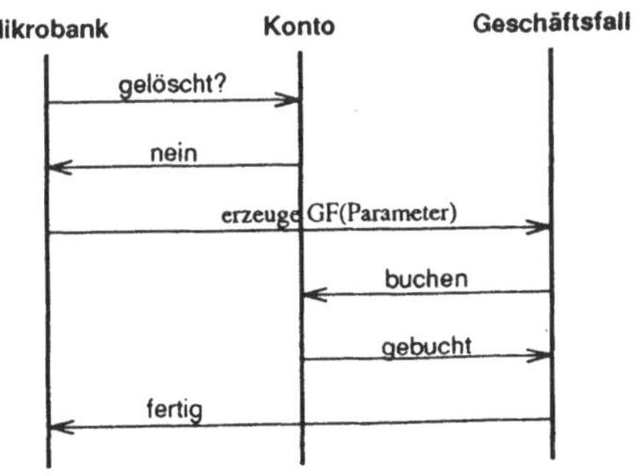

Abb. 3.4.b Event-Trace

Die OMT-Empfehlungen zur Erstellung des Funktionsmodells werden hier nicht wiederholt, da wir den Umgang mit Datenflußdiagrammen als bekannt voraussetzen.

4. Die Anwendung Mikrobank

Bei der Auswahl eines Anwendungsbeispiels für den eingangs genannten Hochschulkurs hatten wir uns drei Rahmenbedingungen vorgegeben:

1. Das Beispiel sollte umfassend genug sein, daß sich daran die wesentlichen Aspekte - sowohl hinsichtlich statischer als auch hinsichtlich dynamischer Aspekte - des objekt-orientierten konzeptuellen Entwurfs demonstrieren und üben ließen.

2. Es sollte in zwei (vollen) Praktikumsstunden vollständig behandelt werden können, d.h. nicht zu umfangreich sein.

3. Das Beispiel sollte dem Gegenstandsbereich nichttechnischer betrieblicher Informationssysteme entstammen. Der Grund hierfür lag weniger in der Tatsache, daß die Mehrzahl der Hochschulkursteilnehmer mit der Planung und Entwicklung solcher Systeme befaßt waren als vielmehr darin, daß die meisten Veröffentlichungen zur objekt-orientierten Analyse dann, wenn es um die Beschreibung dynamischer Aspekte geht, auf technische Gegenstandsbereiche ausweichen [Ru91], [CY91], [SM92]. Dies mag damit zusammenhängen, daß infolge der jahrzehntelangen konventionellen Behandlung sogenannter "kommerzieller" Anwendungen im Sinne einer strikten Trennung zwischen funktionsorientierter Geschäftsvorfallsmodellierung einerseits und strukturorientierter Datenmodellierung andererseits eine objekt-orientierte Behandlung - insbesondere mit entsprechendem Schwerpunkt auf der Dynamik des einzelnen Objekts - ungewöhnlich und damit weniger zugänglich schien. Erst in jüngster Zeit finden sich vermehrt Arbeiten [FS91], die diese Hürde überwinden. Da auch wir hierzu etwas beitragen wollten, fiel die Wahl auf die Kontoverwaltung einer Bank.

Aufgrund der wegen Rahmenbedingung 2 erforderlichen sehr starken Vereinfachung nennen wir diese Anwendung "Mikrobank".

Mikrobank hat zwei Klassen von Konten zu verwalten: ***Sparkonten*** und ***Girokonten***. Sparkonten können ein ***Losungswort***, Girokonten können eine Menge von ***Zeichnungsberechtigten*** haben. Sparkonten kürfen nicht ins ***Soll*** geraten, bei Girokonten ist diesbezüglich ein ***Überziehungsrahmen*** zu beachten. Während Girokonten jederzeit ***gesperrt*** werden können und dann keine ***Auszahlung*** an den ***Kunden*** mehr möglich ist, können Sparkonten nur zur ***Eröffnungszeit*** gesperrt werden. In diesem Fall ist ein ***Datum*** anzugeben, wann die Sperre endet.

Die Anwendung Mikrobank kommuniziert mit einem Bankbediensteten und erfaßt die Daten der ***Überweisung*** oder der ***Ein- bzw. Auszahlung***, die ein Kunde durchführen lassen möchte. Bevor die Daten persistent gemacht werden, müssen sie validiert werden. Dies schließt im Falle der Ansprache eines ***Eigenkontos*** die Prüfung ein, ob das angesprochene Konto gelöscht oder gesperrt ist, ob das gegebenenfalls eingegebene Losungswort korrekt ist und ob im Falle einer Auszahlung von einem Girokonto der ***Verursacher*** des Geschäftsfalles auch zeichnungsberechtigt ist.

Überweisungen werden als Paar bestehend aus einer Auszahlung und einer Einzahlung angesehen. Bewegungsdaten, die ***Fremdkonten*** ansprechen, werden (nicht validiert) als ***Fremdbewegungen*** abgelegt.

Nach erfolgreicher Validierung der eingegebenen Daten wird ein ***Geschäftsfall*** erzeugt und die zu Eigenkonten gehörenden Bewegungen als ***nicht gebuchte Eigenbewegungen*** abgelegt. Jeder Geschäftsfall besteht aus einer oder aus zwei Bewegungen.

Automatisch wird, nachdem die Daten in die Datenbasis aufgenommen sind, die ***Buchung*** durchgeführt. Dabei werden die Eigenbewegungen eines Geschäftsfalles als ***nicht abgerechnete gebuchte Eigenbewegungen*** abgelegt.

Die elementaren Funktionen wie ***eröffnen***, ***löschen***, ***freigeben***, ***sperren***, ***abrechnen*** etc. sind zu spezifizieren (unter Abrechnung ist hier der übliche Quartalsabschluß zu verstehen).

5. Erfahrungen

5.1 Allgemeine Verwendungsaspekte

OMT ist leicht erlernbar und verwendbar:
Die Objektmodellierung fiel uns mit Ausnahme von Multiplicity und Qualification leicht, was wir auf die enge Verwandtschaft mit dem ER-Modell zurückführen. Ähnliches gilt, wenn auch vielleicht nicht im gleichen Ausmaß, für die Verwendung der anderen Teilmodelle. Als günstig weil praktikabel empfanden wir insbesondere den Einsatz endlicher Automaten zur Verhaltensspezifikation. Beispiele siehe Abb. 5.1 und 5.2.

Es fehlen die Mittel zur expliziten Integration von Objekt-, Dynamik- und Funktionsmodell:
Während unserer Entwurfsdiskussion stellten wir fest, daß wir gelegentlich des gewünschten Zusammenhangs der entwickelten Teilschemata nicht mehr sicher waren. Die Ursache hiervon sehen wir darin, daß mit der zunehmenden Größe und Komplexität unsere Schemata unübersichtlich und ihre Zusammenhänge intransparent wurden. Insbesondere lassen sich dann Auswirkungen lokaler Änderungen kaum noch abschätzen.

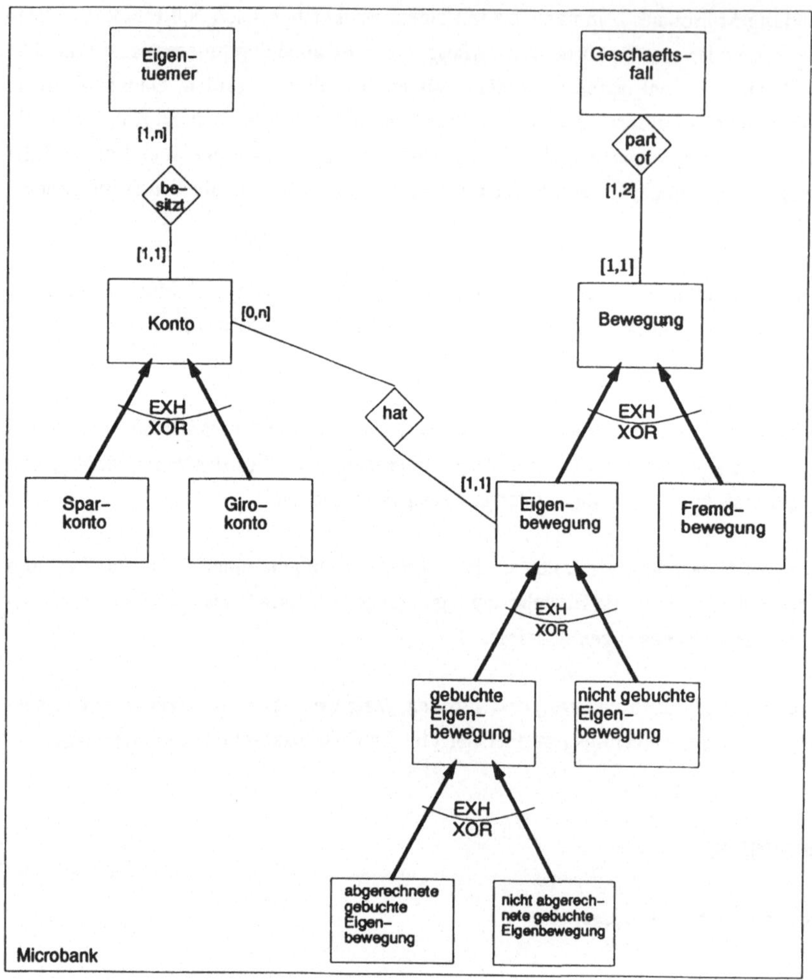

Abb. 5.1: Objektschema von Mikrobank

Voraussetzung zur Behebung dieses Problems z.B. auf der Basis rechnergestützter Entwurfswerkzeuge ist die Integration der Teilmodelle. Hierfür ist ein entsprechendes Metamodell erforderlich, mit dessen Hilfe Schemazusammenhänge ausgedrückt werden können. In Verbindung mit einer Restriktion der Entwurfstätigkeit auf die Verwendung noch zu identifizierender Entwurfsprimitive (im Sinne von [BCN92]) wäre dann unter Umständen die Möglichkeit gegeben, die Wechselwirkungen lokaler und globaler Aspekte eines Schemas automatisch festzustellen und dem Entwerfer bekannt zu machen. Zu diesem Zweck ist OMT selbst einer vollständigen objekt-orientierten Analyse zu unterziehen.

a.)

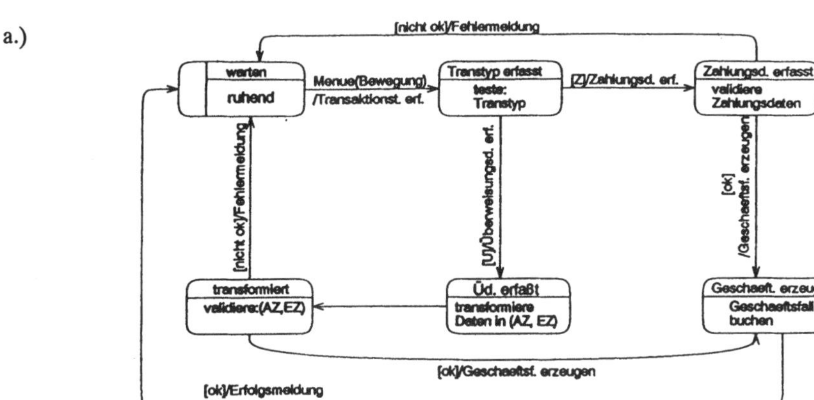

b.)

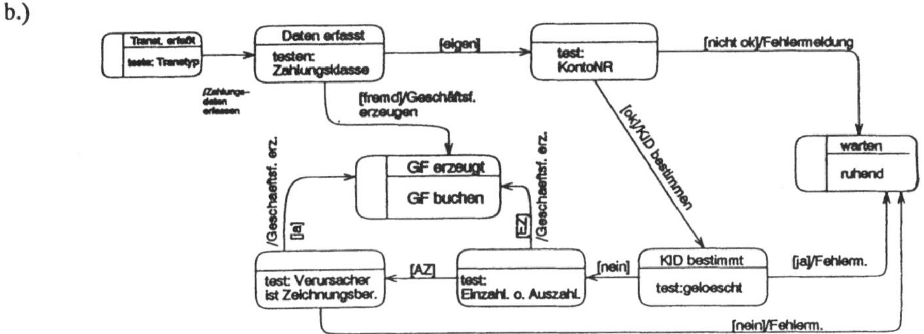

c.)

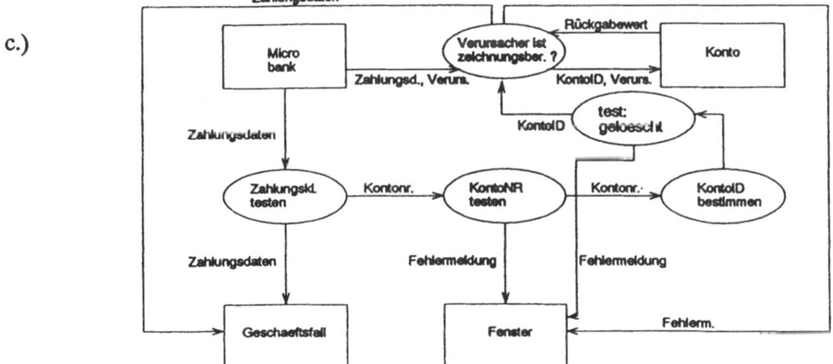

Abb. 5.2 a) Teil des Zustandsdiagramms vom Konto,
b) Verfeinerungen des Zustandes 'Zahlungsdaten erfaßt'
c) Datenflußdiagramm der Aktivität 'validieren Zahlungsdaten'

Fließende Grenzen zwischen Objekt- und Dynamikmodell:
Bei oberflächlicher Betrachtung scheinen die drei Teilmodelle hinsichtlich ihrer Anwendungsbereiche orthogonal. Unsere Erfahrung zeigt aber, daß die Art und Weise, wie die statischen Aspekte modelliert werden, spezifische Auswirkungen auf die zu modellierende Dynamik hat. Beispielsweise erwies es sich während unserer Entwurfsdiskussion gelegentlich als schwierig zu begründen, welche Aspekte des UoD nun mit welchem Mittel zu modellieren sei. So stellte sich etwa die Frage, ob den Bewegungen Merkmale *gebucht?*, *abgerechnet?* zuzubilligen seien, die ihren jeweiligen Zustand zum Ausdruck bringen könnten, oder ob es besser sei, die Bewegungen abhängig von ihrem Status durch verschiedene Klassen migrieren zu lassen. Die Entscheidung fiel zugunsten der zweiten Möglichkeit (siehe Abb. 5.1), weil wir dadurch nicht gezwungen waren, den Objekten aus unserer Sicht "unnatürliche" Merkmale anzudichten. Als Preis hierfür mußten wir mit drei neuen Klassen bezahlen, die lediglich als Behälter dienten. Diese Situation zeigt, daß der Entwerfer einen gewissen Spielraum bei Verwendung der verschiedenen Teilmodelle hat, wobei wir davon ausgehen, daß Vergleichbares auch für den Übergang zwischen Dynamik- und Funktionsmodell gilt.

5.2 Objektmodellierung

Abhängigkeiten zwischen Merkmalen sind nicht beschreibbar:
OMT problematisiert nicht den Umstand, daß zwischen Merkmalen von Objekten Abhängigkeiten bestehen können und bietet dementsprechend auch keine Schreibweise zur Behandlung solcher Abhängigkeiten an. Nach Meinung der Autoren bedeutet dies eine erhebliche Einschränkung der semantischen Mächtigkeit, da Abhängigkeiten zwischen Merkmalen desselben Objekts aber auch zwischen verschiedenen Objekten gegebenenfalls verschiedener Klassen in UoD's der realen Welt häufig auftreten. In der Datenbanktheorie ist dies seit langem bekannt und führte unter anderem beim logischen Entwurf relationaler Datenbanken zur Herausbildung der Normalisierungstheorie. [BPR88] und [SM89] weisen im übrigen darauf hin, daß relationale Implementierungen objekt-orientierter Entwürfe zu dritter Normalform tendieren würden. Dies setzt aber voraus, daß man z.B. funktionale Abhängigkeiten zwischen Merkmalen eines Objekts bereits auf der konzeptuellen Ebene dokumentiert.

Die Modellierungsbegriffe sind mit Ausnahme der Qualification intuitiv anwendbar:
Wie bereits in Abschnitt 5.1 bemerkt, ließen sich bei dem Entwurf unserer verhältnismäßig kleinen übersichtlichen Anwendung die meisten Modellierungsbegriffe von OMT intuitiv anwenden. Ausdrücklich auszunehmen hiervon ist aber die Qualifikation von Beziehungen, deren a priori-Semantik sich uns nicht vollständig erschloß. Spätestens hier machte sich das Fehlen einer formalen Semantik-Definition negativ bemerkbar.

5.3 Dynamik-Modell

Zustandsbegriff ist weiter zu untersuchen:
Geht man entsprechend den Vorschlägen von OMT bei der dynamischen Modellierung vor, so wird der hier verwendete Zustandsbegriff intuitiv einsichtig. Bei näherer Betrachtung zeigt

sich allerdings, daß man zwischen zwei verschiedenen Arten von Zuständen unterscheiden müßte: Mit Aktivitäten verbundene "aktive" Zustände und "auf Ereignis wartende, passive" Zustände, wobei letztere als Äquivalenzklassen von Merkmalsausprägungen aufgefaßt werden können, und damit in etwa den in der Umwelt beobachtbaren Objektzuständen entsprechen. Nach Meinung der Autoren ist hier eine genauere Untersuchung und entsprechende verschärfte Definition erforderlich.

Abstraktionen auch im Dynamik- und Funktionsmodell:
Als konsequent und hilfreich erschien uns die Verwendung der Abstraktionen Generalisation und Aggregation auch im Bereich des Dynamikodells (und später auch des Funktionsmodells). Konkret bietet OMT die Möglichkeit, Ereignisse und Zustände zu verallgemeinern bzw. zu verfeinern, sowie sie zusammenzufassen bzw. zu zerlegen.

Aggregation von Automaten unvollständig definiert:
Eine konzeptuelle Lücke ergibt sich allerdings bei der Aggregation ganzer Automaten entsprechend der Aggregation der zugehörigen Objekte [Ru91]. Die Autoren von OMT sehen hier eine Quelle von Parallelität, allerdings bleibt völlig offen, welchen Beschränkungen diese unterworfen ist, es gibt keine Mittel, Zustandsabhängigkeiten zwischen Komponenten eines Objektes zu formulieren.

5.4 Spezifische Defizite

Unzureichende Behandlung von Parallelität:
In unmittelbarer Erweiterung der mangelnden Behandlung paralleler Zustandsübergänge innerhalb eines (gegebenenfalls aggregierten) Objektes läßt sich auch eine mangelnde Unterstützung der Ausnutzung der dem UoD inhärenten Parallelität diagnostizieren. Zwar behauptet OMT (vergleiche [Ru91, p.202]), daß alle Objekte des UoD grundsätzlich unabhängig voneinander aktiv sein können, daß dies aber im allgemeinen für eine Implementation nicht gelte, sodaß es ein wesentliches Ziel des Systementwurfs sei, herauszufinden für welche Objekte die Möglichkeit gleichzeitiger Aktivität erhalten bleiben müsse, bzw. für welche Objekte dies nicht erforderlich sei. Allerdings wird zur Identifikation dieses Sachverhalts das Dynamikschema herangezogen und festgelegt, daß Objekte dann inhärent parallel sind, wenn sie gleichzeitig Ereignisse erfahren können, ohne miteinander kommunizieren zu müssen. Diese Festlegung führt dazu, daß die oben genannte wesentliche Aufgabe des Entwurfs nicht durch eine semantische Analyse des UoD, sondern durch Analyse von Entwurfsdokumenten "gelöst wird", die nicht zu diesem Zweck angefertigt wurden. Folglich bietet OMT nicht Gewähr, den UoD's inhärente Parallelität zu nutzen und bringt andererseits die Gefahr mit sich, daß aufgrund von Entwurfsfehlern Parallelität unterstellt wird, wo das Gegenteil zu unterstellen wäre. Doch diese Fehler sind nicht leicht zu erkennen.

OMT unterstützt Wiederverwendbarkeit nicht explizit:
Ausmaß und Art der Unterstützung eines an Wiederverwendung orientierten Entwurfs sind unzureichend. Dies ist insofern bemerkenswert, als höhere Wiederverwendbarkeit häufig als

ein wesentlicher Vorteil objekt-orientierter Vorgehensweisen herausgestellt wird ([Su91, p.24], [He92, p.51]). Unser Eindruck von OMT war, daß hier kein Automatismus besteht, sondern daß auf Wiederverwendung ausgerichtete Vorgehensmodelle erforderlich sind. So schien es uns während des Entwurfs manchmal zwingend, zur Konzipierung einer Operation auf Operationen anderer Objekte zurückzugreifen. OMT unterstützte uns in dieser Situation nicht, sondern argumentiert [Ru91, p.169], daß man nicht versuchen solle, Wiederverwendbarkeit zu erzwingen; vielmehr könne man diese am ehesten erreichen, wenn eine neue Aufgabe in einem Kontext zu lösen ist, der ähnlich ist zu einem bereits erfolgreich behandelten. In einem solchen Fall soll ein Schema konstruiert werden, das sowohl eine Verallgemeinerung des neuen als auch des alten Schemas ist. Dies kann sicher dazu beitragen, bereits geleistete Entwurfsarbeit zu nutzen. Allerdings ist zu beachten, daß das allgemeinere Schema gegebenenfalls mehr Arbeit erfordert, als die Lösung der eigentlichen Aufgabe.

Eingeschränkte Wiederverwendbarkeit wird von [Za88] als grundsätzliches Problem top down-orientierter Vorgehensweisen eingeschätzt, solange dabei der Kommunikationsfluß zwischen Komponenten unberücksichtigt bleibt. Dieses Problem läßt sich auf den Entwurf mit OMT übertragen, da keine Methodik zur Gewinnung in sich abgeschlossener (Kommunikations)Zusammenhangskomponenten im Sinne wiederverwendbarer Bausteine angeboten wird. Mit Hilfe der oben schon erwähnten Szenarien und event-traces findet zwar eine Analyse des Kommunikationsflußes statt. Es wurde uns aber nicht klar, wie gewährleistet wird, daß man diesen Fluß auf hinreichend kleine Subsysteme eingrenzt. Damit scheint uns mit OMT Wiederverwendbarkeit von Entwicklungsarbeit nicht wesentlich über das Niveau von Anwendungsbibliotheken gesteigert werden zu können. Diese Steigerung ist bestimmt durch die Effizienz mit der bestehende Entwürfe bzw. Software geändert werden können. Ein erster Schritt in Richtung expliziter Unterstützung von Wiederverwendbarkeit könnte unseres Ermessens die Offenlegung der Import-Schnittstelle von Objekten sein. D.h. zusätzlich sollten Objekte durch die von ihnen "benutzten" Objekte (d.h. solche, deren Operationen sie aufrufen) charakterisiert werden.

6. Logischer Entwurf und Implementierung

Als Demonstrationsbeispiel zum Themenkreis "Objekt-orientierte Datenbanken", der im Rahmen des eingangs erwähnten Hochschulkurses auf die Behandlung des objekt-orientierten konzeptuellen Entwurfs folgte, wurde Mikrobank unter Zuhilfenahme des objekt-orientierten Datenbanksystems O_2 ([Ba88], [De90], [De91], [LR89], [LRV88], [VBD89]) implementiert. Die Möglichkeiten, aus dem konzeptuellen Schema d.h. der Kombination aus Objektmodell, Dynamikmodell und Funktionsmodell unmittelbar ein logisches Schema für O_2 ableiten zu können, standen dabei im Mittelpunkt der Untersuchungen.

Die Überleitung der Klassen des Objektmodells verursachte keine Schwierigkeiten, da sie unmittelbar auf O_2-Klassen abgebildet werden können. Eine ebenso einfache Abbildung von Assoziationen ist dagegen nicht möglich, da das logische Modell von O_2 solche nicht kennt.

Zur Modellierung von Beziehungen zwischen Klassen werden hier vielmehr objektwertige Attribute angeboten. Dies bedeutet insbesondere, daß Assoziationen mit einer Valenz größer zwei bei der Abbildung aufzulösen oder auf eine eigene Klasse abzubilden sind. Dasselbe gilt für nichtfunktionale Assoziationen (allgemeine Relationen) insbesondere dann, wenn sie eigene Attribute haben. Assoziationen ohne eigene Attribute können grundsätzlich durch ein System objektwertiger Attribute realisiert werden, allerdings werden hierfür weder von OMT noch von O_2 Verfahrensregeln angegeben, z.B. betreffend der Richtung der realisierten Attribute. Bei näherer Untersuchung stellt man fest, daß in manchen Fällen bidirektionale Objektreferenzen eingerichtet werden müssen (siehe Abb. 6.1); das hierdurch entstehende Konsistenzproblem hat der Entwickler/die Entwicklerin durch entsprechende Methoden selbst zu behandeln. Detaillierte Untersuchungen hierzu werden in [Kr93] angestellt.

In der vorliegenden Realisierung von Mikrobank wurden sämtliche Assoziationen auf Klassenreferenzen abgebildet, eigene Beziehungsklassen wurden nicht verwendet, da keine mehrstelligen oder funktionalen Assoziationen mit Attributen auftraten. Die Entscheidung, wo derartige Referenzen anzubinden sind und wo gegebenenfalls bidirektionelle Referenzen anzulegen sind, wurde anhand der aus den Datenflußdiagrammen des Funktionsmodells ersichtlichen Input/Output-Beziehungen getroffen. Die Zuordnung von Operationen zu Methoden der einzelnen O_2-Klassen bzw. die Ableitung der diese Operationen implementierenden Algorithmen verlangte eine Kombination von Objekt-, Dynamik- und Funktionsmodell. Im Vergleich zur Strukturableitung verursachte sie größeren Aufwand.

```
class Konto
/* Typdefinition */
type tuple (read knr : integer,                     /* Kontonummer                      */
            read eroeffnungs_dat    : Date,         /* Eröffnungsdatum
            read saldo              : real,         /* Kontostand                       */
            public haben_zinssatz   : real,         /* Haben-Zinsen                     */
            public abrech_dat       : Date,         /* letztes Abrechnungsdatum         */
            read    abrech_saldo    : real,         /* letztes Abrechnungs-Saldo        */
            private kontobewegungen: set(Eigenbewegung),
                                                    /* Menge aller Kontobewegungen */
            read besitzer           : Eigentuemer,  /* Konto-Eigentümer                 */
            private zeichnungsberechtigt: set(string),
                                                    /* Menge der Zeichungsberechtigten */
            private gesperrt        : boolean,      /* gesperrt-Flag                    */
            private aufgeloest      : boolean)      /* gelöscht-Flag                    */

class Bewegung
/* Typdefinition */
public type tuple (bnr: integer,          /* Bewegungsnummer           */
                   b_dat: Date,           /* Datum der Generierung     */
                   art  : string,         /* Art der Bewegung (EZ/AZ)  */
                   betrag:real,           /* Betrag                    */
                   verursacher:string)    /* Verursacher               */

class Eigenbewegung
/* Typdefinition */
inherit Bewegung
public type tuple ( konto  : Konto)  /* Konto-Identifikation des zugehörigen Kontos */
```

Abb. 6.1: O_2-Schema-Ausschnitt von Mikrobank; beachte die Realisierung der Assoziation "hat" durch die Komponente "Kontobewegungen" der Klasse Konto und die Komponente "Konto" der Klasse Eigenbewegung

Welche Operation welcher O_2-Klasse als Methode zuzuordnen sei, konnte zwar je nach Detaillierungsgrad den OMT-Zustandsdiagramm direkt entnommen werden. Wie sie zu implementieren seien und insbesondere, welche Methoden anderer Objekte sie (über message passing) zu referieren hätten, war nicht in ausreichendem Maße erkennbar. Dies lag aber nicht an fehlender Unterstützung durch OMT sondern an der Tatsache, daß wir die Analyseaufgabe im Funktionsmodellbereich zu leicht nahmen und die Datenflußdiagramme zu wenig detailliert ausführten. Ein weiterer Grund ist darin zu sehen, daß wir von der von OMT vorgeschlagenen Vorgehensweise des auf die objekt-orientierte Analyse folgenden objekt-orientierten Designs abgewichen sind, um im Sinne klassischen logischen Entwurfs das konzeptuelle Schema unmittelbar auf die logische O_2-Ebene abzubilden. Wie sich bei einer im nachhinein durchgeführten systematischen Weiterverfolgung im Sinne von OMT zeigte, hätte zumindest das Ausmaß dieser Probleme verringert werden können, da bereits eine stärkere Eingrenzung des Kontexts auf der konzeptuellen Ebene stattgefunden hätte. Um bei der Realisierung der Methoden die durch die einzelnen Zustandsdiagramme des Dynamikmodells vorgebenen Zustandsübergänge einzuhalten, wurde analog der von OMT vorgeschlagenen Methode *(procedure driven approach)* vorgegangen.

Erwähnenswert ist noch die Stellung der einzigen Instanz der Klasse Mikrobank in der Implementierung: Sie bildet ein Aggregat der gesamten Datenbasis und erfüllt damit neben der Rolle des Vorgangsobjektes für die gesamte Benutzerführung auch diejenige der zentralen Verwaltung der erforderlichen Einstiegspunkte in die objekt-orientierte O_2-Datenbasis *(persistency roots)*.

7. Schlußbemerkungen

Anstelle einer Zusammenfassung verweisen wir auf die kursiven Überschriften in Abschnitt 5: Es zeigt sich, daß OMT ein semantisch mächtiges Instrumentarium für den objekt-orientierten konzeptuellen Entwurf bietet, aber dabei allerdings auch einige, nach unserer Ansicht teilweise unnötige, Grenzen hat. Ein Teil davon liegt in der unzureichenden formalen Fundierung begründet, ein anderer Teil darin, daß unseres Ermessens unadäquate Konzepte eingeführt werden.

Wir denken aber, daß sich diese Probleme beheben lassen, entsprechende Untersuchungen stellen wir in unserer Forschungsgruppe derzeit an.

Möchte man allerdings OMT in Projekten der betrieblichen Praxis einsetzen, so scheint uns dies ohne durchgängige Unterstützung durch Entwurfswerkzeuge unmöglich zu sein. Insbesondere müssen solche Werkzeuge mehr als nur grafische Editoren sein, also z.B. Konsistenz- und Vollständigkeitsprüfungen über Teilschemagrenzen hinweg unterstützen, Entwurfsprimitive anbieten, die Simulation endlicher Automaten unterstützen und ähnliches.

8. Literatur

[Ab83] Abbot, R.J.: Program Design from Informal English Descriptions. CACM 26(11) 1983. pp. 882-894.

[Ba88] Bancilhon, F. et al.: The Design and Implementation of O_2, an Object Oriented DB-System. In: Proceedings of Advances in Object Oriented Database Systems. Springer. LNCS 3354. Sept. 1988. pp. 1-22.

[Bo91] Booch, G.: Object-Oriented Design with Applications. Benjamin/Cummings. Redwood City, CA. 1991.

[BCN92] Batini, C.; Ceri, S.; Navathe S.B.: Conceptual Database Design. The Benjamin/Cummings Publ.Co.. 1992.

[BPR88] Blaha, M.; Premerlani, W.; Rumbaugh J.:Relational Database Design Using an Object Oriented Methodology. CACM 31,4(1988). pp. 414-427.

[Br92] Bruegge, B.; Blythe, J.; Jackson, J.; Shufelt, J.: Object-Oriented System Modeling with OMT. OOPSLA'92. pp. 359-376.

[Ce83] Ceri, S. (ed.): Methodology and Tools for Database Design. North-Holland Publ.Co.. 1983.

[Ch76] Chen, P.: The Entity Relationship Model-Toward a Unified View of Data. ACM TODS. 1,1(1976). pp. 9-36.

[CY91] Coad, P.; Yourdon, E.: Object Oriented Analysis. Prentice Hall. Englewood Cliffs. 1991.

[De90] Deux, O. et al.: The Story of O_2. IEEE Trans. on Knowledge and Data Eng. 2,1(1990). pp. 91-108.

[De91] Deux, O. et al: The O_2-System. CACM 34,10 (1991). pp. 34-48.

[EGL89] Ehrich, H.; Gogolla, M.; Liepeck, U.: Algebraische Spezifikation abstrakter Datentypen. Teubner. Stuttgart. 1989.

[Fe92] Felderer, A.: Zur Tabellarisierung natürlich-sprachlicher Anforderungsbeschreibungen. Diplomarbeit. Klagenfurt. 1992.

[FK92] Fichman, R.G.; Kemerer, C.F.: Object-Oriented and Conventional Analysis and Design Methodologies. IEEE Computer 25,10(1992). pp. 22-39.

[FS91] Ferstl, O.K.; Sinz, E.J.: Ein Vorgehensmodell zur Objektmodellierung betrieblicher Informationssysteme im semantischen Objektmodell (SOM). Wirtschaftsinformatik 33,6(1991). pp. 477-491.

[Gr91] Graham, I.:Object Oriented Methods. Addison-Wesley Publishing Company. 1991.

[HC92] Hayes, F.; Coleman, D.: Coherent Models for Object Oriented Analysis. OOPSLA'91. pp. 171-183.

[He92] Henderson-Sellers, B.: A Book of Object-Oriented Knowledge. Prentice Hall. 1992.

[Kr93] Kramer, E.: Objekt-orientierter logischer Datenbankentwurf für O_2. Diplomarbeit. Klagenfurt. Wird fertiggestellt in 1993.

[KS91] Kappel, G.; Schrefl, M.: Object/Behaviour Diagrams. Proceedings of the 7th. International Conference on Data Engineering. 1991. Kobe, Japan.

[LB82] Lawrence Berkeley Laboratory: Integrated Control System: Methodology (bt.dd.20), Electrification (bt.dd.23), Interlockings (bt.dd.62), Run Trains (bt.dd.25), Support Facilities (bt.dd.26), Database (bt.dd.50). 1982.

[LM78] Lockemann, P.C.; Mayr, H.C.: Rechnergestützte Informationssyteme. Springer. 1978.

[LRV88] Lecluse, C.; Richard, P.; Velez,F.:O_2 an Object-Oriented Data Model. In: Proceedings of Advances in Database Technology. Springer LNCS 303. 1988. pp. 556-562.

[LR89] Lecluse, C.; Richard, P.: The O_2 Database Programming Language. In: Proceeedings of the 15th. International Conference on Very Large Databases. 1988. pp. 411-422.

[LSR87] Loomis, M.; Shah, A.; Rumbaugh, J.: An Object Modeling Technique for Conceptual Design. European Conference on Object Oriented Programming. Springer LNCS 276. pp. 192-202.

[MDL87] Mayr, H.C.; Dittrich, K.R.; Lockemann, P.C.: Datenbankentwurf. In: Lockemann, P.C.; Schmidt, J.W.: Datenbank-Handbuch. Springer. 1987.

[Pa89] Paredaens, J.;De Bra, P.; Gyssens, M.; Van Gucht, D.: The Structure of the Relational Database Model. Springer. 1989.

[Ru91] Rumbaugh, J.; Blaha, M.; Premerlani, W.; Eddy, F.; Lorensen, W.: Object Oriented Modelling and Design. Prentice Hall. 1991.

[Rup92] Rupietta, W.: Organisationsmodellierung zur Unterstützung kooperativer Vorgangsbearbeitung. Wirtschafts Informatik 34,1(1992). pp. 26-37.

[SM89] Shlaer, S.; Mellor, S.: An Object Oriented Approach to Domain Analysis. ACM SIGSOFT Software Engineering Notes 14,5(1989). pp. 66-77.

[SM92] Shlaer, S.; Mellor, S.: Object Lifecycles. Prentice-Hall, Inc.. 1992.

[Su91] Sutcliffe, A.G.: Object Oriented Systems Analysis: The Abstract Question. In: Van Assche, F.; Moulin, B.; Rolland, C. (Ed.): Object Oriented Approach in Information Systems. North Holland. 1991. pp. 23-37.

[VBD89] Velez, F.; Bernard, G.; Darnis, V.: The O_2 Object Manager: an Overview. In: Proc. of the 15th International Conference on VLDB. 1989. pp. 357-366.

[WO80] Wedekind, H.; Ortner, E.: Systematisches Konstruieren von Datenbankanwendungen - zur Methodik der Angewandten Informatik. Carl-Hanser-Verlag. 1980.

[Za88] Zahniser, R.: The Perils of Top-Down Design. ACM SIGSOFT Software Engineering Notes 13,2(1988). pp.22-24

Objekt-orientiertes Design und relationale Implementierung eines Standard-Systems für die Personalwirtschaft

Klaus E. Tschira
SAP AG
Neurottstr. 16
D-6900 Walldorf

Abstract

Einige Aspekte der Bildung von Modellen betriebswirtschaftlicher Anwendungsgebiete werden diskutiert. Dabei wird gezeigt, daß die verschiedenen Modelltypen je nach Anwendungsgebiet einen unterschiedlichen Grad der Verbindlichkeit (für eine Vielzahl von Unternehmen) haben. Ein weitgehend verbindliches Modell ist aber die zwingende Voraussetzung für die Entwicklung standardisierter Anwendungssoftware. - Eine flexible und individuelle Organisation gilt immer mehr als kritischer Erfolgsfaktor marktwirtschaftlich operierender Unternehmen. Daher ist für ihre Organisation ein verbindliches, detailliertes Modell weder möglich noch überhaupt wünschenswert. Standardsoftware für die Unternehmens-Organisation muß sich daher auf ein abstrakteres, ein Meta-Modell gründen. Trotzdem ist, wie gezeigt wird, die Konstruktion nicht nur eines geeigneten Tools, sondern einer standardisierten Anwendungssoftware möglich.

1 Betriebswirtschaftliche Modelle

1.1 Modellierung und betriebswirtschaftliche Arbeitsgebiete

1.1.1 Einführung

Die Modellierung der Daten, Prozesse und Organisation von Unternehmen hat in den letzten Jahren weitgehende Anerkennung gefunden als Hilfsmittel zur Entwicklung neuer und zur Beurteilung vorhandener betriebswirtschaftlicher Software-Systeme. An die Modellierung selbst werden unterschiedliche Anforderungen gestellt, je nachdem, ob es sich um firmen-spezifische oder standardisierte Software handelt. Die Anwendbarkeit der verschiedenen Modellierungs-Ansätze hängt zudem vom betrachteten Anwendungsgebiet ab. Wir fassen zur Einführung drei große Anwendungsgebiete ins Auge:

1.1.2 Logistik

Den Gegenstand der Logistik bilden weitgehend pragmatisch-ingenieurmäßig gestaltete, reale Güter und die Prozesse, die zu deren Beschaffung, Erzeugung oder Umwandlung und schließlich zu deren Verteilung dienen. Das Umfeld ist zwar sehr vielgestaltig, doch sind die Modelle - wie die Erfahrung zeigt - weitgehend unternehmens-übergreifend portabel, wenn auch nicht alle Teile eines umfassenden Modells überall anwendbar sein mögen.

1.1.3 Finanzwesen

Verglichen mit der Logistik behandelt das Finanzwesen deutlich abstraktere Dinge. Es blickt jedoch auf eine jahrhunderte-alte Denktradition und Konvergenz der anzuwendenden Begriffe und Methoden zurück - seit einst in der Lombardei die Anfänge der modernen Buchhaltung gelegt wurden. Daher sind auch hier die Daten- und Prozessmodelle weitgehend unternehmensübergreifend portabel. Dementsprechend sind die ältesten Beispiele betriebswirtschaftlicher Standard-Anwendungen durchweg aus dem Bereich des Finanzwesens, speziell der Buchhaltung.

1.1.4 Personalwesen

Ganz anders das Personalwesen. Es entstand als eigene Disziplin erst zaghaft gegen Ende des letzten Jahrhunderts. Seine Abgrenzung gegenüber anderen Funktionsbereichen im Unternehmen variiert in weiten Grenzen. Für unsere Zwecke definieren wir das Personalwesen bzw. die Personalwirtschaft als alles das umfassend, was direkt mit der Beschäftigung von Menschen in einem Unternehmen (oder auch in einer not-for-profit Organisation) zu tun hat.

Die historische Entwicklung sah viele Fachrichtungen, die in häufigem Wechsel nacheinander das personalwirtschaftliche Weltbild prägten.

Als standardisierbar galt daher für lange Zeit nur der Teilbereich der unmittelbar personenbezogenen Datenverwaltung und Personalabrechnung. Hingegen entzog sich das Arbeitsumfeld bis in die jüngste Vergangenheit der Umsetzung in integrierte und standardisierte Anwendungs-Software.

In der Wissenschaft herrscht zwar Klarheit und sogar weitgehender Konsens über die Begriffe, mit denen das Umfeld der menschlichen Arbeit beschrieben wird. In der betrieblichen Praxis werden aber meist (zur tatsächlichen oder vermeintlichen Vereinfachung) nur Teile des BegriffsSystems implementiert.

In den Betrieben und im öffentlichen Sprachgebrauch herrscht zudem ein beträchtlicher Wirrwarr der Begriffe. Davon kann sich jeder täglich überzeugen: Werden tatsächlich Mitarbeiter entlassen oder eingestellt, so kann man in der Zeitung lesen, daß angeblich Arbeitsplätze abgebaut (oder dramatischer: vernichtet) wurden oder daß Stellen geschaffen wurden; einige Seiten weiter wird unter der Rubrik Stellenangebote mitgeteilt, daß eine Planstelle neu besetzt werden soll.

1.2 Problematik der Organisations-Modellierung

1.2.1 Ist Organisation standardwürdig?

Hinsichtlich der zweckmäßigen Organisation von Unternehmen gibt es so viele unterschiedliche Modell-Vorstellungen wie Sand am Meer, schlimmer noch: es gibt ständig neue. Weder ist damit zu rechnen, daß sich eine bestimmte Organisationsform durchsetzt, noch ist dies überhaupt wünschenswert: vielmehr wird zunehmend klarer, daß die organisatorische Flexibilität selbst als ein kritischer Erfolgsfaktor eines Unternehmens angesehen werden muß. Die (Ablauf- und Aufbau-) Organisation variiert daher nicht nur von Unternehmen zu Unternehmen; sie wechselt potentiell auch innerhalb eines Unternehmens, einerseits im Laufe der Zeit und andererseits zwischen Unternehmensteilen.

1.2.2 Das SoftwareAngebot im Arbeitsumfeld

Angesichts dieser Situation ist es nicht verwunderlich, daß die Software-Landschaft des Personalwesens durch viele 'Insel-Lösungen' für einzelne Teilgebiete - sowohl bei firmenspezifischer als auch bei standardisierter Software - geprägt ist. Durchgängige, umfassende Software-Systeme für die Personalwirtschaft hingegen sind, sowohl als individuelle Entwicklung wie als standardisierte Anwendung, ziemlich selten.

1.3 Zur Portabilität der verschiedenen Modellklassen

1.3.1 Unternehmensdatenmodell: UdM (DM) oder UDm (OM)?

Der Terminus UnternehmensDatenModell ist mehrdeutig und daher klärungsbedürftig. Ich plädiere dafür, die zwei möglichen Bedeutungen scharf zu trennen.

Ein Unternehmensdaten-Modell ist ein Modell der Daten, mit denen das Unternehmen umgeht. Es ist die Meta-Beschreibung des Zustands oder Bestands der (finanziellen, materiellen und personellen) Ressourcen und der Ereignisse, die ebendiese Zustände oder Bestände verändern. Wir wollen es der Klarheit wegen das 'Daten-Modell' (DM) nennen.

Davon wohl zu unterscheiden ist das Unternehmens-Datenmodell als datenmäßiges Modell des Unternehmens selbst, oder genauer: seiner Aufbau- und Ablauf-Organisation. Wir wollen es das 'Organisations-Modell' (OM) nennen.

1.3.2 Interdependenz von DM und OM

Im Sprachgebrauch und in der Modellierungspraxis schwingt stets etwas von beiden Bedeutungen mit. Das Organisations-Modell ist zwar noch ohne das Daten-Modell und ohne das Funktions-Modell denkbar, doch bleibt es so völlig unverbindlich und ist bestenfalls von theoretischem Interesse. Das Daten-Modell kommt nur im trivialen Grenzfall (eines nicht gegliederten Unternehmens) ohne jegliche Aspekte des Organisations-Modells aus, denn selbstverständlich müssen die Daten (zumindest in gewissem Umfang) organisatorischen Einheiten zugeordnet werden.

1.3.3 Vermischung von DM und OM ist teuer

Für die Modellierung eines einzelnen Unternehmens mag die Unterscheidung spitzfindig erscheinen und entbehrlich sein. Wenn während der mutmaßlichen Nutzungsdauer der nach einem Modell gebauten Software nicht mit organisatorischen Änderungen gerechnet werden braucht, kann man guten Gewissens Daten beider Art gemeinsam modellieren. (Das bekannt hohe Verhältnis von Wartungskosten zu Entwicklungskosten insbesondere bei betriebswirtschaftlicher Software spricht allerdings nicht dafür, daß der betrachtete Fall besonders häufig in der Realität vorkommt. Wohl aber wird er immer wieder unterstellt.)

Daher tut man ganz allgemein gut daran, das Daten-Modell so weit wie irgend möglich vom Organisations-Modell zu trennen. Je besser diese Trennung gelingt oder je allgemeinverbindlicher die Rudimente der Organisation im Datenmodell sind, umso leichter ist das Gesamtmodell auf andere Unternehmen portabel und desto stabiler ist es im Laufe der Zeit.

Wir erkennen daraus, daß ein geschickter Kompromiß zwischen zuviel und zuwenig Organisationsmodellierung entscheidend (im Sinne einer notwendigen, aber nicht hinreichenden Bedingung) für die Portabilität und den Wartungsaufwand von Standard-Anwendungssoftware im Finanzwesen, der Logistik und im Personalwesen ist. Wie bereits einleitend bemerkt, gelingt die Datenmodellierung mit einem Minimum an Organisation in den beiden erstgenannten Bereichen hinreichend, in der Personalwirtschaft kommt man um eine explizite Modellierung der Organisation nicht mehr herum.

1.3.4 Standardisierung der OM?!

Personalwirtschaft umfaßt neben den administrativen und abrechnenden Funktionen auch planerische Aufgaben und Dienste, die ohne detaillierten Bezug zur Organisation nicht sinnvoll angegangen werden können.

Für die Organisation von Unternehmen ist ein Modell mit demselben Grad an Konkretheit wie wir ihn beim Datenmodell anstreben, nicht wünschenswert: Auf einem konkreten Modell basierende Individual-Software würde die immer wichtiger werdende organisatorische Flexibilität hemmen; so konzipierte Standard-Software hätte keinen ausreichend großen Markt, der ihre Entwicklung, Vermarktung und Wartung für Anbieter wie Anwender wirtschaftlich interessant machte.

Als Lösung bietet sich die Organisations-Modellierung auf einer höheren Abstraktionsebene an. Wie aber soll dann noch konkrete Anwendungslogik als Standard-Software realisierbar sein?

2 Organisations-Modellierung mit besonderer Berücksichtigung der personalwirtschaftlichen Aspekte

2.1 Das Organisationsmodell aus Sicht der objektorientierten Analyse

Die Objekte und Begriffe, mit denen man in der Organisationslehre und in der Personalwirtschaft umgeht, haben geläufige Klassen-Bezeichnungen, die aus der Umgangssprache bekannt sind. Sie stehen zueinander in mannigfachen, unmittelbar aus dem Wortlaut intuitiv einsichtigen, Beziehungen. Die Objekte und ihre Beziehungen untereinander betreffen etwa ...

* Die Gliederung eines Unternehmens im weitesten Sinne: Konzern, Unternehmensgruppe, (Dach-, Konzern- Tochter-, Auslands-, Beteiligungs-) Gesellschaft, Niederlassung, Region, Division, Sparte, Ressort, Direktionsbereich, (Haupt-, Unter-, Stabs-) Abteilung, (Haupt-, Ober-, Unter-) Gruppe, Team, Task-Force, Arbeitskreis, Special-Interest-Group und viele andere mehr. Sie alle abstrahieren wir zur Objektklasse 'Organisationseinheit'.

  Eine Organisationseinheit kann zu anderen in mannigfachen Beziehungen stehen. Sie 'ist Teil von', 'gliedert sich in', 'besitzt einen Anteil von ...% an', 'untersteht', u.s.w..

  Organisationseinheiten 'haben' (qualitative) 'Aufgaben' und (quantitative und qualitative, terminierte) 'Zielvorgaben', die ihrerseits in untergeordnete Aufgaben und Zielvorgaben 'zerfallen'.

* Das Umfeld der menschlichen Arbeit: Die Aufgaben werden in sinnvoller Weise zu 'Stellen' zusammengefaßt, die die Arbeitsinhalte qualitativ beschreiben. Nach Arbeitsanfall im Rahmen einer Organisationseinheit und nach vorgesehener Arbeitszeit werden 'Planstellen' geschaffen und den Organisationseinheiten zugeordnet. Planstellen beschreiben also den organisatorischen Kontext, während die physikalischen Umstände der Arbeit als 'Arbeitsplatz' beschrieben werden. Ein Mensch wird aus Sicht der Personalwirtschaft zum 'Mitarbeiter', der eine Planstelle 'besetzt' oder 'als potentieller Nachfolger für' andere Planstellen gilt.

  Mitarbeiter 'besitzen' Kenntnisse, Fähigkeiten, Fertigkeiten, kurz 'Qualifikationen', während Aufgaben, Stellen, Planstellen, Arbeitsplätze diese Qualifikationen 'anfordern'; Vielleicht stellt auch ein Team oder eine Task-Force (als Unterklasse der Organisationseinheit) gewisse qualitative und quantitative 'Anforderungen'. Schließlich bilden Qualifikationen/Anforderungen untereinander Spezialisierungs- und Generalisierungs-Beziehungen.

2.2 Implementierungs-Optionen

2.2.1 RDBMS?

Angesichts dieser, noch lange fortsetzbaren Vielfalt von ObjektKlassen und unterschiedlichen Verknüfungstypen, angesichts auch der uneinheitlichen, teils sogar widersprüchlichen Verwendung der Begriffe stößt eine unmittelbare Implementierung nach dem inzwischen standardisierten und in der Wirtschaft akzeptierten Relationenmodell auf enorme Schwierigkeiten.

Nach dem RDBM würde man die normalisierten Attribute der Objekte als Relationen darstellen, die wie üblich durch Fremdschlüssel miteinander verbunden sind. Die semantische Vielfalt der unterschiedlichen Verknüpfungen wäre nicht formal darstellbar; zudem wäre die unterschiedliche Behandlung von 0/1:1- und m:n-Beziehungen unbefriedigend. Die verschiedenen Tabelleneinträge, die ein einziges Objekt betreffen,

Das Datenmodell der Personalplanung

Gesamt-Überblick

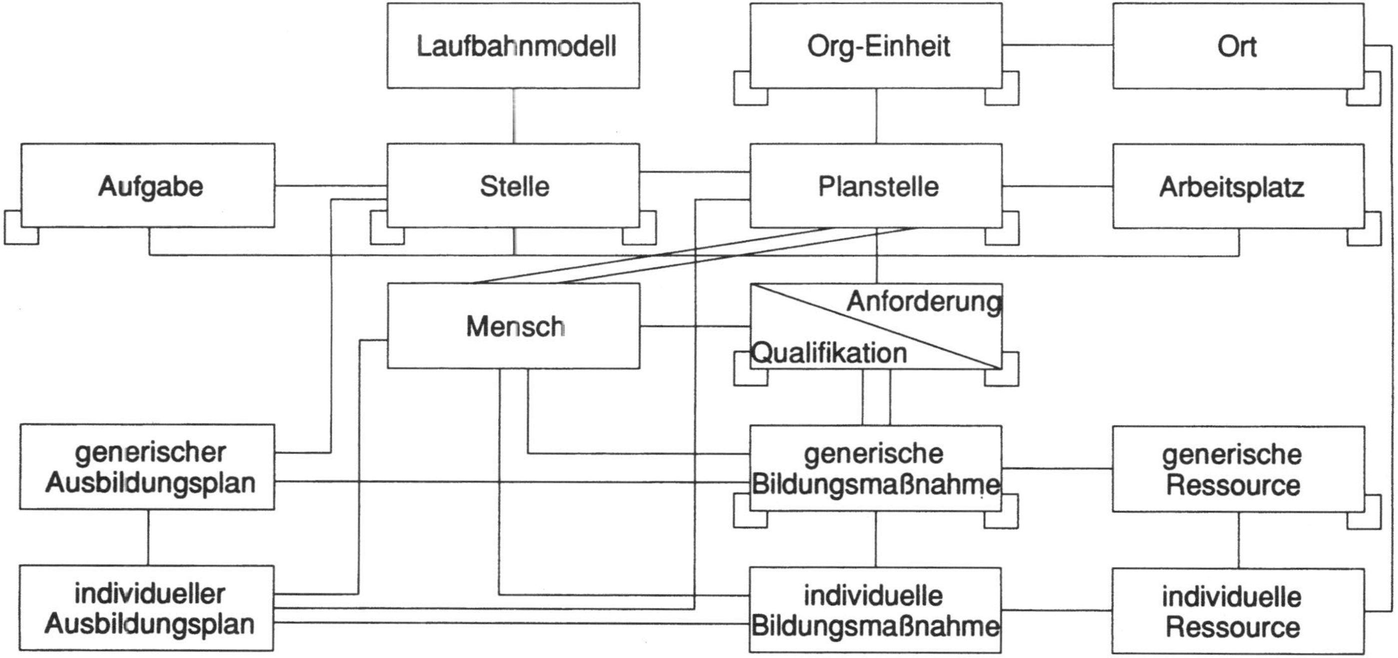

SAP Aktiengesellschaft / D-6909 Walldorf

hätten jeweils gleiche Partialschlüssel, die auf den eben dieses Objekt identifizierenden Tabelleneintrag in einer natürlich objektklassen-spezifischen Tabelle hinweisen. Wahlweise Zuordnung eines Attributs zu Objekten verschiedener Klassen würde eine Aufblähung des Codes zur Folge haben; ebenso würde jede Erweiterung des Katalogs von Attributtypen und Objektklassen oder die Änderung der Zuordnung zwischen Attributtypen und Objektklassen den Code aufblähen, und zwar auch für triviale Funktionen, die beispielsweise neue Attribute nur unspezifisch bearbeiten. Die einheitliche Modellierung im Großen und im Kleinen ließe zudem die Übersichtlichkeit verschwinden.

2.2.2 OO Entwicklungs- und Ablauf-Umgebungen?

Andererseits sind die inzwischen zahlreich angebotenen, objekt-orientierten Programmierungswerkzeuge und Datenbanken noch weit von einer Standardisierung durch ANSI oder ISO entfernt; es existiert nicht einmal ein de facto Industrie-Standard. Jedes eventuell taugliche OO System für sich hat nur eine geringe Verbreitung in dem für Standard-Personalwirtschafts-Systeme relevanten Markt der mittleren und großen Unternehmen. Die OOPLs und OODBMSs schieden daher für unsere Zwecke von vornherein aus; damit ist nichts über ihre eventuelle Tauglichkeit für individuelle Implementierungen ausgesagt.

Als Implementierungssprache wählten wir stattdessen ABAP/4, die 4GL der SAP. Damit ist die Portierung in sämtliche Hard- und Software-Umgebungen, die von den SAP-Systemen R/2 (Mainframes) und R/3 (verschiedene Client/Server Systeme) unterstützt werden, sichergestellt. Gleichermaßen ist die Portierung in Länder mit anderer Sprache, Schrift etc vorbereitet.

2.2.3 OO und RDBMS!

Die oben geforderte Notwendigkeit zur flexiblen Abbildung unterschiedlichster Organisations-Philosophien besteht nur im Großen. Im Kleinen gibt es, wie in anderen Anwendungsgebieten, natürlich auch im Personalwesen Inseln des Pragmatismus. Für bestimmte Aufgabenstellungen benötigt man ebenso bestimmte Grunddaten. Das legt eine mehrschichtige Modellbildung nahe.

3 Das Zwei-Schichten Modell der Personalwirtschaft

Deshalb wurde eine Zwei-Schichten-Architektur gewählt.

In der 'O-Schicht' werden allgemeine Objekte bearbeitet, miteinander verknüpft, und Strukturen, die aus Objekten und Verknüpfungen gebildet werden, ausgebeutet und dargestellt.

In der 'A-Schicht' werden die Attribute der Objekte behandelt. Die Attribute der Objekte sind als Relationen in einem relationalen Datenbank-System dargestellt.

3.1 Systemsteuerungen der O-Schicht

Jedes Objekt ist eindeutig einer Objektklasse zugeordnet und durch eine Objekt-Nummer identifiziert. Es wird als eine Menge von Attributen dargestellt. In Steuerungstabellen werden folgende Systemeigenschaften definiert:

* Die zulässigen Objektklassen. und ihre Bezeichnungen in mehreren Sprachen.
* Die Zusammenfassung von Objektklassen zu Superklassen.
* Die Anwendbarkeit der Attributtypen pro Objektklasse und die Existenzeigenschaften der Attribute.

Die Verknüpfung zweier Objekte wird durch je ein Attribut der beiden verknüpften Objekte symmetrisch dargestellt. Damit verschiedenste Verknüpfungen einheitlich bearbeitet werden können, wird für alle Verknüpfungen ein einziger Attributtyp verwendet, der bei jeder Objektklasse anwendbar ist. Die Verknüpfungen sind ihrerseits typisiert. Wiederum werden in Steuerungstabellen festgelegt:

* Die definierten Verknüpfungstypen, ihre Bezeichnung in mehreren Sprachen und in beiden Richtungen. (Beispiel: <Planstelle> 'ist besetzt durch' <Mitarbeiter>, <Mitarbeiter> 'besetzt' <Planstelle>.)
* Die Zulässigkeit der Verknüpfung pro Objektklassen-Paar und Verknüpfungstyp.

Durch die Verknüpfungen werden Objekte zu homogenen oder heterogenen Hierachien oder Netzen verbunden. Der interaktive Benutzer kann zwischen verbundenen Objekten innerhalb einer solchen Struktur längs der existierenden Verknüpfungen beliebig navigieren. Für die automatische, interaktionsfreie Bearbeitung von Strukturen können sogenannte Pfade vordefiniert werden; ein Pfad ist eine benannte, alternierende Folge von Objektklassen und Verknüpfungstypen.

Es gibt eine Vielzahl von Methoden, die auf alle Objekte beliebiger Objektklassen angewendet werden können. Unter anderem sind implementiert:

* Transaktionen für die Erfassung, Pflege und Anzeige aller anwendbaren Attribute eines Objektes beliebiger Klasse.
* Transaktionen für das Kopieren, Löschen, Anzeigen und Ausdrucken, Versenden innerhalb eines Rechnerverbundes (z.B. zwischen Server und Client oder zwischen Database Servern), sowie auf die Änderung von Statusvariablen und die Änderung der zeitlichen Gültigkeit. Diese Methoden beziehen sich auf ...
  * einzelne Objekte,
  * alle Objekte, die spezifizierte Selektionsbedingungen erfüllen, oder auf

* alle Objekte, die mit einem angegebenen Wurzelobjekt einer Baumstruktur durch einen angegebenen Pfad verbunden sind, die also eine wohldefinierte Teilstruktur bilden.

* Prüfung der Zugriffsberechtigung nach Maßgabe einer ausgezeichneten Hierarchie.

Zur Realisierung ihrer Aufgaben greifen die Methoden der O-Schicht gegebenenfalls auf die der A-Schicht zurück, etwa beim Anzeigen der vorhandenen Attribute eines Objektes. Die Mehrzahl der Methoden bearbeitet jedoch ganze Objekte, d.h. alle Attribute ohne Beachtung des Attributtyps oder gar der speziellen Inhalte.

3.2 Systemsteuerungen der A-Schicht

Die Steuerungsmechanismen der A-Schicht beziehen sich auf die speziellen Attributtypen. Diese sind ihrerseits als Relationen definiert.

Die in der A-Schicht implementierten Methoden beziehen sich auf die konkreten Dateninhalte der verschiedenartigen Attribute. Sie sind größtenteils ad hoc codiert, je nach der Zweckbestimmung der Attributtypen.

Formalisiert sind jedoch u.a.:

* Steuerung der optionalen oder obligatorischen, Einfach- oder Mehrfach-Existenz von Attributen vom selben Attributtyp pro Objekt.

* Normierung von Gewichtsfaktoren auf 100%.

* Prüfung der Zugriffsberechtigung je nach Attributtyp, Zugriffsart (gar nicht, nur lesend, uneingeschränkt, Vier-Augen-Prinzip).

4 Erfahrungen im praktischen Einsatz

Die dargestellte Zwei-Schichten-Architektur ist die Grundlage eines umfassenden Systems für die Personalwirtschaft. Sie kommt voll zum Tragen in den Bereichen Organisation, Planung und Controlling, in eingeschränktem Umfang auch in der Personal-Administration und Zeitwirtschaft.

Das beschriebene System ist unter den Bezeichnungen SAP R/2 RP (Realtime Personalwirtschaft) für Mainframes und SAP R/3 HR (Human Resource Management) kommerzialisiert.

4.1 System-Konfigurierbarkeit

Bei Erweiterungen des Leistungsumfangs des Systems, sei es durch zusätzliche Installation bereits existierender Komponenten, sei es durch Hinzunahme gänzlich neuer Einrichtungen, erweist sich das System als sehr änderungsfreundlich und erweiterungsfähig.

Die Unterstützung zusätzlicher Funktionen erfordert eine oder mehrere der folgenden Maßnahmen:

* Die Erweiterung des O-Modells um zusätzliche Objektklassen.
* Die Erweiterung des O-Modells um zusätzliche Verknüpfungstypen.
* Die Erweiterung der A-Schicht um zusätzliche Attributtypen und diesbezügliche Methoden.
* Die Einführung zusätzlicher Methoden der O- oder A-Schicht oder (in seltenen Fällen) die Änderung bereits bestehender Methoden.

Dabei sind die Erweiterungen des O-Modells besonders einfach durch bloße Tabelleneinträge zu realisieren. Die Methoden der O-Schicht sind davon nicht betroffen. Alt-Daten brauchen in der Regel nicht umgesetzt zu werden. Die O-Methoden sind gegen solche Änderungen immun. Bei einer streng-relationalen Implementierung würden derartige Änderungen stattdessen stets auch Erweiterungen im Code zur Folge haben, sodaß die Programme bei gleichbleibender Funktionalität (etwa: Transportieren eines ganzen Objektes) beständig größer würden.

4.2 Das Modell als Kommunikations-Unterstützung

Das O-Modell kommt - wie dargetan - ohne großen technischen Ballast aus. Erklärt man es an anwendungsnahen Beispielen ohne viel Abstraktion, dann stellt sich auch bei von OO-Technologie unbelasteten Zuhörern schnell ein zutreffendes, intuitives Verständnis ein. Insofern ist der Modellierungsansatz gewissermaßen ein natürlicher Ansatz auf dem richtigen Abstraktionsniveau. Auf dieser Grundlage können dann leicht bereits implementierte Funktionen erklärt und gewünschte Zusatzfunktionen diskutiert werden.

4.3 Akzeptanz des vorgeschlagenen Modells

Wie bereits erwähnt, sind in der Organisationspraxis unvollständige Näherungen des vollständigen Modells des Arbeitsumfeldes sehr verbreitet; so denkt man oft, je nach Hintergrund, 'vereinfachend' statt in Stellen, Planstellen und Arbeitsplätzen nur in Stellen oder Planstellen oder Arbeitsplätzen. Verständlicherweise hängt jeder an seinem hergebrachten Modell. Ein im Wettbewerb stehendes Produkt für denselben Funktionsbereich war nahezu unverkäuflich, weil es nur das vollständige Modell der

Organisationslehre unterstützte, welches hier lediglich als empfohlenes Muster angeboten wird. Durch das Fehlen des Zwanges, das eigene Modell aufgeben zu müssen, werden die meisten Anwender zur Erkenntnis der Vorzüge des vollständigen Modells geführt.

Literaturhinweise

M.L. Brodie, J. Mylopoulos, J.W. Schmidt, (Eds.) (1984): On Conceptual Modelling - Perspectives from Artificial Intelligence, Databases, and Programming Languages; Springer, New York.

P. Coad, E. Yourdon (1990): Object-Oriented Analysis; Prentice Hall, Englewood Cliffs.

B. Cox, (1986): Object-Oriented Programming; Addison-Wesley, Reading.

K.R. Dittrich, U. Dayal, A.P. Buchmann, (Eds.) (1991): On Object-Oriented Database Systems; Springer, New York.

A. Goldberg (1984): Smalltalk-80 The Interactive Programming Environment; Addison-Wesley, Reading.

A. Goldberg, D. Robson (1985): Smalltalk-80 The Language and its Implementation; Addison-Wesley, Reading.

W. Kim, F.H. Lochovsky, (Eds.) (1989): Object-Oriented Concepts, Databases, and Applications; Addison-Wesley, Reading.

G. Krasner (ed.) (1984): Smalltalk-80 Bits of History, Words of Advice; Addison-Wesley, Reading.

B. Meyer (1988): Object-Oriented Software Construction; Prentice Hall, Englewood Cliffs.

S. Shlaer, S. Mellor (1988): Object-Oriented Systems Analysis; Prentice Hall, Englewood Cliffs.

J.F. Sowa, (1984): Conceptual Structures - Information Processing in Mind and Machine; Addison-Wesley, Reading.

ooSEM - Eine objektorientierte Entwicklungsmethode für Software (Entstehung und Anwendung)

Reinhard Patels

Programm- und Systementwicklung (PSE)

Abteilung für Qualitätssicherung (PSE QS)

Siemens Österreich

Gudrunstraße 11

A-1100 Wien, Österreich

1 Einleitung

1.1 Entwicklung der Methode

Objektorientierte Entwicklung ist nicht nur die gezielte Anwendung von Sprachmitteln angepaßter oder neugeschaffener Programmiersprachen, sondern erfordert auch ein entsprechend methodisches Vorgehen bei Analyse und Design. Dies erfordert eine Adaptierung des bisherigen strukturierten Entwicklungskonzeptes, um auch das "neue" Paradigma abdecken zu können.
So entstand die Idee, eine eigene Entwicklungsmethode zu schaffen, die sich zwar so eng wie möglich an der bisherigen strukturierten Methode orientieren, aber eben auf die speziellen Bedürfnisse bei objektorientierter Entwicklung eingehen und damit eine Alternative darstellen sollte.

2 ooSEM - eine Entwicklungsmethode

2.1 Prinzipieller Aufbau

Die Methode ooSEM bietet einen Rahmen, der alle gängigen Entwurfsmethoden für objektorientierte Entwicklung umfaßt. Dabei werden ungenaue oder gar nicht vorhandene Aussagen dieser Methoden über Phaseneinteilung, auszuführende Tätigkeiten und entstehende Ergebnisse des Entwicklungsprozesses präzisiert bzw. ergänzt. Es wird ein eigenes Lebenszyklusmodell definiert. Der Entwicklungsprozeß wird dabei in mehrere getrennte Phasen

aufgeteilt, für die jeweils alle Voraussetzungen, typischen Tätigkeiten und geforderten Ergebnisse aufgelistet sind. Diese Struktur bildet einen Vorschlag (auf der Basis eines "Baukastensystems"), wie die genannten Elemente sinnvoll kombiniert werden können, wobei für jedes durchgeführte Projekt die tatsächlich verwendete Struktur definiert werden muß.
Die Beschreibung der Methode besteht aus einem Entwicklunghandbuch (Beschreibung des strukturellen Aufbaus) und einem Entwicklungsverfahrenshandbuch (Beschreibung der technischen Durchführung der Einzelschritte).

2.2 Lebenszyklusmodell

Der Entwicklungsprozeß für Software wird in die Phasen **Planung** (Anstoß, Studie), **Entwurf** (Klassenentwurf, Subsystementwurf), **Realisierung** (Klassenspezifikation, Klassenimplementierung, Integration, Systemtest, Produktabnahme) und **Einsatz** eingeteilt.
Eine Phase besteht aus einer geordneten Menge von Aufgaben, die zu einer geordneten Menge von Resultaten führt, die normalerweise wieder die Eingangsgrößen für die nächste Phase darstellen.
Eine Produktdatenbank verwaltet die Ergebnisse des aktuellen Projekts (Configuration-Management).

2.3 Phasentätigkeiten

Verschiedene Phasen betrachten das System aus verschiedenen Blickwinkeln und produzieren entsprechend unterschiedliche Modelle (gegebenenfalls Wiederverwendung bestehender Elemente): Die **Planung** beschreibt die eigentliche Problemstellung (WAS soll entwickelt werden). Der **Entwurf** betrachtet die Lösungsmöglichkeiten (WIE sollen die Anforderungen realisiert werden). Das Planungsmodell wird dabei durch implementierungs- und umgebungsspezifische Objekte, Methoden und Verbindungen ergänzt (Darstellung der gewählten Algorithmen). Die **Realisierung** - zielt auf die Umsetzung der objektorientierten Modelle auf eine Programmiersprache ab.

2.4 Phasenergebnisse

Die Resultate einer Phase bei objektorientierter Entwicklung bestehen u.a. aus objektorientierten Modellen, die das System aus dem gerade gegebenen Blickwinkel beschreiben. Jedes objektorientierte Modell repräsentiert dabei eines von vier "Standbeinen": Die **statische Sicht** beschreibt die Objekte eines Systems mit all ihren Eigenschaften und ihren Verbindungen untereinander. Die **dynamische Sicht** beschreibt die Zustandswechsel von Objekten als Reaktion auf Ereignisse im System und die Versorgung des Systems mit Ablaufkontrollsignalen durch die Objekte. Die **funktionale Sicht** beschreibt die Verarbeitung von Daten durch Methoden der Objekte des Systems. Die **Sicht des strukturellen Aufbaus** des Systems beschreibt die Subsysteme des Systems, die interne Struktur und die externen Zusammenhänge mit anderen Subsystemen oder Objekten.

2.3 Vergleich zur nicht-oo Methode (SEM)

Prinzipiell bleibt ooSEM unverändert bei Projektmanagement, Projektorganisation, Configuration-Management und Qualitätssicherung, wenngleich für die Erstellung eines Projektplanes zusätzlich eine Entscheidung über die Entwicklungsmethode getroffen werden muß, und das Configuration-Management die neue Dokumentenstruktur zu berücksichtigen hat.

Die Dokumente sind objektorientiert und über den gesamten Projektverlauf einheitlich ausgerichtet.

Subsystementwurf und Testkonzepte sind völlig auf die klassen- und objektorientierten Strukturen angepaßt.

3 Probleme bei Anlauf der oo-Technik

- Erste Implementierungen zu Beginn 1987 (Schwierigkeiten mit Compilern und anderen Werkzeugen).
- Unsere Auftraggeber schrieben (und schreiben) den Einsatz der verschiedensten Analyse- und Entwurfsmethoden vor (SNI-MOOD, SOM usw.)

Methoden und Werkzeuge

Objektspezifikation von Benutzerschnittstellen in TROLL*

Gunter Saake
Thorsten Hartmann
Ralf Jungclaus

Abt. Datenbanken, Techn. Universität Braunschweig
Postfach 3329, W-3300 Braunschweig
E-mail {saake|hartmann|jungclau}@idb.cs.tu-bs.de

Zusammenfassung

Die konzeptionelle Modellierung des Weltausschnittes, der durch ein Informationssystem dargestellt werden soll, ist die erste Phase des Systementwurfes. Das konzeptionelle Modell ist damit die Grundlage der Implementierung. In diesem Modell sind das später zu implementierende System *und* seine Umgebung integriert. Zwischen diesen beiden Komponenten ist die Benutzerschnittstelle einzuordnen. Die Definition dieser Schnittstelle ist damit der konzeptionellen Modellierung zuzuordnen, während ihre konkrete Darstellung im Verlaufe des Designs gestaltet wird.

In unserem Ansatz erfolgt die Modellierung der Benutzerschnittstelle in dem Formalismus, der auch zur Modellierung des Gesamtsystems verwendet wird. Das Systemdesign trennt dabei die Teile des im Modell dargestellten Weltauschnittes, die in eine interne Repräsentierung des Systems abgebildet werden, von den Teilen, die eine Abstraktion des Benutzers bzw. der Außenwelt repräsentieren. Der beschriebene Ansatz *integriert* die Beschreibung persistenter Datenbestände, deren Manipulation sowie die Beschreibung (re)aktiver Komponenten wie der Benutzer bzw. der Systemumgebung.

1 Einleitung

Die Phase des *konzeptionellen Systementwurfs* hat die Erstellung einer Spezifikation eines abstrakten Modells des Informationssystems zum Ziel. Diese Spezifikation wird oft auch *konzeptionelles Modell* genannt. Das konzeptionelle Modell sollte soweit als möglich *formal* sein, da es die Grundlage der Systementwicklung und somit einen Vertrag zwischen Anwendern und Systementwicklern darstellt. Um dieser Forderung nachzukommen, muß das konzeptionelle Modell von Implementierungsentscheidungen abstrahieren. Es muß lediglich festlegen, *was* realisiert werden soll, nicht jedoch *wie* dieses geschehen soll.

Die Betrachtungsweise eines Weltausschnitts als ein System interagierender Komponenten ist prinzipiell der *objektorientierten* Sichtweise sehr nahe. Beim objektorientierten

*Die Arbeit wurde teilweise gefördert von der EG in der ESPRIT WG IS-CORE II (Information Systems – COrrectness and REusability). Die Arbeit von Thorsten Hartmann und Ralf Jungclaus wird von der Deutschen Forschungsgemeinschaft unter Sa 465/1-2 gefördert. Projektleiter sind G. Saake und H.-D. Ehrich.

Entwurf von Softwaresystemen [Boo90, RBP+90, CF92] werden die Systemkomponenten durch Objekte repräsentiert, die sowohl statische Struktur als auch dynamisches Verhalten aufweisen. Wesentlich ist dabei, daß Objekte eingekapselt sind, somit einen *lokalen Zustand* und *lokale Aktionen* beinhalten. Das Systemverhalten ergibt sich dann aus dem lokalen Verhalten der Komponentenobjekte und der Kommunikation zwischen ihnen.

Der TROLL-Ansatz zur Spezifikation von Informationssystemen versucht die Konzepte semantischer Datenmodelle mit objektorientierten Konzepten sowie Konzepten formaler Ansätze zur Softwarespezifikation zu integrieren. Wesentliche Einflüsse kommen aus den Gebieten algebraische Spezifikation abstrakter Datentypen [EGL89, Wir90], der algebraischen Spezifikation von Prozessen [Hoa85, Mil90], der temporallogik-basierten Spezifikation reaktiver Systeme [MP92], der objektorientierten Programmierung [Weg90] und den objektorientierten Datenbanken [ABD+89, Heu92]. TROLL basiert auf dem OBLOG-Modell, das zuerst in [SSE87] vorgestellt wurde. Weitere Darstellungen und Erweiterungen sind u.a. in [SFSE89, ES91, ESS92] zu finden.

Da Informationssysteme relevante Aspekte eines Weltausschnittes implementieren, sind sie immer in eine ihre Dienste nutzende Umgebung eingebettet. In den ersten Phasen des Entwurfs liegt es daher nahe, den betrachteten Weltausschnitt als *geschlossenes System* mit seiner Umgebung zu spezifizieren.

In den späteren Phasen des Systementwurfes, die im allgemeinen als *Design* bezeichnet werden, muß – im Gegensatz zu den frühen Phasen – die Einbettung der Systemumgebung in das Modell aufgehoben und die *Schnittstelle* zwischen System und Umgebung formalisiert werden. Während ein Teil der Modellierung mit geeigneten Mitteln in eine interne Repräsentation transformiert wird, bleibt die modellierte Welt der Benutzer von dieser Transformation unberührt. Die Schnittstelle ist damit als die Grenze zwischen *Weltrepräsentation innerhalb eines Systems* und der *realen Welt anzusehen.*

Die Bausteine von TROLL-Modellierungen sind Objekte, deren Struktur in Form von Attributen sichtbar ist und deren mögliches Verhalten in Form von möglichen *Aktionensequenzen* (Prozessen) modelliert wird. Schnittstellen zwischen Benutzern und Computersystemen zeichnen sich durch nach „außen" vermittelte Information und an das System übermittelte Befehle aus. Ebenso ist aber auch die umgekehrte Sichtweise denkbar, bei der Informationen als Eingaben dienen und Befehle vom System an die Umgebung gegeben werden (letzteres bevorzugt im Falle von Schnittstellen mit anderen Systemen). Bei beiden Sichtweisen treten bestimmte *Aktionensequenzen* auf, die manchmal auch als *Protokolle* bezeichnet werden. Mit Protokollen wird das wechselseitige *Verhalten* von Kommunikationspartnern beschrieben und es liegt somit nahe, Benutzerschnittstellen als *Objekte* zu spezifizieren. Wenn wir im folgenden von Benutzern und Benutzerschnittstellen sprechen, sind natürlich ebenfalls Benutzerinnen und Benutzerinnenschnittstellen gemeint.

Der Vorteil des in dieser Arbeit beschriebenen Ansatzes liegt in der *einheitlichen Repräsentation* der informationsspeichernden Komponente (i.a. Datenbanken), der Benutzerschnittstelle und sogar der Systemumgebung, d.h. der Benutzer selber. Damit werden Aspekte der Beschreibung persistenter Datenbestände, Operationen auf diesen Daten und die Schnittstelle zum Benutzer integriert dargestellt. Wir werden hier besonders auf die Schnittstelle und deren Beschreibung im Verlaufe des *Designs* eingehen. Dazu müssen Aspekte wie aktives Verhalten, Bedienungssequenzen und Ein- und Ausgabe von Daten deklarativ modelliert werden.

Die Sprache TROLL stellt dazu, neben den deklarativen Sprachmitteln zur konzeptionellen Modellierung, auch eine operationale Kernsprache bereit [HJ92], die als Zielsprache für den Designprozeß und auch zur Animation von Spezifikationen dienen kann [HJSE92]. Da Spezifikationen *deklarativ* formuliert sind, d.h., nicht ausführbare Konstrukte enthalten [HJ89], muß eine TROLL Spezifikation analysiert werden um direkt ausführbare und nicht direkt ausführbare Teile zu identifizieren und den Transformationsprozeß zu steuern. Wir werden diese Aufgabe hier nicht weiter betrachten. Wir bemerken nur, daß der hier beschriebene Ansatz damit auch Möglichkeiten der *Schnittstellen-Validierung* durch Prototyping bereitstellt [Rot91].

Die Arbeit ist wie folgt gegliedert. Im Abschnitt 2 werden wir die zum weiteren Verständnis notwendigen TROLL Sprachmittel einführen. In Abschnitt 3 wird dann ein Beispiel für die Modellierung einer einfachen Benutzerschnittstelle in TROLL angeben, die auf einem Beispiel in einem etablierten Formalismus basiert. Die Vorteile der TROLL-Modellierung werden motiviert. In Abschnitt 4 folgt dann eine kurze Zusammenfassung und die Identifizierung der notwendigen weiterführenden Arbeiten.

2 TROLL

Um die im nächsten Abschnitt dargestellte Modellierung von Benutzerschnittstellen im TROLL-Modell verständlich zu machen, wollen wir hier zunächst einen Überblick über die Sprache geben. Dabei werden wir uns auf die wesentlichen Konstruktionen beschränken, die für die Beispiele wichtig sind und verweisen den interessierten Leser auf [HJS93, JSHS91, JHS93, HJS92, HJSE92].

TROLL-Objekte sind *eingekapselte* Einheiten im Sinne einer Menge von Ereignissen, die auf einem nicht sichtbaren lokalen Zustand arbeiten. Die Ereignisse bilden die *Operationenschnittstelle* eines Objekts. Sichtbare Eigenschaften von Objekten werden als datenwertige Attribute modelliert, deren Wert vom internen Objektzustand abhängig ist. Einer Spezifikation unterliegend wird ein Datentyp-Universum angenommen, welches in einem Formalismus zur Spezifikation von ADT's dargestellt werden kann (z.B. [EM85, VHL89]). In einer Objektbeschreibung muß in TROLL nur die Signatur der benutzten Datentypen bekannt gemacht werden.

Objekte sind, intuitiv gesprochen, *beobachtbare Prozesse*, d.h., wir betrachten Sequenzen von Ereignissen und Beobachtungen über Anfangsstücken solcher Sequenzen. Ein wesentlicher Teil einer TROLL-Spezifikation besteht damit aus einer Prozeßbeschreibung, die die möglichen Sequenzen von Ereignissen festlegt. Ein weiterer Teil besteht aus der Beschreibung der aus den Prozessen abgeleiteten Attributbeobachtungen. Die Kommunikation von Objekten wird als *Synchronisation* von Prozessen modelliert.

Im folgenden soll nun eine Beispielspezifikation von Objekten kurz dargestellt werden. In TROLL besteht eine Objektspezifikation aus der Angabe eines *Objektnamens* und einer *Objektbeschreibung*, die nach dem Schlüsselwort **template** gegeben wird. Die Objektbeschreibung beinhaltet die Deklaration von Attributen (**attributes**) und Ereignissen (**events**) sowie verschiedene Abschnitte zur Spezifikation der zulässigen Beobachtungen (**valuation**) und des zulässigen Verhaltens (**behavior**).

In der Signaturbeschreibung werden die importierten Datentypen, Attributsymbole und Ereignissymbole festgelegt. Attribute sind typisiert, Ereignissymbole können optional mit Parametern versehen sein, die später zur Beschreibung der Auswirkungen von Ereignissen auf Attributbeobachtungen bzw. den Datenaustausch bei Objektinteraktionen verwendet werden.

Beispiel 2.1 Wir geben nun als Beispiel eine einfache Beschreibung eines Kontos an, mit dem die wesentlichen Komponenten einer TROLL-Spezifikation verdeutlicht werden.

```
object Konto
template
   data types money;
```

```
attributes
   KontoStand:money;
   DispoKredit:money;
events
   birth ErzeugeKonto(InitialerStand:money, Kredit:money);
   death LoeseKontoAuf;
   Abheben(Betrag:money);
   Einzahlen(Betrag:money);
valuation
   variables I,D:money;
   [ErzeugeKonto(I,D)] KontoStand = I, DispoKredit = D;
   [Abheben(I)] KontoStand = KontoStand - I;
   [Einzahlen(I)] KontoStand = KontoStand + I;
behavior
   permissions
      variables I,K:money;
      { I >= 0 } ErzeugeKonto(I,K);
      { (KontoStand + DispoKredit) > I } Abheben(I);
      { KontoStand = 0 } LoeseKontoAuf;
   obligations
      LoeseKontoAuf;
end object Konto
```

Als zu beobachtende Eigenschaften stellt dieses so spezifizierte Konto die Attribute `KontoStand` und `DispoKredit` zur Verfügung, die Werte des Datentyps `money` annehmen können. `Money` muß dabei extern spezifiziert sein und muß im **data types** Abschnitt importiert werden. Um Kontenobjekte zu erzeugen wird das mit dem Schlüsselwort **birth** qualifizierte Ereignis `ErzeugeKonto` modelliert. Dieses Ereignis besitzt zusätzlich zwei Parameter, die den initialen Kontostand sowie den Dispositionskredit modellieren. Analog zu Geburtsereignissen können mit dem Schlüsselwort **death** Ereignisse deklariert werden die ein Objekt vernichten, in diesem Falle `LoeseKontoAuf`.

In den folgenden Abschnitten einer Objektbeschreibung werden nun die Auswirkungen von Ereignissen auf Attribute und das erlaubte Verhalten eines Objektes beschrieben. Auswirkungen von Ereignissen werden mit *Auswertungsregeln* dargestellt. Die Regel

```
variables I:money;
[ Einzahlen(I) ] KontoStand = KontoStand + I
```

beschreibt dabei den Sachverhalt, daß die Einzahlung eines Geldbetrages auf ein Konto mit einer Erhöhung des Kontostandes einhergeht. Die Regel ist als Formel einer (eingeschränkten) positionalen Logik [FSMS91, FS90] anzusehen und muß gelesen werden als

> *„Nach dem Eintreten des Ereignisses* `Einzahlen`*, instantiiert mit dem Parameter* `I`*, hat der Kontostand einen Wert, der durch den Datenterm* `KontoStand+I`*, ausgewertet vor Eintreten des Ereignisses, beschrieben ist“.*

Wie im Falle des Ereignisses `ErzeugeKonto` können als syntaktische Erleichterung Auswirkungen auf verschiedene Attribute in einer Regel beschrieben werden.

Im **behavior** Abschnitt einer Objektbeschreibung wird nun das erlaubte Verhalten eines Objektes in Form von *Vorbedingungen* (**permissions**) und *Anforderungen* (**obligations**) an das Eintreten von Ereignissen beschrieben. Eine Vorbedingung der Form

```
variables I:money;
{ (KontoStand + DispoKredit) >= I } Abheben(I)
```

beschreibt, daß ein Ereignis `Abheben`, instantiiert mit dem Parameter `I` im konkreten Lebenslauf des Objektes nur dann stattfinden kann, wenn die Formel

```
( KontoStand + DispoKredit ) >= I
```

im Zustand direkt vor Eintreten des Ereignisses zu *wahr* ausgewertet wird. Die Auswertung erfolgt mit der konkreten Belegung der Variablen `I`. Als allgemeinere Formeln für Vorbedingungen sind auch *temporale* Formeln in einer vergangenheitsgerichteten temporalen Logik zugelassen, die auf den bisherigen Lebenslauf des Objektes zurückgreifen. Ein Beispiel dafür ist im nächsten Abschnitt zu finden.

In einfachen Kontenobjekten werden weiter keine Vorbedingungen an Ereignisse gestellt. Möglich ist in TROLL auch die Bedingung, daß ein bestimmtes Ereignis, eine Kombination von Ereignissen oder eine Sequenz aus Ereignissen in einem Lebenslauf enthalten sein *müssen*. Diese Anforderungen werden als **obligations** notiert. Im Beispiel wurde die in diesem Falle etwas künstliche Modellierung des Todesereignisses als Anforderung gewählt. Die Bedeutung ist in diesem Falle also, daß ein Lebenslauf des Kontenobjektes erst dann vollständig ist, wenn dieses Ereignis in einem Lebenslauf auch eingetreten ist. □

Die Darstellung von Objektlebensläufen geschieht in der oben beschriebenen Form *deklarativ*. Es werden *Anforderungen* gestellt, die für einen konkreten Lebenslauf erfüllt sein müssen. Für manche Modellierungsbeispiele ist es jedoch einfacher auf einen expliziten Formalismus zur Beschreibung von Lebensläufen zurückzugreifen, die Spezifikation von *Mustern* für Ereignissequenzen, sogenannte *patterns*. Dieser Formalismus eignet sich besonders für deterministische *Abläufe* wie sie unter anderem auch in Benutzerschnittstellen auftreten.

Beispiel 2.2 Als einfaches Beispiel sei eine Spezifikation einer Uhr angegeben, deren Lebenslauf durch einen einfachen Prozeß beschrieben ist:

```
object UHR
template
  attributes
    Stunden:nat; Minuten:nat;
  events
    birth New(Stunden:nat, Minuten:nat);
    active Tick;
    active Tack;
    StundenTack;
  valuation
    variables S,M:nat;
    [New(S,M)] Stunden = S, Minuten = M;
    { Minuten<59 } ==> [Tack] Minuten = Minuten + 1;
    { Minuten=59 } ==> [Tack] Minuten = 0;
    { Stunden<23 } ==> [StundenTack] Stunden = Stunden + 1;
    { Stunden=23 } ==> [StundenTack] Stunden = 0;
  behavior
    patterns
      variables H,M:nat;
```

```
        process START = case New(H,M) esac -> RUN
            with
                process
                    RUN = Tick -> Tack -> RUN
                end process; /*RUN*/
        end process; /*START*/
        START;
    interaction
        { Minuten = 59 } ==> Tack >> StundenTack;
end object UHR
```

In diesem Beispiel wurden *bedingte Auswertungsregeln* benutzt, um die Auswirkungen der Ereignisse auf Attribute vom Zustand abhängig zu machen. Eine bedingte Auswertungsregel kommt nur zur Anwendung, wenn die vorangestellte Bedingung mit *wahr* ausgewertet wird. Dies gilt ebenso für andere bedingte Spezifikationsformeln (Ereignisaufruf, s.u.).

Der wichtigste Bestandteil dieser Spezifikation ist die Darstellung eines *Verhaltensmusters* in Form einer expliziten Prozeßbeschreibung. Nach der Erzeugung eines Uhrobjektes verhält sich die Uhr wie im Prozeß `RUN` beschrieben: jeweils auf ein `Tick`-Ereignis folgt ein `Tack`-Ereignis und der Teilprozeß startet von vorne (Rekursion).

Die beiden Ereignisse `Tick` und `Tack` sind als **active** gekennzeichnet, da sie aus der Initiative der Uhr stattfinden. Aktive Ereignisse sind ein Modelierungsmittel um darzustellen, daß keine äußere Bedingung für das Stattfinden des Ereignisses modelliert wurde. Dieses Mittel wird wichtig bei der abstrahierenden Darstellung von Benutzern bei denen nicht alle möglichen Aktionen kausal beschrieben werden können und sollen.

Der `START` Prozeß selbst beginnt mit einem Auswahloperator (**case**). Die Parameter von `New` bestimmen dabei die Menge der möglichen Ereignisse, d.h., es wird *ein* `New` Ereignis von der Umgebung des Uhr-Objektes über seine Parameter ausgewählt. Eine Auswahl wird in diesem Falle *extern* erfolgen, z.B. durch einen Ereignisaufruf der konkrete Parameterwerte festlegt. Die Sprache zur Prozeßbeschreibung enthält neben den hier aufgeführten Operatoren *Sequenz*, *Rekursion* und *Auswahl* außerdem noch einen *Mengen-Iterator* (**foreach**).

Am Ende der Uhr-Spezifikation wird dann ein Ereignisaufruf beschrieben. Mit jedem `Tack` Ereignis wird, wenn die entsprechende Anwendungsbedingung erfüllt ist, *synchron* ein `StundenTack`-Ereignis aufgerufen. Im Fall der Uhr findet genaugenommen keine Kommunikation statt wie das Schlüsselwort **interaction** vermuten läßt. Bei Objektbeziehungen (**relationships**) wird jedoch der gleiche Aufrufmechanismus auf die Kommunikation von Objekten untereinander verallgemeinert. Da wir in der kurzen Sprachbeschreibung nur auf die wichtigsten Konstrukte eingehen können, sei auf den nächsten Abschnitt verwiesen, in dem wir ein Beispiel für Objektbeziehungen geben werden. □

Die in diesem Abschnitt gegebene Darstellung der Sprache TROLL berücksichtigt nur die für diese Arbeit notwendigen Sprachkonstrukte. In [JSHS91] und [HJS93] werden darüberhinaus Sprachmittel zur Spezifikation von Klassen, Spezialisierungen, Generalisierungen und zusammengesetzten Objekten angegeben. Wir werden im nächsten Abschnitt nun genauer auf die Benutzung von Prozeßbeschreibungen in expliziter und deklarativer Form eingehen und ein Beispiel zur Spezifikation einer Benutzerschnittstelle angeben.

3 Benutzerschnittstellen als Objekte

Benutzerschnittstellen sind zwischen implementiertem System und der Außenwelt einzuordnen. Eine Formalisierung dieser Schnittstelle wird durch die Spezifikation der Benutzerschnittstelle erreicht. Die objektorientierte Spezifikation hat den Anspruch, die folgenden beiden Aspekte dieser Schnittstelle formal zu definieren:

- die *Schnittstelle* selber als Systemkomponente
- und den Benutzer aus der Außenwelt, d.h. natürlich nur eine *Abstraktion eines echten Benutzers.* Dieser „Benutzer" kann - als Sonderfall - natürlich auch ein anderes System sein.

Sowohl die Eingabeschnittstellen als auch der abstrakte Benutzer können sowohl *spontane* als auch *reaktive Aktivität* zeigen — in den meisten Anwendungen wird die spontane Aktivität jedoch wohl beim Benutzer und die reaktive Aktivität bei der Systemschnittstelle zu finden sein. Unter spontaner Aktivität verstehen wir dabei das ohne eine (modellierte) Kausalbeziehung zu beobachtende Eintreten von Ereignissen. Reaktive Aktivität tritt dagegen auf, wenn ein Objekt von außen (z.B. durch Ereignisaufruf) in einen Zustand gelangt, in dem nachfolgende Ereignisse zwingend eintreten müssen.

Beginnen wir mit der Modellierung von Schnittstellen als Systemkomponenten. Übliche Modellierungen von derartigen Schnittstellen setzen etwa Zustandsgraphen als Modellierungprinzip ein [Den91]. Ein Beispiel von Benutzerschnittstellen als Zustandsgraph (dort Interaktionsdiagramm genannt) kann in Abbildung 1 gefunden werden (angelehnt an das Beispiel in [Den91, Seite 130]).

Der Beispielgraph modelliert Teile des Eingabeverhaltens eines Geldautomaten. Das Dreieck bezeichnet dabei den initialen Zustand. Kreise entsprechen Zuständen des Zustandsgraphen (hier mit **Z1** bis **Z3** bezeichnet). Pfeile entsprechen Zustandsübergängen eventuell gesteuert durch Eingaben (genannt virtuelle Tasten, hier etwa der Eingabe einer 'Geheimzahl'), während Rechtecke (aufgerufenen) Aktionen entsprechen. Die Aktivitäten nach der Prüfung der Geheimzahl (Geldauszahlung, Drucken des Kontostandes, etc.) wurden der Einfachheit halber weggelassen.

Zustandsgraphen entsprechen deterministischen Prozessen. Somit liegt es nahe, derartige Zustandsgraphen direkt als Objekte zu kodieren [Saa92]. Im folgenden Beispiel wird erst eine Benutzerschnittstelle eines Geldautomaten mit einer aktiven Phase, nämlich einer Automatenbedienung entsprechend einer Bildschirmsitzung modelliert und anschließend in den folgenden Beispielspezifikationen ein abstrakter Benutzer und seine Kommunikation mit dieser Schnittstelle beschrieben.

Beispiel 3.1 *(Schnittstellen-Signatur)* Wir beginnen mit der Spezifikation der Benutzerschnittstelle angelehnt an das in Abbildung 1 dargestellte Beispiel. Zuerst geben wir nur einen Teil der Signatur an.

```
object GASchnittstelle
template
   data types Zustände, KartenInfo, ZiffernFolge, bool;
   attributes
      Zustand:Zustände;
   events
      birth ErzeugeSchnittstelle;
      AktiviereSchnittstelle;
      active KartePrüfen(Karte: KartenInfo, ok?:bool);
```

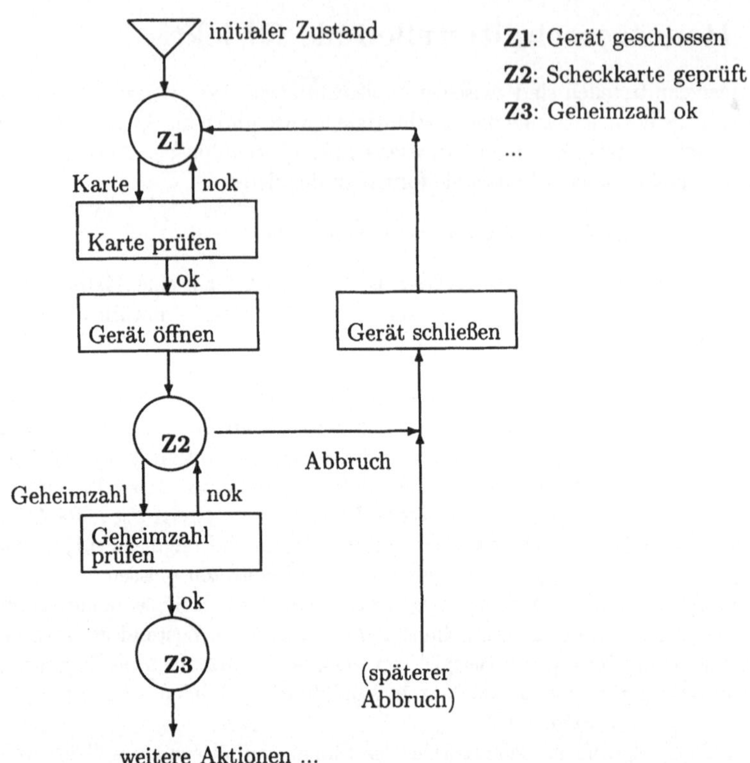

Abbildung 1: Zustandsgraph einer Benutzerschnittstelle (nach [Den91]).

```
active GerätÖffnen;
active KarteAuswerfen;
active GerätSchließen;
active GeheimzahlPrüfen(Zahl:ZiffernFolge, ok?:bool);
...;
KarteAnnehmen(Karte:KartenInfo);
GeheimzahlEingegeben(Zahl:ZiffernFolge);
AbbruchTasteGedrückt;
active AbbruchAkzeptiert;
...
```

Wir unterbrechen hier die Spezifikation des Objekts, um auf einen Unterschied zum Übergangsautomaten in Abbildung 1 hinzuweisen: In der Objektspezifikation werden Übergange durch Eingaben von außen, also vom Benutzer, als passive Ereignisse modelliert und damit von den Übergängen durch interne Entscheidungen (in Abbildung 1 ok versus nok) unterschieden, die hier Ergebnisparametern von Ereignissen oder Attributwerten entsprechen. Wir gehen im Beispiel davon aus, daß die Werte des ok? Parameters durch eine Anfrage (per Ereignisaufruf) bei einem anderen Objekt (z.B. einer Bank) gesetzt werden, die hier nicht weiter ausspezifiziert wird. □

Beispiel 3.2 *(Verwaltung der Zustandsinformation)* (Forts. von 3.1) Auch wenn in der TROLL Modellierung die Zustände nicht unbedingt benötigt werden, so soll hier diese Information analog zu der Beschreibung von Denert mit modelliert werden.

```
valuation
   variables z: ZiffernFolge;
   [AktiviereSchnittstelle] Zustand = Z1;
   [GerätÖffnen] Zustand = Z2;
   [GerätSchließen] Zustand = Z1;
   [GeheimzahlPrüfen(z,true)] Zustand = Z3;
   ...
```

Für die TROLL Spezifikation ist dieser Teil entbehrlich, da die Zustandsinformation implizit in einem Prozeß verwaltet wird (s.u.). Hier soll sie nur der einfachen Zuordnung zum Zustandsgraphen aus Abb. 1 dienen. □

Bisher haben wir die Objektsignatur und die Verwaltung der Zustandsinformation spezifiziert. Die eigentliche, fest vorgegebene Abarbeitung wird durch das Prozeßmuster in der GASchnittstelle gesteuert. Zusätzlich sollte auch eine aktive Phase eingeleitet werden um ein garantiertes Ende der Sitzung (etwa nach einer bestimmten Zeitspanne ohne Benutzerinteraktion) zu erzwingen. Hier wäre es z.B. möglich, daß Uhr-Objekt des vorigen Abschnittes zu verwenden um eine Art *TimeOut* zu spezifizieren. Darauf wurde hier verzichtet, da dieses in dem Originalbeispiel in Abbildung 1 nicht modelliert war und auch im dort verwendeten Formalismus nur auf einer Metaebene formulierbar wäre.

Beispiel 3.3 *(Verhalten der Schnittstelle)* (Forts. von 3.2) Die reaktive Aktivität wird nun durch die Gestalt des Prozesses und aktive Ereignisse spezifiziert.

```
patterns
   variables z:ZiffernFolge, k:KartenInfo;
   process GAS =
         case KarteAnnehmen(k) esac ->
         case
            KartePrüfen(k,false) -> KarteAuswerfen;
            KartePrüfen(k,true) -> GerätÖffnen -> KARTEOK?
         esac
      with
         process KARTEOK? =
               case GeheimzahlEingeben(z) esac ->
               case
                  GeheimzahlPrüfen(z,true) -> FORTSETZEN;
                  GeheimzahlPrüfen(z,false) -> KARTEOK?;
                  AbbruchTasteGedrückt -> ABBRUCH;
               esac
            with
               process ABBRUCH =
                  KarteAuswerfen -> GerätSchließen -> AbbruchAkzeptiert;
               end process;
               process FORTSETZEN = ... end process;
         end process;
   end process;
   GAS;
end object GASchnittstelle
```

Natürlich hätten wir in einer realistischen Anwendung eine Klasse von Geldautomatenschnittstellen spezifiziert anstatt wie hier eines einzelnen Objekts. Wir verzichten hier auf die Klassenspezifikation, da wir im Abschnitt 2 den Begriff der Klasse nicht eingeführt haben. □

Dieses Beispiel zeigt, daß Objektspezifikationen von Schnittstellen sich (halb-) automatisch aus Zustandsgraphen generieren lassen. Die erhaltenen Spezifikationen sehen allerdings nicht besonders gut lesbar aus; man sollte aber bedenken, daß auch Objektspezifikationen graphisch (und damit besser übersehbar) dargestellt werden können, und daß die Stärke der Objektspezifikation bei deskriptiven Beschreibungen und nicht bei der Umsetzung von operationalen Vorgaben liegt.

Beispiel 3.4 *(Benutzermodellierung)* (Fortsetzung von Beispiel 3.1–3.3) Nach der Spezifikation der Schnittstelle des Geldautomatens deklarieren wir jetzt eine spezielle Rolle von Personen, nämlich Personen in der Rolle eines `GeldAutomatBenutzers`. Rollen wurden bisher nicht eingeführt. In TROLL erbt ein Rollenobjekt die Struktur, das Verhalten und die konkrete Zustandsinformation des Elternobjektes [JSHS91].

```
object GeldAutomatBenutzer
  role of Person;
template
  data types KartenInfo, ZiffernFolge, TastenSymbole;
  attributes
    Karte: KartenInfo;
    GeheimZahl: ZiffernFolge;
  events
    birth active SchiebeKarteInSchlitz(Karte:KartenInfo);
    active GebeZiffernfolgeEin(ZiffernFolge);
    active DrückeTaste(TastenSymbole);
    ...
    EmpfangeAbbruchBestätigung;
    EmpfangeGeld;
    death active BeendeSitzung;
  valuation
    variables K: KartenInfo;
    [ SchiebeKarteInSchlitz(K) ] Karte = K;
    ...
  permissions
    { sometime(after(EmpfangeAbbruchBestätigung)
                  or after(EmpfangeGeld) ) } BeendeSitzung;
  patterns
    process GAB = SchiebeKarteInSchlitz(Karte) ->
                        case GebeZiffernfolgeEin(GeheimZahl);
                             DrückeTaste(Abbruch);
                        esac -> ...-> BeendeSitzung
    end process;
    GAB;
end object GeldAutomatBenutzer
```

Das Symbol `Abbruch` bezeichnet hier eine Konstante des Datentyps `TastenSymbole`, der die Tastenbeschriftungen der einzelnen Tasten des Geldautomaten als Werte enthält. Die vom Benutzer erwarteten Tätigkeiten werden als Prozeß mit aktiven Ereignissen modelliert, der vom Benutzer selbst initiiert wird.

Ein Benutzer hat die Verpflichtung (sich selbst gegenüber) die Bedienung des Geldautomaten zu beenden — er muß dazu aber eine Reaktion des Automaten abwarten, entweder die Herausgabe des Geldes oder die Meldung, daß der Automat einen Abbruch akzeptiert (wer würde auch einen Geldautomaten verlassen, solange noch Geld zu erwarten ist...).

Spezifikationsteile, die zum Verständnis der Modellierung des Benutzerverhaltens nicht unbedingt notwendig sind, wurden der Übersichtlichkeit halber hier weggelassen. □

Bereits bei diesem einfachen Beispiel zeigt sich ein Vorteil der Benutzung von Objektspezifikationen gegenüber einfachen Zustandsdiagrammen. Objektspezifikationen können auch auf die Sprachmittel allgemeiner Beschreibungsformalismen zurückgreifen; so könnte etwa mittels eines Attributes die Anzahl der Fehlversuche bei der Eingabe der Geheimzahl bestimmt und gegebenenfalls eine Reaktion (etwa Abbruch) bei zu hoher Anzahl (etwa > 3) ausgelöst werden. Bei Zustandsdiagrammen müßte der entsprechende Teilgraph mit dem Zustand **Z2** hierbei dreimal kopiert werden, um das Hochzählen zu realisieren [Den91].

Die Interaktion zwischen dem Geldautomaten und der Benutzerrolle wird nun in Form einer Beziehung etabliert, um den Kommunikationsvorgang konzeptionell von den betroffenen Objekten zu trennen [JHS93]. Eine derartige Trennung erhöht unter anderem den Grad der Wiederverwendbarkeit der beteiligten Objekte und die Implementierungsunabhängigkeit der Modellierung.

Beispiel 3.5 *(Interaktionsbeschreibung)* (Fortsetzung von Beispiel 3.1–3.4) Als letzter (unvollständiger) Teil der Spezifikation der Interaktion zwischen Geldautomaten und Kunden wird eine Beziehung definiert, die die Kommunikation zwischen beiden steuert.

```
relationship GeldAutomatBenutzung
   between GeldAutomatBenutzer B, GASchnittstelle GAS;
   variables gz:ZiffernFolge, ki:KartenInfo;
   interaction
      B.SchiebeKarteInSchlitz(ki) >> GAS.KarteAnnehmen(ki);
      B.GebeZiffernfolgeEin(gz) >> GAS.GeheimzahlEingegeben(gz);
      B.DrückeTaste(Abbruch) >> GAS.AbbruchTasteGedrückt;
      GAS.AbbruchAkzeptiert >> B.EmpfangeAbbruchBestätigung;
      ...
end relationship GeldAutomatBenutzung
```

In diesem Beispiel besteht die Interaktion aus unbedingten Ereignisaufrufen. Allgemein können an dieser Stelle auch komplexere Interaktionsmuster und Integritätsbedingungen auftreten. Hier findet nun Ereignisaufruf nicht mehr innerhalb eines Objektes sondern zwischen verschiedenen Objekten statt. Wie schon oben erwähnt, wird damit die Interaktion explizit beschrieben und nicht innerhalb der Objekte versteckt. □

Analog zu Beispiel 3.5 kann nun auch die Kommunikation der Schnittstelle mit dem unterliegenden System spezifiziert werden. Hier würden zum Beispiel Ereignisaufrufe wie `GeheimzahlPrüfen` an die entsprechenden Stellen weitergeleitet. Da wir diese Systemteile in dieser Arbeit nicht spezifiziert haben, verzichten wir an dieser Stelle darauf. Zu bemerken ist, daß auf die Art der hier vorgestellten Modellierung die Schnittstelle klar zu beiden Seiten – den Benutzern und dem unterliegenden zu implementierenden System – abgegrenzt ist.

Ziel der Arbeit war es, zu zeigen, daß auch interaktive Benutzerschnittstellen eines Informationssystems mittels der ursprünglich für den Entwurf persistenter dynamischer

Objekte und deren zeitlichen Verhaltens entworfenen Spezifikationssprache TROLL modelliert werden können. Dazu wurde als Beispiel eine deterministische Schnittstelle eines Geldautomaten mit Hilfe der in TROLL integrierten expliziten Prozeßsprache skizziert.

4 Zusammenfassung und Ausblick

Bei der Modellierung von Informationssytemen, die ja im besonderen Maße Teile der realen Welt abbilden und somit mit der realen Welt in engem Kontakt stehen, muß besonderes Augenmerk auf die Schnittstelle zwischen dieser Abbildung und den Benutzern des Systems gelegt werden. In der hier kurz vorgestellte Sprache TROLL ist die Modellierung der Benutzerschnittstelle mit Hilfe von *Objekten* möglich, die ebenso zur Modellierung des verwalteten Datenbestandes wie der (Abstraktion von) Benutzer(n) selber geeignet sind.

Ein integriertes Vorgehen – wie hier demonstriert – ist wünschenswert um eine einheitliche Beschreibung des gesamten Systems zu ermöglichen. Die Adaption anderer Formalismen ist nur dann sinnvoll, wenn die semantischen Grundlagen der benutzten Sprachen kompatibel sind. Es war daher unser Ziel, die prinzipielle Vorgehensweise einer Benutzerschnittstellen-Modellierung in TROLL darzustellen, die durch die Mächtigkeit der Sprache selbst außerdem noch Vorteile gegenüber anderen Formalismen hat.

Die Vorteile eines integrierten Vorgehens sind im wesentlichen die einheitliche Sichtweise auf alle Modellierungskomponenten und die Mächtigkeit des Objektkonzeptes gegenüber Formalismen wie z.B. Zustandsdiagrammen, die im allgemeinen nur einfache Automaten beschreiben. Zusätzlich zur Objektabstraktion wurde auch die Benutzung von Relationships als über Objekte hinausgehende Sprachmittel kurz präsentiert und damit die Eigenständigkeit der Schnittstelle im Gegensatz zu Benutzer wie System hervorgehoben.

In Gebiet Schnittstellenmodellierung in TROLL fehlen allerdings noch eine Entwurfsmethodik für den Entwurf und deren Validierung anhand realistischer Anwendungen. Auch der Bezug zu anderen Verfahren der Schnittstellenmodellierung, die nicht auf Übergangsautomaten basieren, muß sicher noch eingehender untersucht werden. In diesem Falle wurde eine Schnittstelle untersucht, die sich auch einfach mit operationalen Beschreibungsmitteln wie Zustandsdiagrammen darstellen läßt. Andere Arten von Schnittstellen verlangen nach deskriptiven Techniken, die noch mit den deklarativen Sprachmitteln von TROLL verglichen werden müssen.

Weitergehende Arbeit hier wird unter anderem die Modellierung von Teilen eines Entwurfssystems zur Unterstützung der Modellierung in TROLL selbst sein. Damit steht eine (aus der Sicht von TROLL) Nicht-Standard Anwendung zur Verfügung, deren Komplexität zur Untersuchung der zur Verfügung stehenden Sprachmittel ausreicht.

Danksagung

Wir danken in erster Linie den Kolleginnen und Kollegen, die im IS-CORE Projekt mit uns zusammengearbeitet haben. Hier sind insbesondere Hans-Dieter Ehrich und Amílcar Sernadas zu nennen, deren Arbeiten zu formalen Objektmodellen die Grundlagen der Sprache TROLL gelegt haben, sowie Cristina Sernadas, die an der Sprachdefinition mitgearbeitet hat.

Ferner danken wir allen Studentinnen und Studenten, die im Verlaufe von Diplom- und Studienarbeiten wertvolle Anregungen zum Sprachdesign lieferten, allen Kolleginnen und Kollegen, die in Diskussionen kritische Anmerkungen lieferten und nicht zuletzt den anonymen Gutachterinnen und Gutachtern für ihre Kommentare zur Vorversion dieser Arbeit.

Literatur

[ABD+89] Atkinson, M.; Bancilhon, F.; DeWitt, D.; Dittrich, K. R.; Maier, D.; Zdonik, S. B.: The Object-Oriented Database System Manifesto. In: Kim, W.; Nicolas, J.-M.; Nishio, S. (Hrsg.): *Proc. Int. Conf. on Deductive and Object-Oriented Database Systems*, Kyoto, Japan, Dezember 1989. S. 40–57.

[Boo90] Booch, G.: *Object-Oriented Design.* Benjamin/Cummings, Menlo Park, CA, 1990.

[CF92] de Champeaux, D.; Faure, P.: A Comparative Study of Object-Oriented Analysis Methods. *Journal of Object-Oriented Programming*, Band 3, Nr. 2, 1992, S. 21–33.

[Den91] Denert, E.: *Software-Engineering. Methodische Projektabwicklung.* Springer-Verlag, Berlin, 1991.

[EGL89] Ehrich, H.-D.; Gogolla, M.; Lipeck, U.W.: *Algebraische Spezifikation abstrakter Datentypen.* Teubner, Stuttgart, 1989.

[EM85] Ehrig, H.; Mahr, B.: *Fundamentals of Algebraic Specification 1. Equations and Initial Semantics.* Springer-Verlag, Berlin, 1985.

[ES91] Ehrich, H.-D.; Sernadas, A.: Fundamental Object Concepts and Constructions. In: Saake, G.; Sernadas, A. (Hrsg.): *Information Systems – Correctness and Reusability.* TU Braunschweig, Informatik Bericht 91-03, 1991, S. 1–24.

[ESS92] Ehrich, H.-D.; Saake, G.; Sernadas, A.: Concepts of Object-Orientation. In: *Proc. of the 2nd Workshop of "Informationssysteme und Künstliche Intelligenz: Modellierung", Ulm (D).* Springer IFB 303, 1992, S. 1–19.

[FS90] Fiadeiro, J.; Sernadas, A.: Logics of Modal Terms for System Specifications. *Journal of Logic and Computation*, Band 1, Nr. 2, 1990, S. 187–227.

[FSMS91] Fiadeiro, J.; Sernadas, C.; Maibaum, T.; Saake, G.: Proof-Theoretic Semantics of Object-Oriented Specification Constructs. In: Meersman, R.; Kent, W.; Khosla, S. (Hrsg.): *Object-Oriented Databases: Analysis, Design and Construction (Proc. 4th IFIP WG 2.6 Working Conference DS-4, Windermere (UK))*, Amsterdam, 1991. North-Holland, S. 243–284.

[Heu92] Heuer, A.: *Objektorientierte Datenbanken.* Addison-Wesley, Bonn (D), 1992.

[HJ89] Hayes, I.J.; Jones, C.B.: Specifications are not (necessarily) executable. Technischer Bericht UMCS-89-12-1, Univ. of Manchester, 1989.

[HJ92] Hartmann, T.; Jungclaus, R.: Abstract Description of Distributed Object Systems. In: Tokoro, M.; Nierstrasz, O.; Wegner, P. (Hrsg.): *Proc. ECOOP'91 Workshop on Object-Based Concurrent Computing. Genf (CH), 1991.* Springer, LNCS 612, Berlin, 1992, S. 227–244.

[HJS92] Hartmann, T.; Jungclaus, R.; Saake, G.: Aggregation in a Behavior Oriented Object Model. In: Lehrmann Madsen, O. (Hrsg.): *Proc. European Conference on Object-Oriented Programming (ECOOP'92).* Springer, LNCS 615, Berlin, 1992, S. 57–77.

[HJS93] Hartmann, T.; Jungclaus, R.; Saake, G.: Spezifikation von Informationssystemen als Objektsysteme. *EMISA Forum, Mitteilungen der GI-Fachgruppe 2.5.2*, Band 1, 1993, S. 2–18.

[HJSE92] Hartmann, T.; Jungclaus, R.; Saake, G.; Ehrich, H.-D.: Spezifikation von Objektsystemen. In: Bayer, R.; Härder, T.; Lockemann, P.C. (Hrsg.): *Objektbanken für Experten.* Springer, Berlin, Reihe Informatik aktuell, 1992, S. 220–242.

[Hoa85] Hoare, C.A.R.: *Communicating Sequential Processes.* Prentice-Hall, Englewood Cliffs, 1985.

[JHS93] Jungclaus, R.; Hartmann, T.; Saake, G.: Relationships between Dynamic Objects. In: Kangassalo, H. (Hrsg.): *Proc. 2nd Eurpean-Japanese Seminar on Information Modelling and Knowledge Bases, 1992, Hotel Ellivuori (SF).* IOS Press, Amsterdam. *Erscheint 1993.*

[JSHS91] Jungclaus, R.; Saake, G.; Hartmann, T.; Sernadas, C.: Object-Oriented Specification of Information Systems: The TROLL Language. Informatik-Bericht 91-04, TU Braunschweig, 1991.

[Mil90] Milner, R.: Operational and Algebraic Semantics of Concurrent Processes. In: Leeuwen, J. van (Hrsg.): *Formal Models and Semantics.* Elsevier Science Publishers B.V., 1990, S. 1201–1242.

[MP92] Manna, Z.; Pnueli, A.: *The Temporal Logic of Reactive and Concurrent Systems. Vol. 1: Specification.* Springer-Verlag, New York, 1992.

[RBP+90] Rumbaugh, J.; Blaha, M.; Premerlani, W.; Eddy, F.; Lorensen, W.: *Object-Oriented Modeling and Design.* Prentice-Hall, Englewood Cliffs, NJ, 1990.

[Rot91] Rothenberg, J.: Prototyping as Modeling: What is being Modeled? In: Sol, H.G.; van Hee, K.M. (Hrsg.): *Dynamic Modeling of Information Systems.* Elsevier Science Publishers, 1991, S. 335–359.

[Saa92] Saake, G.: Objektorientierte Spezifikation von Informationssystemen: Konzepte und Sprachvorschläge. Habilitationsschrift, TU Braunschweig, 1992.

[SFSE89] Sernadas, A.; Fiadeiro, J.; Sernadas, C.; Ehrich, H.-D.: The Basic Building Blocks of Information Systems. In: Falkenberg, E.; Lindgreen, P. (Hrsg.): *Information System Concepts: An In-Depth Analysis*, Namur (B), 1989. North-Holland, Amsterdam, 1989, S. 225–246.

[SSE87] Sernadas, A.; Sernadas, C.; Ehrich, H.-D.: Object-Oriented Specification of Databases: An Algebraic Approach. In: Stoecker, P.M.; Kent, W. (Hrsg.): *Proc. 13th Int. Conf. on Very Large Databases VLDB'87.* VLDB Endowment Press, Saratoga (CA), 1987, S. 107–116.

[VHL89] Van Horebeek, I.; Lewi, J.: *Algebraic Specifications in Software Engineering.* Springer-Verlag, Berlin, 1989.

[Weg90] Wegner, P.: Concepts and Paradigms of Object-Oriented Programming. *ACM SIGPLAN, OOPS Messenger*, Band 1, Nr. 1, 1990, S. 7–87.

[Wir90] Wirsing, M.: Algebraic Specification. In: Van Leeuwen, J. (Hrsg.): *Handbook of Theoretical Computer Science, Vol. B: Formal Models and Semantics.* Elsevier Sci. Publ. B.V., Amsterdam, 1990, S. 675–788.

vis-A-vis: Ein objekt-orientiertes Application Framework für grafische Entwurfswerkzeuge

Horst Lichter, Kurt Schneider
Abt. Software Engineering
Universität Stuttgart
Breitwiesenstr. 20/22
7000 Stuttgart 80

Zusammenfassung

Viele Ingenieurwissenschaften verwenden graphische Notationen mit wohldefinierter Semantik, wie Petri-Netze oder Blockschaltbilder. Diagramme, die mit Hilfe dieser Notationen erstellt werden, repräsentieren semantische Modelle, auf denen anwendungsspezifische Operationen ausgeführt werden können. Um diese Art von Notationen und ihre semantischen Modelle komfortabel handhaben zu können, empfiehlt es sich, sie durch einen grafischen Editor zu unterstützen. Dabei sollte allgemeine Editor-Funktionalität nicht für jede einzelne Notation neu implementiert, sondern wiederverwendet werden, um Editoren mit geringem Aufwand erstellen zu können.

vis-A-vis ist ein objekt-orientiertes Application Framework, das diesem Zweck dient. In diesem Beitrag geben wir die wichtigsten Anforderungen an, die wir bei der Konstruktion von vis-A-vis beachtet haben. Der Anwendungsbereich von vis-A-vis-basierten Werkzeugen wird definiert und es wird ein Überblick über die grundlegenden Konzepte gegeben. Das Beispiel eines System Dynamics-Editors illustriert diese Konzepte und zeigt, wie ein Werkzeugbauer ein neues Werkzeug erstellen kann und welcher Aufwand dafür zu treiben ist.

1. Einführung und Motivation

Grafische Notationen werden in jeder Ingenieurwissenschaft eingesetzt, wenn ausdrucksstarke Modelle zu erstellen sind. Diese Modelle heißen - je nach Anwendungsgebiet - oft auch "Pläne", "Entwürfe" usw. Um diese Modelle interaktiv erstellen und bearbeiten zu können, sind Werkzeuge nötig. Diese Werkzeuge müssen:

- Umfangreiche grafische Fähigkeiten besitzen,
- einfach zu bedienen sein,
- die Semantik der Diagramme "verstehen", also ein internes Modell der Diagramme bilden.

Hochauflösende Monitore, Workstations und Fenstersysteme erlauben, interaktive grafische Werkzeuge zu verwenden, um Modelle zu entwickeln. Es ist jedoch ein schweres Stück Arbeit, solche Werkzeuge zu implementieren, wenn man jedesmal von vorne beginnen muß. Gamma (1989) weist darauf hin, daß eine objekt-orientierte Klassenbibliothek, die als Application Framework organisiert ist, vorteilhaft eingesetzt werden kann, wenn Anwendungen realisiert werden sollen, die in den dadurch vorgegebenen Rahmen passen.

Unser Beitrag erklärt die Grundkonzepte und den Aufbau des objekt-orientierten Application Frameworks *vis-A-vis*. Das Framework ist speziell darauf ausgerichtet, interaktive Entwurfswerkzeuge (im weitesten Sinne) einfach und schnell konstruieren zu können. Es legt eine einheitliche Architektur und eine einheitliche Benutzungsschnittstelle nahe und bietet eine Menge grafischer Repräsentationsmöglichkeiten an. Sie können verwendet werden, um ein spezielles Entwurfswerkzeug zu realisieren.

Der Beitrag ist wie folgt gegliedert: In Abschnitt 2 definieren wir das Anwendungsfeld des Frameworks. Abschnitt 3 faßt einige Anforderungen zusammen, die die Entwicklung von vis-A-vis beeinflußt haben. Abschnitt 4 gibt einen kurzen Überblick über das Framework; Abschnitt 5 zeigt an einem Beispiel, wie ein neuer Editor mithilfe von vis-A-vis konstruiert wird. In Abschnitt 6 berichten wir über unsere Erfahrungen, die wir inzwischen gesammelt haben, über den Stand der Arbeit und geben einen Ausblick auf die Punkte, die wir als nächstes angehen wollen.

In diesem Beitrag verwenden wir abkürzend den Begriff "vis-A-vis-Werkzeug" oder auch nur "Editor", wenn wir ein spezielles Entwurfswerkzeug meinen, das mit vis-A-vis erstellt worden ist. "vis-A-vis" steht dagegen für das Application Framework selbst.

2. Das Anwendungsfeld von vis-A-vis

vis-A-vis ist ein Application Framework. Die Anwendungen, die dadurch unterstützt werden, und die man also damit erstellen kann, sind Editoren für grafische Notationen. Es stellt Mechanismen und wiederverwendbare Klassen zur Verfügung, mit denen schnell und auf einheitliche Weise ein spezieller Editor entwickelt werden kann.

Mit vis-A-vis werden grafische Notationen unterstützt, die aus Symbolen für Objekte und Relationen bestehen. vis-A-vis erlaubt, sowohl auf einzelnen semantischen Elementen des Modells (also auf einzelnen Objekten und Relationen) als auch auf dem gesamten Modell Operationen auszuführen. Simulationen, Konsistenzprüfungen und Transformationen zählen zu den häufigsten derartigen Operationen.

Da vis-A-vis auf diese Art von Werkzeugen zugeschnitten ist, bietet sein Einsatz die folgenden Vorteile:

- Das Framework ist relativ klein und kann somit schnell "erlernt" und eingesetzt werden; es umfaßt rund 60 Klassen, die direkt verwendet werden können, um spezielle Editoren zu bauen.

- Mechanismen, die für jeden Editor notwendig sind, werden bereits fertig zur Verfügung gestellt. Dadurch braucht nicht mehr viel Aufwand in allgemeine Funktionalität gesteckt zu werden. In Abschnitt 5 zeigen wir die Vorgehensweise, in dem man mit vis-A-vis Editoren erstellt.

Andererseits eignet sich vis-A-vis nicht, um Werkzeuge zu implementieren, die außerhalb der Anwendungsklasse liegen. Darin besteht der Hauptunterschied zu mächtigeren Application Frameworks wie etwa ET++[1]. Auch ist vis-A-vis nicht darauf ausgelegt, daß beliebige Benutzungsschnittstellen erzeugt werden können, wie dies etwa das System VICK erlaubt[2]. Vielmehr sind Aussehen und Bedienungsweise aller vis-A-vis-Werkzeuge weitgehend vorgegeben und einheitlich. Sie sollten nicht vom Werkzeugbauer verändert werden. Andererseits beschränkt sich vis-A-vis nicht auf die Visualisierung von existierendem Smalltalk-Code und seiner Attribute (wie VICK), sondern ist für eine viel größere und allgemeinere Klasse von grafischen Notationen geeignet.

In jeder Ingenieurdisziplin gibt es grafische Notationen, die sich für die Unterstützung durch vis-A-vis eignen. In unserem eigenen Fach, Software Engineering, sind beispielsweise die Strukturierte Analyse (Datenflußdiagramme), Jackson Structured Programming, SADT, die objekt-orientierte Analysemethode nach Coad/Yourdon, Automatendiagramme oder Booch-Diagramme zu nennen. In anderen Bereichen können Organigramme, Schaltbilder oder Netzpläne durch vis-A-vis-Werkzeuge unterstützt werden.

Ein Beispiel für eine Grafische Notation mit Semantik

Jede grafische Notation besteht aus Symbolen, die in den meisten Notationen eine wohldefinierte Semantik haben. Diese Symbole können in zwei Gruppen aufgeteilt werden:

- Symbole, die Objekte (Entitäten) der Modelle darstellen;
- Symbole für Relationen zwischen diesen Objekten.

Bei der bekannten Petri-Netz-Notation sind dies (vgl. Baumgarten, 1990): Bedingungen (Stellen) und Transitionen als Objekte und Abhängigkeitspfeile zwischen diesen Objekten. Die Transitionen, die durch einen Strich dargestellt sind, können "feuern", wenn alle Bedingungen, von denen sie abhängen, erfüllt sind. Eine Bedingung wird durch einen Kreis symbolisiert, eine erfüllte Bedingung beinhaltet (mindestens) einen schwarzen Punkt, eine sogenannte "Marke".

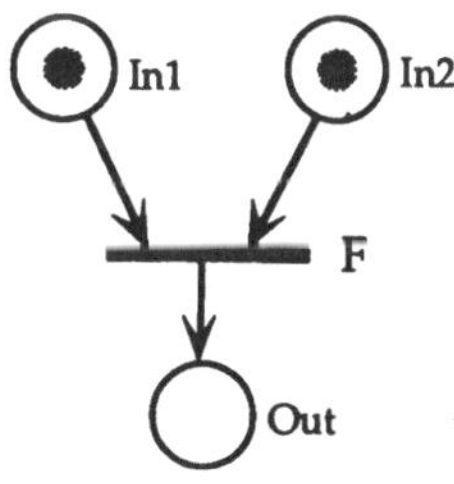

Abb. 1: Ein Petri-Netz

1 siehe dazu Weinand (1989)

2 siehe dazu Böcker (1992)

Feuert nun die Transition F, so wird dadurch aus jeder Eingangsbedingung (In1 und In2) eine Marke entfernt, und jede Ausgangsbedingung (Out), erhält eine Marke.

Man kann Netze aus solchen Symbolen zur Untersuchung von Synchronisationsmechanismen und von Nebenläufigkeit verwenden. Abbildung 1 zeigt ein einfaches Petri-Netz mit einer Transition F, die von zwei Eingangsbedingungen (In1 und In2) abhängig ist, und die eine Ausgangsbedingung Out hat. Üblicherweise ist Out dann wieder Eingangsbedingung für andere Transitionen, wodurch sich schließlich ein Netz von Stellen und Transitionen, ein "Petri-Netz" ergibt.

3. Anforderungen an vis-A-vis

Bei der Entwicklung von vis-A-vis hatten wir drei Perspektiven im Hinterkopf: Die des Anwenders eines vis-A-vis-Werkzeugs, die des Werkzeugbauers, der einen speziellen Editor erstellen will, und die allgemeinen Anforderungen an die Konstruktion des Frameworks aus der Sicht des Software Engineering.

3.1 Anforderungen des Werkzeugbenutzers

Wer ein Entwurfswerkzeug benutzt, erwartet vermutlich:

- Ein *einfach zu handhabendes* Werkzeug, das den üblichen Zeichenwerkzeugen ähnelt, und das mit Basisoperationen wie Verschieben, Löschen und Ausrichten von Symbolen oder Speichern und Laden ganzer Modelle ausgerüstet ist.
- *Einheitliches look & feel*: Wer ein vis-A-vis-Werkzeug zu bedienen gelernt hat, sollte damit auch alle anderen vis-A-vis-Werkzeuge bedienen können. Das gilt besonders für grafische Operationen, trifft aber auch auf den Aufruf von semantischen Operationen zu.
- *Anwendungsspezifische Symbole und Verbindungen*: Mit einem Mausklick sollten auch komplizierte Symbole plaziert und verschoben werden können. Es sollte für den Benutzer unnötig sein, Symbole erst aus Basissymbolen (Kreis, Rechteck) zusammenzusetzen. Die angebotenen Symbole sollten wie die aus der Literatur zu der Notation gewohnten aussehen.
- Anders als herkömmliche Zeichenwerkzeuge sollte vis-A-vis sich der *Modellstruktur* bewußt sein: Beschriftungen und Verbindungen zu Symbolen sollten mit diesen Symbolen eine Einheit bilden und zusammen mit diesen verschoben und gelöscht werden.
- Es sollen *semantische Konsistenzprüfungen* auf den Modellen möglich sein: Alle Möglichkeiten, die eine Notation prinzipiell auf dem Papier bietet, sollten auch im Werkzeug bereit stehen; in der Notation nicht definierte Diagramme sollten nicht erstellt werden können.
- Die semantischen Modelle sollten so *unabhängig* wie möglich von vis-A-vis sein, um leicht in anderen Kontexten verwendet werden zu können. So kann

ein Modell von verschiedenen vis-A-vis-Werkzeugen unterschiedlich visualisiert werden, ohne daß das Modell mehrfach zu erstellen ist.

3.2 Anforderungen des Werkzeugbauers

Wer einen speziellen grafischen Editor mit Semantik bauen will, hofft:

- Einen problemspezifischen Editor so *schnell* wie möglich und mit möglichst *wenig Aufwand* implementieren zu können. Dazu sollte eine große Bibliothek wiederverwendbarer Bausteine angeboten werden.
- Kleine, gut beschriebene *Schnittstellen* sollten die Entwicklung eines vis-A-vis-Werkzeugs erlauben, ohne zuvor vis-A-vis in allen Einzelheiten verstehen zu müssen. Nebenbei sollte eine einheitliche Architektur entstehen, wenn die Bausteine verwendet und die Schnittstellen eingehalten werden.
- Jeder Baustein muß *anpaßbar* sein. Insbesondere müssen nicht benötigte Fähigkeiten eines Bausteins vor dem Werkzeugbenutzer verborgen werden können, um nur notationskonforme Diagramme erzeugen zu können.
- Problemspezifische Symbole, Semantik, Hilfe-Texte und Beschriftungen sollen leicht *integrierbar* sein, ohne sich über interne Details weiter den Kopf zerbrechen zu müssen.
- Einfacher Zugriff auf das *Dateisystem* und auf eine *Datenbank* sollen die dauerhafte Speicherung der Modelle ohne viel Codierung ermöglichen.

3.3 Anforderungen an die Konstruktion

Um Software-Qualitäten wie Wartbarkeit und Erweiterbarkeit zu gewährleisten, sollte vis-A-vis folgenden Anforderungen genügen:

- Strikte Trennung der grafischen Notation und des entsprechenden semantischen Modells, um unabhängige Veränderung und Entwicklung zu erlauben.
- Hochgradig generischer Code sollte zu geringer Redundanz und folglich zu minimalen Änderungsanomalien führen.
- Die Beachtung allgemeiner Anforderungen an Werkzeuge, wie sie z.B. in Schneider (1991) eingeführt werden, ist obligatorisch.

3.4 Unsere Konsequenzen aus den Anforderungen

vis-A-vis ist, als Folgerung aus den Anforderungen, objekt-orientiert entworfen und implementiert worden. Ein neues vis-A-vis-Werkzeug wird dementsprechend erzeugt,

- indem von den zur Verfügung gestellten abstrakten Klassen geerbt wird, um diese zu konkreten, problemspezifischen Klassen zu spezialisieren,
- indem existierende Klassen durch Parametrisierung angepaßt und im neuen Werkzeug wiederverwendet werden.

Entsprechend dem Konzept der objekt-orientierten Application Frameworks bietet vis-A-vis eine Menge von Klassen als Bausteine an. Sie werden entweder unverändert eingebaut, oder als Oberklassen verwendet. Dieser Ansatz ist dem herkömmlichen Bibliotheks-Ansatz insofern überlegen, als Architekturgerüste automatisch ausgefüllt werden. Dadurch entstehen einheitliche Architekturen, es ist weniger Dokumentationsaufwand zu leisten, und eine bessere Wartbarkeit wird erreicht.

vis-A-vis ist in Smalltalk-80 realisiert, weil es über eine umfangreiche Bibliothek verfügt, die den Umgang mit grafischen Oberflächen wesentlich erleichtert.

4. Ein Überblick über vis-A-vis

In diesem Abschnitt erklären wir einige Eigenschaften von vis-A-vis. Zuerst zeigen wir, wie die Benutzungsschnittstelle von vis-A-vis aufgebaut ist und führen die Visualisierungsarten ein, die vis-A-vis zur Unterstützung grafischer Notationen anbietet. Dann gehen wir auf die Standardarchitektur ein, die vis-A-vis für jedes Werkzeug definiert.

4.1 Das Look & Feel von vis-A-vis

Im vis-A-vis Fenster werden vier Bereiche unterschieden:

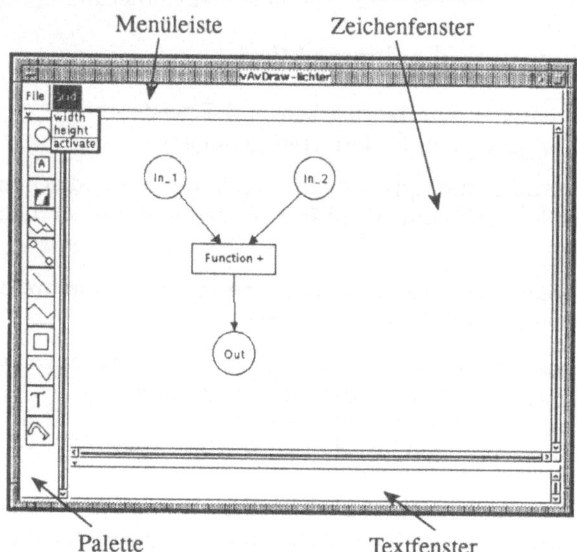

Abb. 2: Die Standard-Benutzungsschnittstelle von vis-A-vis-Werkzeugen

Die *Palette* zeigt Icons, die die angebotenen Symboltypen (Elemente des Modells) der grafischen Notation zeigen. Nachdem der Benutzer einen Symboltyp ausgewählt hat, kann er entsprechende Symbole im Zeichenfenster plaźieren.

Das *Zeichenfenster* dient dazu, das Modell in der grafischen Notation zu entwickeln. Der Fensterinhalt kann horizontal und vertikal gerollt werden. Die Symbole können verschoben und selektiert werden, um über ihr semantisches Menü Operationen anzustoßen.

Die *Menüleiste* bietet werkzeugspezifische Menüs. vis-A-vis stellt von vorneherein zwei Menüs zur Verfügung, die in jedem vis-A-vis-Werkzeug auftreten: Das "File-Menü" bietet Funktionen wie Speichern, Laden, Drucken der Modells oder Verlassen des Editors. Das "Grid-Menü" erlaubt, die Symbole an einem Raster auszurichten.

Das *Textfenster* informiert den Benutzer über Fehler, das Ergebnis von Konsistenzprüfungen und zeigt Hilfe-Informationen an.

Visualisierungsformen in vis-A-vis

vis-A-vis bietet eine Menge von Grundvisualisierungsformen, die der Werkzeugbauer benutzen kann, um daraus die Symbole für die grafische Notation eines speziellen vis-A-vis-Werkzeugs zusammenzubauen. Abbildung 3 zeigt die Grundvisualisierungsformen, die vis-A-vis derzeit anbietet, und wie sie vom Werkzeugbauer zu einem komplexeren Symboltyp zusammengebaut werden können.

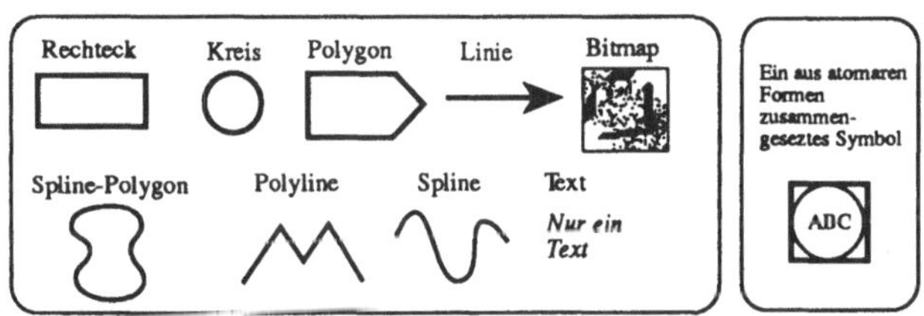

Abb. 3: Grundvisualisierungsformen und ihre Kombination zu einem komplexen Symbol

Die Visualisierungsformen haben typspezifische grafische Attribute. Rechtecke, Kreise usw. haben eine Innenfarbe; Linien können in unterschiedlichen Stilen (durchgehend, gestrichelt, dick) dargestellt werden. Texte können in unterschiedlichen Stilen und Hervorhebungsarten gestaltet werden. Pfeilspitzen können Linien zugeordnet werden.

4.2 Die Architektur der vis-A-vis-Werkzeuge

vis-A-vis definiert eine Standardarchitektur für jedes damit erzeugte Werkzeug. Diese Architektur wurde hauptsächlich von den folgenden Aspekten beeinflußt:

- Die in Budde (1992) beschriebene "Werkzeug-Material-Metapher", die angibt, wie interaktive Werkzeuge intern aufgebaut sein sollen.
- Die strikte Trennung zwischen grafischer Notation (Symbole für Objekte und Relationen) und semantischem Modell.

- Der Aufbau von Benutzungsschnittstelle nach dem Model-View-Controller-Paradigma, wie es in Krasner (1988) beschrieben ist.

Die Architektur gliedert sich in drei Schichten: Die Interaktions-Schicht, die Werkzeug-Schicht und die Material-Schicht. Deren Zusammenhang zeigt die folgende Abbildung.

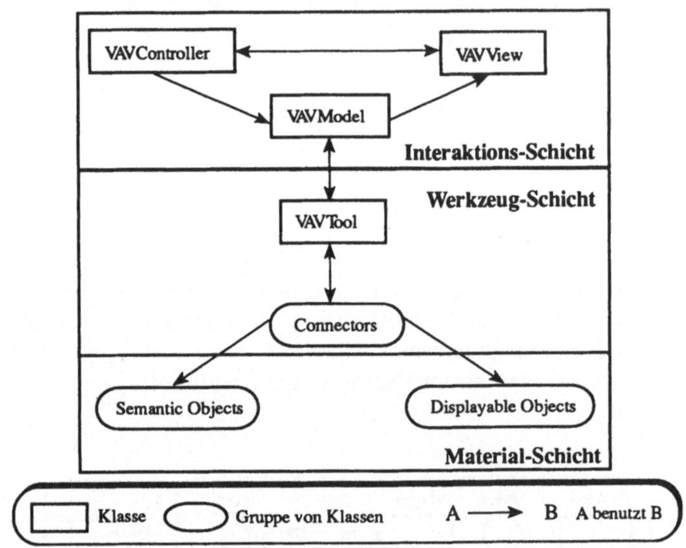

Abb. 4: Die Standardarchitektur von vis-A-vis-Werkzeugen

Die Interaktions-Schicht
enthält alle Klassen, die das look&feel von vis-A-vis-Werkzeugen prägen. Diese Klassen wurden entsprechend dem Model-View-Controller-Paradigma entworfen. Die Controller-Klasse ist jeweils für die Interaktion zwischen dem Benutzer und dem Werkzeug verantwortlich. Die View-Klasse bestimmt, wie die Benutzungsoberfläche aussieht, die Model-Klasse speichert den aktuellen Zustand der Interaktion und verbindet die Benutzungsschnittstelle mit dem eigentlichen Werkzeug.

Die Werkzeug-Schicht
besteht aus einer Reihe von Komponenten:

- Die Hauptkomponente *VAVTool* ist für die gemeinsamen Grundmechanismen und für allgemeine Funktionen wie Speichern. Laden etc. verantwortlich. VAVTool wird stets als Oberklasse verwendet, wenn ein neues Werkzeug mit erweiterter, problemspezifischer Funktionalität gebaut wird.
- Sogenannte *Konnektoren* verbinden die semantischen Objekte des Modells mit ihrer grafischen Visualisierung und reichen die Operationsaufrufe weiter.

Für jeden Symboltyp, den ein vis-A-vis-Werkzeug anbieten soll, muß eine Konnektor-Klasse vorhanden sein. Damit diese Konnektor-Klassen einfach konstruiert werden können, bietet vis-A-vis häufig verwendete abstrakte Konnektor-Klassen an, die spezialisiert werden können, so daß jeweils nur wenige Teile neu implementiert werden müssen.

Die Material-Schicht
enthält die semantischen Klassen, die die eigentlichen Modellelemente implementieren, und die entsprechenden Visualisierungsklassen. Wie erwähnt, stellt vis-A-vis bereits einige Visualisierungsklassen zur Verfügung.

4.3 Grundlegende Konzepte und Mechanismen in vis-A-vis

Zuerst erläutern wir detailliert das zentrale Konzept der Konnektoren, das ein Schlüssel zur Struktur von vis-A-vis ist. Dann zeigen wir, wie ein neues Werkzeug erzeugt wird.

Konnektoren verbinden Modellelemente und deren Visualisierung

vis-A-vis unterscheidet klar zwischen den *semantischen Objekten* (als den Elementen des internen Modells), und ihren *grafischen Visualisierungen*. Um dies zu erreichen, haben wir einige Basismechanismen und ein Nachrichtenprotokoll entwickelt, über das die semantischen Objekte sehr lose mit ihren Visualisierungen gekoppelt sind. Die Mechanismen sind in einem Klassenbaum realisiert, den *Konnektor*-Klassen. Die folgende Abbildung zeigt den Zusammenhang zwischen einem vis-A-vis-Werkzeug, seinen Konnektoren, den semantischen und den Visualisierungs-Objekten.

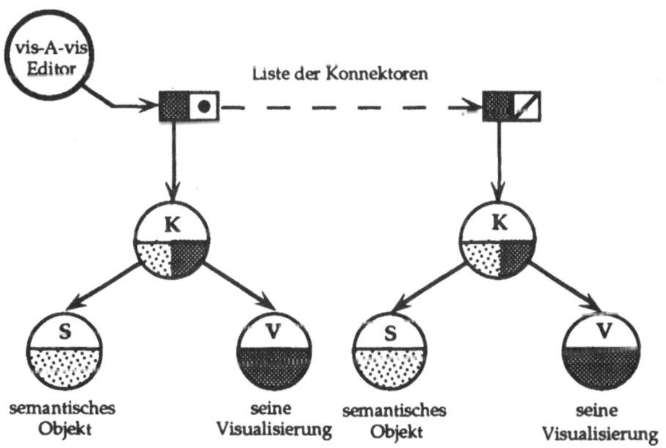

Abb. 5: Die interne Struktur eines vis-A-vis-Werkzeugs

Das vis-A-vis-Werkzeug hält die Konnektoren für alle semantischen Objekte des gesamten Modells in einer internen Liste. Jeder Konnektor verbindet über zwei Referenzen das semantische Objekt mit seiner Visualisierung. Ein Konnektor übernimmt die Kontrolle, wenn das zugehörige Symbol auf dem Bildschirm selektiert ("angeklickt") wird. Über den Konnektor wird das Menü des semantischen Objekts an den Benutzer weitergereicht; umgekehrt wird der

Aufruf einer Operation vom Konnektor an das semantische Objekt weitergeleitet.

Ein Konnektor legt weiterhin fest, wie das semantische Objekt visualisiert werden soll, und wie sich Veränderungen im Zustand des semantischen Objekts auf seine Visualisierung auswirken. Um Teile der Visualisierung einzeln verändern zu können, kann jeder Konnektor beliebig viele sogenannte *interne Konnektoren* haben. Die internen Konnektoren sind dann zwar eng mit dem Hauptkonnektor verbunden; sie visualisieren aber jeweils einen Aspekt des semantischen Objekts und können insofern unabhängig modifiziert werden. Das Symbol auf dem Bildschirm erscheint dann wie ein komplex zusammengesetztes, zusammengehöriges Symbol (das insbesondere in einem Zug verschoben oder gelöscht werden kann).

Im Beispiel der Petri-Netz-Notation könnte z.B. eine Bedingung einen Hauptkonnektor haben, der diese mit einem Kreis als Visualisierung verknüpft. Der Hauptkonnektor enthält zwei interne Konnektoren: Der eine verbindet das "markiert"-Attribut einer Bedingung mit einem kleinen, schwarzgefüllten Kreis, der zweite verbindet die Bezeichnung der Bedingung mit einem darstellbaren Text. Die nächste Abbildung zeigt die Struktur des *ConditionToCircleConnectors* mit seinen zwei internen Konnektoren.

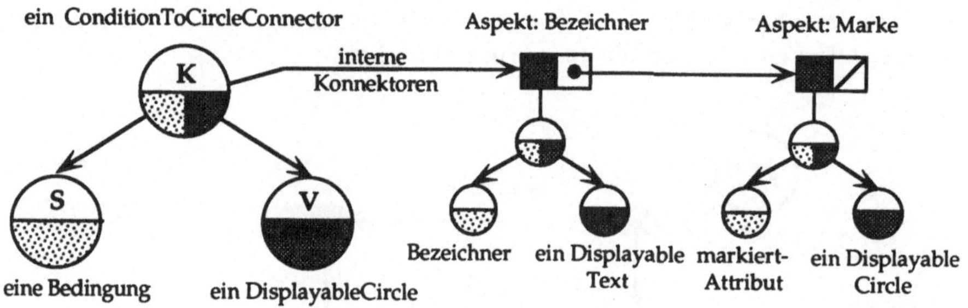

Abb. 6: Die Verwendung interner Konnektoren

Das oben beschriebene Konzept, semantische mit grafischen Objekte zu verbinden, garantiert, daß die semantischen Klassen ohne Rücksicht auf Visualisierungen in einem speziellen Werkzeug erstellt und verändert werden können. Ebenso kann man die Visualisierung einer semantischen Klasse auswechseln, ohne in die semantische Klasse selbst eingreifen zu müssen.

Die Installation eines neuen vis-A-vis-Werkzeugs

Folgende Komponenten muß ein Werkzeugbauer schreiben, wenn er ein neues Werkzeug erzeugen möchte:

- Für jedes Symbol der grafischen Notation müssen eine *semantische Klasse*, ein *Icon* für die Werkzeugpalette und ein *Hilfetext* geliefert werden.
- Zu jeder semantischen Klasse muß es eine *Konnektor-Klasse* geben.

- Eine *Werkzeugklasse* (als direkte Unterklasse der Klasse VAVTool) muß alle Operationen implementieren, die über die Default-Operationen hinausgehen, und die auf dem Modell als Ganzes ausgeführt werden sollen.

Eine Installations-Routine von vis-A-vis erleichtert den Zusammenbau des gewünschten Werkzeugs. Diese Routine entnimmt ihre Anweisungen einer werkzeugspezifischen Konfigurationsdatei, deren Inhalt einer definierten Syntax entsprechen muß. Sie faßt alle benötigten Informationen zusammen, die die Routine braucht, um ein Werkzeug zu generieren. Diese Datei muß der Werkzeugbauer zur Verfügung stellen.

4.4 Die Klassenbibliothek von vis-A-vis

Die Klassenbibliothek von vis-A-vis besteht aus ungefähr 60 Smalltalk-80-Klassen. Dabei kann man zwei Teil-Bibliotheken unterscheiden: Die der Konnektoren und die der Visualisierungen. Der Baum der Konnektor-Klassen wurde bereits eingeführt; er basiert auf einem entsprechenden Baum von Visualisierungs-Klassen, z.B. *DisplayableRectangle, DisplayablePolygon* oder *DisplayableLine*. Wir beschränken uns in den folgenden Erläuterungen auf die Konnektor-Klassen, weil sie praktisch immer als Oberklassen wiederverwendet werden, wenn ein neues Werkzeug gebaut wird. Sie implizieren dann zum Teil schon die Visualisierung, auf der sie basieren.

Die Konnektor-Bibliothek

Alle Konnektor-Klassen in vis-A-vis sind Unterklassen von *XtoYConnector;* dabei steht X für irgendeine semantische Klasse, Y für eine Visualisierungsklasse. Abbildung 7 zeigt einen Ausschnitt aus dieser Bibliothek. In der Klasse *XtoYConnector* sind alle allgemeinen Mechanismen der Konnektoren implementiert: Verbinden der Objekte, Operationsweitergabe usw.

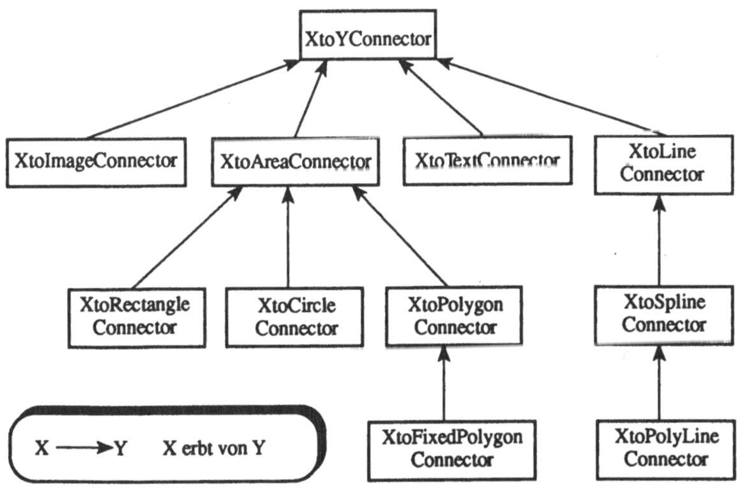

Abb. 7: Ein Ausschnitt aus der Konnektor-Bibliothek

In der abstrakten Oberklasse *XtoYConnector* sind aber X und Y noch unbekannt. Sie auszufüllen und damit eine konkrete Konnektor-Klasse zu erzeugen, ist Aufgabe des Werkzeugbauers. Alle allgemeinen Mechanismen erbt er dabei einfach von *XtoYConnector* – oder von einer bereits etwas spezielleren Unterklasse davon. So legt *XtoCircleConnector* zum Beispiel bereits fest, daß die Visualisierung mit einem Kreis erfolgen soll. Die Verbindung zum *DisplayableCircle* ist also in dieser Klasse bereits angelegt. Erbt man von ihr, um *ConditionToCircleConnector* zu realisieren, so muß dort nur noch implementiert werden, wie die die Eigenschaften der Bedingung (*Condition*) auf die bereits vorgegebene Visualisierung (*Circle*) abgebildet werden soll.

5. Wie man ein neues vis-A-vis-Werkzeug erzeugt - ein Beispiel

In diesem Abschnitt zeigen wir, wie ein einfaches vis-A-vis-Werkzeug konstruiert wird. Mit diesem Werkzeug können Modelle nach System Dynamics, einem weitverbreiteten Simulationsansatz mit grafischer Notation, erstellt werden. Wir zeigen, was ein Werkzeugbauer im einzelnen tun muß, wenn er den System Dynamics Editor implementieren will, und was vis-A-vis dazutut.

5.1 Die Anwendung: System Dynamics

Die Geschichte von System Dynamics geht auf die 60er Jahre zurück. Forrester (1961) führte den Ansatz zunächst unter dem Namen "Industrial Dynamics" ein und taufte ihn später in "System Dynamics" um, als sich erwies, daß eine sehr viel größere Klasse dynamischer Modelle damit modelliert und simuliert werden können.

System Dynamics benutzt die mathematische Form von Differenzengleichungen, um ein Modell aufzustellen. Die Simulationszeit schreitet in festen Schritten von Δt voran. Dabei geht System Dynamics davon aus, daß Δt klein genug gewählt ist, um durch die sprungartige Zeitfortschaltung keine Modellverfälschungen einzubauen (quasi-kontinuierliche Simulation mit fester Schrittweite). In gewissem Sinn ist eine Simulation also eine Folge von Transformationen, ausgehend vom Anfangszustand des Systems. Der nächste Zustand wird jeweils als Funktion des vorhergehenden Zustandes und der Länge von Δt berechnet. Der Zustand eines Systems ist definiert als die Menge der Werte von sogenannten *Levels*. Diese Levels stehen für die relevanten Systemgrößen. Ein Schritt der Simulationszeit berechnet und transformiert gleichzeitig alle Level-Werte auf ihren nächsten Wert.

Eine grafische Notation erlaubt, die Struktur von System Dynamics - Modellen zu skizzieren. Dabei gibt man an, welche Levels von welchen (anderen) Levels abhängen, wodurch sich die Systemgrößen erhöhen oder erniedrigen. Wenn mehrere Levels sich gegenseitig beeinflussen, kommt es zu Rückkopplungsschleifen, einer für System Dynamics geradezu charakteristischen Erscheinung. Bisher mußten die Diagramme dann von Hand in eine textuelle Sprache, üblicherweise *DYNAMO*, übersetzt werden. Dabei waren noch einige Details zu ergänzen, die aus den Diagrammen nicht zu ersehen sind. Die Diagramme dienen als Kommunikationsmedium zwischen Anwendungs- und Simulationsexperten und sollen deshalb nicht mit Details überladen werden: Sie zeigen nur die Struktur des Modells.

Erst seit kurzem gibt es interaktive grafische Werkzeuge, die die direkte Manipulation von Diagrammen erlauben. Nachdem man die fehlenden Zusatzangaben gemacht hat, kann das Modell dann animiert werden. STELLA ist ein Vertreter solcher Werkzeuge. Wir entschlossen uns, mithilfe von vis-A-vis auch ein solches Werkzeug zu entwickeln.

Die Elemente der grafischen System Dynamics - Notation sind:

Dabei bedeuten:

- *Levels* sind die Systemgrößen, für deren Entwicklung man sich interessiert. Sie speichern ihren Wert und aktualisieren ihn nach jedem Simulationsschritt.
- *Raten* erhöhen oder erniedrigen Level-Werte. Dadurch bringen sie Dynamik ins Modell. Sie steuern den Materialfluß zwischen Leveln. Dabei kann auch einer der Partner statt eines Levels eine Senke oder Quelle sein.
- *Quellen* oder *Senken* haben weder Namen noch zeigen sie irgendwelches Verhalten. Sie stehen lediglich für "Irgendetwas außerhalb des Systems" und versorgen und entsorgen das System von dem darin fließenden Material.
- Um die Richtung des *Materialflusses* anzugeben, verbindet man Levels und Quellen oder Senken mit durchgehenden Pfeilen.
- Wie stark eine Rate einen Level verändert, hängt üblicherweise von (zum Teil anderen) Levels ab. Gestrichelte Pfeile zeigen solche *Abhängigkeiten*.
- Werden die Berechnungsformeln in den Raten zu komplex, so kann man *Hilfsvariablen* einführen, die als Zwischenergebnisse fungieren. Dies dient oft auch der Klarheit der Modellstruktur. Hilfsvariablen speichern keine Werte (wie Levels), sie unterstützen lediglich Raten bei der Rechnung. Deshalb treten Hilfsvariablen nur zwischen Abhängigkeitspfeilen auf.

Abbildung 8 ist ein Bildschirmabdruck und zeigt, wie der Editor schließlich aussieht. Wir haben ein problemspezifisches *Simulations*-Menü in die Menüleiste eingefügt, zusätzlich zu den schon vorhandenen *File*- und *Grid*-Menüs, die ja von jedem Werkzeug ererbt werden. Das Simulation-Menü ist hier aufgeklappt zu sehen: Der Benutzer kann die Simulationsuhr zurücksetzen, Parameter für die Simulation bestimmen und die Simulation starten. Sollte das grafische Modell unvollständig sein oder gegen eine grafische Syntaxregel verstoßen, erscheint eine Fehlermeldung im Textfenster.

In Abbildung 8 ist ein einfaches Räuber-Beute-Modell skizziert. Hilfsvariablen waren nicht nötig, weil die Abhängigkeiten ausgesprochen trivialer Natur sind: Sowohl Räuber als auch Beute werden geboren und sterben eines natürlichen Todes. Außerdem ist die Beute aber ein wichtiges Zubrot für die Räuber, durch das deren Lebensverhältnisse sich bessern und die Fruchtbarkeit steigt. Andererseits führt das natürlich zu einer "unnatürlichen" Todesrate bei der Beute, die gefressen wird. Das Zubrot wird damit wieder geschmälert, eine Rückkopplungsschleife ist entstanden.

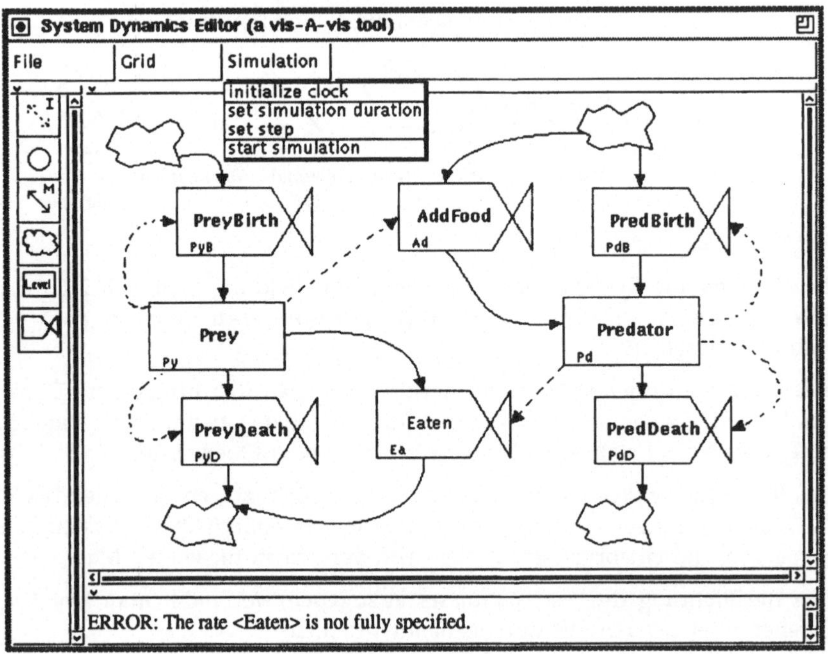

Abb. 8: Der System Dynamics-Editor

Wir entschlossen uns, den Namen vollständig spezifizierter Modellelemente fett zu setzen und unvollständige Objekte mit normaler Schrift zu kennzeichnen. Von einem unvollständigen Objekt sprechen wir, wenn ein Level keinen Anfangswert oder eine Rate keine Formel zugewiesen bekommen hat (in diesem Fall hat "Eaten" keine Formel). Um diese nicht sichtbaren Teile des Modells festzulegen oder zu verändern, klickt der Benutzer auf das Symbol und erhält ein Menü mit den verfügbaren Operationen. In unserem Beispiel kann er Anfangswerte oder Formeln und Bezeichner wählen. Das führt zu einer sofortigen Aktualisierung des Erscheinungsbildes (z.B. fetter Bezeichner). Im unteren linken Eck von Levels und Raten sieht man ein Kürzel. Der Editor leitet es aus dem Namen ab und prüft es auf modellweite Eindeutigkeit. Diese Kürzel dienen im Beispiel dazu, Formeln kompakter schreiben zu können. Vor allem aber illustrieren sie das Konzept der internen Konnektoren, denn sowohl der

Bezeichner als auch das Kürzel werden durch interne Konnektoren dargestellt; durch diesen Mechanismus ist es einfach, sie zu plazieren und zu gestalten.

5.2 Schritt für Schritt zum System Dynamics - Editor

Wir schlagen folgende Vorgehensweise vor, um ein neues vis-A-vis-Werkzeug zu erzeugen:

1. *Semantische Objekte der Anwendung identifizieren und implementieren*

   Die Klasse Rate hat zum Beispiel Name, Kürzel und Formel-Attribute. Sie kann ihre Formel auswerten und einige andere simulationsbezogene Aufgaben erfüllen. Semantische Klassen haben auch grundsätzlich das semantische Menü und die darin aufgeführten Operationen anzubieten.

2. *Grundsymbole für die semantischen Objekte festlegen.*

   Für den System Dynamics-Editor konnten wir die Klassen *DisplayableCircle* und *DisplayableRectangle* unverändert aus der vis-A-vis-Bibliothek übernehmen. Zur Visualisierung von Raten und Quellen bzw. Senken verwendeten wir das angebotene *DisplayFixedPolygon* und parametrisierten es mit den die Form ausmachenden Eckpunkten, so daß das "Ventilsymbol" und die "Wolke" entstanden. Außerdem war zu jedem semantischen Objekt ein Icon zu zeichnen, das in der Palette gezeigt wird. Die Icons können mit einem zu vis-A-vis gehörenden Bitmap-Editor gezeichnet und verändert werden. Schließlich kann ein Hilfetext dem Symbol zugeordnet werden, der auf Benutzeranfrage im Text-Fenster erscheint.

3. *Festlegen, welche Aspekte des semantischen Objekts wie visualisiert werden sollen.*

   Ohnehin muß für jede semantische Klasse eine Konnektor-Klasse geschrieben werden, die die Verbindung zur Visualisierung herstellt (z.B. verbindet *RateConnector* das semantische Objekt *Rate* mit einem *FixedPolygon*). Als Unterklasse von *XtoFixedPolygonConnector* aus der vis-A-vis-Bibliothek mußte der Werkzeugbauer darin nur noch Raten-spezifische Operationen implementieren, nicht mehr aber Menüzugriff, Operationsweitergabe, Symbolverschiebemöglichkeiten und die restliche Integration in alle anderen vis-A-vis-Dienste.

4. *Unterklasse von VAVTool schreiben.*

   Man möchte natürlich nicht nur Modelle mit Semantik zeichnen, sondern von dieser Semantik auch in anwendungstypischer Weise Gebrauch machen. In unserem Beispiel kann man mit den Menüpunkten des *Simulations*-Menüs einen Simulationsrahmen bedienen, der dadurch mit dem Editor verbunden ist. In vielen Fällen liegt in der Praxis ja zunächst ein Anwendungsprogramm vor, das allerdings noch nicht mit einer grafischen Notation bedient werden kann. Der in unserem Beispiel verwendete Simulationsrahmen war ein solches, über Kommandos und Texteingaben bedientes Werkzeug. Das mit vis-A-vis realisierte Werkzeug erlaubt nun, den manuellen Übersetzungsschritt einzusparen und die Modelle direkt zu animieren.

5.3 Die Implementierung im Detail

In diesem Abschnitt wird beispielhaft die Realisierung der Klasse *RateConnector* vorgestellt. Dadurch soll deutlich werden, was der Werkzeugbauer im Normalfall tun muß, wenn er Konnektor-Klassen implementiert.

Der *RateConnector* ist als Unterklasse von *XtoFixedPolygonConnector* realisiert, da eine Rate durch ein Polygon – und zwar durch ein Polygon mit festgelegter Form – dargestellt werden soll. Daher ist das grafische Objekt ein *FixedPolygon*.

```
XtoFixedPolygonConnector subclass: #RateConnector
  instanceVariableNames: ''
  classVariableNames:    ''
  poolDictionaries:      ''
  category: 'vAv-SD-Connectors'
```

Bei der Initialisierung der Klasse werden in der Klassenmethode *initialize* die internen Konnektoren eingebaut: Jeder interne Konnektor wird mit einem Symbol (z.B. *#formel*) identifiziert, und es wird festgelegt, welcher Konnektor-Typ verwendet werden soll (hier: *StringToTextConnector*). Im Prinzip kann jeder Konnektor auch als interner Konnektor verwendet werden.

```
initialize

  super initialize.

  internalConnectors at: #name    put: #StringToTextConnector.
  internalConnectors at: #kuerzel put: #StringToTextConnector.
  internalConnectors at: #formel  put: #StringToTextConnector.
```

In der Klassenmethode *initializeFixedPolygon* wird angegeben, wie das spezielle Polygon aussieht. Diese Methode wird bei der Initialisierung einer Unterklasse von *XtoFixedPolygonConnector* aufgerufen. Der Werkzeugbauer muß sie also zur Verfügung stellen.

```
initializeFixedPolygon
  | points |
  points := OrderedCollection new.
  points addLast: (0@0);
    addLast: (0@50);
    addLast: (70@50);
    addLast: (100@0);
    addLast: (100@50);
    addLast: (70@0);
    addLast: (0@0).

  fixedPolygon := Polygon new collectionOfPoints:points
```

Die Klassen-Methode *defaultSemanticClass* liefert den Namen der semantischen Klasse, auf die sich der Konnektor bezieht. Diese Information ist notwendig, damit der Konnektor sein semantisches Objekt erzeugen kann.

```
defaultSemanticClass

    ^'SDRate'
```

Ein Konnektor und damit sein semantisches Objekt wird folgendermaßen erzeugt: vis-A-vis instanziiert eine neues Objekt der Klasse *RateConnector* und schickt ihm die Nachricht "*createSemanticObject: aRepresentation*". Da sichergestellt wollen soll, daß sofort, nachdem das Polygon im Editor angezeigt wird, nach dem Namen und nach der Formel gefragt wird, wird diese Methode überschrieben und angepaßt. Zuerst wird mithilfe derselben Methode der Oberklasse das semantische Objekt erzeugt (*super createSemanticObject:* verwendet dazu die *defaultSemanticClass*), dann wird der Benutzer nach Name und Formel gefragt. Innerhalb der aufgerufenen Methoden *getName* und *getFormula* werden dabei auch gleich die entsprechenden Aspekte des semantischen Objekts gesetzt.

```
createSemanticObject: aRepresentation

  super createSemanticObject: aRepresentation.
  self getName.
  self getFormula

getName

  semanticObject name: (DialogView request: ´Enter name´).
```

Soll nachträglich Name, Kürzel oder Formel der Rate verändern, so muß mit der Maus das Symbol der Rate selektiert werden. Daraufhin erscheint das „semantische Menü". Dieses Menü erhält vis-A-vis von der semantischen Klasse des Konnektors. Es enthält in unserem Beispiel die Einträge *editKuerzel*, *editName* und *editFormel*. Wählt der Benutzer beispielsweise *editName* aus, so wird dadurch dieselbe Operation des Konnektors aufgerufen, die schon bei *createSemanticObject:* verwendet wurde.

Die Methode *displaySemanticObjectOn:at:refresh:* wird von einem vis-A-vis-Werkzeug an alle Konnektoren versandt, wenn Änderungen im inneren Zustand eines semantischen Objekts nach außen sichtbar gemacht werden sollen. In unserem Beispiel sollen vollständig spezifizierte Raten durch fettgedruckte Namen gekennzeichnet werden. Weiterhin sollen die Formel und das Namenskürzel an einer geeigneten Stelle im Raten-Symbol angezeigt werden, wenn dies möglich ist. Dazu muß die allgemeine Konnektor-Methode *displaySemanticObjectOn:at:refresh:* überschrieben werden.

```
displaySemanticObjectOn: aGC at: aPoint refresh: aBool
  | nameConnector |
  nameConnector := internalConnectors at: #name
  (semanticObject vollstaendig)
    ifTrue: [ nameConnector graphicObject format:#bold ]
    ifFalse:[ nameConnector graphicObject format:#normal ].

  "Der Name wird 10 Punkte links vom Zentrum angezeigt "

  semanticObject name notEmpty
    ifTrue:
      [nameConnector
        displayCenteredOn:  aGC
        at: (self centerTextDisplayPoint + (aPoint-(10@0)))
        refresh: aBool
      ].

  "Das Kuerzel wird im Abstand 10@12 rechts von der linken
   unteren Ecke angezeigt"

  semanticObject kuerzel notEmpty
    ifTrue:
      [(internalConnectors at: #kuerzel)
          displayOn:    aGC
           at: (((graphicObject left)@(graphicObject bottom))-
                 (-10@12))
           refresh: aBool
      ]
```

vis-A-vis stellt eine Reihe von Methoden zur Verfügung, um Positionen zu berechnen, an denen Aspekte eines semantischen Objekts dargestellt werden sollen. Die Methode *centerTextDisplayPoint* liefert zum Beispiel einen Punkt, um einen Text zentriert in ein flächiges geometrisches Objekt zu plazieren. Diese wird verwendet, wenn der Name einer Rate angezeigt wird. Reichen die vordefinierten Methoden nicht aus, so muß der Punkt, an dem ein Aspekt angezeigt werden soll, ausgerechnet werden. Dies wird im Beispiel für den internen Konnektor getan, der das Namenskürzel darstellt.

5.4 Aufwand zur Implementierung des System Dynamics - Editors

Bei der Implementierung des System Dynamics-Editors brauchten wir uns nicht um die Symbolhandhabung zu kümmern. *DisplayableSplineLines* konnten eingesetzt werden, um Pfeile mit abgerundeten Ecken zu erzeugen. Alle Pfeile und Beschriftungen folgen, wenn ein Symbol verschoben wird. Ohne Zusatzaufwand für den Werkzeugbauer werden die semantischen Objekte benachrichtigt, wenn ihre Repräsentationen durch Pfeile verbunden werden. Icons und Hilfetexte müssen nur in der Konfigurationsdatei zur Verfügung gestellt werden; sie in die Palette bzw. in das Textfenster zu bringen, obliegt der Installationsroutine und vis-A-vis selbst.

Die semantische Klassen und die Werkzeugklasse müssen eine Beschreibung aller semantischen Menüs liefern (im wesentlichen eine Liste der Menüpunkte) und die entsprechenden Menüoperationen zur Verfügung stellen. vis-A-vis setzt aus den Beschreibungen funktionierende Menüs zusammen, blendet sie auf, wenn das Symbol angeklickt ist und löst die ausgewählte Operation im semantischen Objekt aus. Speichern und Laden der erstellten Modelle erledigt vis-A-vis alleine.

Ein Student hat den System Dynamics - Editor (ohne den Simulationsrahmen) innerhalb von 40 Mann-Stunden implementiert. Da der Editor eine der ersten Anwendungen von vis-A-vis war, erwarten wir, vergleichbare Anwendungen in Zukunft noch wesentlich schneller realisieren zu können, wenn wir mehr Erfahrungen gesammelt und die Dokumentation weiter verbessert haben.

6. Ausblick: Gegenwärtige und zukünftige Entwicklungsschritte

Der Entwicklungsstand von vis-A-vis läßt sich heute folgendermaßen beschreiben:

- vis-A-vis verbindet erfolgreich semantische Objekte eines Modells mit ihren Visualisierungen;
- vis-A-vis unterstützt, jedoch nur unzureichend, die Speicherung von Modellen und allgemeine Operationen auf den semantischen Modellen. vis-A-vis sieht vor, daß die Modelle in der objekt-orientierten Datenbank GemStone gespeichert und von dort geladen werden können.
- vis-A-vis bietet außer einem einfachen Icon-Editor und der Installationsroutine keine Unterstützung des Werkzeugbauers im Sinne von Meta-Werkzeugen, die verwendet werden könnten, um einen neuen Editor weitgehend ohne Programmierung zu erstellen.

Unsere Arbeit hat derzeit eine Konsolidierungs- und Evaluationsphase erreicht. Einige Anwendungen sind in Angriff genommen und haben bereits einige Schwächen gezeigt und zu Verbesserungen geführt. Dazu zählt

- der vorgestellte System Dynamics-Editor,
- ein Editor mit dem Software-Architekturen modelliert werden können (siehe Lichter, 1992)
- und verschiedene Editoren, die im Rahmen des Projekts SESAM eingesetzt werden, um der Software-Entwicklungsprozeß zu modellieren und zu simulieren (siehe Schneider, 1993).

Hand in Hand mit der Entwicklung von vis-A-vis erweitern und verbessern wir auch ständig die Dokumentation in verschiedener Hinsicht: Neben der existierenden Architektur- und Code-Dokumentation erarbeiten wir ein allgemeines vis-A-vis Benutzerhandbuch und ein Werkzeugbauer-Handbuch (mit ausführlichen Beispielen) Mit systematischen Code-Reviews streben wir ein hohes Qualitätsniveau und größtmögliche Wartungsfreundlichkeit an.

Zukünftig werden wir die folgenden beiden Aspekte in vis-A-vis realisieren:

Komfortable Mechanismen für die Verwendung semantischer Modelle

Bisher werden semantische Modelle aufgebaut und entsprechend der visualisierten Grafik (also des Diagramms) ein Graph erzeugt; dieser semantische Graph ist ein strukturgleicher "Schatten" der Grafik. Bei dessen Aufbau werden bisher bereits einige Konsistenzbedingungen beachtet.

Wir werden demnächst dem Werkzeugbauer wesentlich mächtigere und komfortablere Möglichkeiten an die Hand geben, um mit dem semantischen Graph umzugehen und ihn im Sinne der Anwendung zu bearbeiten:

- Einfache Navigation im Graphen: Durch sehr einfache Operationen soll es möglich sein, den Graphen von einem Knoten über eine Relation zum nächsten Knoten usw. zu durchwandern.
- Mengenorientierte Abfrage nach Graphstrukturen: Der Werkzeugbauer soll durch einfache Operationen ganze Mengen von Knoten und Relationen erfragen können. So kann er Teilmodelle extrahieren und bearbeiten oder z.B. auch feststellen, durch welchen Pfad (von Relationen) zwei Objekte im Graph verbunden sind.
- Einheitlich spezifizierte und unterstützte Graphveränderungen: Entsprechend dem Formalismus der Graph-Grammatiken von Göttler (1988) wollen wir dem Werkzeugbauer Möglichkeiten anbieten, um strukturelle Umbauten des Graphen einheitlich zu beschreiben und einfach zu implementieren. Natürlich bewirkt der Umbau des semantischen Graphen automatisch auch eine Anpassung der Visualisierung in vis-A-vis.
- Strengere Trennung der semantischen Objekte in vis-A-vis: In Zukunft werden semantische Objekte nicht mehr direkt am Konnektor hängen. Wir führen statt dessen eine Indirektionsstufe, die sogenannten "Umschläge", ein, in denen nun wiederum die semantischen Objekte stecken. Der Vorteil: Alle Navigations- und vis-A-vis-typischen Operationen und Daten, die ein semantisches Objekt persistent speichern und beherrschen muß, werden im zugehörigen Umschläge gekapselt. Das semantische Objekt "merkt" dann gar nicht mehr, wenn es in vis-A-vis eingesetzt wird; es muß in keinerlei Weise verändert oder darauf vorbereitet werden. Das erleichtert die Anwendung von vis-A-vis auf bestehende Systeme, deren Objekte nun nicht mehr angepaßt, sondern nur noch in die Umschläge eingepackt werden müssen.

Unterstützung des Werkzeugbauers durch Meta-Werkzeuge

Es lassen sich einige Aktivitäten, die zur Zeit noch mühsam von Hand durchgeführt werden müssen, durch Werkzeuge unterstützen. Folgende Werkzeuge sind denkbar:

Symbol-Editor
Mit diesem Werkzeug sollen interaktiv die Symbole der grafischen Notation aus den Grundvisualisierungsformen zusammengesetzt werden. Weiterhin soll damit die Abbildung der Attribute semantischer Modellelemente auf deren Visualisierung im Werkzeug angegeben werden können.

Menü-Editor
Damit sollen alle semantischen Menüs (die der Modellelemente und die des Werkzeugs) interaktiv definiert werden können.

Konfigurations-Werkzeug
Es soll dazu dienen, die Konfigurationsinformationen für ein neues vis-A-vis-Werkzeug zu erstellen und den Installationsschritt anzustoßen

Diese Werkzeuge werden dazu beitragen, daß der für ein vis-A-vis-Werkzeug notwendige Programmieraufwand auf den Teil reduziert wird, der anwendungsspezifisch ist und somit nicht generiert werden kann.

Literatur

Baumgarten, B. (1990): Petri-Netze Grundlagen und Anwendungen. Bibliographisches Institut, Mannheim.

Böcker, H.-D., Pawlitschek, M (1992): VICK: a visualization construction kit. Journal of Object-Oriented Programming, Vol. 4, No. 8, pp, 8-14.

Budde, R., M.-L. Christ-Neumann, K.-H. Sylla (1992): Tools and Materials, an Analysis and Design Metaphor. G.Heeg, B. Magnussen, B. Meyer (eds.), Proceedings of the Seventh International Conference TOOLS Europe '92, Prentice Hall.

Forrester, J. W. (1961): Industrial Dynamics, M.I.T.-Press, Cambridge, MA.

Forrester, J. W. (1972): Grundzüge einer Systemtheorie, Betriebswirtschaftlicher Verlag Dr. Th. Gabler, Wiesbaden.

Gamma, E., A. Weinand, R. Marty (1988): Integration of a Programming Environment into ET++ A Case Study, Proc. of ECOOP '89, Cambridge University Press, pp. 283-287.

Göttler, H. (1988): Graphgrammatiken in der Softwaretechnik, Springer, Berlin.

Krasner, G., S. Pope (1988): A Cookbook for using the Model-View-Controller User Interface in Smalltalk-80, Parc Place Systems.

Lichter, H. (1992): Architecture Prototyping - A Seamless Transition into the Final System. Proc. of the NordDATA'92 conference, Tampere, Finland.

Schneider, K. (1993): Object-Oriented Simulation of the Software Development Process in SESAM; Proc. of Western Multiconference on Computer Simulation, San Diego, 17.-20.1. 1993.

Schneider, K. (1991): Systematische Evaluierung von CASE-Tools, Tagungsband zur TOOL 91, Karlsruhe, 27.-28. 11.91; vde-Verlag, Berlin.

Weinand, A., E. Gamma, R. Marty (1989): Design and Implementation of ET++, a Seamless Object-Oriented Application Framework. Structured Programming, Vol. 10, No 2.

Warenzeichen

STELLA ist ein Warenzeichen von High Performance Systems, Inc.
GemStone ist ein Warenzeichen von SERVIO Logic.
Smalltalk-80 ist ein Warenzeichen von Parc Place Systems, Inc.

Rational Rose: Objektorientierte Analyse und objektorientiertes Design nach der Booch-Methode

Peter Wehrum und Dorothea Mehling

Rational GmbH

Rosenstraße 7

8023 Pullach im Isartal

1 Einleitung

Die Booch-Methode wurde 1991 publiziert [1]. Ergänzungen finden sich in weiteren Papieren [2, 3]. Die Booch-Methode ist aus der Praxis heraus in einem 10-jährigen Entwicklungsprozeß bei Rational entstanden. Sie kann in allen Anwendungs- und Einsatzbereichen benutzt werden, da sie **programmiersprachenunabhängig** ist. Sie stellt eine reichhaltige, umfassende **graphische Notation** sowie ein durchgängiges **Vorgehensmodell** bereit. Eine **Werkzeugunterstützung** für diese Methode wird seit Mitte 1992 von Rational unter dem Namen *Rational Rose* (Rational Object-oriented Software Engineering) angeboten. In diesem Beitrag sollen das Vorgehensmodell, die Notation und Rational Rose näher erläutert werden.

2 Das Vorgehensmodell

Der Lebenszyklus für die objektorientierte Softwareentwicklung nach Booch setzt sich aus vier Phasen zusammen: Analyse, Design, Evolution, Modifikation. Die Softwareentwicklung wird als *Rundreise* durch die Phasen, d. h. als inkrementeller, iterativer Prozeß verstanden, bei dem die genannten Phasen mehrfach durchlaufen werden. Jede der einzelnen Phasen ist durch unterschiedliche Zielsetzungen und Ergebnisse charakterisiert.

Während der Analyse liegt der Schwerpunkt der Aktivitäten auf der Entdeckung der wesentlichen Abstraktionen aus der gegebenen Problemdomäne, d. h., es werden Klassen und Objekte identifiziert, die das gewünschte Verhalten des Systems bescheiben (*knowledge acquisition*). Unter Berücksichtigung der gegebenen Anforderungen an das zukünftige System wird ein Domänenmodell erstellt, das konsistent, lesbar und überprüfbar für alle am Entwicklungsprozeß beteiligten Entwickler und Benutzer ist.

In der Designphase findet eine Verfeierung des in der Analysephase entstandenen Domänenmodells statt. Hier liegt der Schwerpunkt der Aktivitäten auf der Erfindung von Klassen und Objekten, die notwendig sind, um das Domänenmodell in eine ablauffähige Form zu überführen. Ziel des Designs ist es, erste Prototypen zu entwickeln, die nur einen Teil der Anforderungen auf einer weniger detaillierten Ebene als das endgültige System implementieren. Diese Prototypen werden bewertet, und deren Ergebnisse werden in den Analyse- und Designprozeß zurückgeführt.

Die nacheinander entwickelten Prototypen werden weiter verfeinert und münden in die endgültige Implementierung (evolutionäres Prototyping). Damit wird erreicht, daß beim iterativen, inkrementellen Entwicklungsprozeß anstelle eines einzigen *big bang* der Systemintegration mehrere Teilintegrationen kontinuierlich während des gesamten Lebenszyklus auftreten.

In der Modifikationsphase wird das System an geänderte Anforderungen angepaßt. Die hier relevanten Aktivitäten umfassen: Hinzunehmen neuer Klassen, Änderung der Implementierung einer Klasse, Änderung der Schnittstelle einer Klasse, usw.

In der Analyse- und Designphase wird dabei weder nur top-down noch nur bottom-up vorgegangen. Das empfohlene Vorgehen kann als Jojo-Verfahren beschrieben werden: Verfeinerung durch das Top-down-Vorgehen und Generalisierung durch das Bottom-up-Vorgehen wechseln sich in der Regel ab.

3 Die Booch-Notation

Die graphische Notation von Booch dient der Beschreibung von Modellen, die in der Analyse- und in der Designphase erarbeitet werden: Entscheidungen und Ergebnisse werden in Form von Diagrammen (und textuellen Spezifikationen) festgehalten, die sich sowohl für die Kommunikation zwischen allen am Softwareentwicklungsprozeß beteiligten Personen als auch für die Erstellung von Dokumentation eignen. Die Booch-Notation sieht Klassen-, Kategorie-, Zustandsübergangs-, Objekt-, Zeit-, Modul-, Subsystem- und Prozeßdiagramme vor. Es gibt sieben verschiedene Arten von Klassen und sechs verschiedene Arten von Klassenrelationen (so z. B. die *Vererbungs*- und die *Benutzt*relation. Diese Diagramme zusammen mit den entsprechenden Spezifikationen erlauben es, Systeme nicht nur aus **logischer**, sondern auch aus **physischer Sicht** zu beschreiben sowie ihre **statische** und **dynamische**

Semantik zu definieren. Beispielsweise dienen Klassendiagramme dazu, die statische Semantik aus logischer Sicht zu beschreiben. Im Gegensatz zu strukturierten Verfahren ermöglicht die Booch-Methode einen **nahtlosen Übergang** zwischen Analyse und Design: Ein und dieselbe Notation wird für Analyse und Entwurf verwendet. Die gesamte Klassenstruktur eines Systems kann durch ein einzelnes Klassendiagramm oder auch mehrere Klassendiagramme ausgedrückt werden.

4 Rational Rose

Das graphische Werkzeug Rational Rose unterstützt die sprachenunabhängige objektorientierte Analyse und den objektorientierten Entwurf, wie oben angedeutet und wie ausführlich in [1] beschrieben. Insbesondere gestattet Rational Rose, alle Diagramme zu zeichnen, die entsprechenden Spezifikationen zu definieren und auf diese Weise logische und physische Sichten von Systemmodellen zu analysieren und zu entwerfen.

Das Herzstück von Rational Rose ist eine zentrale Datenbasis, ein Repositorium, in dem alle semantischen Projektinformationen feinkörnig abgelegt sind und auf dem alle Komponenten von Rose operieren (*single-source*-Prinzip). Rational Rose kann mit Hilfe dieser feinkörnigen Abspeicherung von Informationen (z. B. bezüglich Klassen, Objekten und Methoden) eine Reihe von **Überprüfungen** eines vorliegenden Modells durchführen. Diese Überprüfungen betreffen zum einen die **Syntax**, die Vergabe von Namen, die Werte der Kardinalität und Aufrufreihenfolge von Methoden, zum anderen die **Semantik**, also z. B. die Sichtbarkeit zwischen Kategorien und allgemein die Konsistenz des gesamten Modells.

Rational Rose ist ein *offenes System*: über Programmschnittstellen und sog. *petal files* kann auf die Information des Repositoriums zugegriffen werden, neue Werkzeuge lassen sich in Rational Rose integrieren, und Rational Rose selbst kann verschiedenen *Frameworks* (wie z.B. Softbench, Workbench) eingegliedert werden. Das Rational Rose-Kernprodukt setzt sich aus folgenden Komponenten zusammen: graphische Benutzeroberfläche, Browser, Tool zur Unterstützung der Dokumentengenerierung, Tool zur Überprüfung der Syntax und Semantik, Online-Hypertext-Hilfefunktion und -Referenzmanual, Tutorial sowie der Entwurf der *Booch Components*, einer wiederverwendbaren Klassenbibliothek in C++. Zusätzlich gibt es in Erprobung befindliche *Forward- und Reverse- Engineering*-Werkzeuge für C++. Mit Forward Engineering sind allgemein Codegeneratoren gemeint, die aus Booch-Diagrammen den Quellcode einer Programmiersprache erzeugen. Reverse Engineering bezieht sich auf den umgekehrten Vorgang, nämlich aus Quellcode graphische Strukturen in der Booch-Notation aufbauen.

Rational Rose steht für verschiedene Plattformen zur Verfügung: Auf UNIX-Systemen läuft Rational Rose als Client/Server-Applikation unter Motif oder OpenWindows ab. Ein *floating-license server* gestattet es, Rational Rose von beliebigen UNIX-Systemen und Terminals (z.B. X-Terminals, PC mit X-Emulation) im Netz aufzurufen. Außerdem steht Rational Rose für IBM-kompatible PC unter Windows 3.0 und für OS/2 zur Verfügung.

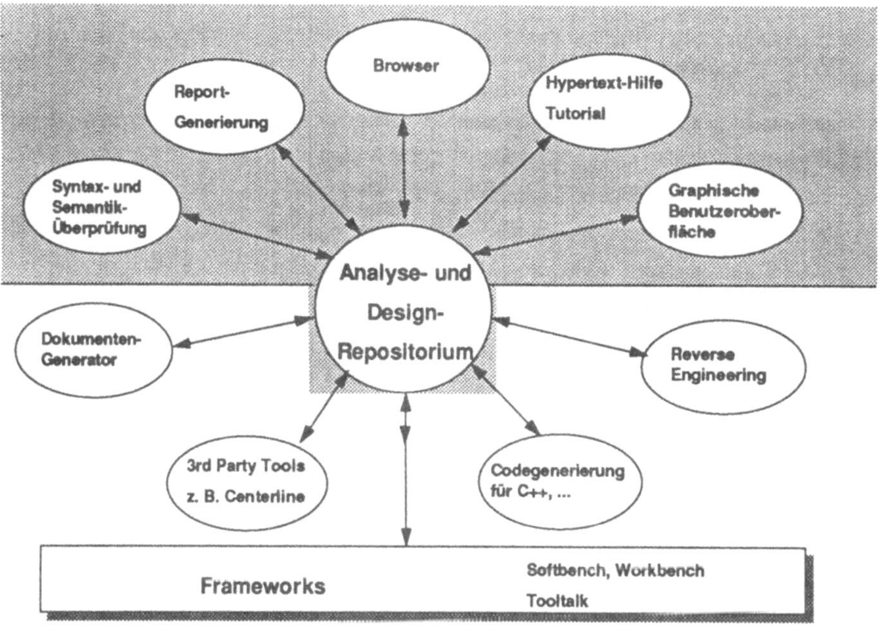

Abb. 1: Die Komponenten von Rational Rose

Zukünftig wird Rational Rose zu einer Produktfamilie erweitert, die aus dem oben beschriebenen Rose-Kernprodukt , den Forward- und Reverse- Engineering-Tools sowie weiteren *layered products* besteht (Abb. 1). Damit wird Rational Rose nicht nur die Phasen Analyse und Design unterstützen, sondern auch die Phasen Evolution und Modifikation des erweiterten Softwarelebenszyklus. Die Forward- und Reverse-Engineering-Werkzeuge sind insbesondere vonnöten, um die Softwareentwicklung zu dem konsistenten *round-trip*-Prozeß auszugestalten, wie er von der Booch-Methode vorgesehen ist. Zukünftige Versionen werden neben der bereits implementierten Notation Zustandsübergangsdiagramme nach Harel [4] und eine neue Version der Zeitdiagramme bedienen.

Rational Rose wird für alle Plattformen **kompatibel** und **interoperabel** sein, d. h., die Projektdatenbasen werden über alle Plattformen hinweg portabel sein.

5 Einsatz

Die Booch-Methode und deren Vorläufer werden seit mehreren Jahren von zahlreichen Firmen in großen Projekten mit Erfolg benutzt. Um zwei Beispiele zu nennen: CelsiusTech in Schweden geht bei der Entwicklung von C^3I-Software für fünf Schiffstypen (1,5 Mill. LoC pro Schiff) nach der Booch-Methode vor. Ein anderes großes Projekt, bei dem die Booch-Methode Verwendung findet, ist das Reengineering eines existierenden, 4 Millionen C-Codezeilen umfassenden Telekommunikationssystems, bei dem 500.000 Codezeilen in C++ umgeschrieben werden (AT&T).

Rational Rose ist seit Sommer 1992 als Produkt verfügbar geworden. Bei der Entwicklung dieses Werkzeugs ist die Booch-Methode erfolgreich eingesetzt worden. Die ersten Prototypen von Rational Rose sind in Smalltalk und die Produktversionen in C++ realisiert worden. Die erste Produktversion umfaßte 800 Klassen in 20 Kategorien/Subsystemen. IBM/USA hat für die interne Systementwicklung rund 1000 Lizenzen von Rational Rose beschafft.

Literatur

[1] Booch G., *Object Oriented Design with Applications*, Benjamin/Cummings, Menlo Park / Redwood City 1991

[2] Booch G., *The Booch Method: Notation*, Santa Clara: Rational, Juli 1992, pp.1-32

[3] Booch G., *The Booch Method: Process and Pragmatics*, Santa Clara: Rational, Juli 1992, pp.1-13

[4] Harel D., *Statecharts: A Visual Formalism for Complex Systems*. Science of Computer Programming, Vol. 8, 1987

Rational® ist ein registriertes Warenzeichen von Rational, Rational Rose™ ist ein Warenzeichen von Rational; UNIX ist ein eingetragenes Warenzeichen der USL; OSF/Motif™ ist ein Warenzeichen der Open Software Foundation

Spezielle Konzepte

Integritätssicherung durch lokale Methoden

Gerhard Koschorreck, Udo W. Lipeck

Institut für Informatik, Universität Hannover
Lange Laube 22, D-W 3000 Hannover 1
{gk|ul}@informatik.uni-hannover.de

1 Motivation

Aufgabe des Datenbank-Entwurfs ist es, ein Modell der realen Welt zu entwerfen. Neben der Entwicklung adäquater Speicherstrukturen kommt dabei der Berücksichtigung von Integritätsbedingungen eine zentrale Bedeutung zu ([TF82], [Lip89], [Lip92], [Saa92]). Es kann sich hierbei um Restriktionen handeln, die sich aus der Struktur der Daten ergeben *(z.B. müssen Kundendaten zu Aufträgen vorliegen)*, um firmenpolitische Richtlinien *(Angestellte dürfen nicht mehr als ihre Vorgesetzten verdienen)* oder auch um gesetzliche Bestimmungen *(z.B. Ordnungsmäßigkeit der Buchführung)*. Während die Spezifikation von Integritätsbedingungen im Rahmen des objekt-orientierten Entwurfs bei Meyer [Mey88] einen breiten Raum einnimmt, fehlt sie bei [Boo91] fast gänzlich.

Um später die Einhaltung von Integritätsbedingungen sicherstellen zu können, müssen sie bereits zur Entwurfszeit spezifiziert werden. Da jedoch auch Datenbankanwendungen dem zeitlichen Wandel unterliegen, muß eine Erweiterung sowohl des Schemas als auch der zugehörigen Integritätsbedingungen möglich sein. Bisherige Arbeiten zur Schema-Evolution (z.B. [NR89], [Su91]) betrachten in erster Linie die strukturellen Änderungen und lassen die Integritätssicherung unberücksichtigt.

Die Überwachung von Integritätsbedingungen durch einen zentralen Monitor führt bei bisherigen Ansätzen zu großen Effizienzeinbußen, da z.B. alle Tupel einer Relation überprüft werden müssen, wenn nur ein einziges Tupel verändert worden ist. Diesem Dilemma kann man entgehen, wenn man vorab Transaktionen, die Grundbausteine von DB-Anwendungsprogrammen sein sollen, festlegt und so entwirft, daß sie die Integrität der Datenbank immer wahren ([Lip89], [Saa91]); damit tut man sich in klassischen Datenbanksystemen schwer, da die Standardoperationen `insert` / `delete` / `update` als Bausteine zur Verfügung stehen und beliebige adhoc-Transaktionen erlauben.

Einen Ansatzpunkt zur Behebung einiger der oben genannten Probleme bietet die objektorientierte Sichtweise. Betrachtet man die konzeptionellen Objekte, die Objekte der realen Welt repräsentieren, auch als die Einheiten der Integritätssicherung, so kann die Überwachung von Integritätsbedingungen objekt-lokal durchgeführt werden. Statt der Transaktionen sorgen dann (dynamisch modifizierbare) Methoden für die Einhaltung der Integritätsbedingungen.

Integritätsbedingungen, die alle Objekte einer Klasse betreffen, beispielsweise ein Maximalwert für ein bestimmtes Attribut, können bereits beim Entwurf der Zugriffsmethoden berücksichtigt werden.

Andererseits kann es jedoch auch Restriktionen geben, die nur eine Teilmenge der Instanzen einer Klasse betreffen. Ein Beispiel hierfür ist, daß alle Angestellten, die Buchhalter sind, keine Gehaltserhöhung bekommen dürfen. Für Buchhalter müssen also die gehaltsändernden Methoden überwacht werden. Es empfiehlt sich jedoch nicht, die Methoden der Klasse zu ändern, weil dann immer ein Test auf den Beruf durchgeführt werden müßte.

Die allgemeinste Gruppe von Integritätsbedingungen sind Restriktionen auf beliebig, homogen wie heterogen zusammengesetzten Objekten (hier einheitlich Aggregationen genannt). Die Bedingungen können also auch Objekte betreffen, die verschiedenen Klassen angehören. In einem solchen Fall ist es sinnvoll, für jede Aggregation von Objekten ein eigenes Objekt einzuführen, in dem dann auch gemeinsam benötigte Informationen gespeichert werden können.

Aufgabe des Datenbank-Entwurfs ist hier, eine Transformation von Integritätsbedingungen durchzuführen: Bedingungen, die die Aggregation als Ganzes betreffen, sind so zu modifizieren, daß sie objekt-lokal in den Komponenten geprüft werden können. Dazu kann es notwendig sein, Hilfsinformationen zu verwalten, die eine effiziente Prüfung von Bedingungen erlauben. Tests, ob eine Restriktion verletzt ist, sollten nur in den Objekten stattfinden, die auch wirklich Teil einer Aggregation sind.

Da nicht alle Objekte einer Klasse an Aggregationen teilnehmen müssen, ist es nicht sinnvoll, die Prüfung der Einhaltung solcher Bedingungen in die Spezifikation der Klasse aufzunehmen. Es besteht somit das Problem, daß sich ein Objekt anders verhalten kann, je nachdem, ob es in einer Aggregation enthalten ist oder nicht.

Aufgrund der Langlebigkeit von Datenbankanwendungen kann der Fall eintreten, daß Objekte einer bereits vorhandenen Klasse an einer neu definierten Aggregation teilnehmen sollen. Formuliert man nun Integritätsbedingungen für die Aggregation, so betreffen diese auch bereits vorhandene Objekte. Um eine objekt-lokale und dynamisch änderbare Integritätsüberwachung durchführen zu können, müssen die Methoden der Komponenten um zusätzliche Integritätsprüfungen angereichert werden. Wiederum ist eine Modifikation der "alten" Spezifikation der Komponenten nicht sinnvoll, da nicht unbedingt alle Objekte der Klasse an Aggregationen teilnehmen.

Für die Spezifikation von Objektsystemen ist eine ähnliche Methodik anzustreben, wie sie Sannella [San90] für allgemeine Programme vorschlägt. Die Spezifikation von Objekten erfolgt zunächst deklarativ, wobei ein besonderer Schwerpunkt auf der Formulierung von Integritätsbedingungen liegt. Durch schrittweise Verfeinerung gelangt man schließlich zu ausführbaren Programmen. In der vorliegenden Arbeit geben wir einen einfachen Mechanismus an, der es erlaubt, Integritätssicherung durch Methoden zu beschreiben *(Methodenkontext)*. Hierbei werden jedoch einerseits die Methodendefinitionen der zu überwachenden Objekte erhalten, andererseits ist aber auch eine dynamische Anpassung an neue bzw. veränderte Integritätsbedingungen möglich.

Im folgenden Abschnitt beschreiben wir den Weg vom Entwurf einer Spezifikation bis zu ihrer Implementierung. Zunächst wird die Beschreibungssprache für Objekte vorgestellt, dann gehen wir auf die Verfeinerung von Spezifikationen ein und geben schließlich einen Ansatz zur Implementierung von integritätssichernden Methoden an. In Abschnitt 3 illustrieren wir an typischen Beispielen die systematische Umsetzung von Integritätsbedingungen für Aggregationen in Methoden.

2 Von der Spezifikation zur Implementierung

2.1 Objekt-Beschreibungssprache

In objekt-orientierten Systemen ist es notwendig, Struktur und Verhalten von Objekten festzulegen. In Programmiersprachen wie z.B. Eiffel [Mey92] können Vor- und Nachbedingungen für die Ausführung von Methoden formuliert werden, so daß die Konsistenz der Einzelobjekte sichergestellt werden kann. Bei der Spezifikation von Datenbankanwendungen liegt jedoch ein besonderer Schwerpunkt auf der Beschreibung von Beziehungen zwischen Objekten unterschiedlicher Klassen. Vor- und Nachbedingungen, die lediglich für Methoden einer Klasse definiert werden, reichen hierzu nicht aus. Außerdem müssen temporale Integritätsbedingungen berücksichtigt werden. In der Spezifikation einer Aggregation muß auch auf die Komponenten Bezug genommen werden können.

Die im folgenden beschriebene Objekt-Beschreibungssprache benutzt eine Notation ähnlich der der Spezifikationssprache TROLL ([JSHS91], [SJ91]), ohne jedoch alle Sprachkonstrukte zu übernehmen.

Eine Objekt-Spezifikation hat folgendes Aussehen:

```
objecttype =

  signature
  integrity
  characterization
  state
  effect
  applicability
  calling
  implementation

end;
```

Die Abschnitte **state**, **applicability**, **calling** und **implementation** brauchen nicht unbedingt sofort alle gleichmäßig ausgefüllt werden, sondern erst schrittweise im Laufe der Verfeinerung (s.u.); sie werden teilweise auch erst dort erklärt.

Im Signatur-Teil wird die nach außen sichtbare Schnittstelle des Objektes spezifiziert. Hierzu gehört z.B. der Typ des vereinbarten Objektes und die Methoden, die auf ein Objekt angewandt werden können.

Um einen Objekttyp EMPLOYEE zu definieren, kann ein Ausschnitt des Signatur-Teils wie folgt aussehen:

```
signature

    type   employee;

    birth  hire       : string * string * int -> employee;
    method set_salary : int ->;
    method set_job    : string ->;
    method get_empno  : -> int;
    method get_ename  : -> string;
    method get_job    : -> string;
    method get_salary : -> int;
    method get_age    : -> int;
```

Bei der Methode `hire` handelt es sich um eine ausgezeichnete Methode, die der Erzeugung neuer Objekte dient. Möchte man das Alter einer Person abspeichern, so spezifiziert man die entsprechende Zugriffsmethode, beispielsweise `get_age`. Ob man wirklich das Alter speichert oder doch das Geburtsdatum und die Altersberechnung dann jeweils beim Zugriff durchführt, ist eine Entscheidung, die nicht auf der konzeptionellen Ebene getroffen werden muß. Deshalb ist es auf dieser Ebene der Spezifikation nicht erforderlich, zwischen Attributen und Zugriffsoperationen zu unterscheiden. Trennt man so Signatur und Repräsentation der Daten, ist es möglich, im nachhinein die Implementierung eines Objektes unter Beibehaltung der Signatur zu ändern. Andere Klassen, die die veränderten Objekte benutzen, werden davon nicht betroffen.

Im Abschnitt `integrity` werden die für diese Klasse gültigen Integritätsbedingungen festgelegt. Es kann sich dabei sowohl um statische als auch um dynamische Bedingungen handeln. Die folgende Bedingung legt ein Mindestgehalt für alle Angestellten fest:

```
integrity
  forall e:employee . e.get_salary >= 2000
```

Der Charakterisierungs-Teil (`characterization`) wird benutzt, um deklarativ Eigenschaften der Gesamtheit aller definierten Objekte zu beschreiben. Für eine Klasse wie `EMPLOYEE` ist die Charakterisierung leer, da klar ist, daß alle durch die Methode `hire` erzeugten Objekte auch Instanzen der Klasse sind. Dieser Teil der Spezifikation wird dann benötigt, wenn z.B. die Zugehörigkeit zu einer bestimmten Menge nicht durch explizite Mengenoperationen beeinflußt wird, sondern durch ein Prädikat beschrieben wird. Ein Beispiel für eine solche Beschreibung findet sich, wenn man eine Klasse von Angestellten hat und dann die Teilklasse aller Angestellten mit einem bestimmten Beruf einführt. Ein Angestellter kann durch Versetzung in eine solche Menge hineinkommen oder sie auch wieder verlassen. Es handelt sich hier um eine dynamische Klassifikation.

Im Zustands-Teil (`state`) wird festgelegt, wie die Daten repräsentiert werden. Hier muß also die Entscheidung getroffen werden, ob ein Attribut physisch gespeichert wird, oder ob es abgeleitet werden kann. Für Angestellte legt man z.B. fest, daß es die nachstehenden Attribute gibt.

```
state
  attributes
    ename  : string;
    job    : string;
    salary : int;
```

Welche Auswirkungen die Anwendung einer Methode haben, wird unter `effect` aufgeführt. So bedeutet beispielsweise

```
[set_job(job)] get_job = job;
```

daß nach Ausführung der Methode `set_job` mit dem Parameter `job` die Zugriffsmethode `get_job` den Wert von `job` liefert. Es wird beschrieben, welche Wirkungen zustandsändernde Methoden auf Zugriffsmethoden haben.

Bei der Spezifikation von Integritätsbedingungen kann es sich als sinnvoll erweisen, die Anwendbarkeit von Methoden unter gewissen Umständen auszuschließen, z.B. wenn die Anwendung zu einer Integritätsverletzung führen würde. Im `applicability`-Teil der

Spezifikation können diese Fälle behandelt werden. Die Entscheidung, unter welchen Umständen eine Methode anwendbar ist, ergibt sich meist durch eine Konkretisierung der deklarativ angegebenen IBen. Geht man beispielsweise von der obigen Bedingung des Mindestgehalts aus, so kann man fordern, daß eine Gehaltsänderung nur ausgeführt wird, wenn der Wert größer als 2000 ist.

```
applicability
  set_salary(sal) only when sal >= 2000;
```

Die im Abschnitt `effect` aufgeführten Auswirkungen der Methodenanwendung gelten natürlich nur, wenn die Methode auch wirklich anwendbar war. Außerdem muß darauf geachtet werden, daß die Einschränkungen der Anwendbarkeit konsistent mit den angegebenen Integritätsbedingungen sind.

Bei der Spezifikation von Aggregationen kann der Fall auftreten, daß der Aufruf einer Methode einen anderen Methodenaufruf auslösen soll. Dies wird im Abschnitt `calling` festgelegt.

Im Implementierungsteil (`implementation`) wird die Implementierung der Methoden angegeben; Methoden, die nicht im Signatur-Teil angegeben wurden, sind dabei lokal. Grundsätzlich muß die Implementierung zum Signatur-Teil "passen", d.h. Anzahl und Typ der Parameter von Methoden müssen übereinstimmen, für alle in der Signatur aufgeführten Methoden muß es eine Entsprechung im Implementierungsteil geben, etc.

2.2 Verfeinerung von Spezifikationen

Der Entwurf von Datenbank-Anwendungen ist ein dynamischer Prozeß, der sich meist in mehreren Stufen vollzieht. Im Anfang geht man von einer deklarativen Beschreibung der interessierenden Objekte aus, die dann immer weiter verfeinert wird, bis am Ende eine konkrete Implementierung in einer ausführbaren (Programmier-)Sprache vorliegt.

Zu Beginn eines Entwurfs ist es notwendig, die Schnittstelle eines Objektes nach außen, d.h. seine Signatur festzulegen. Hierbei spielt die Repräsentation von Objekten durch Speicherstrukturen noch keine Rolle. Vielmehr sollte der Entwerfer die Freiheit besitzen, zu einem späteren Zeitpunkt zu entscheiden, wie Daten repräsentiert werden und diese Entscheidung ggf. revidieren können. In einem solchen Fall bleibt der Signatur-Teil unverändert, während im Zustands-Teil (`state`) eine andere Repräsentation gewählt werden kann. Dieses Vorgehen hat den Vorteil, daß alle anderen Klassen nicht verändert werden müssen, da sich die Schnittstelle der modifizierten Objekte nicht verändert hat.

Ein weiteres wichtiges Entwurfsziel ist die Spezifikation des Verhaltens von Objekten. Hierbei gilt es einerseits zu beschreiben, wie sich der Zustand eines Objektes verändert, und andererseits, welche Restriktionen, d.h. Integritätsbedingungen, zu beachten sind.

Zu Beginn des Entwurfsprozesses wird im Abschnitt `effect` der Spezifikation festgelegt, wie die verschiedenen Methoden zusammenwirken. Im obigen Angestellten-Beispiel wurde spezifiziert, daß nach dem Setzen der Berufsbezeichnung ein Zugriff mit `get_job` diesen Beruf als Ergebnis liefert. In einer verfeinerten Spezifikation muß nun der Bezug zu den im Zustands-Teil angegebenen Attributen hergestellt werden. In unserem Beispiel heißt dies, daß sich in der Implementierung die folgende Methodendefinition findet:

```
set_job(j:string) is
  job := j
end;
```

Integritätsbedingungen werden zunächst im Abschnitt `integrity` definiert. Falls der Spezifizierende aus diesen Bedingungen bereits Rückschlüsse auf die Anwendbarkeit von Methoden ziehen konnte, so finden sich diese Angaben im Abschnitt `applicability`. Die Angabe von Restriktionen in deklarativer Form liefert in den seltensten Fällen direkte Hinweise auf eine effiziente Überwachung. Im weiteren Entwurfsprozeß muß deshalb dafür gesorgt werden, daß die angegebene Implementierung der Methoden die Einhaltung der IBen garantiert. Ziel eines jeden Verfeinerungsschrittes ist somit, die Anzahl der im `integrity`-Abschnitt angegebenen Bedingungen zu reduzieren und stattdessen Implementierungen der Methoden anzugeben, die keine Integritätsverletzung mehr zulassen. In der endgültigen Spezifikation brauchen dann die IBen nicht mehr auftauchen. Sie können als Kommentare betrachtet werden, die angeben, was implementiert worden ist.

Beim Übergang von einer Verfeinerungsstufe zur nächsten muß natürlich sichergestellt sein, daß die Spezifikationen äquivalent sind. Äquivalenz bedeutet, daß sich die spezifizierten Objekte gleich verhalten.

2.3 Methodenkontext / Implementierung

Die Überwachung einer Integritätsbedingung kann vom Zustand eines Objektes abhängig sein. Hat z.B. ein Attribut einen speziellen Wert, muß eine IB geprüft werden, andernfalls nicht. Um eine effiziente Integritätssicherung durchzuführen, sollten die zusätzlichen Überprüfungen nur dann durchgeführt werden, wenn das Attribut den speziellen Wert hat. Eine Zustandsänderung kann also die Aktivierung bzw. Deaktivierung von Überprüfungen zur Folge haben.

Bestimmte IBen können nur dann effizient überwacht werden, wenn zusätzliche Informationen gespeichert werden. Während der Laufzeit eines Objektes muß nun sichergestellt werden, daß diese Zusatzinformationen konsistent bleiben. Auch hier können Zustandsänderungen von Objekten weitere Aktionen auslösen, um diese Informationen zu manipulieren.

Integritätssicherung mit Hilfe eines globalen Monitors zu realisieren, bedeutet, daß alle Methoden möglichst vor ihrer Ausführung auf Verletzung von Integritätsbedingungen überprüft werden. Dies verursacht einen erheblichen Aufwand, der es fraglich erscheinen läßt, ob dieser Ansatz in der Praxis anwendbar ist.

Das Hauptproblem der globalen Überwachung besteht darin, daß alle Methodenaufrufe kontrolliert werden müssen, insbesondere auch diejenigen, die nicht zu einer Integritätsverletzung führen können. Eine mögliche Optimierung besteht darin, die Spezifikation einer Klasse zu untersuchen und festzustellen, welche Methoden keiner Integritätsprüfung bedürfen.

Eine solche Analyse kann natürlich nur statische Gesichtspunkte berücksichtigen. Können Objekte Komponenten einer Aggregation werden und gelten dann für sie besondere Integritätsbedingungen, so müssen bei einem globalen Monitor alle Objekte dieser Klasse überwacht werden, obwohl nur ein Teil zu einem Zeitpunkt wirklich Komponente einer Aggregation ist.

Um eine effiziente Prüfung solcher IBen zu ermöglichen, sollten Bedingungsprüfungen zur Laufzeit aktiviert bzw. deaktiviert werden können. Hierzu kann der Methodenaufruf-Mechanismus modifiziert werden: Für jede Instanz einer Klasse soll es für jede Methode der Klasse einen *Methodenkontext* geben, der eine Liste von Methoden enthält, die vor bzw. nach dem eigentlichen Methodenaufruf ausgeführt werden (`pre`- und `post`-Aktionen).

Die Einführung eines solchen Methodenkontextes schlagen wir als eine wünschenswerte Erweiterung objekt-orientierter Programmiersprachen vor. Er unterscheidet sich von den sogenannten *daemon methods* des Commen Lisp Object Systems (siehe [Moo89]) dadurch, daß ein Kontext je Objekt existiert; die Modifikation des Methodenaufrufs erfolgt nicht für alle Objekte einer Klasse gleichzeitig.

Soll nun eine Methode ausgeführt werden, so wird zunächst die Liste der `pre`-Aktionen abgearbeitet. Hierin befinden sich dann z.B. die Bedingungen, die die Anwendbarkeit einer Methode festlegen. Stellt sich heraus, daß die Methode bei Ausführung eine Integritätsbedingungen verletzen würde, so kann die Verarbeitung an dieser Stelle abgebrochen werden. Nach Ausführung der aufgerufenen Methode werden alle `post`-Aktionen ausgeführt. Diese Aktionen können beispielsweise dazu benutzt werden, Zusatzinformationen zur effizienten Integritätsüberwachung zu verändern.

Die Ausführung einer Methode kann als "Mini-Transaktion" aufgefaßt werden, die dem ACID-Prinzip [HR83] genügt. Tritt innerhalb des Methodenkontextes eine Ausnahmesituation auf, so werden alle Änderungen rückgängig gemacht. Mit Hilfe des Methodenkontextes lassen sich somit sowohl optimistische Verfahren, bei denen zunächst Änderungen durchgeführt werden und anschließend (in einer `post`-Aktion) der Test auf Integritätsverletzung durchgeführt wird, als auch pessimistische Verfahren, bei denen die Bedingungsprüfung vor einer Aktion durchgeführt wird, realisieren.

Der Methodenkontext eines Objektes gibt zu jedem Zeitpunkt an, welche zusätzlichen Aktionen bei einem Methodenaufruf auszuführen sind. Da der Inhalt des Kontextes vom Objektzustand abhängen kann, benötigt man (Meta-)Methoden, um den Methodenkontext einer Methode eines bestimmten Objektes um Aktionen anzureichern oder um bestimmte Aktionen zu reduzieren. Insbesondere müssen die Methoden zur Kontextmanipulation selbst wieder in Methodenkontexten benutzt werden können. Aktivierung bzw. Deaktivierung von Bedingungsprüfungen finden besonders bei der Behandlung von Aggregationen Anwendung.

Soll eine IB überwacht werden, die nur in einem bestimmten Objektzustand geprüft werden muß, so beginnt die Überwachung mit Eintritt des speziellen Zustands. Der Eintritt dieses Zustands kann durch eine `post`-Aktion festgestellt werden, was dann die Anreicherung des Methodenkontextes des betreffenden Objekts zur Folge hat. Verläßt ein Objekt den ausgezeichneten Zustand, so kann eine Reduktion des Kontextes erfolgen.

Durch dynamische Änderungen des Methodenkontextes können unnötige Bedingungsprüfungen vermieden werden. Es ist eine effizientere Integritätssicherung möglich als mit einem globalen Monitor, da jeweils nur die Objekte überwacht werden, bei denen potentiell eine Integritätsverletzung möglich ist. Die Überwachung erfolgt lokal in den Objekten. Ein anderer Vorteil des Methodenkontextes besteht darin, daß auch bereits existierende Objekte überwacht werden können. "Alte" Objekte können Bestandteil einer neu definierten Aggregation werden, und mit Hilfe des Methodenkontextes ist es möglich, auch für diese Komponenten Integritätsbedingungen zu überwachen, ohne daß die Klassendefinition verändert werden müßte. Bei Eintritt in eine Aggregation wird lediglich der Methodenkontext des betreffenden Objektes erweitert.

Bei unserem Ansatz wird die Anwendung von Methoden nicht auf eine bestimmte Menge vorgefertigter Transaktionen eingeschränkt, von denen man weiß, daß sie die Konsistenz der Datenbank nicht gefährden. Es können beliebige Methoden benutzt werden; es kommen jedoch nur die Methoden zur Anwendung, die keine Integritätsverletzung zur Folge haben.

3 Exemplarischer Einsatz von Entwurfsmethoden

Im folgenden geben wir typische Beispiele an, wie durch die Verfeinerung von Spezifikationen unter Verwendung von Methodenkontexten eine effiziente Überwachung von Integritätsbedingungen auf komplexen Objekten möglich ist. Das erste Beispiel behandelt eine typische IB für Mengen von Objekten; Beispiel zwei verdeutlicht, wie eine dynamische Klassifikation von Objekten durchgeführt werden kann.

3.1 Explizite Definition von Mengen

Gegeben seien Zähler mit den Methoden `inc` und `dec` zum Inkrementieren und Dekrementieren des Zählerstandes sowie einer Methode `value`, die den aktuellen Zählerstand als Ergebnis liefert. Es sollen Mengen von Zählern zusammengefaßt werden, bei denen die Summe der Zählerstände kleiner als eine Maximalsumme (`max`) ist. Eine mögliche Anwendung ist die Überwachung von mehreren Haushaltstiteln. Ein Aggregationsobjekt kann dann z.B. die folgende Spezifikation besitzen:

```
objecttype COUNTER_SET (c: COUNTER) =

  signature

    type   counter_set;

    birth  create          : -> counter_set;

    method insert_counter : counter ->;
    method remove_counter : counter ->;
    method instances      : -> set of counter;
    method max            : -> int;
    method set_max        : int -> ;

  integrity

    forall cs:counter_set .
        sum_up(apply(value, cs.instances)) <= cs.max

  effect

    [create] max = 0;
    [create] instances = emptyset;
    [insert_counter(c)] c in instances;
    [delete_counter(c)] not (c in instances);
    [set_max(n)] max = n;
end;
```

In der Signatur der Zählermengen wird zunächst nur der Typ `counter_set` angegeben. Wie der Typ repräsentiert wird, bleibt der Verfeinerung der Spezifikation in einem der nächsten Schritte vorbehalten. Es gibt zwei Methoden, um Zähler in eine Zählermenge aufzunehmen (`insert_counter`) bzw. wieder aus ihr zu entfernen (`remove_counter`).

Die Spezifikation (`effect`-Teil) legt fest, wie die Initialisierung zum Zeitpunkt der Erzeugung zu erfolgen hat und welche Auswirkungen die zustandsändernden Methoden besitzen.

Die Integritätsbedingung legt fest, daß die Summe aller Zählerstände der Zählermenge kleiner als **max** sein müssen. Die Methode **apply** wende dabei eine Methode auf alle Objekte einer Menge an; **sum_up** summiere alle Elemente einer Multimenge auf.

In der obigen Spezifikation ist die Integritätsbedingung für die Summe noch rein deklarativ beschrieben. Um zu einer Implementierung zu gelangen, kann die Spezifikation verfeinert werden. Eine Entwurfsentscheidung kann beispielsweise darin bestehen, ein zusätzliches Attribut **sum** einzuführen, in dem zu jedem Zeitpunkt die Summe aller beteiligten Zähler enthalten ist. Eine Veränderung eines Zählers muß also eine Auswirkung auf die Summe besitzen. Es handelt sich hierbei um die typische Überwachungsmethode der differentiellen Prüfung, wie sie etwa von [QW86] für das relationale Modell beschrieben wird. Eine weitere Entwurfsentscheidung besteht darin, festzulegen, daß es ein Attribut für die Maximalsumme und ein listenwertiges Attribut für die Instanzen gibt. Es ergeben sich somit einige Ergänzungen der Spezifikation:

```
objecttype COUNTER_SET (c: COUNTER) =

  signature ...

  state
    attributes
      sum       : int;
      max       : int;
      instances : list of counter;

  integrity

    forall cs:counter_set .
        sum_up(apply(value, cs.instances)) = cs.sum

    forall cs:counter_set . cs.sum <= cs.max

  effect
    ...
    [create] sum = 0;

    forall c:counter . c in instances =>
        [c.inc(n)] sum = sum + n;

    forall c:counter . c in instances =>
        [c.dec(n)] sum = sum - n;

    [insert_counter(c)] sum = sum + c.value;
    [delete_counter(c)] sum = sum - c.value;


  applicability

    set_max(n) only when n >= sum;

    insert_counter(c) only when
        not(c in instances) and (sum + c.value <= max);
```

```
    forall c in instances . c.inc(n) only when
        sum + n <= max;
end;
```

Die Integritätsbedingung, die die Maximalsumme der Zählerstände festlegte, wurde in zwei Bedingungen aufgeteilt, die das neue Attribut `sum` berücksichtigen. Die Summe aller Zählerstände muß zu jedem Zeitpunkt gleich dem Wert von `sum` sein. Außerdem muß `sum` kleiner oder gleich `max` sein.

Um den Wert in `sum` konsistent zu halten, ist es notwendig, nach jeder Veränderung eines Zählers der Menge das Summenattribut ebenfalls zu ändern. Dies ist ein Beispiel dafür, daß in einer Spezifikation auch auf andere Objekttypen (hier Zähler) Bezug genommen wird.

Im Abschnitt `applicability` wird angegeben, wann bestimmte Methoden überhaupt angewandt werden dürfen. In der ursprünglichen Spezifikation war festgelegt worden, welche Auswirkung eine Anwendung hat. Einschränkungen, die die Einhaltung der Integritätsbedingung garantieren, waren noch nicht vorgenommen worden. Hier wird nun festgelegt, daß z.B. die `inc`-Methode eines Zählers einer Zählermenge nur dann aufgerufen werden darf, wenn die Summe der Zählerstände plus die Erhöhung kleiner als die Maximalsumme ist.

Für diese Spezifikation gilt es nun, eine geeignete Implementierung zu finden.

Aus der Spezifikation läßt sich ablesen, daß einige Bedingungen nur dann geprüft werden müssen, wenn ein Zähler sich in einer Zählermenge befindet. Die Aktivierung dieser Tests kann also an die `insert_counter`-Methode gekoppelt werden. Nach erfolgreicher Ausführung dieser Methode kann der Methodenkontext des Zählerobjektes angereichert werden. Die Reduzierung um diese Tests kann erfolgen, wenn ein Zähler aus einer Zählermenge entfernt wird.

Der Test, ob eine Integritätsverletzung vorliegt, wird in Form einer Methode formuliert. Diese Methode muß die gleichen Parameter besitzen wie die Methode, dessen Methodenkontext sie anreichert. Der Test muß natürlich vor der eigentlichen Methodenausführung erfolgen (`pre`-Aktion), um einen Abbruch zu ermöglichen, falls eine Integritätsverletzung auftreten würde. Nach erfolgreicher Ausführung von `inc` muß hingegen die Summe der Zählermenge auf den aktuellen Stand gebracht werden. Hier handelt es sich um eine `post`-Aktion. Im `implementation`-Teil der Spezifikation können dann die folgenden Methodendefinitionen benutzt werden:

```
pre_increment(x:int) is
  if x + sum > max
  then raise exception increment_failure
end;

post_increment(x:int) is
  sum := sum + x
end;
```

In der `insert_counter`-Methode erfolgt nun die Anreicherung:

```
insert_counter(c:counter) is
   ...
```

```
    enrich_pre_action(c, inc, pre_increment);
    enrich_post_action(c, inc, post_increment);
    ...
end;
```

Wird ein Zähler aus einer Zählermenge entfernt, so kann der Methodenkontext des entsprechenden Objektes um die Integritätstests und die Änderung des Summenattributes reduziert werden. Dies geschieht wie folgt:

```
reduce_pre_action(c, inc, pre_increment); ...
```

Bei dem hier angegebenen Beispiel sind die Operationen zum Einfügen und Entfernen aus Zählermengen explizit angegeben, so daß sofort einsichtig ist, wo Anreicherungen des Methodenkontextes vorgenommen werden müssen.

3.2 Implizite Definition von Mengen

Bei der Spezifikation von Integritätsbedingungen kommt es häufig vor, daß eine Menge von Objekten nur implizit definiert werden soll. Man möchte z.B., daß eine bestimmte IB für eine Menge von Objekten erfüllt wird, die durch ein Prädikat charakterisiert ist.

Für die in Abschnitt 2.1 erwähnte Klasse der Angestellten (EMPLOYEE) soll die nachstehende IB sichergestellt werden:

Buchhalter dürfen nicht mehr als DM 4000,- verdienen, d.h.

```
forall e:employee .
    e.get_job = "book-keeper" => e.get_salary <= 4000
```

Um diese Integritätsbedingung sicherzustellen, wird ein neuer Objekttyp eingeführt, der durch ein Prädikat charakterisiert wird:

```
objecttype BOOK_KEEPER_SET =

  signature

    virtual type  book_keeper;

    birth activate : ;
    virtual_method book_keeper_set : set of book_keeper;
    virtual_method insert          : employee ->;
    virtual_method delete          : employee ->;

    const max_sal = 4000;

  characterization

    forall e:employee .
        e.get_job = "book-keeper" => e in book_keeper_set;
```

```
integrity

  forall bk:book_keeper .
      bk.get_salary <= max_sal;

effect

  [activate]  forall e:employee .
      e.get_job = "book-keeper" <=> e in book_keeper_set;
  [insert(e)] e in book_keeper_set;
  [delete(e)] not(e in book_keeper_set);

end;
```

Der virtuelle Typ `book_keeper` umfaßt die Instanzen von `employee`, deren Beruf gleich "`book_keeper`" ist. Der Typ ist virtuell, da es keine explizite Möglichkeit gibt, Objekte dieses Typs zu erzeugen. Ein Angestellter wird zum Buchhalter, wenn das Attribut Beruf den entsprechenden Wert annimmt. Es findet somit eine dynamische Klassifikation statt.

Für alle Elemente des Typs `book_keeper` soll nun das Gehalt kleiner als das in der Spezifikation angegebene Maximalgehalt sein. Es wird eine virtuelle Buchhaltermenge (`book_keeper_set`) und zwei zugehörige Methoden `insert` und `delete` definiert. Mit ihrer Hilfe können Angestellte in die Menge der Buchhalter übernommen und wieder aus ihr entfernt werden.

Da diese beiden Methoden als virtuell deklariert sind, muß in der Spezifikation festgelegt werden, welche "realen" Methoden ihre Ausführung steuern. Dies geschieht im unten angegebenen Abschnitt `calling`. Hier wird festgelegt, daß das Erzeugen eines neuen Angestellten mit Beruf Buchhalter zu einem Einfügen dieses neuen Objektes in die Buchhaltermenge führt. Wird bei einem Angestellten, der kein Buchhalter ist, der Beruf auf "`book_keeper`" gesetzt, so hat das den gleichen Effekt. Falls ein Angestellter bereits Buchhalter ist, so führt ein Berufswechsel zu einem Entfernen aus der Buchhaltermenge. Der nachstehende Teil der Spezifikation beschreibt die Verwaltung der Buchhaltermenge:

```
calling

  hire(_,j,_) where j = "book-keeper" >>
      insert(new);

  e.set_job(j) where e.get_job <> "book-keeper"
      and j = "book-keeper" >> insert(e);

  e.set_job(j) where e.get_job = "book-keeper"
      and j <> "book-keeper" >> delete(e);
```

Mit Hilfe der Methode `activate` wird sichergestellt, daß die Integritätsbedingung auch für alle zum Zeitpunkt der Aktivierung existierenden Buchhalter gilt. Falls es Angestellte gibt, die die IB verletzen, so soll `activate` nicht anwendbar sein. Eine Verfeinerung der Spezifikation des Objekttyps `BOOK_KEEPER_SET` enthält nun Angaben zur Anwendbarkeit von Methoden. Für Buchhalter wird festgelegt, wie die Integrität sichergestellt werden kann.

```
applicability

  activate only when
      forall e:employee .
          get_job = "book-keeper" => get_salary <= max_sal;

  hire(_,j,sal) only when
      j <> "book-keeper" or sal <= max_sal

  var bk:book_keeper . bk.set_salary(sal) only when
      sal <= max_sal;

  var e:employee . e.set_job(j) only when
      j = "book_keeper" and  e.get_salary <= max_sal;
```

Für den Objekttyp EMPLOYEE wird spezifiziert, daß Buchhalter nur eingestellt werden dürfen, wenn sie die obige Integritätsbedingung erfüllen. Für Buchhalter muß zudem die set_salary-Methode überwacht werden, um die Einhaltung des Maximalgehalts sicherstellen zu können. Schließlich muß auch ein Berufswechsel (set_job) überwacht werden.

Die Überwachung der Gehaltsänderungen erfolgt durch eine entsprechende Methode:

```
pre_set_salary(x:int) is
  if x > max_sal
  then raise exception book_keeper_limit
end;
```

Die Implementierung der activate-Methode muß dafür Sorge tragen, daß die Methodenkontexte von bereits existierenden Objekten so ergänzt werden, daß einerseits bei Buchhaltern die Gehaltsänderungen überwacht werden und andererseits ein Berufswechsel ggf. zum Beginn / Ende der Überwachung führt. Außerdem wird durch activate die hire-Methode angereichert. Die anderen Methoden, die virtuell zu einem insert oder delete führen (set_job(job) für job = "book_keeper" bzw. job <> "book_keeper") können mit den folgenden Methoden angereichert werden:

```
pre_set_job(job:string) is
  if job = "book_keeper" and self.get_salary > max_sal
  then raise exception change_job_failure
end;

post_set_job(job:string) is
  if job = "book_keeper"
  then enrich_pre_action(self, set_salary, pre_set_salary)
  else begin
    reduce_pre_action(self, set_salary, pre_set_salary);
    enrich_pre_action(self, set_job, pre_set_job)
  end;
end;

post_hire(name:string, job:string, salary:int) is
  if job = "book_keeper"
  then
```

```
    if salary > max_sal
    then raise exception hire_failure
    else begin
      enrich_pre_action(self, set_salary, pre_set_salary);
      enrich_post_action(self, set_job, post_set_job)
  end else
    enrich_pre_action(self, set_job, pre_set_job)
end;
```

Für einen existierenden Angestellten ist vor einem Berufswechsel zu prüfen, ob ein solcher Wechsel aufgrund der Integritätsbedingungen überhaupt zulässig ist. Nachdem ein Berufswechsel stattgefunden hat, kann entschieden werden, ob eine weitere Überwachung der `set_salary`-Methode noch notwendig ist. Die Aktivierung dieser Methoden erfolgt nach der Erzeugung eines Angestelltenobjektes durch `hire`. Das hier angegebene Beispiel zeigt, daß der Methodenkontext dynamisch, in Abhängigkeit von Zustandsänderungen, manipuliert werden kann.

Implementierungsbedingt existiert für die Menge `book_keeper_set` kein Objekt, das alle Instanzen enthält; jedes einzelne Angestellten-Objekt trägt die Information, ob es zur Buchhaltermenge gehört, im Methodenkontext mit sich. Änderungen des Zustands beeinflussen die Zugehörigkeit zur Buchhaltermenge.

4 Zusammenfassung und Ausblick

Ziel des Datenbank-Entwurfs ist es, aus deklarativ vorgegebenen Anforderungen für Objekte eine Implementierung zu erzeugen, die einerseits effizient ist, andererseits aber auch alle geforderten Konsistenzbedingungen erfüllt. Durch Einführung eines Methodenkontextes ist es möglich, Methoden zu spezifizieren, die die Konsistenz von Datenbank-Anwendungen sicherstellen und trotzdem die notwendige Flexibilität im Falle von Schema-Änderungen besitzen. Für bestehende Objekte können neue Integritätsbedingungen formuliert werden, ohne daß eine Änderung der Klassendefinition zwingend notwendig ist.

Die beiden vorangehenden Beispiele haben gezeigt, daß sich aus einer entsprechend strukturierten Spezifikation systematisch eine mögliche Implementierung ableiten läßt. Die im `applicability`-Teil einer Spezifikation angegebenen Bedingungen, unter denen eine Methode ausgeführt werden darf, lassen sich in entsprechende `pre`-Aktionen transformieren. Die im `effect`-Teil spezifizierten Auswirkungen auf Zusatzinformationen können durch `post`-Aktionen realisiert werden.

Das zweite Beispiel hat insbesondere gezeigt, wie eine dynamische Klassifikation mit Hilfe von Methodenkontexten realisiert werden kann. Aufgabe des Entwurfs ist es, das implizite Einfügen und Löschen von Elementen einer Menge zu entdecken. Zustandsänderungen zur Laufzeit führen zu einer Modifikation der Methodenkontexte der betroffenen Objekte.

Die mit einem Methodenkontext versehenen Objekte führen die Überprüfung von Integritätsbedingungen objekt-lokal durch, so daß auf einen globalen Monitor verzichtet werden kann. Trotzdem ist sichergestellt, daß auch adhoc-Transaktionen nicht zu einer Integritätsverletzung führen können.

Die vorgestellten Konzepte lassen sich auch auf heterogene Aggregationen übertragen. Ein Standardbeispiel hierfür ist die Modellierung der Situation, daß Angestellte in einer bestimmten Abteilung arbeiten. Als Integritätsbedingung kann hier etwa gefordert werden, daß die Summe der Gehälter kleiner als das Abteilungsbudget ist. In diesem Fall müssen auch Methoden, die auf Abteilungen definiert sind, z.B. Budgetänderungen, mit Methodenkontexten angereichert werden.

Eine Erweiterung der Methodik kann darin bestehen, nicht nur Methodenkontexte, sondern auch *Bedingungskontexte* zu betrachten, die angeben, welche Vor- und Nachbedingungen für die Ausführung von Methoden gelten müssen. Hierbei ist insbesondere daran zu denken, eine Unterstützung zur automatischen Erkennung der Methoden zu geben, die aufgrund einer impliziten Definition von Mengen überwacht werden müssen. Aufgrund der Spezifikation von Zustandsänderungen im `effect`-Teil läßt sich ermitteln, welche Methoden ein bestimmtes Attribut verändern. Wird eine Teilmenge durch ein Prädikat definiert, so kann zumindest festgestellt werden, welche Methoden mit Sicherheit nicht überwacht zu werden brauchen. Aus einer deklarativen Teilmengendefinition lassen sich dann Methodenkontexte erzeugen, die die Integritätsbedingungen wahren, die für die Teilmenge gelten sollen.

Ziel weiterer Forschung wird sein, Konzepte zur automatischen Erzeugung von Triggern aus Spezifikationen temporaler Integritätsbedingungen ([GL93]) vom relationalen Modell auf objekt-orientierte Systeme zu übertragen. Außerdem muß untersucht werden, wie die oben gezeigten Konzpte mit einem Transaktionsmechanismus harmonieren. Für komplexe Objekte gilt es, eine Systematik zu entwickeln, wie Integritätsbedingungen, die das Gesamtobjekt betreffen, auf die Komponenten verteilt werden können.

Literatur

[Boo91] G. Booch: *Object-Oriented Design with Applications.* Addison-Wesley, Reading (Mass.), 1991.

[GL93] M. Gertz, U. W. Lipeck: Deriving Integrity Maintaining Triggers from Transition Graphs. to appear: Proc. of The Ninth IEEE Int. Conf. on Data Engineering, Vienna, April 1993.

[HR83] T. Härder, A. Reuter: Principles of Transaction-Oriented Database Recovery. *ACM Computing Surveys 15:4 (1983)*, 287–317.

[JSHS91] R. Jungclaus, G. Saake, T. Hartmann, C. Sernadas: Object-Oriented Specification of Information Systems: The TROLL Language (Version 0.01). Informatik-Berichte 91-04, Technische Universität Braunschweig, Braunschweig, December 1991.

[Lip89] U. W. Lipeck: *Dynamische Integrität von Datenbanken: Grundlagen der Spezifikation und Überwachung.* Informatik-Fachberichte 209. Springer, Berlin, 1989.

[Lip92] U. W. Lipeck: Integritätszentrierter Datenbank-Entwurf. *EMISA Forum 2 (1992)*, 41–55.

[Mey88] B. Meyer: *Object-Oriented Software Construction.* Prentice Hall International Series in Computer Science. Prentice-Hall, Englewood Cliffs, N.J., 1988.

[Mey92] B. Meyer: *Eiffel — The Language.* Prentice Hall, Hempel Hempstead, 1992.

[Moo89] D. A. Moon: The Common Lisp Object-Oriented Programming Language Standard. In W. Kim, F. Lochovsky (eds.), *Object-Oriented Concepts, Databases and Applications*, 49–78. Addison-Wesley, 1989.

[NR89] G. Nguyen, D. Rieu: Schema Evolution in Object-oriented Database Systems. *Data & Knowledge Engineering 4 (1989)*, 43–67.

[QW86] X. Qian, G. Wiederhold: Knowledge-based Integrity Constraint Validation. In *Proceedings of the 12th Int. Conf. on Very Large Data Bases — Kyoto, 1986*, 3–12, August 1986.

[Saa91] G. Saake: Descriptive Specification of Database Object Behaviour. *Data & Knowledge Engineering 6:1 (1991)*, 47–73.

[Saa92] G. Saake: Objektorientierte Modellierung von Informationssystemen. Informatik-Skripten 28, Technische Universität Braunschweig, Braunschweig, August 1992.

[San90] D. Sannella. Formal Programm Development in Extended ML for the Working Programmer, 1990. appeared: Proc. 3rd BCS/FACS Workshop on Refinement, Hursley Park, 1990. Springer Workshops in Computing, 99-130 (1991).

[SJ91] G. Saake, R. Jungclaus: Specification of Database Applications in the TROLL Language. In D. Harper, M. E. Norrie (eds.), *Specifications of Database Systems - 1st Int. Workshop on Specifications on Database Systems, 1991*, 228–245, Springer, Berlin, 1991.

[Su91] J. Su: Dynamic Constraints and Object Migration. In G. M. Lohmann, A. Sernadas, R. Camps (eds.), *Proceedings of the 17th Int. Conf. on Very Large Data Bases - 1991*, 233–242, Morgan Kaufmann Publishers, 1991.

[TF82] T. J. Teorey, J. P. Fry: *Design of Database Structures.* Prentice-Hall, Englewood Cliffs (N.J.), 1982.

Zur verteilten Synchronisation von Objekten

Torsten Wittkugel
Projektinitiative Medizin Informatik[1]
am Deutschen Herzzentrum Berlin und an der Technischen Universität Berlin
Voltastraße 5, Geb. 10, Aufg. 1
W-1000 Berlin 65
torsten@DHZB.DE

Zusammenfassung

Seit einiger Zeit wird versucht, das aus DBMS bekannte Konzept der Transaktion auch für die Anwendungsprogrammierung verfügbar zu machen. Besonders erfolgversprechend sind dabei objektbasierte und objektorientierte Ansätze; u. a. da sie die Möglichkeit bieten, die Anwendungs- von der Synchronisationsfunktionalität konzeptionell sauber zu trennen. Die bisher vorgestellten Überlegungen schränken jedoch die Objektautonomie und die Flexibilität der Transaktionen teilweise erheblich ein. Zudem brauchen sie oftmals zentralisierte Instanzen für das Transaktionsmanagement. Es wird ein Konzept skizziert, das viele dieser Einschränkungen aufhebt — die Synchronisation wird von den beteiligten Objekten selbst durchgeführt, Datenzugriffe sind in jedem Objekt möglich, Transaktionen müssen keinem statischen, vorher festgelegten Schema folgen. Zudem gestattet die Einführung eines objektlokalen Konfliktbegriffes die Berücksichtigung spezieller Synchronisationsmöglichkeiten bei jedem Objekt.

Abstract

Attempts are being made to utilise the concept of transactions used in DBMS for application programming. Especially promising are in this respect object-based approaches; one reason is that they offer the possibility of a conceptional separation of application and synchronisation functionality. The ideas introduced so far, however, impose, to some extent, serious limits on the object autonomy and the flexibility of transactions. Moreover, they require an often centralised instance for transaction management. A concept is outlined, in which these restrictions are removed — the synchronisation ist performed by the objects involved, data access is possible in each object, transactions need not follow a static, previously defined pattern. The introduction of an object-local conflict notion allows the possibility of special synchronisation in each object.

---

[1] Diese Arbeit entstand im Rahmen des BERMED-Projekts in der Projektinitiative Medizin Informatik (PMI) am Deutschen Herzzentrum Berlin (DHZB), der Technischen Universität Berlin (TUB) und der Stahlen- und Poliklinik des Universitätsklinikums Rudolf Virchow (UKRV) unter der wissenschaftlichen Leitung von Prof. Dr. E. Fleck (DHZB), Prof. Dr. B. Mahr (TUB) und Prof. Dr. R. Felix (UKRV). BERMED wird gefördert von der Deutschen Telepost Consulting GmbH (DETECON).

1 Einleitung

Das Paradigma der Objektorientierung hat in kurzer Zeit sowohl in der Welt der Informatik-Forschung als auch schon in der der Anwendungen und Produkte Verbreitung gefunden. Dieser Erfolg hat viele Gründe: Objektorientiertheit als konzeptionelle Grundlage von Informationssystemen gestattet eine *integrierte Sicht von Daten und Funktionalität* und bezieht dadurch Aspekte des Verhaltens in die „Daten"-Modellierung mit ein. Die Beschränkung des Entwurfs objektorientierter Informationssysteme auf eine rein statische Modellierung ist daher nicht ausreichend. Vielmehr muß auch das *dynamische Verhalten* solcher Systeme beachtet und in geeigneter Weise modelliert und kontrolliert werden.

Ein weiteres zentrales Merkmal objektorientierter Systeme ist das durch die Objektkapselung realisierte Prinzip des *information hiding*. Außer strukturellen können auch Verhaltensaspekte nach außen verborgen werden. Dadurch eignet sich die Objektorientierung auch als Mittel zur Integration bereits bestehender Systeme, die so mit einer einheitlichen Schnittstelle versehen werden können. Man hat also ein mächtiges Werkzeug zur *Bewältigung der Software-Heterogenität* in der Hand.

Schließlich erweisen sich Objekte als adäquater Ansatz zur Realisierung verteilter Systeme. Das Konzept des *message passing* zwischen Objekten ist gut dazu geeignet, von Objektlokalitäten zu abstrahieren, ein Aspekt, der in der stetigen Verbreitung kleinerer, leistungsfähiger und vernetzter Rechner zunehmend an Bedeutung gewinnt.

Wir wollen Objekte als prinzipiell *autonom* betrachten. Die Methoden sind auch aus Sicht der Autonomie die Schnittstelle zur Außenwelt. Sie definieren die Syntax der Kommunikation zwischen Objekten und ihren Klienten — gleichzeitig verbindet sich mit ihnen eine gewisse Semantik, die die Auswirkungen auf den Datenbestand des Gesamtsystems und auf das Resultat beschreiben. Genau diese Semantik kann einem Klienten garantiert werden. *Wie* ein Objekt diesen Effekt erzielt, bleibt jedoch verborgen und kann auch von Methodenaufruf zu Methodenaufruf variieren. Man kann also insbesondere keine Aussage darüber machen, *welche* Objekte an der Bearbeitung einer Methode beteiligt sein werden (und in welcher Reihenfolge sie zum Einsatz kommen). Erst zur Laufzeit können wir das Verhalten der Objekte *beobachten* (vgl. auch [SaJu 91]: „Objekte sind beobachtbare, kommunizierende Prozesse"). Auch Ansätze aus dem ODP-Bereich [Herb 92] (etwa *Trading*-Konzepte) scheinen zu belegen, daß diese Sichtweise in Zukunft eher an Bedeutung gewinnen wird.

Der vorliegende Artikel bettet sich in den Kontext der Arbeiten in der Projektinitiative Medizin Informatik ein. Hier wurde ein objektorientiertes, verteiltes Datenmodell entwickelt (vgl. [Kuts 91], [HKS 92]), aus dem das HDMS (Heterogeneous Distributed Information Management System) entstand. Der Wunsch nach besserer Kontrolle konkurrierender Methodenausführungen im HDMS war der Ausgangspunkt des hier umrissenen Konzeptes.

Diese Arbeit gliedert sich wie folgt: In Abschnitt 2 beschreiben wir Anforderungen an ein Transaktionskonzept für objektbasierte Systeme, in Abschnitt 3 wird ein objektlokaler Konfliktbegriff eingeführt, der dazu beiträgt, jedes Objekt nach seinen spezifischen Möglichkeiten und Anforderungen zu synchronisieren. Danach werden wir uns dem verteilten Scheduling zuwenden, das ohne zentrale Transaktionsmanager o. ä. auskommt. Abschließend wird in Abschnitt 5 untersucht, welche Funktionalität die Objekte, die an Transaktionen teilnehmen wollen, zur Verfügung stellen müssen und wie sie strukturiert werden kann. Wir schließen mit einer Einordnung der Arbeit in den wissenschaftlichen Kontext und einem Ausblick auf weitere Arbeiten.

2 Transaktionen in objektbasierten Systemen

Aus der Dynamik objektorientierter Systeme ergeben sich auch eine Reihe neuer Probleme. Der Klient eines Objektes, der bei diesem eine Methode aufruft, kann also weder Aussagen über das Verhalten dieses Objektes, noch über das Verhalten eventuell daraus weiter aufgerufener Objekte treffen. Ihm erscheint die Ausführung seines Auftrages als unteilbare Einheit. Das ist jedoch — besonders in verteilten, parallel arbeitenden Systemen — keineswegs der Fall.

Nun hat die Annahme der Unteilbarkeit einer Methodenausführung durchaus einen wünschenswerten Aspekt[2]; ein Benutzer, der mit der Maus einen „OK"-Knopf drückt, sollte davon ausgehen können, daß seine (dadurch ausgelöste) Methodenausführung

- entweder den von ihm gewünschten oder — im Falle eines Fehlers — keinen Effekt hat (*Atomicity*),
- sich nicht mit anderen Methodenausführungen in einer Weise überschneidet, die zu Anomalien führt (*Isolation*).

Diese Forderungen sind aus Datenbanksystemen bekannt — zusammen mit den weiteren Eigenschaften *Consistency* und *Durability* bilden sie das bekannte ACID-Paradigma [HäRe 83]. Wir wollen im folgenden untersuchen, wie wir sie in einem objektbasierten System gewährleisten können.

Die objektlokale Isolation von Methoden mit herkömmlichen Techniken (Semaphore, kritische Bereiche, etc.) reicht nicht aus, um sich vor Anomalien zu schützen. Selbst eine sequentielle Bearbeitung von Methoden in jedem Objekt kann aus der Datenbankforschung (vgl. etwa [Reut 87]) bekannte Fehler und Anomalien wie *lost update* oder *inconsistent analysis* nicht verhindern.

In DBMS gibt es Komponenten, die die Transaktionseigenschaften sichern; bei verteilten DBMS arbeiten mehrere solcher Komponenten mittels geeigneter Protokolle zusammen [ÖzVa 91]. In unserem Fall ist eine Beschränkung auf eine solch eher kleine Anzahl von Koordinationskomponenten unerwünscht — prinzipiell kann ja jedes Objekt, das an einer Transaktion beteiligt ist, auf einem anderen Rechnerknoten laufen. Der Knoten, auf dem ein Objekt abläuft, ist nicht charakteristisch für das Objekt (Idealerweise möchte man vielmehr von Verteilungsaspekten möglichst vollständig abstrahieren können). Betrachtet man Objekte schließlich als aktive Prozesse, so können Fehlersituationen nicht nur durch den Absturz des entsprechen-

[2] Eine echte Unteilbarkeit wäre allerdings einem parallel arbeitenden System nicht angemessen, der Grad der Parallelität sollte vielmehr möglichst hoch sein, um die vorhandenen Ressourcen effektiv auszunutzen.

den Rechnerknotens, sondern auch durch den Absturz des jeweiligen Prozesses entstehen.

Wir haben es also mit einer hochgradig dynamischen Situation zu tun; Anzahl und Art der beteiligten Objekte können stark variieren. Die Verteiltheit (und damit auch die Parallelität) der Abläufe in einem objektorientierten System sollte auch für Synchronisierungsaufgaben eingesetzt werden, um verteilte Rechenkapazitäten nutzen zu können und einen Flaschenhals bei einem zentralisierten Transaktionsmanager zu vermeiden, der für alle Transaktionen zuständig ist, an denen ein Knoten beteiligt ist. Gleichzeitig können wir bei einem solchen Vorgehen die spezifischen Synchronisationsprobleme einzelner Objekte (oder Objektklassen) besser berücksichtigen.

3 Objektlokale Konflikte als Basis für die globale Isolation

Der Ansatzpunkt für die Isolierung von Methodenausführungen (wir wollen isolierte Methodenausführungen als *Transaktionen* bezeichnen) liegt im Konfliktbegriff. Die Existenz eines objektlokalen Konfliktes (zwischen zwei Methodenausführungen) ist eine notwendige Voraussetzung dafür, daß es zu Anomalien kommen kann — es muß also erst dann in das Geschehen regulierend eingegriffen werden. In welchen Fällen ein Konflikt vorliegt und in welchen nicht, kann von Objekt zu Objekt verschieden sein. Es wird sich zeigen, daß der Konfliktbegriff zur Vorgehensweise beim *Scheduling* weitgehend orthogonal ist.

Anders als z. B. in relationalen Datenbanken sind die Objekte in unserem System von stark unterschiedlicher Granularität und Struktur. Haben wir es dort mir einer gleichförmigen logischen Struktur aller Datenobjekte (Relationen, Tupel, Attribute, ...) zu tun, die auch eine gleichförmige Behandlung der anfallenden Synchronisierungsarbeiten rechtfertigt, so wollen wir hier versuchen, die Heterogenität der Objekte zu nutzen, um eine flexiblere Synchronisierung zu ermöglichen. Das beginnt mit der Erkennung von Konflikten: Ob zwei Methoden in Konflikt sind, kann ganz allgemein durch ein Prädikat festgestellt werden, das bei dem betreffenden Objekt zur Ausführung gelangt. Argumente für dieses *objektlokale Konfliktprädikat* sind:

- die Kennungen der Transaktionen, für die die Methoden ausgeführt werden (sollen)
- der momentane *lokale Konfliktzustand* des Objektes (s. u.)
- die Namen der auszuführenden Methoden
- die Parameter der Methoden
- bestimmte Informationen über den Objektzustand

Nicht in jedem Objekt *müssen* alle diese Parameter verwendet werden; man kann in verschiedenen Objekten unterschiedliche Argumente und dadurch unterschiedliche Synchronisationsanforderungen dieser Objekte berücksichtigen.

Die Methoden müssen mindestens nach ihrer Beziehung zum Zustand (der privaten Daten) eines Objektes klassifiziert werden. Das herkömmliche *read/write*-Modell ist für unsere Zwecke nicht ganz ausreichend: Es gibt nicht nur den Objektzustand lesende und schreibende Methoden, sondern auch solche, die vom Objektzustand unabhängig sind — die z. B. nur weitere Objekte aufrufen oder nur *unveränderliche* interne Informationen (wie die Objekt-ID oder archivierte Daten) verwenden. Es gibt also lesende (*r*), schreibende (*w*) und zustandsfreie (*f*) Methoden mit folgenden Konflikten:

	r	w	f
r	○	●	○
w	●	●	○
f	○	○	○

● Konflikt
○ kein Konflikt

Abb. 1: Konflikttabelle für lesende, schreibende und zustandsfreie Methoden

Um zu einem einfachen objektlokalen Konfliktprädikat zu kommen, spalten wir zunächst den (privaten Daten-) Zustand D eines Objektes in mehrere disjunkte Teile: $D = \{d_1, ..., d_n\}$. Weiterhin definieren für das Objekt (mit der Methodenmenge $M = \{m_1, ..., m_m\}$) eine lokale Klassifikationsfunktion $\kappa\colon M \times D \rightarrow \{r, w, f\}$. Zwei Methoden m_1, m_2 eines Objektes stehen offensichtlich in Konflikt ($m_1 \# m_2$), wenn gilt:

$$m_1 \# m_2 :\Leftrightarrow$$
$$\exists\, d_i \in D:\quad (\kappa(m_1, d_i) = w \;\wedge\; \kappa(m_2, d_i) \neq f) \;\vee$$
$$(\kappa(m_1, d_i) \neq f \;\wedge\; \kappa(m_2, d_i) = w)$$

Wir wollen allerdings im allgemeinen Fall nicht Konflikte zwischen Methoden eines Objektes, sondern zwischen Methodenausführungen bei einem Objekt erkennen können. Die obige Definition wird jedoch auch wesentlicher Bestandteil der Konfliktprädikate sein — u. U. in abgewandelter Form, beispielsweise dann, wenn spezielle Synchronisierungstechniken auf ein d_i angewandt werden können. Zudem kann man — ggf. auch nachträglich — durch eine feinere Granulierung ein *conflict tuning* vornehmen.

Der Konfliktbegriff läßt sich auch objektspezifisch erweitern: Berücksichtigt man die Transaktionskennungen, so kann zusätzlich bestimmt werden, ob Methodenausführungen für unterschiedliche Transaktionen anders isoliert werden, als solche für dieselbe Transaktion — es läßt sich also *für jede Methode jedes Objektes* der Grad der gewünschten Isolation separat einstellen.[3] So kann man u. a. rekursive Methodenaufrufe implizit erlauben oder verbieten.

Weitere Möglichkeiten ergeben sich aus der Berücksichtigung der bei den Methodenaufrufen übergebenen aktuellen Parameter und des Objektzustandes, u. a. die objektlokale Anwendung von Techniken, wie sie zur Synchronisierung von *hot spots* [Reut 82] vorgeschlagen wurden.[4] [Weih 89] macht einen Vorschlag für *application specific concurrency control*,

3 Wir wollen unser Augenmerk hier zunächst auf die Behandlung der Inter-Transaktions-Parallelität beschränken.

4 Beim Übergang von einem objektbasierten zu einem objektorientierten System müssen zusätzlich noch Klassenhierarchien (oder Vererbungshierarchien) betrachtet werden, um zu entscheiden, ob ein Konflikt vorliegt.

der zeigt, daß ein objektlokaler Konfliktbegriff eingesetzt werden kann, um eine größere Parallelität zu erreichen. Wir wollen dabei aber darauf achten, daß die eigentliche Funktionalität eines Objektes (seine Methoden) von der Synchronisationsfunktionalität streng getrennt bleibt und aus der Sicht eines Objektentwicklers weitgehend automatisch generiert wird. Insgesamt führt dieser Ansatz zu einer hohen Flexibilität bei der Synchronisierung der Objekte.

4 Verteiltes Scheduling

Wie kann man nun auf objektlokalen Konflikten aufbauend die Isolation von Transaktionen gewährleisten? Die Ausführungen von Methoden bei den Objekten müssen in eine Reihenfolge gebracht werden, die Anomalien ausschließt. Dazu müssen wir — jeweils objektlokal — Methodenaufträge betrachten, die zu verschiedenen Transaktionen gehören und die in Konflikt stehen. Wird einer dieser Aufträge ausgeführt, während der andere (oder die anderen) warten müssen, so wird dadurch eine Ordnungsrelation auf den Transaktionen definiert, die bei weiteren Konflikten der beteiligten Transaktionen (auch bei anderen Objekten) eingehalten werden muß. Eine solche Ordnung wird in der Serialisierbarkeitstheorie i. allg. als gerichteter Graph dargestellt, dessen Knoten Transaktionen und dessen Kanten Elementen der Ordnungsrelation entsprechen. Gewähr für die Serialisierbarkeit eines Schedules ist die Zyklenfreiheit des Graphen (vgl. etwa [BHG 87]).

In unserem Fall gewährleistet die Zyklenfreiheit, daß — wenn es zwischen zwei Transaktionen Konfliktsituationen gibt — alle im Konflikt stehenden Methodenausführungen für diese Transaktionen stets in der gleichen Reihenfolge stattfinden. Unser Korrektheitskriterium für Schedules unterscheidet sich aufgrund des anderen Konfliktbegriffes von der klassischen Serialisierbarkeit (schließt diese aber für den Fall, daß alle Objekte lokale Konflikte nur als *r/w*-Konflikte definieren, ein).

Es ist nun nicht notwendig, zentral *einen* Graphen zu verwalten, der *alle* im System aktiven Transaktionen enthält. Vielmehr interessieren jede Transaktion nur die anderen, mit denen es überhaupt zu Synchronisationsproblemen kommen kann. Die Verwaltung der Transaktionsgraphen muß daher auch nicht von einer zentralen Instanz, sondern kann von den Wurzelobjekten der Transaktionen vorgenommen werden. Es soll nun der Ablauf mehrerer paralleler Transaktionen und der dazu notwendigen Synchronisierungsmaßnahmen grob skizziert werden. Wir gehen dabei von der Grundannahme aus, daß ein Konflikt in einem objektorientierten System ein eher seltenes Ereignis ist (d. h. daß weitaus mehr Methodenausführungen bei den Objekten ohne Konflikt ablaufen), so daß besonders die Fälle, in denen keine Konflikte vorliegen, objektlokal und schnell behandelt werden sollen.

Mehrere Transaktionen, die in der Folge weitere Objekte aufrufen, werden gestartet. Jedes Objekt nimmt eingehende Methodenaufrufe entgegen und prüft, ob diese zu noch aktiven, bereits beendeten (deren Transaktion noch läuft) oder ebenfalls wartenden Methoden im Konflikt steht. Falls nicht, kann die Methode einfach gestartet werden. Falls doch, findet ein *Konfliktpropagationsschritt* statt. Der Konflikt wird einem der beteiligten Wurzelobjekte gemeldet, das sich mit den anderen in Verbindung setzt und einen *gemeinsamen Konfliktgraphen* erstellt, den dann jedes der Wurzelobjekte erhält. Welche Objekte dabei anzusprechen sind, kann es dem eigenen Konfliktgraphen und der Konfliktmeldung des betreffenden Objektes entnehmen. Falls der gemeldete Konflikt bereits im angesprochenen Wurzelobjekt aufgelöst werden kann, weil die beiden Transaktionen bereits in seinem Konfliktgraphen enthalten und geordnet sind, kann der zusätzliche Kontakt mit den anderen Wurzelobjekten unterbleiben. Durch dieses Vorgehen werden automatisch alle Transaktionen berücksichtigt, mit denen es zu unerwünschten Überlagerungen kommen kann.

Der so entstandene Graph wird dann an das Objekt übermittelt, das den Konflikt gemeldet hat. Anhand der Transaktionsordnung im Graphen kann das Objekt entscheiden, welche Methode im aktuellen Konfliktfall auszuführen ist und welche zu warten hat (also das *objektlokale Scheduling* ausführen). Der globale Konfliktgraph wird aufgehoben; im Falle eines weiteren Konfliktes bei diesem Objekt kann dann zunächst objektlokal überprüft werden, ob dieser bereits registriert wurde (dann sind alle für das Scheduling relevanten Informationen objektlokal vorhanden) oder nicht (dann muß ein weiterer Konfliktpropagationsschritt erfolgen). Durch dieses Vorgehen besorgen sich die Objekte die für das Scheduling notwendige nichtlokale Information immer dann, wenn sie benötigt wird und aktualisieren sie dabei gleichzeitig zur Verwendung für andere Objekte.

Während eines Konfliktpropagationsschrittes kann durch das Einfügen einer Kante zwischen zwei bereits im Konfliktgraphen enthaltenen Transaktionen ein Zyklus entstehen. In diesem Fall muß eine Transaktion zurückgesetzt werden. Die beteiligten Wurzelobjekte müssen sich dazu auf ein geeignetes Opfer einigen, wobei das Wurzelobjekt, auf dessen Initiative der Zyklus entdeckt wurde, wiederum eine Koordinationsfunktion übernimmt.

Außer den gemeinsamen Konfliktgraphen müssen noch weitere Informationen für das Scheduling verwaltet werden, *allerdings alle objektlokal* (so daß hier kein weiterer Kommunikationsaufwand entsteht). Dazu gehört die konkrete Information über Methodenaufrufe; die Transaktion, für die sie ausgeführt werden sollen, ihr Ausführungsstatus (*waiting, scheduled, running, ready, prepared, committed, aborted*) und die für die Auswertung des objektlokalen Konfliktprädikats benötigten Argumente. Wir wollen diese Information (zusammen mit dem jeweils lokal bekannten Teil des gemeinsamen Konfliktgraphen) als *lokalen Konfliktzustand* bezeichnen.

Bei der Rückgabe der Ergebnisse einer Methode werden auch die Objekt-IDs der Objekte übermittelt, die an der Transaktion beteiligt waren. So sammelt sich schließlich bei den Wurzelobjekten die Information an, die sie für den Transaktionsabschluß brauchen.

Für die Realisierung dieser Mechanismen werden diverse Protokolle benötigt. Während eines Konfliktpropagationsschrittes muß sich ein Wurzelobjekt mit mehreren anderen in Verbindung setzen, um den gemeinsamen Konfliktgraphen auf den neusten Stand zu bringen und ggf. einen globalen, nicht auflösbaren Konflikt zu erkennen. Dabei muß beachtet werden, daß mehrere Wurzelobjekte praktisch gleichzeitig aktiv werden können. Die Wurzelobjekte der Transaktionen können schließlich auch die Koordination der Transaktionsabschluß- und -abbrucharbeiten unter Verwendung bekannter Protokolle — wie *2-phase-commit* o. ä. — übernehmen, die *atomic commitment* [Raz 92] gewährleisten.

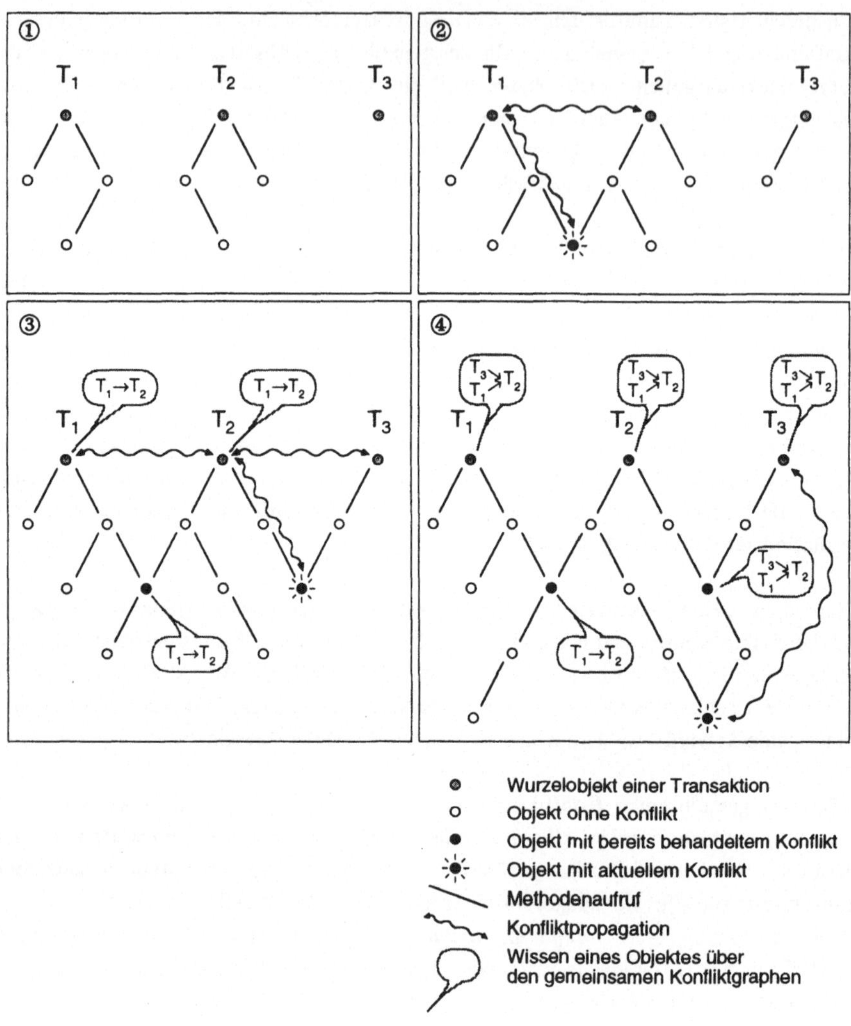

Abb. 2: Beispiel zur Konfliktpropagation

Wir wollen uns das Prinzip der Konfliktpropagation an einem Beispiel (s. Abb. 2) verdeutlichen. Die Darstellung wird hierbei u. a. dadurch stark vereinfacht, daß wir Objekte nicht mehrmals in einer Transaktion vorkommen lassen. Das ist jedoch keine Voraussetzung für die Verwendung des vorgestellten Verfahrens:

① Drei Transaktionen T_1, T_2 und T_3 werden gestartet. Solange keine objektlokalen Konflikte auftreten, arbeiten sie parallel weiter.

② Ein Konflikt zwischen T_1 und T_2 tritt auf, und ein Konfliktpropagationsschritt wird durchgeführt. Die Objekte, bei denen keine Konflikte auftreten, arbeiten weiter.

③ Nach der Konfliktpropagation gibt es den gemeinsamen Konfliktgraphen, der aussagt, daß in weiteren Konfliktfällen T_1 vor T_2 Vorrang hat. T_1 kann dann von dem Objekt aus weiterarbeiten, in dem der Konflikt auftrat, T_2 muß an dieser Stelle warten.
Zwischen T_2 und T_3 tritt ein weiterer Konflikt auf, der einen neuen Konfliktpropagationsschritt nach sich zieht.

④ Nach der Konfliktpropagation hat sich der gemeinsame Konfliktgraph erweitert. Das Objekt, bei dem der erste Konflikt auftrat, braucht diese Information nicht. Es wird sie erhalten, wenn ein Konflikt auftritt, an dem andere Transaktionen als T_1 und T_2 beteiligt sind.
Bei einem weiteren Objekt tritt ein Konflikt zwischen T_2 und T_3 auf. Der Konfliktpropagationsschritt involviert nur ein Wurzelobjekt, da der Konflikt dort bereits bekannt ist. Somit muß nur der gemeinsame Konfliktzustand unverändert an dieses Objekt übermittelt werden.

5 Synchronisationsfunktionalität von Objekten

Wir gehen davon aus, daß Objekte aus privaten Daten bestehen, die durch Methoden eingekapselt sind. Eine aktive Komponente sorgt dafür, daß ein eingehender Methodenaufruf die Ausführung der entsprechenden Methode und eventuell die Rückgabe eines Ergebnisses bewirkt. Zur Realisierung des beschriebenen Transaktionskonzeptes müssen wir diese Komponente so erweitern, daß sie die nötigen Arbeiten bewerkstelligen kann. Da diese Funktionalität in wesentlichen Teilen für alle Objekte gleich ist, kann man sie auch standardisiert zur Verfügung stellen (die objektlokalen Konfliktprädikate können allerdings von Objekt zu Objekt variieren).

Folgende Komponenten sind zur Realisierung eines Objektes (das nicht das Wurzelobjekt einer Transaktion ist) notwendig:

- Ein *objektlokales Konfliktprädikat*, mit dem sich anhand der eingehenden Methodenaufrufe und des lokalen Konfliktzustandes entscheiden läßt, ob eine Methodenausführung in Konflikt mit einer anderen bei diesem Objekt steht oder nicht.

- Eine Komponente zur *Verwaltung des lokalen Konfliktzustandes* mit Operationen zum Eintragen und Löschen von Methodenaufrufen, zum Ändern des Status, zur Aufnahme des objektlokal bekannten Teiles des gemeinsamen Konfliktgraphen und einfachen Operationen darauf (Löschen eines Knotens bei Beendigung einer Transaktion, Test ob ein Konflikt zwischen zwei Transaktionen bereits objektlokal erfaßt ist).

- Eine Komponente *Kommunikation und Konfliktpropagation*. Sie ist für die Aufnahme von Methodenaufrufen und Rückgabe der Resultate zuständig. Zusätzlich müssen Verwaltungsinformationen für die Transaktionen mit übergeben werden (Transaktions-ID[5], Informationen über die bisher an der Transaktion beteiligten Objekte, ...). Auch

[5] Die Transaktions-ID könnte die Objekt-ID des zuständigen Wurzelobjektes enthalten, damit ein Objekt, bei

die für die Konfliktpropagation notwendigen Kommunikationsschritte werden von dieser Komponente ausgeführt.

- Eine Komponente zur *Koordination der Transaktionsabschluß und -abbrucharbeiten*, die in der Lage ist, geeignete Protokolle zu bearbeiten, die Aktualisierung des lokalen Konfliktzustandes zu initiieren und die Recovery-Komponente anzustoßen.

- Eine *Recovery-Komponente*, die eine geeignete Protokollierung betreibt, mit deren Hilfe sich Atomarität und Persistenz gewährleisten lassen. Die Recovery-Strategien werden insofern in den Objekten unterschiedlich sein, als sie gewisse Teile der Semantik der objektlokalen Konfliktprädikate berücksichtigen müssen. Sie können aber auch (bis zu einem gewissen Grad) speziellen Eigenschaften der Daten eines Objektes[6] angepaßt werden.

- Eine *Scheduling-Komponente*, die die Ausführung von Methoden anhand des lokalen Konfliktprädikates und des lokalen Konfliktzustandes steuert. Die Scheduling Komponente muß erkennen können, wenn das lokale Wissen nicht mehr ausreicht, um einen Konflikt zu behandeln und dann einen Konfliktpropagationsschritt auslösen.

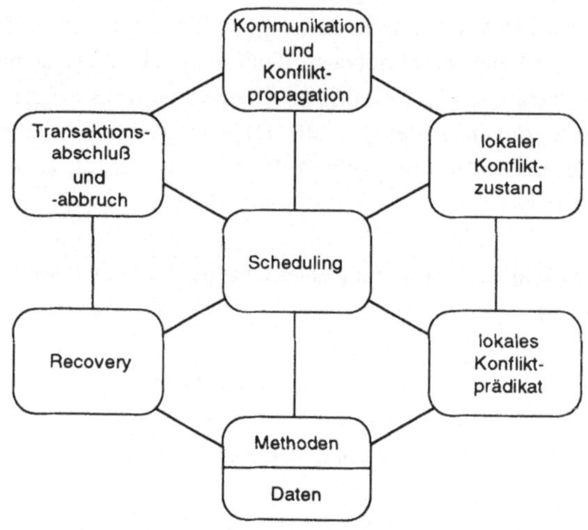

Abb. 3: Struktur eines Objektes und seiner Transaktionsfunktionalität

Die Objekte, die über Methoden verfügen, die als Transaktion markiert sind (d. h. Wurzelobjekte von Transaktionen) brauchen zusätzlich Funktionalität zur *Bearbeitung der Protokolle für Konfliktpropagation, Transaktionsabschluß und -abbruch*.

dem ein Konflikt auftritt, seinen Anspechpartner ermitteln kann.

6 Es kann z. B. sinnvoll sein, in Objekten mit großer Datengranularität — man denke etwa an digitalisierte Bilder — mit Undo-Operationen zu arbeiten (um nicht den ganzen Zustand kopieren zu müssen). Dabei muß man allerdings beachten, daß Recovery-Strategien (leider) nicht orthogonal zu Scheduling-Strategien sind.

6 Zusammenfassung, Einordnung und Ausblick

Das skizzierte Transaktionskonzept kommt ohne zentrale Komponenten (wie z. B. Transaktionsmanager bei jedem Rechnerknoten) aus. Die Synchronisierung erfolgt direkt durch und bei den betroffenen Objekten. Dadurch unterscheidet sich der vorgestellte Ansatz von vielen anderen, beispielsweise dem von Camelot [EMZ 91], oder dem verteilter DBMS [ÖzVa 91]. Objekte werden als aktive Prozesse betrachtet, die selber arbeiten und nicht, wie in DBMS (auch in vielen OODBMS) eher „gearbeitet werden" (Das macht ihn eher den *Communicating Sequential Processes* von [Hoar 85] ähnlich. Dort werden allerdings nur Mechanismen für die Synchronisierung „im Kleinen" vorgestellt, die gleichwohl zur Realisierung von übergreifender Synchronisationsfunktionalität verwendet werden könnten).

Ansätze, die auf *Nested Transactions* [Moss 85] beruhen, erlauben Zugriffe auf die privaten Daten von Objekten lediglich an den Blättern von Aufrufstrukturen, d. h. nur in solchen Objekten, die selbst zur Ausführung ihrer Methoden nicht wiederum Methoden bei anderen aufrufen (Dies ist z. B. bei [FLW 92] der Fall). Das entspricht aber nicht der Realität in objektbasierten Systemen. Unser Ansatz erlaubt daher Datenzugriffe in jedem an einer Transaktion beteiligten Objekt.

In [FLW 92] wird auch versucht, das zur Synchronisierung nötige Wissen so weit wie möglich lokal in den Objekten zu halten; das vorgestellte Konzept der *Hybrid Atomicity* (dabei werden Techniken von Zeitmarken- und Sperrverfahren kombiniert) funktioniert aber nur deshalb, weil die Transaktionen immer in gleicher Form ablaufen, d. h. auch immer die genau gleichen Objekte in der gleichen Art und Weise (an gleicher Stelle in einer Aufrufstruktur) involvieren — aus unserer Sicht ein Verstoß gegen das Konzept der Objektautonomie (oder, wenn man so will, gegen das Prinzip der verhaltensmäßigen Objektkapselung).

Die Heterogenität der Objekte (strukturell wie verhaltensmäßig) kann für die Synchronisierung gewinnbringend (d. h. zur Erhöhung der Parallelität) eingesetzt werden. Durch einen objektlokalen Konfliktbegriff können Objekte bis auf die Methodenebene herab nach ihren spezifischen Bedürfnissen und Möglichkeiten synchronisiert werden. *Der Grad der Isolation ist damit nicht mehr ein Charakteristikum des Transaktionskonzeptes, sondern ein Charakteristikum eines Objektes.* Erweist sich ein Objekt im Betrieb als Flaschenhals, kann auch nachträglich ein *conflict tuning* vorgenommen werden, ohne daß Änderungen an der Anwendungsfunktionalität (oder an anderen Objekten) nötig werden. Das gelingt dadurch, daß Anwendungs- und Synchronalisierungsfunktionalität getrennt werden. Das Konzept der Konfliktpropagation sorgt dafür, daß die Information, die ein Objekt zum lokalen Scheduling benötigt, bei Bedarf ermittelt wird.

Die hier vorgestellten Ideen bieten eine Fülle von Ansatzpunkten für die weitere Arbeit. Die verwendeten Protokolle müssen spezifiziert werden — dabei können Verfahren aus dem Gebiet der verteilten Algorithmen [LaLy 90] verwendet werden. Formale Beschreibungen der objektlokalen Konflikte, der Konfliktzustände, (korrekter) Schedules und der Abläufe während der Konfliktpropagation und während des Scheduling sind notwendig für das Verständnis vieler Detailprobleme (Erste Ansätze einer solchen formalen Beschreibung finden sich in [Witt 93]). Es kann auch untersucht werden, welche Arten von objektlokalen Konflikten prinzipiell denkbar sind (sind z. B. *check-in/check-out*-Mechanismen sinnvoll einsetzbar?) und inwiefern sich „Standard"-Konfliktbegriffe aus vorhandenen Objektspezifikationen oder -programmen generieren lassen.

Danksagung

Mein Dank gilt an dieser Stelle den Kolleginnen und Kollegen der Projektinitiative Medizin Informatik für ihre Unterstützung; im besonderen danke ich Bernd Mahr, Horst Hansen und Ralf-Detlef Kutsche für wertvolle Hinweise.

Literatur

[BHG 87] P. A. Bernstein, V. Hadzilacos, N. Goodman, *Concurrency Control and Recovery in Database Systems*, Addison-Wesley 1987.

[EMZ 91] J. L. Eppinger, L. B. Mummert, A. Z. Spector, *Camelot and Avalon: A Distributed Transaction Facility*, Morgan Kaufmann Publishers, 1991.

[FLW 92] A. Fekete, N. Lynch, W. E. Weihl, *Hybrid Atomicity for Nested Transactions*, in: J. Biskup, R. Hull (eds.), *Proc. International Conference on Database Theory — ICDT '92*, Berlin, October 1992, LNCS 646, pp. 216-230, Springer 1992.

[HäRe 83] T. Härder, A. Reuter, *Principles of Transaction-Oriented Database Recovery*, ACM Computing Surveys, Vol. 15 (1983), No. 4, pp. 287-317.

[Herb 92] A. Herbert, *The Challenge of ODP*, in J. de Meer, V. Heymer, R. Roth (eds.), *Proc. of the IFIP TC6/WG6.4 International Workshop on Open Distributed Processing*, Berlin, Nov. 1991, North-Holland, 1992, pp. 15-28.

[HKS 92] H. Hansen, R.-D. Kutsche, J. Steffens, *The PADKOM System Model — an Open Platform for Medical Applications in a Distributed Environment*, in in: J. de Meer, V. Heymer & R. ROTH (eds.), *Open Distributed Processing*, Proc. of the IFIP TC6/WG6.4 Int. Workshop on Open Distributed Processing, Berlin, October 1991, Elsevier Science Publishers (North Holland), 1992.

[Hoar 85] C. A. R. Hoare, *Communicating Sequential Processes*, Prentice-Hall, 1985.

[Kuts 91] Ralf-Detlef Kutsche, *PADKOM — Ein objektorientiertes, verteiltes Datenmodell für medizinische Anwendungen*, in H.-J. Appelrath (Hrsg.), *Datenbanksysteme in Büro, Technik und Wissenschaft*, GI-Fachtagung, Kaiserslautern 1991, IFB 270, Kaiserslautern, März 1991, pp. 238 - 257, Springer 1991.

[LaLy 90] L. Lamport, N. Lynch, *Distributed Computing: Models and Methods*, in J. v. Leeuven (ed.), *Handbook Of Theoretical Computer Science, Volume B, Formal Models and Semantics*, Elsevier Science Publishers 1990, pp. 1157-1199.

[Moss 85] J. E. B. Moss, *Nested Transactions: An Approach to Reliable Distributed Computing*, Cambridge, MIT Press, 1985.

[ÖzVa 91] M. T. Özsu, P. Valduriez, *Principles of Distributed Database Systems*, Prentice Hall, 1991.

[Raz 92] Y. Raz, *The Principle of Commitment Ordering*, Proc. 18th VLDB Conference, Vancouver, British Columbia, Canada 1992.

[Reut 82] A. Reuter, *Concurrency on high traffic data elements*, Proc. 1982 Conf. on Principles of Database Systems, pp. 83-93, Los Angeles, 1982.

[Reut 87] A. Reuter, *Maßnahmen zur Sicherung von Sicherheits- und Integritätsbedingungen*, in: P. C. Lockemann, J. W. Schmidt, *Datenbank-Handbuch*, Springer, 1987.

[SaJu 91] G. Saake, R. Jungclaus, *Konzeptioneller Entwurf von Objektgesellschaften*, in H.-J. Appelrath (Hrsg.), *Datenbanksysteme in Büro, Technik und Wissenschaft,* GI-Fachtagung, Kaiserslautern, März 1991, IFB 270, 1991, pp. 327-343, Springer 1991.

[Weih 89] W. E. Weihl, *Using Transactions in Distributed Applications*, in S. Mullender (ed.), *Distributed Systems*, Addison Wesley, 1989.

[Witt 93] T. Wittkugel, *Isolation von Methodenausführungen in Objektsystemen*, Proc. 5. GI-Workshop Grundlagen von Datenbanken, Rostock, Juni 1993.

Objekt-Orientierung und CIM

Visuelle Objektmodellierung in der rechnerintegrierten Fertigung

Reinhard Schauer Siegfried Schönberger Roland Wagner

Johannes Kepler Universität Linz
FAW - Forschungsinstitut für Anwendungsorientierte Wissensverarbeitung
(Research Institute For Applied Knowledge Processing)

Schloß Hagenberg, A-4232 Hagenberg, AUSTRIA
Email: oodb @ faw.uni-linz.ac.at

Kurzfassung

Schlanke Produktion, Just In Time sind Produktionsphilosophien zur Erhöhung der Unternehmensrentabilität durch eine Verringerung der benötigten Resourcen an Personal, Kapital und Materialien unter Wahrung der Produktionsrahmenbedingungen, wie Produktqualität, Termintreue und Flexibilität. Ihre Durchsetzung erfordert neben den technischen Voraussetzungen flexible Modelle zur Planung, Terminierung, Steuerung und Simulation des Fertigungsgeschehens. Die Modellierung technischer Systeme dieser Art erfordert aber bislang einen überdimensionalen Aufwand in den letzten Phasen des Software Lebenszyklus, der Implementierung und Wartung. Der Grund hierfür liegt vor allem in der mangelnden Unterstützung des Modellentwurfs durch geeignete Software-Engineering-Methoden und -Werkzeuge. Die vorliegende Arbeit soll einen Beitrag zur Verringerung dieses Defizits leisten.

In dieser Arbeit wird die Methode VOM *(Visual Object Modelling)* und deren Anwendung auf die konzeptionelle Modellierung von Teilen eines flexiblen Fertigungssystems vorgestellt. Aufbauend auf den objektorientierten Ansatz wird eine Notation für einen realitätstreuen Modellentwurf eingeführt. Die Unterteilung der Diskurswelt in *Basisobjekte*, *Steuerobjekte* und *Schnittstellenobjekte* ermöglicht eine hierarchische Modellierung des Systemverhaltens unter Einbeziehung von Benutzer- und Geräteschnittstellen. Den Anforderungen technischer Systeme hinsichtlich Prozeßmodellierung wird durch die Einführung sequentieller und paralleler *Tasks* begegnet. Durch die Anwendung objektorientierter Techniken wie Datenkapselung, Vererbung, Polymorphismen usw., können gut verständliche, in hohem Ausmaß wiederverwendbare Modellkomponenten aufgebaut werden.

1. Einleitung

Der Stellenwert der Produktionsplanung und -steuerung hat im letzten Jahrzehnt durch einen immer härter werdenden internationalen Wettbewerb immens an Bedeutung gewonnen. Auf der Basis immer leistungsfähiger werdender Arbeitsplatzrechner konnten die dispositiven und technischen Komponenten von Produktionssystemen stärker gekoppelt werden. Dies führte zum Entstehen einer neuen Forschungs- und Entwicklungsdisziplin, dem *Computer Integrated Manufacturing* (CIM). Neue Metamodelle [Sche88], basierend auf der Drei-Schichtenarchitektur "Planung - Durchsetzung - Realisierung", entstanden für eine stärkere Integration der Produktion in die aufbau- und ablauforganisatorischen Unternehmensstrukturen. Die Umsetzung dieser Metamodelle in reale Produktionssysteme bereitete aber bislang den Software-Entwicklern große Probleme. Den gestiegenen Anforderungen hinsichtlich Entwicklungseffizienz, Produktqualität und Wartbarkeit kann mit den heute angewandten Software-Entwicklungsmethoden nicht mehr entsprochen werden. Bis in jüngster Zeit war man darauf beschränkt, CIM-Systeme in einer sehr vereinfacht dargestellten Weise zu modellieren. Eine strukturierte Darstellung des technischen Systems auf mehreren Abstraktionsebenen wurde aber weitgehend vernachlässigt. Die isolierte Betrachtung einzelner CIM-Teilsysteme und die Vernachlässigung der Wechselwirkungen zu anderen Systemen führten zum Entstehen realitätsfremder CIM-Modelle, die in ihrer Struktur den realen Systemen nicht mehr entsprachen. Hoher Wartungsaufwand und eine mit einem vertretbaren Änderungsaufwand nicht durchzuführende Anpassung derartiger CIM-Modelle an die sich rapide weiterentwickelnden technischen Fertigungskomponenten sind die Konsequenzen des Fehlens dieser realitätskonformen Modellierung. Die Entwicklung neuer Modellierungsmethoden, mit denen modulare und realitätstreue Modelle, leicht erweiterbare und wiederverwendbare Softwarebausteine, eine übersichtliche Schnittstellengestaltung und letztendlich eine automatische Software-Implementierung realisiert werden können, ist daher eine unabdingbare Notwendigkeit.

Im Rahmen dieser Arbeit wird die Modellierungsmethode VOM (*Visual Object Modelling*) [ScSc92] als Methode für eine durchgängige, integrierte Modellierung der Planung, Terminierung und Steuerung von Produktionsprozessen vorgestellt. VOM ist eine graphische Modellierungssprache, die primär auf dem objektorientierten Paradigma des Software-Engineerings basiert. Die Objektorientierung, d.h die Idee, ein Modell als direktes Abbild der Diskurswelt zu strukturieren, kann als konzeptionelles Fundament dieser Sprache angesehen werden. Der VOM-Modellierer sieht ein reales System nicht mehr als eine Sequenz auszuführender Funktionen, sondern als eine Menge interagierender Objekte mit eigenen Zuständen und eigenem Verhalten. Objekte, zusammengefaßt und beschrieben durch Objektklassen, bilden die Bausteine des VOM-Modells. Strukturelle und funktionale Sichten auf die abzubildende Realität sind in diesen Objekten vereint. Um den Anforderungen einer umfassenden Modellierungssprache zu entsprechen, enthält die objektorientierte Modellierungstechnik in VOM neben Konstrukten zur strukturellen Modellierung auch Konstrukte der Verhaltensmodellierung. Dazu zählen Zustandsüberführungsdiagramme zur Beschreibung der internen Objektlebenszyklen, regelbasierte Objektzustandsbeschreibungen und vor allem *Tasks* zur Beschreibung parallel auszuführender Prozesse.

VOM ist eine durchgängige Methode, die alle drei Hauptphasen der Software-Entwicklung, die Analyse, den Entwurf und die Implementierung umfaßt. Das Vorgehensmodell von VOM basiert auf einem iterativen Modellierungsprozeß. Auf der Basis des meist unvollständigen Wissens des Modellierers über die Diskurswelt wird am Beginn ein Modellgerüst als Abbild des Ergebnisses der Systemanalyse aufgebaut. Modellierungsaufgaben dieser ersten Phasen sind

- die Abgrenzung des relevanten Objektsystems,
- die Beschreibung der grundlegenden Objektverhaltensweisen,

- die hierarchische Anordnung der Objekte, wobei die unteren Ebenen dieser Objekthierarchie die Struktur und das Basisverhalten (*Basisobjekte*) und die oberen Ebenen vor allem Steuerungsmechanismen (*Steuerobjekte*) für Basisobjekte beschreiben, und
- die Identifikation von sequentiellen und parallelen Systemprozessen zur Abbildung von Informations- und Steuerflüssen durch Tasks.

In einem iterativen Verfeinerungszyklus wird in der anschließenden Entwurfsphase dieses Gerüst zu einem einheitlichen Ganzen erweitert. Entscheidungen über

- Objektbeziehungen,
- das interne und externe Objektverhalten,
- Interaktionen zwischen Objekten,
- Schnittstellen zur Wirklichkeit (Benutzerschnittstellen, Geräteschnittstellen) und
- die Einführung von Parallelität

müssen in dieser Phase getroffen werden.

Die letzte Phase der Software-Entwicklung, die Implementierung, kann aufgrund der exakten Abbildungsmöglichkeit der Wirklichkeit und der exakten Spezifikationsmöglichkeit der Problemlösung weitgehend automatisch durchgeführt werden. Ein VOM-Werkzeug kann aus dem VOM-Modell eine umfassende *Objektbank* - das ist ein ausführbares Softwaresystem, bestehend aus einem Steuerungsteil, persistenter Objekthaltung und Schnittstellen zur Kommunikation mit der Wirklichkeit - generieren.

2. Beispielspezifikation

Zur Präsentation von VOM wurde ein vereinfacht dargestelltes Beispiel eines flexiblen Fertigungssystems ausgewählt. Im folgenden wird die Konfiguration dieses Systems beschrieben.

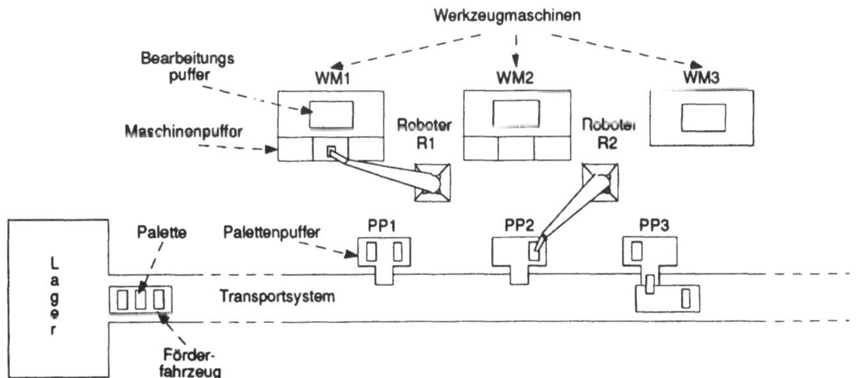

Die Konfiguration des Fertigungssystems besteht aus folgenden Hardwarekomponenten:

- ein Transportsystem, mit dem Paletten vom Lager zu den Palettenpuffern der Werkzeugmaschinen und wieder zurück befördert werden können;
- drei Palettenpufferplätze - PP1, PP2, PP3;
  In jedem der Palettenpuffer ist Platz für zwei Paletten zur Ein- und Auslagerung von Bearbeitungsteilen. Das Einschleusen einer Palette vom Transportsystem in einen Palettenpuffer erfolgt automatisch.
- 3 DNC-Werkzeugmaschinen - WM1, WM2, WM3;
  - Die Werkzeugmaschinen WM1 und WM2 besitzen jeweils drei Maschinenpuffer zur Zwischenlagerung von zu bearbeitenden oder bereits bearbeiteten Teilen. Das Laden der Teile vom Palettenpuffer in die Maschinenpuffer erfolgt über einen Roboter. Die Ein- bzw. Auslagerung eines Teils zwischen Maschinenpuffer und Bearbeitungspuffer wird automatisch von der Werkzeugmaschine durchgeführt.
  - Werkzeugmaschine WM3 besitzt keinen maschineneigenen Zwischenpuffer. Die zu bearbeitenden Teile werden vom Roboter R2 direkt von einer Palette der Palettenpuffer PP2 oder PP3 in den Bearbeitungspuffer der Maschine befördert.
- 2 stationäre Roboter - R1, R2;
  - Roboter R1 kann die Werkzeugmaschinen WM1 und WM2 von den Palettenpufferplätzen PP1 und PP2 beschicken.
  - Roboter R2 kann die Werkzeugmaschinen WM2 und WM3 von den Palettenpufferplätzen PP2 und PP3 beschicken.

3. VOM - Konzepte

Das fundamentale Konzept von VOM basiert auf der Idee, Systemdynamik als eine globale Funktion, die die zeitliche Änderung des Systemzustandsraumes beschreibt, zu sehen. Die hohe Komplexität dieser Funktion verlangt aber nach einer Zerlegung des Systems in Teilsysteme, deren Verhalten durch Zustandsüberführungsfunktionen minderer Komplexität beschrieben werden können. Die Komplexität der globalen Funktion verringert sich somit auf die Beschreibung des Zusammenwirkens der Teilsysteme. Eine kontinuierliche Fortführung dieser Systemzerlegung führt zum Entstehen einer Systemhierarchie, in der auf unterster Ebene Kleinstsysteme mit überschaubarem Systemverhalten zu finden sind. Struktur und Verhalten dieser Kleinstsysteme bilden die Basis des Gesamtsystems. Allgemein gesehen beschreiben Systeme auf den oberen Ebenen dieser Hierarchie vor allem Steuerungsmechanismen (Steuersysteme) für die unteren Ebenen (Basissysteme). Diese Unterscheidung zwischen Basissystemen und Steuersystemen bildet die Grundlage für den Vorgang der Modellierung mit VOM. VOM-Modellierung ist die realitätstreue Abbildung der Diskurswelt durch Objektbeschreibungen in Form von Objektklassen. Dazu unterscheidet VOM zwischen drei Arten von Objekten:

- *Basisobjekte* repräsentieren die Struktur und das Grundverhalten der zu beschreibenden Realität. Sie stehen für die Entitäten der Realität, die man als die interessierenden Objekte identifizieren würde. Typische Vertreter von Basisobjekten im Bereich der rechnerintegrierten Fertigung sind Werkzeugmaschinen, Roboter, Paletten, Pufferplätze, usw.

- *Steuerobjekte* stellen den Kontrollfluß eines Systems dar. Ihre Aufgabe ist die Entkopplung komplexer Verhaltensweisen, in denen mehr als ein Objekt involviert ist, von den Basisobjekten. Sie sorgen für ein geordnetes Zusammenwirken zwischen Basisobjekten und sind die Impulsgeber für die Ausführung deren Operationen. Steuerobjekte sind somit die Träger des Informations- und Steuerflusses innerhalb der Modellwelt. Zellensteuerungen, Transportsteuerungen aber auch Leitstände als Schnittstelle zwischen Produktionsplanung und Fertigung sind Beispiele für Steuerobjekte.

- *Schnittstellenobjekte* sind die Kommunikationsträger zwischen Modellwelt und Wirklichkeit. Sie versorgen einerseits das Modellsystem mit Informationen, die im realen System erzeugt wurden, andererseits geben sie dem realen System Informationen des Modellsystems zur Steuerung realer Systemkomponenten. Eine der wichtigsten Gruppen dieser Objekte sind Benutzerschnittstellenobjekte. Diese warten auf Benutzereingaben und reichen diese an Steuerobjekte weiter. Sie übernehmen aber auch Daten von Steuerobjekten und stellen diese visuell dar. Andere Schnittstellenobjekte sind Zeitgeber (timers) und Geräteschnittstellen.

Ein weiteres wichtiges Konzept ist die Unterscheidung zwischen internem und externem Verhalten von Objekten. *Internes Verhalten* eines Objekts bezieht sich auf jene Verhaltensweisen des Objekts, die nur die eigenen Attribute und Operationen ansprechen, jedoch keine Auswirkung auf andere, fremde Objekte haben. *Externes Verhalten* stellt im Gegensatz dazu die Interaktion zwischen Objekten dar. Das bedeutet, daß externes Verhalten eines Objekts diese dazu veranlaßt, aktiv zu werden, d.h. andere, fremde Objekte dazu zu bewegen, Operationen auszuführen. Basisobjekte führen nur ihr internes Verhalten aus, wohingegen ihr externes Verhalten von Steuerobjekten übernommen und ausgeführt wird. Demnach können Basisobjekte auch als passive Objekte bezeichnet werden.

4. VOM - Methode und Notation

Das zentrale Konzept der Modellierungsmethode VOM ist die Unterteilung der Objektwelt in Basisobjekte, Steuerobjekte und Schnittstellenobjekte. Zu deren Modellierung wurden für VOM folgende methodische Schwerpunkte definiert:

- visuelle Modellierung, basierend auf einem intelligenten Graphikeditor
- die strukturellen und verhaltensmäßigen Komponenten der realen Welt können hierarisch, auf unterschiedlichen Abstraktionsebenen, modelliert werden
- der Modellierungsvorgang basiert auf einem iterativen Entwurfsprozeß
- Beachtung der *Golden Rules* objektorientierter Datenbanksysteme [Atki90]
- Einbindung der Benutzerschnittstelle in den Modellierungsprozeß
- vollständige Modellierung, wodurch eine automatische Transformation des Modells auf eine Objektbank ermöglicht wird

4.1. Basisobjektmodellierung

In der Basisobjektmodellierung wird der Lebenslauf von Basisobjekten dargestellt. Die zentrale Aufgabe ist die Modellierung der internen Struktur und des internen Verhaltens eines

Basisobjekts von dessen Geburt bis zu dessen Tod, d.h. von der Erzeugung bis zum Löschen, zusammen mit allen Zuständen, in denen sich das Objekt befinden kann. Die Modellierung der Basisobjekte erfolgt in den beiden aufeinader aufbauenden Ebenen der Strukturmodellierung und der Verhaltensmodellierung.

4.1.1. Strukturmodellierung

In der Strukturmodellierung wird durch Klassifikation, Generalisation, Gruppierung und Assoziation das Modellgerüst als direktes Abbild der Wirklichkeit definiert.

- *Klassifikation* ist die Abstraktion gleicher realer Objekte mit gleichen Eigenschaften und gleichen Verhaltensweisen zu einer gemeinsamen Objektklasse. Die Menge der Objekte im betrachteten Realitätsausschnitt wird durch die Klassifikation in eine Anzahl von Klassen eingeteilt. Objekte werden als Exemplare (oder Instanzen) dieser Klassen bezeichnet. Beispielsweise werden alle Fertigungsmaschinen (WM1, WM2, WM3) zur Klasse `Maschine` zusammengefaßt.

- *Generalisation* ist die Abstraktion ähnlicher Objekte mit ähnlichen Eigenschaften und ähnlichen Verhaltensweisen zu einer gemeinsamen Objektklasse. In der objektorientierten Denkweise wird die Generalisation von Klassen zu einer Oberklasse durch den Vererbungsmechanismus (einfach, mehrfach) realisiert. VOM stellt den Vererbungsmechanismus durch die "is a"-Beziehung zwischen zwei Klassen dar.

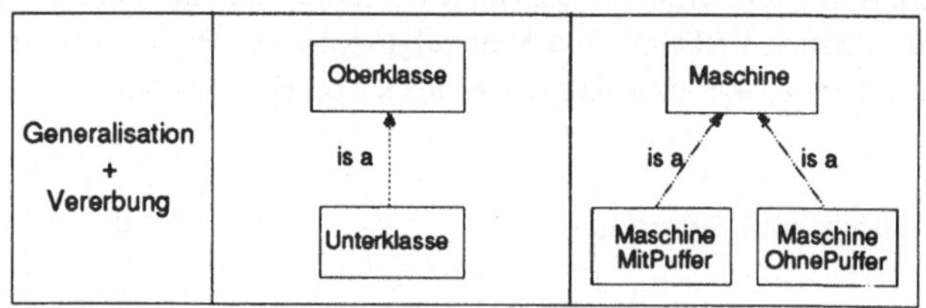

  Beispielsweise können Maschinen mit eigenem Zwischenpuffer (`MaschineMitPuffer`) und Maschinen ohne derartigen Zwischenpuffer (`MaschineOhnePuffer`) zur allgemeinen, generalisierenden Objektklasse `Maschine` zusammengefaßt werden.

- *Gruppierung* ist die Zusammenfassung von Objekten einer oder mehrerer Klassen zur Beschreibung ihrer Zusammengehörigkeit. Durch die Einführung der Objektgruppe als Exemplar der Kasse `Collection` können Objekte zu ihrer Identifikation zu Gruppen zusammengefaßt werden. Jeder Klasse kann bei ihrer Definition eine Gruppe zugeordnet werden. Dadurch ist es in VOM möglich, eine Klasse nach ihren Objekten zu fragen. Unterklassen der generalisierenden Objektklasse `Collection` sind `Bag`, `Set`, `Array`. Die Anzahl der Elemente innerhalb einer Gruppe wird durch ihre Kardinalität angegeben. Diese wird entweder durch eine natürliche Zahl (1, 5, 100) zur Definition einer genau definierten Anzahl von Elementen, oder durch ein Intervall ([0:5] - maximal 5, [1:100] - mindestens 1, maximal 100, n - beliebig viele) zur Beschreibung einer möglichen Anzahl von Elementen, spezifiziert. Durch die Spezifikation einer Einschränkung kann eine Objektgruppe auf Objekte mit bestimmten Eigenschaften oder Objekte bestimmter

Klassenzugehörigkeit eingeengt werden. Wird keine Einschränkung angegeben, wird implizit die Objektgruppe auf Objekte der gleichnamigen Objektklasse eingeschränkt.

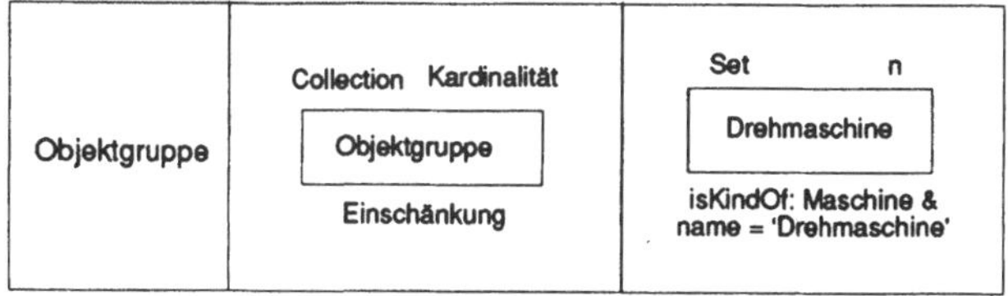

Assoziationen beschreiben Beziehungen zwischen den Objekten der Diskurswelt. In den meisten Modellierungsmethoden, wie *Entity-Relationship-Modelling* (ERM) [Chen70] oder *Object-Modelling-Technique* (OMT) [Rumb91], werden Beziehungen durch die explizite Angabe einer Beziehung modelliert. VOM sieht diese Benennung einer Objektbeziehung nicht vor. Es gibt nur zwei Arten, wie Objekte zueinander in Beziehung stehen können, die Eigentumsbeziehung und die Verwendungsbeziehung. Durch die Definition einer Eigentumsbeziehung zwischen zwei Objektgruppen `a` und `b` wird eine existenzielle Abhängigkeit des Objekts `b` von `a` modelliert. Wird Objekt `a` gelöscht, so wird auch Objekt `b` gelöscht. In der VOM-Notation wird eine *Eigentumsbeziehung* durch einen Pfeil zwischen den zueinander in Beziehung stehenden Klassen dargestellt.

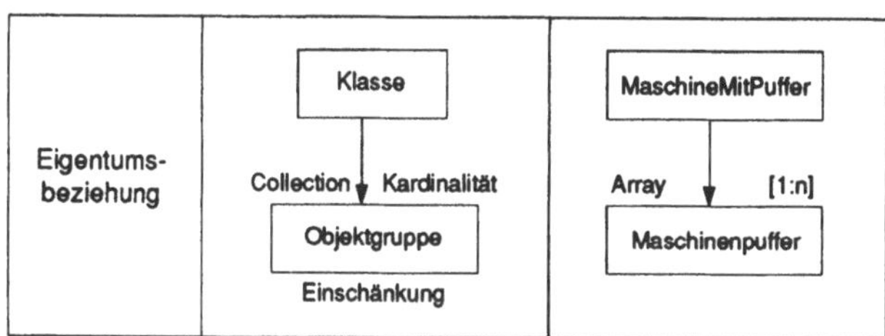

Beispielsweise können Maschinen eigene Zwischenpuffer zur Ein-/Auslagerung von Bearbeitungsteilen besitzen. Dazu wird jedem Objekt der Unterklasse `MaschineMitPuffer` eine Objektgruppe `MaschinenPuffer` zugeordnet. Die Objekte innerhalb dieser Gruppe haben nur dann ihre Existenzberechtigung, wenn ihr übergeordnetes Objekt der Klasse `MaschineMitPuffer` existiert.

Per definitionem kann ein Objekt nur Eigentum *eines* anderen Objektes sein. Kann diese Forderung nicht aufrechterhalten werden, da beispielsweise ein Objekt mehreren anderen Objekten zur Ausführung bestimmter Verhaltensweisen zugeordnet werden muß, kann diese durch eine *Verwendungsbeziehung* modelliert werden. Durch die Verwendungsbeziehung wird eine lose Beziehung zwischen zwei Objekten definiert. Ein Objekt `a` verwendet ein Objekt `b`, ohne es zu besitzen. Wird Objekt `a` gelöscht, bleibt die Existenz von Objekt `b` sehrwohl erhalten. In der VOM-Notation wird eine Verwendungsbeziehung durch einen strichlierten Pfeil dargestellt.

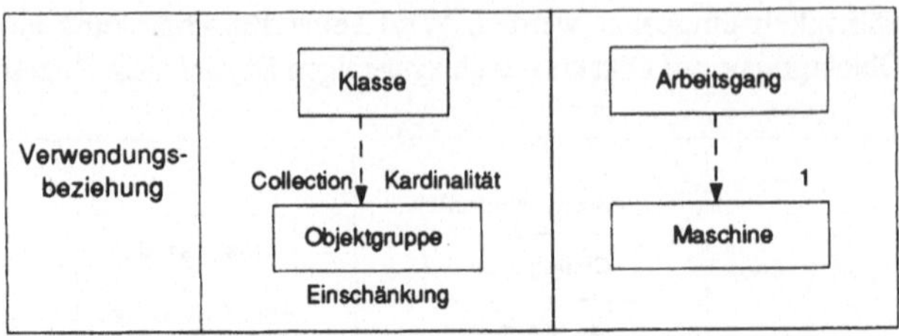

Die Beziehung zwischen Objekten der Klassen `Arbeitsgang` und `Maschine` wird als Verwendungsbeziehung modelliert. Bei der Ausführung eines Arbeitsganges wird eine Maschine zur Bearbeitung eines Teiles verwendet. Der Arbeitsgang ist aber keinesfalls Eigentümer einer Maschine. Wird ein Arbeitsgang gelöscht, bleibt die Bearbeitungsmaschine erhalten.

4.1.2. Verhaltensmodellierung

Das graphische Konstrukt zur Modellierung der Verhaltensanteile von Basisobjekten ist ein erweitertes Zustandsüberführungsdiagramm. Dieses basiert auf der Grundlage der Petrinetz-Theorie [Rose82], in der Transitionen den Zustandsraum der Objekte verwalten. Die Komponenten des VOM-Zustandsüberführungsdiagramms werden im folgenden anhand eines vereinfacht dargestellten Roboter-Zustandsüberführungsdiagrammes diskutiert:

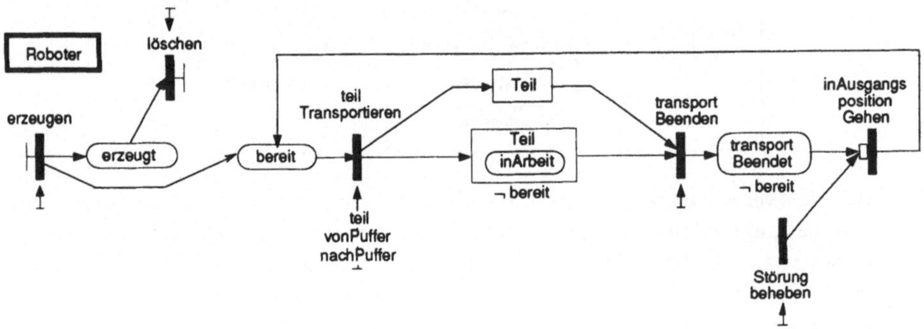

Transitionen sind die Operationen zur Verwaltung des Objektzustandsraumes. Eine Transition wird automatisch ausgeführt, sobald alle Vorbedingungen (interne Zustände, Anstoß von anderen Objekten) gültig sind. Die Richtung der Zustandsüberführung wird durch einen einfachen Pfeil definiert, welcher auf der rechten Seite der Transition austritt.

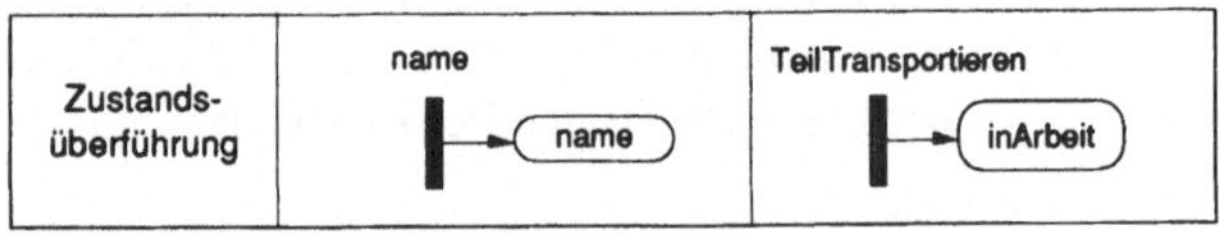

Zum Erzeugen und zum Löschen von Objekten gibt es zwei spezielle Arten von Transitionen, die *Konstruktortransition* und die *Destruktortransition*. Die Konstruktortransition erzeugt am

Beginn der Transitionsausführung ein Objekt der Klasse, für die das Zustandsüberführungsdiagramm definiert wurde, und versetzt es in seinen Anfangszustand. Konstruktortransitionen sind somit immer die Beginntransitionen innerhalb von Zustandsüberführungsdiagrammen. Die Destruktortransition löscht ein Objekt nach Ausführung der Transition. Das Objekt verliert dadurch seine Existenz in der Modellwelt.

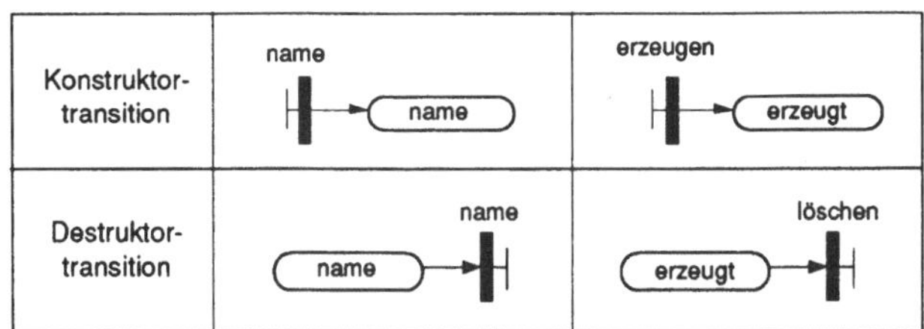

Über die Verbindungslinie vor der Transition werden die Vorzustände, die für die Ausführung der Transition gegeben sein müssen, definiert. Falls der Vorzustand bei Ausführung der Transition gültig bleiben soll, muß dies durch eine Linie ohne Pfeil zur Transition modelliert werden. Ansonsten führt ein Pfeil vom Zustand weg, wodurch bei Ausführung der Transition der Vorzustand weggenommen wird.

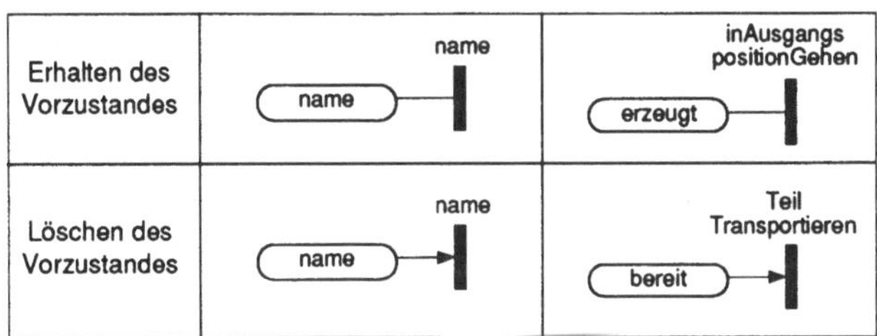

Es besteht jedoch keine Verpflichtung, Transitionen über Zustände zu verketten. Es ist auch möglich, daß eine Basisobjekttransition eine andere Transition anstößt.

Vorzustände für die Ausführung von Transitionen können auch *oder-verknüpft* werden. Die Oder-Verknüpfung von Vorzuständen wird in VOM durch das Einmünden der Verbindungslinien in ein der Transition vorangestelltes Rechteck definiert. Auf diese Weise können UND/ODER verknüpfte Vorbedingungen für die Ausführung von Transitionen formuliert werden.

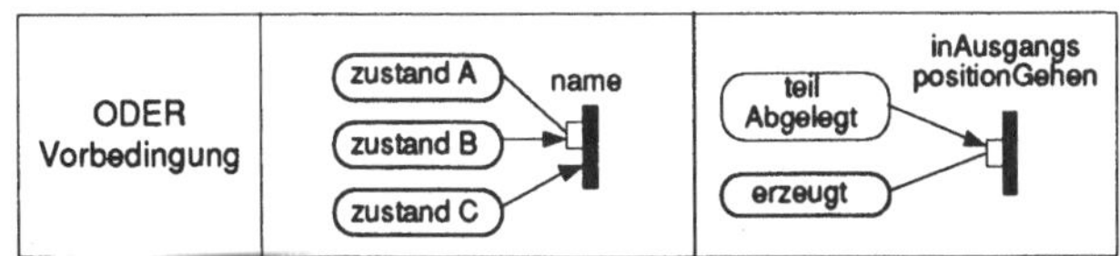

Wie bereits dargestellt, werden Transitionen bei Erfüllung all ihrer Vorbedingungen automatisch ausgeführt. Dies würde aber bislang bedeuten, daß sofort nach dem Setzen eines Zustandes, alle von diesem Zustand abhängigen Transitionen sofort ausgeführt würden. Ein derartiges Modellverhalten ist aber in den wenigsten Fällen erwünscht. Deshalb wird ein Modellkonstrukt benötigt, von dem eine Transition blockiert wird und auf einen Anstoß von außen, von einem Steuerobjekt, wartet. Ein derartiger Transitionsanstoß von seiten eines Steuerobjektes wird wie ein Vorzustand als Vorbedingung betrachtet. Erst wenn die Basisobjekttransition von einem Steuerobjekt angestoßen wird und alle internen Vorzustände erfüllt sind, kann sie ausgeführt werden. Optional können bei einem Transitionsanstoß Parameter, die der Transition zu übergeben sind, definiert werden.

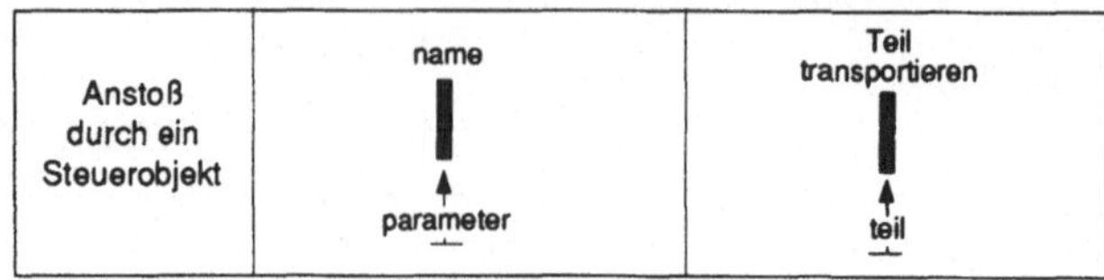

Zur Beschreibung des Aufbaus von Objektbeziehungen (Eigentums- oder Verwendungsbeziehungen) bedarf es der Modellierungsmöglichkeit, Transitionsparameter in die interne Objektstruktur aufzunehmen, d.h. zu speichern. Die graphische Notation hierfür ist ein auf ein Rechteck zeigender Pfeil. Unterscheidet sich das Objektattribut vom Transitionsparameter, so kann explizit eine Zuweisung (param --> attribut) spezifiziert werden.

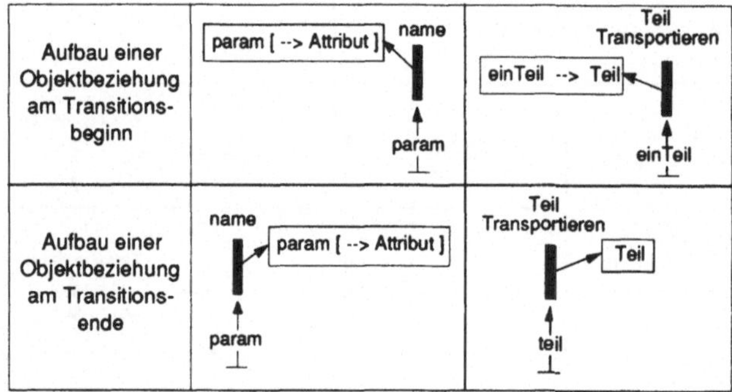

Das Ändern einer Objektbeziehung, d.h. das Ersetzen eines Fremdobjektes durch ein anderes, erfolgt mit einer ähnlichen Notation. Anstelle des Zuweisungspfeiles (-->) wird ein Änderungspfeil (<-->) verwendet.

Das Löschen einer Objektbeziehung erfolgt durch einen Pfeil vom Attribut zur löschenden Transition.

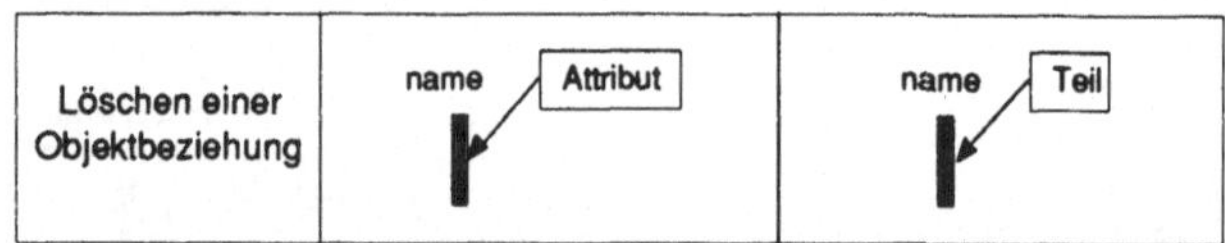

Zustände wurden bislang den Basisobjekten direkt zugeordnet. Häufig besteht aber die Notwendigkeit, Zustände für Objektbeziehungen zu definieren. Dies ist der Fall, wenn ein Objekt andere Objekte, meistens in Form von Objektgruppen, über Eigentums- oder Verwendungsbeziehungen referenziert. Für jedes Element innerhalb der Objektgruppe müssen Zustände definiert werden können, welche Informationen über die Beziehung zwischen diesem Element und dem Basisobjekt enthalten.

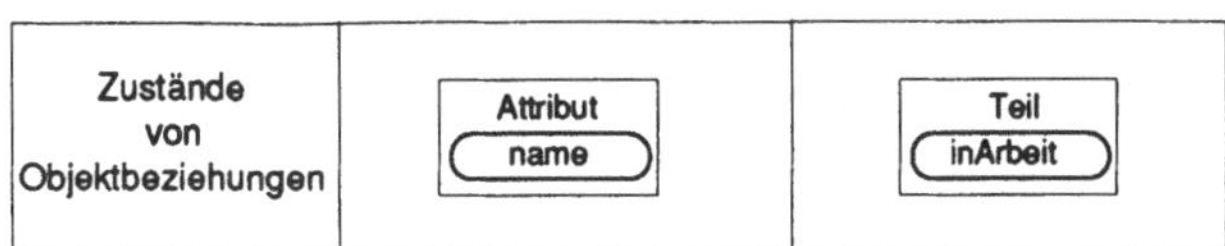

Zustandsbedingungen sind Modellierungskonstrukte zur Formulierung zusätzlicher Bedingungen für die Gültigkeit von Zuständen. Bislang mußte der Gültigkeitswert eines Zustandes explizit durch die Ausführung einer Transition gesetzt und wieder gelöscht werden. Die Komplexität der zu modellierenden Basisobjektklasse ist aber meist zu hoch, um sie in Form von sequentiellen Ketten von Zustandsüberführungen übersichtlich zu beschreiben. Häufig gibt es Ausnahmesituationen, die während des gesamten Objektlebenszyklus eintreten können und sich auf die Gültigkeit sehr vieler Zustände von Basisobjekten auswirken.

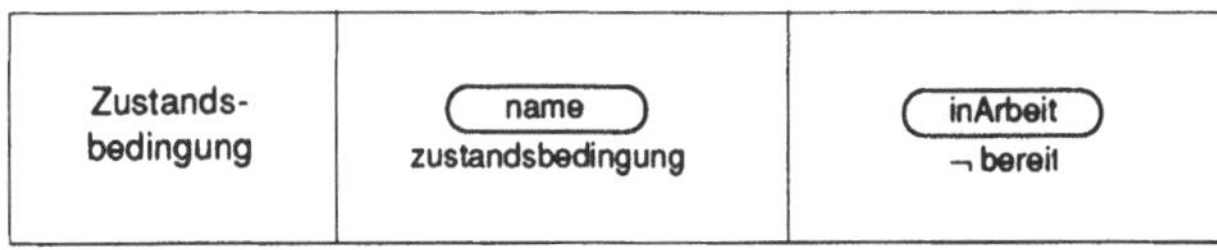

In unserem Beispiel kann die Transition `StörungBeheben` jederzeit angestoßen werden. Auf diese Weise kann im Falle einer Störung der Roboter in seinen Initialzustand zurückgesetzt werden. Durch den Anstoß der Transition `inAusgangspositionGehen` wird der Folgezustand `bereit` gesetzt. Da sich der Roboter vor der Störung in einem beliebigen Zustand befinden kann, müssen diese Zustände gelöscht werden. Durch die Formulierung von Zustandsbedingungen erfolgt das Löschen von Zuständen automatisch. Die Zustände `inArbeit` und `transportBeendet` sind nur dann gültig, wenn der Zustand `bereit` gesetzt ist (¬ `bereit`). Wird der Zustand `bereit` gesetzt, verlieren die beiden anderen Zustände sofort ihre Gültigkeit.

4.2. Steuerobjektmodellierung

Steuerobjekte sorgen für die Steuerung des Gesamtmodells durch ihre Interaktionen mit den großteils passiven Basisobjekten und Schnittstellenobjekten. Sie enkoppeln die externe Komplexität zwischen den Basisobjekten und stellen diese auf einer höheren Ebene der Modellhierarchie zur Verfügung. Ihre primäre Aufgabe ist die Abbildung des Informations- und Steuerflusses innerhalb komplexer Systemprozesse.

Steuerflüsse werden durch die Verkettung von Steuerobjekttransitionen dargestellt. Der Begriff der Steuerobjekttransition deutet bereits darauf hin, daß Steuerflüsse wie die Lebenszyklen von Basisobjekten ebenfalls durch Zustandsüberführungsdiagramme dargestellt werden. Das bedeutet, daß zwischen den Steuerobjekttransitionen optional Zustände als Informationsträger des aktuellen Steuerzustandes definiert werden können. Hinzu kommt, daß zur Modellierung des Informationsflusses zwischen Steuerobjekttransitionen Parameter definiert werden können.

Steuerobjekttransitionen können auch polymorphe Operationen darstellen. Polymorphismus kann in zwei verschiedenen Formen auftreten. Von *Einfach-Polymorphismus* wird gesprochen, wenn eine Operation in verschiedenen Klassen unterschiedlich implementiert ist. *Mehrfach-Polymorphismus* liegt vor, wenn zusätzlich zum Einfach-Polymorphismus innerhalb einer

Klasse mehrere Methoden für eine Operation existieren. In diesem Fall wird die passende Methode aufgrund der Operationsparameter, d.h. deren Anzahl und Typen, ausgewählt. Dies entspricht den Konzepten, die durch C++ bekannt sind.

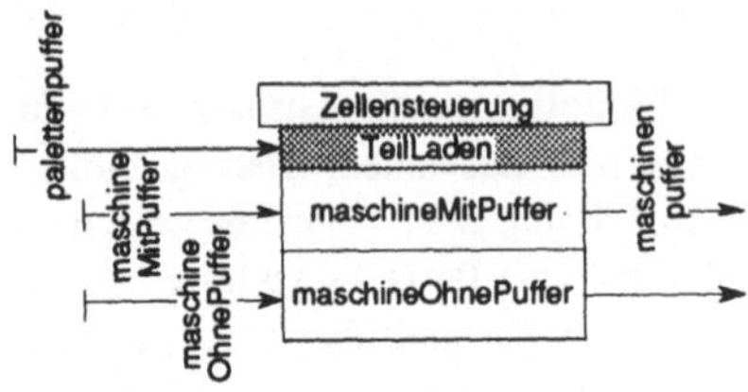

In diesem Beispiel werden für die Steuerobjekttransition `TeilLaden` zwei verschiedene Methoden (`maschineMitPuffer` und `maschineOhnePuffer`) definiert. Der erste Parameter beider Methoden ist ein `palettenpuffer`. Im zweiten Parameter unterscheiden sich die Methoden. Die Auswahl der passenenden Methode hängt somit vom Typ des zweiten Parameters ab. Wird eine `MaschineMitPuffer` übergeben, wird die erste Methode ausgewählt. Wird eine `MaschineOhnePuffer` übergeben, wird die zweite Methode ausgewählt. Im obigen Beispiel ist auch ersichtlich, daß der nachfolgende Steuerfluß für verschiedene Methoden unterschiedlich sein kann.

In VOM wird zusätzlich gefordert, daß unterschiedliche Methoden einer Operation auch gleiche formale Parameter besitzen können. Durch die Angabe einer Bedingung für die Parameterwerte kann zur Laufzeit die jeweils passende Methode ausgewählt werden.

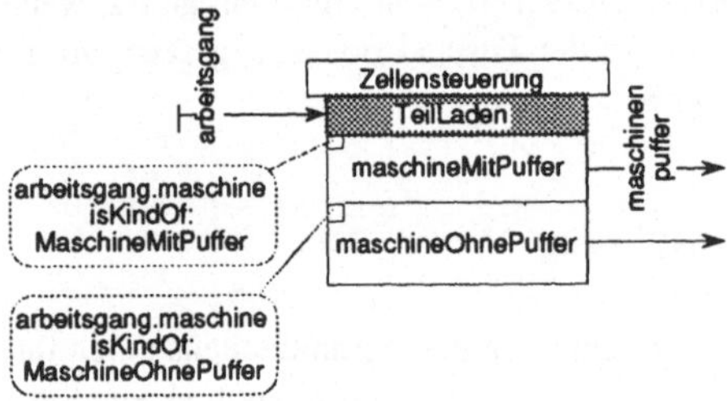

In diesem Beispiel wird der Parameter `arbeitsgang` der Steuerobjekttransition `TeilLaden` für beide Methoden definiert. Die Ausführung einer Methode von `TeiLaden` hängt von der Maschine, auf der der Arbeitsgang ausgeführt wird (`arbeitsgang.maschine`), ab. Dies wird durch die Angabe der obigen Auswahlbedingungen modelliert.

4.2.1. Interaktionsmodellierung

Die Modellierung von Steuerobjekttransitionen als Bindeglied zwischen den internen Verhaltenskomponenten von Basis- und Schnittstellenobjekten erfolgt über Interaktionsdiagramme. Steuerobjekte können mit Basisobjekten und/oder Schnittstellenobjekten interagieren. Dazu gibt es in VOM drei Arten von Interaktionen, die *Eingabeinteraktion*, die *Ausgabeinteraktion* und die *EinAusgabeinteraktion*.

Eingabeinteraktionen ermöglichen es, am Beginn einer Steuerobjekttransition Informationen von Basis- oder Schnittstellenobjekten einzuholen.

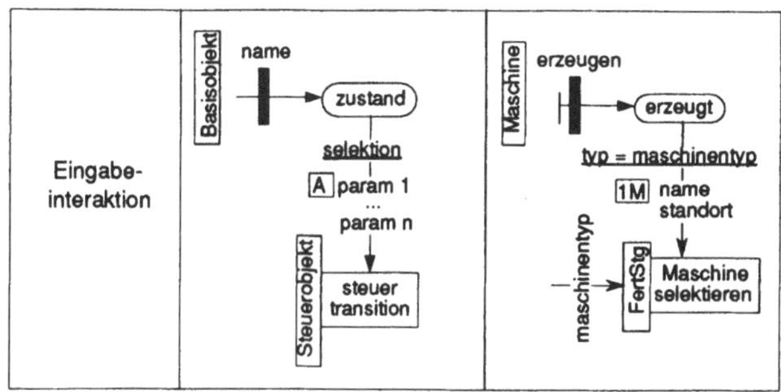

Die grundlegende Idee, die einer Interaktion mit Basisobjekten zugrunde liegt, ist, alle Objekte einer Klasse, die in jenem Zustand sind, von welchem der Interaktionspfeil wegführt, abzurufen. Falls entlang des Pfeiles zusätzliche Selektionsanweisungen angegeben werden, werden die von dieser Klasse gelieferten Objekte auf jene reduziert, die diese Bedingungen erfüllen. Eine Selektionsanweisung besteht primär aus zwei Komponenten, einem *Auswahlindikator* (A) und einem *Parameter*.

```
Auswahlindikator      := ManuelleAuswahl | AutomatischeAuswahl.
ManuelleAuswahl       := [ <natürliche Zahl> ] "M".
AutomatischeAuswahl   := [ <natürliche Zahl> ].
```

Eine *manuelle Auswahl* von Objekten wird an die Benutzerschnittstelle weitergeleitet. Der Benutzer wird dazu aufgefordert, die durch <natürliche Zahl> angegebene Anzahl von Elementen zu selektieren. Wird keine Quantifizierung vorgenommen, so bestimmt der Benutzer, wieviele Elemente selektiert werden. Im Gegensatz dazu wird eine *automatische Auswahl* vom System durchgeführt. Falls die Objektmenge der Quellklasse die definierte Quantifizierung übersteigt, wird eine nicht bestimmte Teilmenge, deren Elementeanzahl der Quantifizierung entspricht, ausgewählt. Die Projektion von Attributen erfolgt durch die Angabe von Parametern, deren Namen den gewünschten Attributen entsprechen. In diesem Fall wird für die selektierten Objekte lediglich eine reduzierte Sicht auf die Attribute weitergegeben.

Im obigen Beispiel wird eine Interaktion zwischen der Transition `MaschineSelektieren` des Steuerobjekts `FertStg` (Fertigungssteuerung) und der Basisobjektklasse `Maschine` definiert. Vorerst wird die Menge der gelieferten Objekte auf jene im Zustand `erzeugt` reduziert. Durch die Selektionsanweisung `typ = maschinentyp` wird die Klasse der Maschinen auf jene Objekte eingeschränkt, deren Wert des Attributs `typ` gleich dem des Steuerflußparameters `maschinentyp` ist. Aus dieser eingeschränkten Objektmenge wird der Benutzer aufgefordert, genau ein Objekt auszuwählen (1M). Von diesem Objekt wird anschließend eine Sicht auf die Attribute `name` und `standort` an die Transition `MaschineSelektieren` weitergegeben. Alle anderen Attribute dieses Objekts sind vor Zugriff geschützt.

Ausgabeinteraktionen stoßen am Ende einer Steuerobjekttransition Transitionen von Basisobjekten oder Schnittstellenobjekten an. Wie bei der Eingabeinteraktion kann auch eine Ausgabeinteraktion die durch die Vorzustände der Basisobjekttransition definierte Objektmenge durch Selektionsanweisungen und einem Auswahlindikator weiter einschränken.

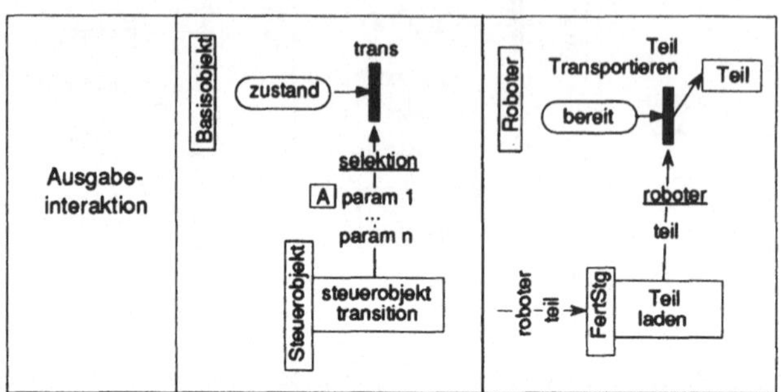

In diesem Beispiel ist eine Ausgabeinteraktion zwischen der Steuerobjekttransition `TeilLaden` des Steuerobjekts `FertStg` und der Basisobjektklasse `Roboter` modelliert. Die Klasse der Roboter wird hierbei genau auf das durch den Parameter `roboter` beschriebene Objekt eingeschränkt. Der Transitionsparameter `teil` wird am Ende von `TeilTransportieren` in die interne Struktur des Roboters eingebaut.

Eine *EinAusgabeinteraktion* ist die Zusammenfassung einer Eingabeinteraktion und einer Ausgabeinteraktion. Der Eingabeteil identifiziert eine Objektmenge, die als Eingangsdatum für die Transition des Steuerobjekts verwendet wird und deren Elemente die Zielobjekte für den Ausgabeteil der Interaktion darstellen.

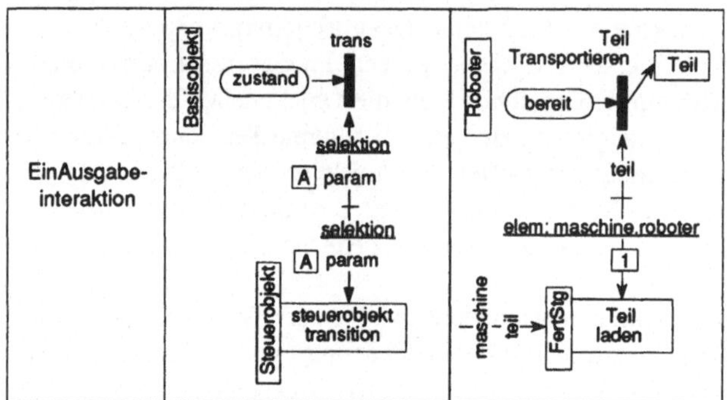

Im allgemeinen Fall werden im Eingabeteil der Interaktion alle Objekte, die sich in dem der Transition der Basisobjektklasse vorangehenden Zustand befinden, ausgewählt. Zusätzlich können, wie bei der einfachen Eingabeinteraktion, optionale Einschränkungen durch einen Auswahlindikator oder Selektionanweisungen diese Objektmenge noch weiter reduzieren. Die auf diese Weise ausgewählten Objekte werden der Steuerobjekttransition zur Verfügung gestellt. Nach deren Ausführung wird der Ausgabeteil der Interaktion abgearbeitet, dessen Zielobjekte die zuvor ausgewählten Basisobjekte sind. Das bedeutet, daß im Standardfall für jedes im Eingabeteil der Interaktion selektierte Basisobjekt die in der Interaktion angegebene

Transition angestoßen wird. Wiederum kann diese Zielmenge wahlweise durch einen Auswahlindikator oder zusätzliche Selektionsanweisungen weiter eingeschränkt werden.

Im obigen Beispiel wird über den Eingabeteil ein Roboter, der zu Beschickung der Maschine `maschine` definiert worden ist, automatisch ausgewählt. Im Ausgabeteil wird für diesen Roboter die Transition `TeilTransportieren` angestoßen. Dieser Transition wird der Parameter `teil` mitgegeben, welcher in die interne Struktur des Roboters (`Teil`) eingebaut wird.

4.2.2. Aufgabenmodellierung

Um eine umfassende Modellierung der Funktionalität eines technischen Systems zu ermöglichen, sind zusätzliche Konstrukte der Prozeßmodellierung erforderlich. Technische Systeme der Produktion sind vor allem durch eine hohes Maß an Parallelität gekennzeichnet. Parallelität kann in zwei verschiedenen Formen auftreten, je nachdem ob mehrere Funktionen unterschiedlichen oder gleichen Typs zeitlich parallel ausgeführt werden. Der erste Fall, in dem mehrere unterschiedliche Funktionen parallel ausgeführt werden, ist in VOM bereits durch die Definition des Begriffs *Transition* realisiert. Transitionen werden automatisch ausgeführt, wenn all ihre Vorbedingungen (Zustände, Anstoß von Steuer- oder Schnittstellenobjekten) erfüllt sind. Die zweite Art der Parallelität bezieht sich auf die gleichzeitige Ausführung mehrerer Exemplare der gleichen Steuertransitionskette. In diesem Fall spricht man von einer Aufgabe bzw. einem *Task*. Eine Aufgabe entspricht einer Menge von Steuerobjekttransitionen, die zusammen eine logische Funktionseinheit bilden.

Neben der Spezifikationsmöglichkeit von Parallelität ist es das charakteristische Merkmal einer Aufgabe, Verhaltensbausteine zu konstruieren, aus denen das Gesamtverhalten des Systems auf höheren Abstraktionsniveaus zusammengesetzt werden kann. Dazu bietet VOM folgende Notation:

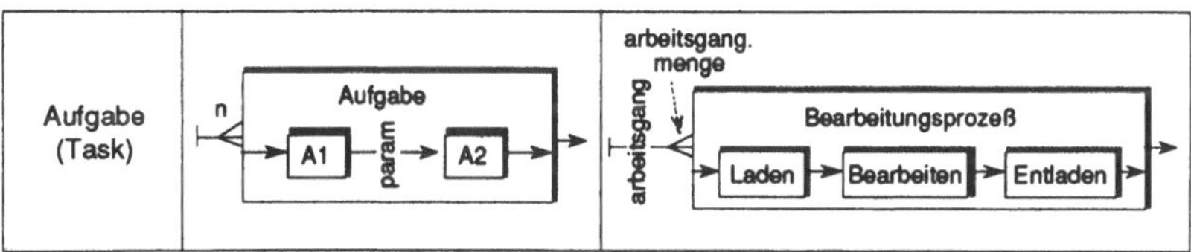

In diesem Beispiel wird ein `Bearbeitungsprozeß` in Form einer Aufgabe dargestellt. Der Bearbeitungsprozeß besteht aus einer Sequenz der Unteraufgaben `Laden`, `Bearbeiten` und `Entladen`. Durch die Verzweigung vor der Aufgabe `Bearbeitungsprozeß` wird angegeben, daß mehrere Aufgaben zu einem Zeitpunkt generiert werden können. Dabei spezifiziert die Quantifizierung (`arbeitsgang.menge`) die Anzahl der beim Anstoß der Aufgabe zu erzeugenden Exemplare. Zwischen den Aufgaben können optional Parameter zur Weitergabe von Informationen spezifiziert werden. Aufgrund des einfachen Pfeils nach der Aufgabe wird für jede generierte Aufgabe des Typs `Bearbeitungsprozeß` die nachfolgende Aufgabe oder Steuerobjekttransition angestoßen. Wäre anstatt des Pfeils eine Zusammenführung der generierten Aufgaben definiert, würde das die Ausführung der nachfolgenden Aufgaben und Steuerobjekttransitionen so lange blockieren, bis alle generierten Exemplare der Aufgabe beendet sind. Dies wird im folgenden Beispiel demonstriert:

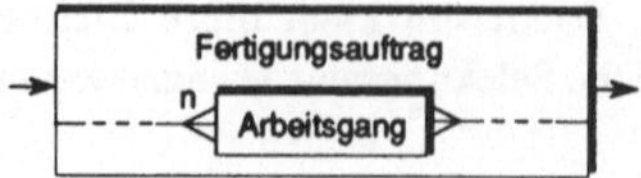

Innerhalb einer Aufgabe des Typs `Fertigungsauftrag` wird für jeden `Arbeitsgang` des Fertigungsauftrags eine Aufgabe generiert. Durch die Weiterführung der Unteraufgabe `Arbeitsgang` mit der Notation der Aufgaben-Zusammenführung werden die nachfolgenden Transitionen innerhalb dieses Steuerflusses blockiert, bis alle Arbeitsgänge des Fertigungsauftrags ausgeführt worden sind.

5. Ein Beispiel

Auf der Basis der im Kapitel 4 eingeführten VOM-Methode und Notation werden Ausschnitte eines vereinfacht dargestellten Beispiels für einen Bearbeitungsvorgang, beginnend mit dem Transport von Bearbeitungsteilen vom Lager zu den Werkzeugmaschinen über die Bearbeitung der Teile bis hin zu ihrem Rücktransport ins Lager, modelliert. Grundlage für die Modellierung bildet die in Kapitel 2 dargestellte Anlagenkonfiguration. Ziel dieses Beispiels ist nicht die vollständige Spezifikation des Modells, sondern das Zeigen der Anwendbarkeit von VOM für die Belange der rechnerintegrierten Fertigung.

Die für unser Beispiel relevanten Komponenten des zu beschreibenden Fertigungssystems können zu den Objektklassen `Maschine`, `Maschinenpuffer`, `Palettenpuffer`, `Roboter`, `Fertigungsauftrag`, `Arbeitsgang` und `Teil` zusammengefaßt werden. Die Klasse der Maschinen kann spezialisiert werden in Maschinen mit eigenen Zwischenpuffern zur Ein- und Auslagerung von Bearbeitungsteilen und Maschinen ohne derartige Zwischenpuffer. Weiters werden die Klassen `Palettenpuffer`, `Maschinenpuffer` und `Bearbeitungspuffer` zur generalisierenden Oberklasse `Puffer` zusammengefaßt.

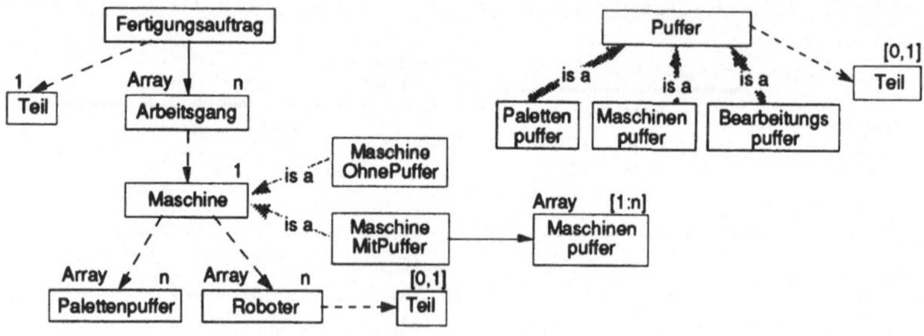

Das Verhaltensmodell entspricht der Spezifikation der Lebenszyklen der im Strukturmodell definierten Basisobjektklassen.

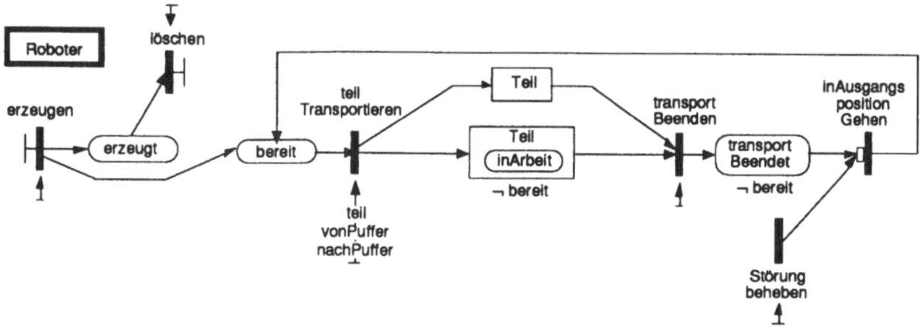

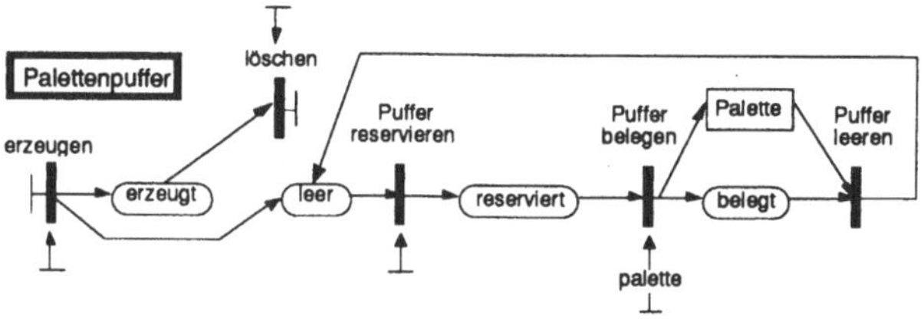

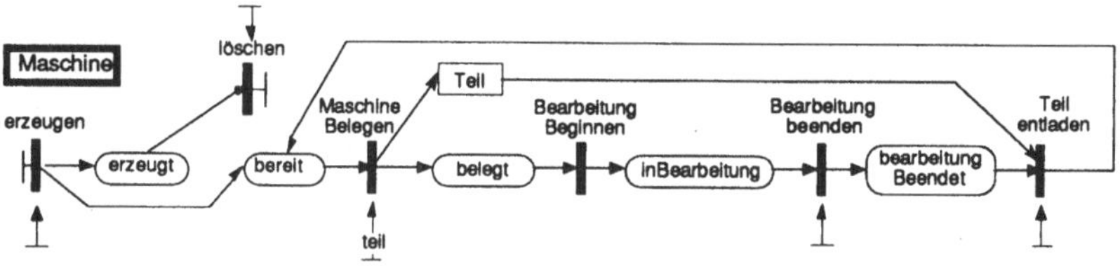

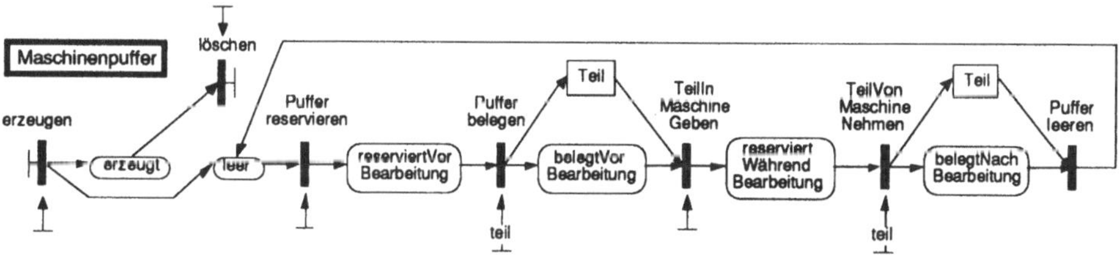

Auf der Basis des in der Strukur- und Verhaltensmodellierung definierten Modellgerüsts können komplexe Aufgaben, wie die Durchführung von Arbeitsgängen, formuliert werden. Eine abstrahierte Darstellung eines Arbeitsganges in Form eines Aufgabenmodells kann folgendes Aussehen haben:

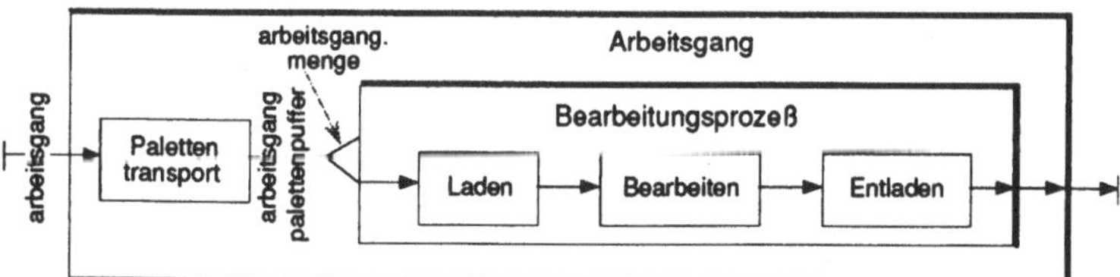

Ein Arbeitsgang besteht aus einer Sequenz auszuführender Aufgaben. Er beginnt mit dem Transport einer Palette zu einem freien Palettenpuffer, von dem die Maschine des Arbeitsganges beschickt wird. Dieser Vorgang wird vom Task `Palettentransport` durchgeführt.

Anschließend kann für jeden Teil auf der Palette der `Bearbeitungsprozeß` begonnen werden. Stehen die benötigten Resourcen an Werkzeugmaschinen, Maschinenpuffern, Robotern, usw. zur Verfügung, können mehrere Bearbeitungsprozesse gleichzeitig gestartet werden. Dies wird durch die Verzweigung vor dem Task `Bearbeitungsprozeß` dargestellt. Ein Bearbeitungsprozeß wird als Folge der Subtasks "`Laden` des Teils auf die Maschine", "`Bearbeiten` des Teils" und "`Entladen` des Teils von der Maschine" angesehen.

Im nächsten Verfeinerungszyklus kann der Task `Arbeitsgang` durch ein Steuerflußdiagramm verfeinert werden. Dabei werden für jede Steuerobjekttransition die Basisobjekt- und Steuerobjektklassen, mit denen die Steuerobjekttransition kommuniziert, definiert. Im folgenden wird der Ladevorgang beispielhaft durch ein Steuerflußdiagramm abgebildet.

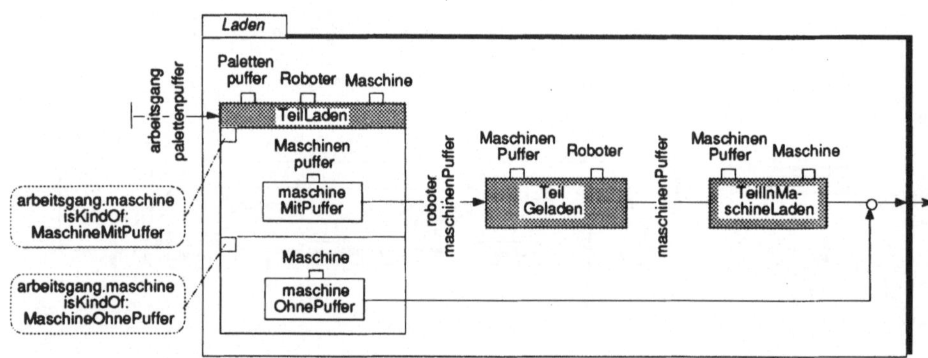

Für den Task `Laden` sind die beiden Parameter `arbeitsgang` und `palettenpuffer`, die in einem übergeordneten Task definiert worden sind, bekannt. `Laden` beginnt mit der polymorphen Steuerobjekttransition `TeilLaden`. Diese veranlaßt den Transport eines Teils von der Palette im `palettenpuffer` zur Bearbeitungsmaschine `arbeitsgang.maschine`. Dieser Transport wird von einem Roboter durchgeführt. Je nachdem, ob die Bearbeitungsmaschine eine `MaschineMitPuffer` oder eine `MaschineOhnePuffer` ist, müssen unterschiedliche Aktionen ausgeführt werden. Ist die Maschine des Arbeitsganges eine `MaschineMitPuffer`, muß der Teil in einen freien Maschinenpuffer abgelegt werden. In der nachfolgenden Transition `TeilGeladen` wartet der Task `Laden` so lange, bis von der Robotersteuerung eine Botschaft einlangt, daß der Ladeprozeß beendet ist. Ist die Bearbeitungsmaschine frei, wird der Teil mit der Transition `TeilInMaschineLaden` vom Maschinenpuffer auf den Bearbeitungspuffer der Maschine geladen. Dieser zweite Ladevorgang wird von der Bearbeitungsmaschine selbst ausgeführt. Handelt es sich um eine `MaschineOhnePuffer`, wird der Teil direkt auf den Bearbeitungspuffer der Maschine geladen.

Im nachfolgenden Interaktionsdiagramm werden die Steuerobjekttransitionen des obigen Steuerflußdiagramms durch deren Interaktionen mit Basisobjektklassen präzisiert.

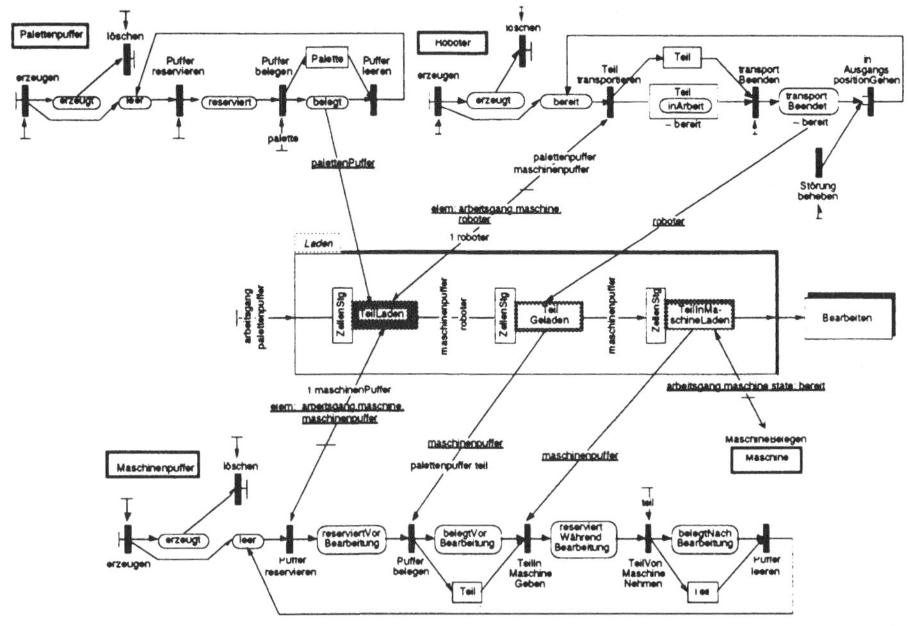

Literaturverweise

[Atki90] Atkinson, M., DeWitt D., Maier, D., Bancilhon, F., Dittrich, K., Zdonik, S.: The Object-Oriented Database System Manifesto. In: Kim, W. et al.: Deductive and Object-Oriented Databases, Elsevier Science Publishers B.V. (North Holland), 1990.

[Booc91] Booch, G.: Object oriented design with applications, The Benjamin/Cummings Publishing Company, Redwood City, CA, 1991.

[Chen70] Chen, P.: The Entity-Relationship Model - Toward a Unified View of Data, ACM Transactions on Database Systems, Vol. 1, No. 1, 1970.

[Coad90] Coad, P., Yourdon, E.: Object-Oriented Analysis, Prentice Hall, Englewood Cliffs, N.J., 1990.

[Meye88] Meyer, B.: Object Oriented Software Construction, Prentice Hall, Hertfordshire, UK, 1988.

[Rose82] Rosenstengel, B.; Winand, U.: Petri-Netze - Eine anwendungsorientierte Einführung, Vieweg, Braunschweig, 1982.

[Rumb91] Rumbaugh, J., Blaha, M., Premerlani, W., Eddy, F., Lorensen, W.: Object-Oriented Modeling and Design, Prentice-Hall, Englewood Cliffs, N.J., 1991.

[ScSc92] Schauer, R., Schönberger, S.: Visual Object Modelling. In: Tjoa, A M., Ramos, I.: Database and Expert Systems Applications, Springer-Verlag, Wien, 1992.

[Sche88] Scheer, A.W.: Wirtschaftsinformatik - Informationssysteme im Industriebetrieb, Springer Verlag, 1988.

Fachtagung

Objektorientierte Methoden für Informationssysteme

Erfahrungen beim Bau eines objektorientierten Klassensystems für anpaßbare anwendungsspezifische Leitstände

Thomas Otterbein
Fraunhofer Institut für Arbeitswirtschaft und Organisation IAO
Senefelder Str. 26
7000 Stuttgart 1
Tel. 0711/970-2346
Fax 0711/970-2300
E-Mail: T_Otterbein@iao.fhg.de

Inhaltsverzeichnis

1. Einführung

Leitstände werden seit geraumer Zeit als das wesentliche Instrument bei der Durchsetzung der Planung in der Fertigung angesehen (/35/, /28/). Hierzu sind unterschiedliche Systeme bekannt, die von der klassischen manuellen Plantafel bis zu dem rechnerbasierten CIM-Leitstand gehen. Eine Beherrschung der in der Werkstatt vorliegenden Informationen ist aufgrund des Umfangs und der Vielfalt nur möglich, wenn es gelingt, den großen Teil der Routinearbeit auf Computersysteme zu übertragen (/21/).

Leider sind in jeder Fertigung unterschiedliche Anforderungen anzutreffen, welche auch andere Eigenschaften von dem steuernden Leitstand fordern. Diese Anforderungen erstrecken sich von der Anpassung an die durch das übergeordnete PPS-System vorgegebene Planungsstrategie (/16/) über die Ankopplung unterschiedlichster Werkzeugmaschinen via DNC bis zum Einsatz spezifisch an eine Fertigung angepaßter Planungsalgorithmen. Die sich hieraus ergebenden Anforderungen lassen sich durch Standardsysteme nur begrenzt erfüllen. Schon beim Einsatz einer bestimmten BDE-Lösung sind häufig Anpassungen vonnöten (/32/). Zwar können die am Markt befindlichen Leitstände spezifische Einzellösungen hierfür anbieten, doch gilt für eine Anpassung dieser Produkte an spezifische Firmeneigenschaften, daß diese nur begrenzt möglich und zumeist sehr aufwendig ist (/29/).

Hieraus ergibt sich die Notwendigkeit, zukünftige Leitstände nach anderen Kriterien zu bauen, als dies bisher geschehen ist (/32/). Ziel muß es vor allem sein, änder-, wart- und erweiterbare Software zu erstellen. Objektorientierung, deren Prinzipien bereits seit den 60er Jahren bekannt sind (/10/), seit Beginn der 80er Jahre in Smalltalk einen bekannten Vertreter hat und in den vergangenen Jahren in den unterschiedlichsten Gebieten eingesetzt wird (objektorientierte Analyse /8/, objektorientierte Programmierung /37/, objektorientierte Systementwicklung /23/, objektorientiertes Design /6/), verspricht hier einen großen Fortschritt: Korrektheit, Robustheit, Erweiterbarkeit, Wiederverwendung und Verträglichkeit von Software können hiermit erzielt werden (/23/, /9/).

Der vorliegende Beitrag beschreibt Erfahrungen bei Design und Implementierung eines Klassensystems, welches zum Bau von anwendungsspezifischen Leitständen am Fraunhofer Institut für Arbeitswirtschaft und Organisation erarbeitet wurde.

2. Ausgangssituation

2.1. Heutige Leitstände

Hauptaufgabe und -einsatzgebiet heutiger elektronischer Leitstände ist in der Steuerung einer werkstattorientierten Fertigung zu sehen (/35/,

/28/). Die bereits vorhandenen Systeme zeichnen sich aus durch eine stark graphisch interaktive Plantafel zur Darstellung des jeweiligen Auftragsbestandes und die gegenwärtige Auslastung (/41/) sowie weitere graphische Menu-Masken zur Verwaltung der vorhandenen Daten: Fertigungsaufträge, Arbeitsgänge, Ressourcen (Maschinen, Material), Schichtpläne u.a.

Die Systeme sind in der Regel geeignet, um Aufträge mit den zugehörigen Arbeitsgängen sowie Maschinen zu verwalten. In einzelnen Fällen können einfache Formen von Arbeitsplänen sowie Reihenfolgebeziehungen zwischen Arbeitsgängen verwaltet werden.

Die Leitstände erhalten von einem übergeordneten PPS-System diese Fertigungsaufträge sowie ihre Arbeitsgänge fertig aufbereitet. Durch einfache Planungsverfahren (Vorwärts-, Rückwärtsterminierung) können sie diese auf die Maschinen einplanen. Die Schnittstellen zu den PPS-Systemen sowie zu untergeordneten BDE-Systemen sind jeweils spezifisch anzufertigen.

Leitstände werden auch in anderen "ähnlichen" Gebieten eingesetzt: Steuerung von Fertigungsinseln (/42/), Wartungsplanung für Flugzeuge (/43/) u.a.

2.2. Stand der Standardisierung, Normung und Modellbildung für Leitstände

DIN (/44/) beschreibt den derzeitige Stand eines allgemeingültigen Verständnisses (Modellbildung) und einer darauf basierenden Normung der Fertigungssteuerung (und damit auch der Leitstände) folgendermaßen:

- Es besteht kein einheitliches Funktionsverständnis
- Eine Standardisierung erfolgt nur durch die Marktpotenz einzelner Anbieter
- CIM-fähige modulare und austauschbare Bausteine existieren derzeit nicht

Der Bericht kommt zu dem Schluß, daß hier zunächst Grundlagen- und Entwicklungsarbeit zu leisten ist. Er sieht als wichtigstes Arbeitsgebiet die Erstellung eines Referenzmodelles. Dabei ist ein sehr wichtiger Aspekt die Erweiterbarkeit und Anpaßbarkeit.

Zwar liegen hier bereits Teilvorschläge vor (/45/, /46/, /47/), doch decken diese jeweils nur einzelne Sichten (Funktionen oder Daten, beschränkter Bereich der Fertigung). Eine Vorschlag für ein solches Modell wurde in Form des vorliegenden Klassensystems erarbeitet.

2.3. Gründe für die Auswahl der Objektorientierung als Methode

2.3.1. Phasenmodell und Softwarekrise

Die Erstellung von Software wird heute idealtypisch nach dem Phasenmodell (Wasserfallmodell, /40/) durchgeführt. Ein Projekt wird in verschiedene Phasen aufgeteilt. Jede Phase wird abgeschlossen, bevor die nächste Phase beginnt (/14/). Die Ergebnisse einer Phase werden als korrekt angesehen, sie brauchen also nur noch in die nächste Phase übertragen und dort entsprechend erweitert werden. Entsprechende Brüche sind auch in den Methoden und Tools zur Unterstützung der einzelnen Phasen zu finden (/2/, /19/). Da eine Phase jedoch als abgeschlossen betrachtet wird, ist der Übertragungsvorgang nur einmal notwendig (/31/).

Die Erfahrungen der vergangenen Jahre zeigen jedoch, daß die verschiedenen Phasen mehrfach durchlaufen werden müssen. Die Arbeiten während einer Phase führen dazu, daß in einer vorangegangenen Phase noch Korrekturen vorgenommen werden müssen. Softwareerstellung wird deshalb immer mehr als ein evolutionärer Prozeß verstanden. Dies wird von Boehm in seinem Spiralmodell dargestellt (Boehm /4/).

Heute sind 70% der Programmierkapazität an die Wartung von Software gebunden ist (Curth/Giebel /7/). 1972 lag dieser Wert noch bei 50%, doch wurde schon in den 60er Jahren der hohe Wartungsanteil für kritisch gehalten. Damals wurde der Begriff der Softwarekrise geprägt. Nach der Interpretation dieser Werte ist davon auszugehen, daß diese Krise nach wie vor nicht behoben ist (Nagl /27/), sondern sie sich im Gegenteil beständig verschärft hat.

Diese Werte gelten auch für den Bau von Leitständen: Leitstandshersteller klagen über den großen Wartungsanteil, den sie zusätzlich zu dem Standardprodukt Leitstand bei dem Verkauf jedes einzelnen Leitstandes erbringen müssen, um das Produkt an die praktischen Erfordernisse einer Fertigung anzupassen. Gängige Werte sind das Verhältnis 2:1 vom Anpassungsaufwand zum Grundkostenpreis des Produktes Leitstand (/29/).

Das Bewußtsein für diesen Zustand hat sich geschärft. Nach einer Studie über die Rangordnung verschiedener Softwareeigenschaften aus dem Jahr 1987 wird Wartbarkeit inzwischen als die wichtigste Eigenschaft von Software angesehen. Interessanterweise halten Mitarbeiter eines großen Softwarehauses die Wiederverwendung von Design als auch Code für den besten Ansatz, um dieses Problem bei der Softwareproduktion zu lösen (/38/).

2.3.2. Objektorientierung

Objektorientierte Systeme werden gebaut in der Erwartung, daß sie später geändert werden (vgl. /15/). Grundlage hierfür ist die Einhaltung einiger Prinzipien des Software-Engineering, die zwar schon lange bekannt sind, von den bisher verwendeten Methoden jedoch nicht erfüllt werden. Diese sind Abstraktion, Kapselung, Modularisierung, die auf das Konzept der abstrakten Datentypen zurückgehen (/30/), sowie Hierarchie oder Vererbung (/10/): Ein abstrakter Datentyp (in objektorientierter Terminologie als Klasse bezeichnet, vgl. z.B. Meyer /23/) wird so definiert, daß er/sie die Eigenschaften einer anderen Klasse übernimmt und ergänzende Eigenschaften definiert werden. So werden schrittweise an die Anwendung angepaßte Bausteine erstellt werden, die die Eigenschaften bereits zuvor erstellter Bausteine wiederverwenden (vgl. /1/, 17/).

Moderne Softwaresysteme sind zunehmend komplex. Auch Leitstände, die in zunehmenden Maß in eine vorhandene CIM-Umgebung eingebunden werden müssen, gewinnen ständig an Komplexität. Zur Lösung komplexer Probleme sind generell zwei unterschiedliche Ansätze bekannt - Vereinfachung, also Abstraktion sowie Delegation, also Modularisierung (vgl. /18/). Durch die Unterstützung beider Ansätze ist Objektorientierung eine sehr gut geeignete Methodik zum Bau komplexer Systeme.

Eine genaue Beschreibung objektorientierter Prinzipien ist z.B. in /6/ oder /23/ zu finden.

Die Verfügbarkeit von Methoden und Sprachen zum Bau von vor allem anpaßbaren Applikationen durch die Objektorientierung fordert eine Anwendung auf den Bau von Leitständen heraus. Die im inneren eines Leitstandes vorhandenen Komponenten - nämlich Klassen - müssen hierzu definiert werden. Sie bilden gleichzeitig das benötigte Modell.

3. Teilaufgaben beim Bau des Klassensystems

3.1. Analyse

Zur Erreichung der Zielvorstellung (Referenzmodell der Fertigungssteuerung), war darauf zu achten, daß die zugrundeliegende Modellvorstellung auf der einen Seite die notwendige Mächtigkeit erhält, um möglichst viele der in der Praxis anzutreffenden Anforderungen zumindest aus struktureller Sicht zu erfüllen. Auf der anderen Seite sollte das System nicht zu komplex werden. Somit war ein schlankes, aber mächtiges Modell der in der Fertigung anzutreffenden Strukturen zu schaffen und in Klassen umzusetzen. Aufgrund dieser Aufgabenstellung unterscheiden sich die verschiedenen Teilaufgaben von den Aufgaben in einem gewöhnlichen Projekt.

Ein Großteil der klassischen Analyse (Aufnahme der Anforderungen beim Kunden/Anwender) war durch eine Recherche der (teilweise extremen) Anforderungen an Leitstände in der Literatur zu ersetzen, um den notwendigen Allgemeinheitsgrad zu erhalten. Schwerpunkt dieser Recherche war weniger die Detailfunktionalität von Leitständen als vielmehr eine Untersuchung, was ein solches Klassensystem denn an generellen Informationen unterstützen sollte, bzw. welche Art von Informationsgehalt darin darstellbar sein sollte. Hierzu gehörten Fragestellungen nach der

- Darstellbarkeit alternativer oder substrukturierter Arbeitspläne,
- Auftragsnetze sowie substrukturierte Aufträge,
- Split und Join von Aufträgen
- substrukturierte Ressourcen, z.B. Maschinengruppen oder Fertigungsinseln
- Beliebige gegenseitige zeitliche Abhängigkeiten von Aufträgen in Form von Reihenfolgen, Überlapp oder Parallelität

3.2. Design

Die wichtigste und auch schwierigste Aufgabe beim Aufbau einer neuen Menge von Klassen für ein beliebiges Applikationsfeld ist in dem Auffinden der gemeinsamen Eigenschaften verschiedener Objekte und der Umsetzung dieser gemeinsamen Eigenschaften in entsprechend abstrakte Klassen zu sehen. Booch und Vilot bezeichnen solche Klassen auch als "key abstractions" (/5/). Diese Aufgabe ist in etwa gleichzusetzen mit der Designphase konventioneller Software-Projekte.

Bezogen auf das Applikationsfeld Leitstand war eine Menge von Klassen zu finden, die auf der einen Seite abstrakt genug sind, der anschließenden Anpassung an die spezielle Anwendung noch genug Raum zu lassen, auf der anderen Seite jedoch schon die typischen in Leitständen vorzufindenden Strukturen, Objekte und Methoden enthält und damit den Anpassungsaufwand so niedrig wie möglich hält.

Diese Suche wurde in zwei sich stark überlappende Teile geteilt: Eine erste Modellbildungsphase, welche auf Basis von Entity-Relationsship-Modell Darstellungen sowie ergänzenden Abbildungen erfolgte sowie die Umsetzung dieses ersten Modelles in Klassen. Das ERM war dabei mit in der Literatur existierenden ERM der Fertigung auf gemeinsame Semantik abzugleichen, um die gewählte Modellierung bezüglich ihrer Allgemeingültigkeit auch absichern zu können.

Für die Umsetzung des ERM in ein Klassensystem wurde eine empirische Methode entworfen und eingesetzt, die im wesentlichen aus 6 Schritten besteht (vgl. Abb. 1).

Auf diese Weise entsteht nach und nach ein tief gestaffelter Klassenbaum, der eine objektorientierte Struktur beschreibt.

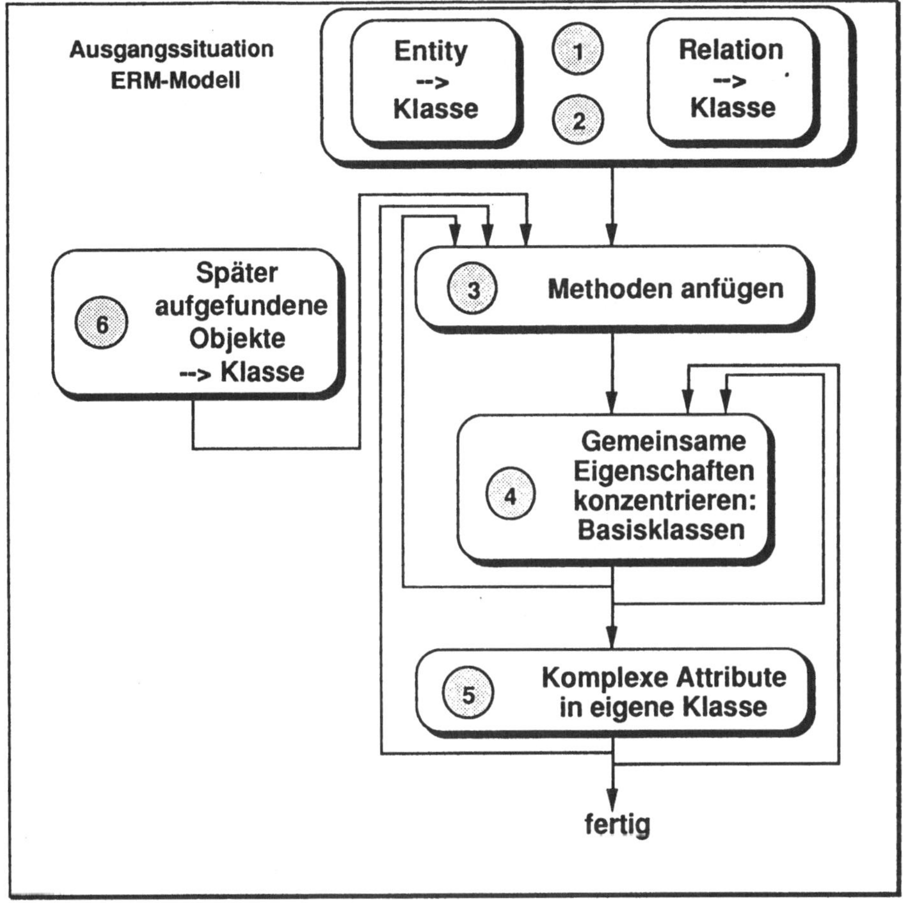

Abb.1 **Methodik zur Erarbeitung der objektorientierten Architektur**

3.3. Implementierung

Die Menge der Klassen war sodann geeignet zu implementieren. Die Erfahrungen bei der Durchführung der Implementierung sind in Kapitel 5 wiedergegeben.

4. Detailmodell am Beispiel des Arbeitsplans

Aufgrund der Analyse wurden die grundlegenden Objekttypen Arbeit (Fertigungsaufträge und Arbeitsvorgänge, zumeist einfach als Auftrag bezeichnet), Arbeitsplan und Ressource vorgefunden. Ihre gegenseitige Beziehung

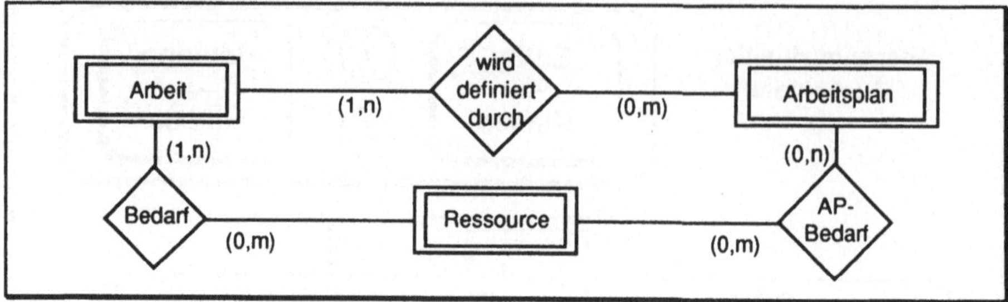

Abb. 2 Stark vereinfachtes Ausgangsmodell

ist in Abb. 2 als ERM dargestellt. Diese Objekttypen wurden weiter strukturiert.

Der Arbeitsplan (AP) ist die aufgabenbezogene Beschreibung der Tätigkeiten, die zur Produktion eines Gutes benötigt werden. Aufgrund der Analyse ergaben sich umfangreiche Anforderungen an die strukturellen Eigenschaften des AP ((AP-1) bis (AP-6)), die in Abb. 3 wiedergegeben sind.

Anf.- Nr.	Eigenschaft	Erfüllung durch heutige Leitstände
(AP-1)	Ein Arbeitsplan muß einen Fertigungsauftrag in eine Menge von kleineren Einheiten (die auch Arbeitsvorgänge sein können), zerlegen (Grundprinzip der Zerlegung einer Aufgabe in Teilaufgaben).	teilweise
(AP-2)	Durch die Zerlegung müssen beliebige zeitliche Beziehungen zwischen den Unteraufträgen möglich werden: Vorgänger/Nachfolger, aber auch Parallelität (Benötigt für Darstellung von Auftrags-/Arbeitsvorgangnetzen).	teilweise
(AP-3)	Für jeden Subauftrag muß es möglich sein, alternative Arten und Weisen der Durchführung anzubieten (Verlagerung der Entscheidungskompetenz in die dezentralen Teile, wichtig z.B. für flexible Fertigungssysteme).	teilweise
(AP-4)	Ein Subauftrag kann seinerseits wieder durch einen eigenen Arbeitsplan in weitere Subaufträge zerlegt werden (Zerlegung einer Aufgabe in Teilaufgaben über mehrstufige Hierarchien hinweg).	nein
(AP-5)	Für die Zerlegung eines Fertigungsauftrages in Arbeitsvorgänge müssen verschiedene alternative Arbeitspläne vorsehbar sein (Verlagerung von Entscheidungskompetenz in die jeweilige Entscheidungsebene)	nein
(AP-6)	Ein Arbeitsplan muß neben der Prozeßstruktur auch die Teilestruktur enthalten (Zusammenlegung von Stückliste und Abarbeitungsablauf)	nein

Abb. 3 Erforderliche Eigenschaften von Arbeitsplänen

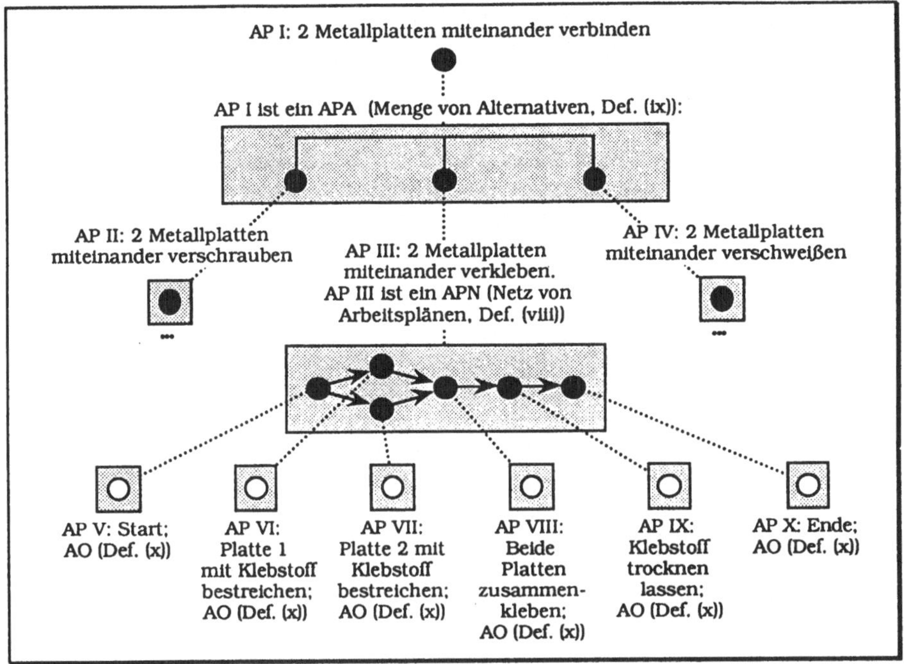

Abb. 5 Beispiel für die Substrukturierung eines Arbeitsplanes

4.1. Makro-Struktur

Aus den Anforderungen konnte die Makrostruktur für APs entwickelt werden. Diese ist Abb. 4 wiedergeben. Durch sie werden (AP-1) bis (AP-5) erfüllt. Abb. 5 gibt ein Beispiel.

(AP-6) stellt eine Beziehung zwischen dem AP und den Ressourcen her. Danach muß der Arbeitsplan Informationen über die benötigten Ressourcen enthalten. Zusätzlich sind die erzeugten Ressourcen von Interesse:

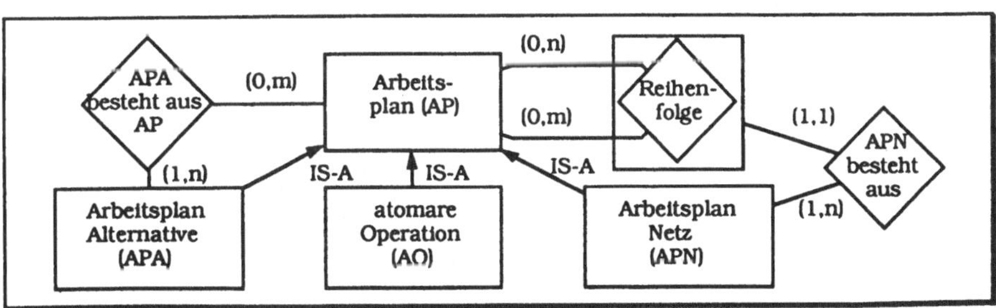

Abb. 4 Struktur-ERM des Arbeitsplanes

(neu erzeugtes) Material oder Abfallprodukte sowie wieder freigegebene Kapazitäten. Diese Information wird in der Relation AP-Bedarf zusammengefaßt.

Hierfür existieren sowohl Eingangs- als auch Ausgangs-AP-Bedarfe: Eingangs-AP-Bedarfe stellen die Beziehung zu benötigten Ressourcen, Ausgangs-AP-Bedarfe zu erzeugten bzw. wieder freigegebenen Ressourcen her. Eingangs-AP-Bedarfe eines AP werden durch die Ausgangs-AP-Bedarfe anderer AP befriedigt, ebenso werden die Ausgangs-AP-Bedarfe eines AP durch die Eingangs-AP-Bedarfe anderer AP befriedigt.

Aufgrund der Definition von AO, APA und APN kann das Verhalten ihrer AP-Bedarfe festgelgt werden. Abb. 6 gibt einen Überblick über die Regeln zur Ermittlung der AP-Bedarfe für AO, APA und APN.

Für eine AO ist die Menge der Eingangs- und Ausgangs-AP-Bedarfe durch die Fertigungstechnologie festgelegt und klar erkennbar. Sie ist immer vollständig, da sonst die betreffende AO nicht durchgeführt werden könnte.

Die AP-Bedarfe des APA sind von der erst später zu treffenden Auswahl eines speziellen AP abhängig. Sie können nur dann Bestandteil des APA sein, wenn alle seine AP diesen AP-Bedarf haben. In allen anderen Fällen sind sie nicht beim APA aufgeführt. Deshalb sind die AP-Bedarfe eines APA häufig unvollständig. Würden alle AP-Bedarfe der Alternativen automatisch AP-Bedarfe des APA, so würden dessen AP-Bedarfe mit jeder neuen Alternative anwachsen, was diese Information vollständig unbrauchbar

	Atomare Operation	Arbeitsplan-Alternativen	APN
Eingangs-AP-Bedarf	Die tatsächlichen Eingangs-Bedarfe. Manueller Wert	Alle Eingangs-Bedarfe, die auch Eingangs-Bedarfe aller Alternativen sind	Die Eingangs-AP-Bedarfe aller AP des APN, soweit sie nicht unmittelbar durch Ausgangs-AP-Bedarfe anderer AP des APN gedeckt sind. AP-Bedarfe können auch additiv zusammengefaßt werden.
Ausgangs-AP-Bedarfe	Die tatsächlichen Ausgangs-Bedarfe. Manueller Wert	Alle Ausgangs-Bedarfe, die auch Ausgangs-Bedarfe aller Alternativen sind.	Die Ausgangs-AP-Bedarfe aller AP des APN, soweit sie nicht unmittelbar durch Eingangs-AP-Bedarfe anderer AP des APN gedeckt sind. AP-Bedarfe können auch additiv zusammengefaßt werden
Bedarfs-Vollständigkeit	Immer TRUE.	FALSE,wenn ein AP-Bedarf aus APA nicht AP-Bedarf aller AP aus APA ist oder wenn Vollständigkeit in einem der AP aus APA FALSE ist.	FALSE, wenn Vollständigkeit in einem der Teilarbeitspläne FALSE ist.

Abb. 6 Aggregation der verschiedenen Bedarfe sowie die Vollständigkeit der Aggregation

macht. Für jeden AP ist deshalb zu beschreiben, ob seine AP-Bedarfe vollständig sind.

Innerhalb eines APN können sich AP-Bedarfe von AP gegenseitig befriedigen: Hier existieren AP, deren Eingangs-AP-Bedarfe durch Ausgangs-AP-Bedarfe anderer AP unmittelbar gedeckt werden. Z.B. wird der Eingangs-AP-Bedarf von AO IX (die zusammengelegten Platten mit Kleber, vgl. Abb 5) durch den Ausgangs-AP-Bedarf von AO VIII gedeckt. Beide werden außerhalb des APN nicht mehr dargestellt. Das APN hat deshalb nur intern nicht gedeckte AP-Bedarfe seiner AP.

4.2. Attribute von Arbeitsplan und AP-Bedarf

Nachdem die Makro-Struktur von AP und AP-Bedarf entwickelt wurde, sind für ein vollständiges ERM die Attribute von AP und AP-Bedarf fest-

Dauer-Typ	Formale Definition	AO	APA	APN
Typische Dauer	D_{typ}: **AP→ZD**, $D_{typ}(x)=a$	Die tatsächliche Dauer. Erfahrungswert	Erfahrungswert. Falls nicht definiert, arithmetisches Mittel	Erfahrungswert. Falls nicht definiert, arithmetisches Mittel.
Min. Dauer	D_{min}: **AP→ZD**, $D_{min}(x)=a$	Minimaler Extremwert. Erfahrungswert. Falls nicht definiert, typische Dauer.	$\min_{x_i \in APA} \{D_{min}(x_i)\}$	$\max_{BF_j \in \mathbf{BF}(APN)} \left\{ \sum_{AP_i \in BF_j} D_{min}(AP_i) \right\}$
Max. Dauer	D_{max}: **AP→ZD**, $D_{max}(x)=a$	Maximaler Extremwert. Erfahrungswert. Falls nicht definiert, typische Dauer.	$\max_{x_i \in APA} \{D_{max}(x_i)\}$	$\max_{BF_j \in \mathbf{BF}(APN)} \left\{ \sum_{AP_i \in BF_j} D_{max}(AP_i) \right\}$
Arithmetisch mittlere Dauer	D_{arith}: **AP→ZD**, $D_{arith}(x)=a$	Aus Erfahrungswert statistisch ermittelt. Falls nicht definiert, typische Dauer.	$\frac{\sum_{x_i \in APA} D_{arith}(x_i)}{n}$	$\max_{BF_j \in \mathbf{BF}(APN)} \left\{ \sum_{AP_i \in BF_j} D_{arith}(AP_i) \right\}$
Geometrisch mittlere Dauer	D_{geo}: **AP→ZD**, $D_{geo}(x)=a$	Aus Erfahrungswert statistisch ermittelt. Falls nicht definiert, typische Dauer.	$\sqrt[n]{\prod_{x_i \in APA} D_{geo}(x_i)}$	$\max_{BF_j \in \mathbf{BF}(APN)} \left\{ \sum_{AP_i \in BF_j} D_{geo}(AP_i) \right\}$
Definition der Bearbeitungsfolgen BF innerhalb eines APN	$BF(APN) := \{(AP_i, AP_j) \in APN \mid (\forall (AP_i, AP_j) \in BF: i \neq 1 \Rightarrow \exists k: (AP_k, AP_i) \in BF \wedge j \neq n \Rightarrow \exists h: (AP_j, AP_h) \in BF) \wedge (AP_i, AP_j) \in BF \wedge (AP_i, AP_k) \in BF \Rightarrow k=j \wedge (AP_i, AP_j) \in BF \wedge (AP_k, AP_j) \in BF \Rightarrow k=i\}$ $\mathbf{BF}(APN) := \{BF_i(APN)\}$			

Abb. 7 Wertbildung für die verschiedenen Einheitsdauern

zulegen. Von besonderem Interesse ist auch hier das Verhalten der Attribute für AO, APA, APN, daß sich aus deren Definition ermitteln läßt.

4.2.1. AP-Dauer

Die AP-Dauer beschreibt den Zeitraum, der für die Ausführung eines AP für eine bestimmte Einheitsmenge benötigt wird (Einheitsdauer). Für die AO kann die Dauer in den meisten Technologien exakt angegeben werden, so daß für die AO die Attributwerte unmittelbar aus der Fertigung übernommen werden können.

Für die APA ist eine exakte Festlegung der Dauer schwierig, da die verschiedenen Alternativen unterschiedliche Dauern haben können. Die Dauer einer APA kann erst nach einer getroffenen Auswahl ermittelt werden. Umgekehrt werden für eine vorrausschauende Planung schon vorher Anhaltspunkte bezüglich der Dauer eines AP benötigt. Deshalb muß für die APA mit Durchschnitts-, Schätz- und Erfahrungswerten gearbeitet werden. Mögliche Arten sind hier die typische Dauer (Erfahrungswert), min. und max. Dauer sowie arithmetisch und geometrisch mittlere Dauer.

Die Ausprägung sowie Regeln zur Generierung der Dauern für AO, APN und APA sind in Abb. 7 aufgeführt. In einem speziellen Applikationsfeld der OOLA (objektorientierte Leitstandsarchitektur) können selbstverständlich noch weitere Arten von Dauern hinzugefügt werden.

4.2.2. Die Dauer bei unterschiedlichen Mengen

AP sind mengenneutral ausgelegt, d.h., sie beziehen sich auf eine Einheitsmenge des zu produzierenden Gutes. Um einen Auftrag mit anderer Menge zu bearbeiten, ist die Ermittlung der Dauer für diese Menge mittels eines Dauerberechnungsverfahren (DBV (Menge)) notwendig.

Proportionalität von Menge und Dauer ist ein häufig genutztes Verfahren und einfach zu implementieren: für den AP muß nur das Attribut Einheitsdauer gespeichert werden. Leider ist dieses Verfahren nicht allgemeingültig: Z.B. spielt es für eine Tauchlackieranlage keine Rolle, wieviele Objekte gleichzeitig getaucht werden, solange diese in das Tauchlackierbad hineinpassen. Sowohl ein einzelnes Stück als auch ein ganzes Los benötigen dieselbe Zeit.

Eine feste Wahl eines DBV in der OOLA würde somit dazu führen, daß a priori Situationen bekannt sind, die durch die OOLA nicht abbildbar sind. Dies würde der Zielsetzung der OOLA widersprechen.

Durch die OO kann alternativ statt eines festen Datenattributes mit festem DBV ein Regelattribut (in Form einer Klasse) eingesetzt werden, wodurch

Gewählte Gestaltungsart für		Auswirkungen			
AO	APA/APN	Flexibilität	Rechenaufwand	Machbarkeit	Bemerkungen
Festes Dauerattribut und festes DBV	Festes Dauerattribut und feste DBV	--	gering	ja	Keine Lose darstellbar
Festes Dauerattribut und festes DBV	Freies Regelattribut	-	gering	als Klasse ja	Vereinfachungen bei Berechnung der Dauern für APA/APN möglich
Freies Regelattribut	Festes Dauerattribut und feste DBV	+	groß	als Klasse ja	Dauern von APA/APN sind jedesmal neu zu berechnen
Freies Regelattribut	Freies Regelattribut	++	wählbar	als Klasse ja	Vereinfachungen bei Berechnung der Dauern für APA/APN möglich, dadurch Rechenaufwand vermeidbar

Abb. 8 Alternativen zur Darstellung mengenabhängiger Dauern

unterschiedliche Formen von DBV darstellbar sind. Abb. 8 zeigt die Auswirkungen der beiden Vorgehensweisen für AO, APA und APN und die verschiedenen Arten von Dauern. Aufgrund der klaren Vorteile in Bezug auf Flexibilität werden Regelattribute ausgewählt. Das Proportionalitätsverfahrens wird durch eine solche Regel abgedeckt; diese ist Bestandteil der OOLA.

4.2.3. Vollständigkeitsflag, Bezeichnung und Beschreibung

Wie in Kap. 4.2.1 festgestellt, muß für einen AP bekannt sein, ob seine AP-Bedarfe vollständig sind. Hierzu ist ein Attribut beim AP mitzuführen. Abb. 6 gibt die verschiedenen Werte für dieses Attribut wieder.

Zusätzlich werden zu einem AP noch Attribute für eine Bezeichnung und eine Beschreibung hinzugefügt. Diese dienen dazu, dem Bediener ergänzende Informationen über den AP zu geben. In der Beschreibung kann nicht nur Text, sondern auch weitere Information wie Zeichnungen u.a. enthalten sein.

4.2.4. Ort, Zeit, Menge und Bedarfsdauer

Ein AP-Bedarf an einer Ressource ist durch den Ort, den Zeitraum, die Menge sowie die Dauer gekennzeichnet. Die deshalb im AP-Bedarf benötigten Attribute sind in Abb. 9 dargestellt. Für die Zeit, Menge und Dauer werden analog zu der AP-Dauer (Kap. 6.2.2.2) Regelattribute benutzt. Eingangs- und Ausgangsbedarfe haben die gleichen Attribute. Die Dauer für den Eingangsbedarf bedeutet, daß die betreffende Ressource erst nach

Ablauf dieser Zeit als Ausgangsbedarf wieder zur Verfügung steht. Für die Dauer des Eingangsbedarfes gilt, daß die Ressource zuletzt vor Beginn dieses Zeitraums verfügbar war.

4.2.5. Unterbrechbarkeit

Für jeden AP-Bedarf muß definiert sein, ob dieser unterbrochen werden darf (z.B. durch eine Ruhepause der betreffenden Ressource, über Nacht oder über Wochenende). Die Unterbrechbarkeit und Folgen der Unterbrechung sind prozeßabhängig:

- Ein chemischer Prozeß kann u.U. alleine weiter laufen, während der Mitarbeiter Mittagspause hat, d.h., die dahinterstehende Arbeit wird dadurch nicht verzögert. Die mitbenutzte Anlage wird nicht frei.
- Die manuelle Montage eines elektronischen Gerätes kann durch die Mittagspause des Mitarbeiters unterbrochen werden, die Unterbrechung führt zu einer Verzögerung. Evt. mitbenutzte Ressourcen (z.B. Werkzeuge) werden frei während der Unterbrechung.
- Die manuelle Spritzlackierung kann nicht unterbrochen werden, da dies zu unterschiedlicher Konsistenz der aufgetragenen Lackschicht führen würde.

Aus diesem Grund wird für jeden AP-Bedarf ein Regelattribut zur Festlegung der Unterbrechbarkeit benötigt.

Attribut-Typ	Beschreibung	Bezug zu AP	Anwendungszeitpunkt
Bedarfs-Zeitraum-Regel	Regel zur Berechnung das Zeitintervall abhängig von Menge des AP, innerhalb dessen Befriedigung dieses Bedarfes beginnen muß	Intervall relativ zum Start oder Ende des AP	Generierung der Bedarfe
Dauer-Berechnungsregel	Regel, womit Dauer des Bedarfes für eine bestimmte Menge des AP ermittelt wird. Dies ist Zeitintervall, für das die Ressource nicht verfügbar ist. Für Verbrauchsmaterial wird Dauer ∞ errechnet. Für jede Dauerart ex. je eine Regel	Dauer (AP-Bedarf) <= Dauer (AP)	Generierung der Bedarfe
Mengen-Berechnungsregel	Regel, aufgrund der die Menge des Bedarfes für eine bestimmte Menge des AP ermittelt wird. Bei Kapazitäten häufig eins.	Menge ist relativ zu AP-Menge	Generierung der Bedarfe
Unterbrechungs-regel	Regel, womit Zulässigkeit einer Bedarfsunterbrechung sowie Auswirkungen auf andere Bedarfe derselben Arbeit ermittelt wird.	Regel wirkt auch auf andere AP-Bedarfe	Einplanung der Bedarfe
Ort	Ort, an dem der Bedarf befriedigt werden muß, d.h., an dem die Kapazität/das Material verfügbar sein müssen	unabhängig vom AP	-
Die Ressource ist Bestandteil der Relation AP-Bedarf und deshalb kein Attribut			

Abb. 9 Attribute des AP-Bedarfes

4.3. Klassen für AP und AP-Bedarf

Aus dem ERM wird eine Menge von Klassen erstellt: Die Klassen *BWorkplan*, *BSingleOp*, *WPNet* und *WPAlternatives* entstehen aus den Entities AP, AO, APN und AP des ER-Modells. Die Beziehung IS_A des ERM wird unmittelbar in eine Ableitung umgesetzt: *BSingleOp*, *WPNet* und *WPAlternatives* sind von *BWorkplan* abgeleitet (Regel 2a).

Die "Besteht aus"-Relation zwischen APA und AP ist eine HAS_A Relation und wird durch die Listenklasse *FreeWPList* repräsentiert, die ein Attribut von *WPAlternatives* ist. Die Reihenfolgerelation zwischen zwei AP ist eine Menge von Assoziationen, die durch eine Graphenklasse *DiGraph-WithRelation* dargestellt wird. Da sie gleichzeitig zu dem APN gehört, ist der Graph ein Attribut von *WPNet*.

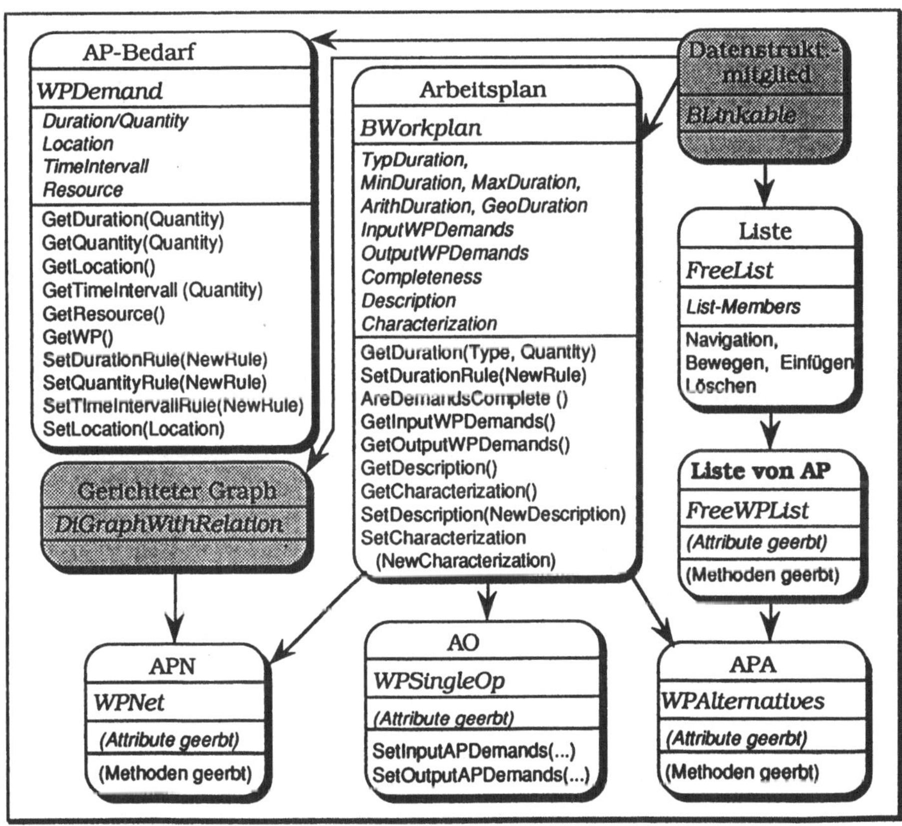

Abb. 10 Klassen für Arbeitspläne und ihre Ableitung

Die Relation des AP-Bedarf ist eine Assoziation zwischen dem AP und den Ressourcen, die durch eine Liste von AP-Bedarfen als Attribut des AP modelliert wird. Für Ein- und Ausgangsbedarfe existieren getrennte Listen im AP. Hierdurch wird auch die Unterscheidung zwischen Ein- und Ausgangs-AP-Bedarfen möglich.

Alle Klassen sind in dem Vererbungsbaum in Abb. 10 dargestellt.

5. Erfahrungen

5.1. Erfahrungen aus der Modellbildung

Der Aufbau des Klassensystems hat die in der Literatur aufgeführte Auflösung der unterschiedlichen Phasen (Analyse, Design etc.) (/17/, /6/) voll bestätigt. Die gesamte Arbeit war durch eine große Durchgängigkeit von der Analyse bis zur Implementierung gekennzeichnet. Die evolutionäre Vorgehensweise war kennzeichnend für den gesamten Projektverlauf, so daß während der Implementierung noch Analyse-Vorgaben geändert wurden. Gleichzeitig bereiteten diese Änderungen keine Schwierigkeiten, da die in der Analyse genannten Objekte auch noch in der Implementierung eindeutig zu identifizieren waren.

Gleichzeitig trat der Effekt ein, daß sowohl Ingenieure des Anwendungsfeldes als auch Informatiker ein sehr gutes gemeinsames Verständnis gewannen, welches eine hervorragende Grundlage für weitere Diskussionen darstellte.

5.2. Erfahrungen aus der Implementierung

Die Implementierung des Klassenbaumes erfolgt geringfügig zeitversetzt, um einerseits Teile des Designs fertigstellen zu können, andererseits neue Erkenntnisse aus der Implementierung (evolutionäre Vorgehensweise) entsprechend übernehmen und das Design anpassen zu können. Letztendlich ist das Design in der Implementierung des Klassenbaumes festgehalten.

Als Implementierungssprache wurde C++ eingesetzt. Diese Wahl wurde wegen der weiten Verbreitung und offensichtlichen Entwicklung zum Industriestandard getroffen. Dabei machte sich die Kompatibilität zu C sehr positiv bemerkbar, da hierdurch zu nahezu allen Tools gängige Schnittstellen verfügbar sind. Im Rahmen des Projektes wurden Schnittstellen zu einer relationalen Datenbank (Oracle) sowie zu einem User-Interface-Management-Tool (ISA Dialog Manager) geschaffen.

Umgekehrt wurde das Fehlen von Metawissen zur Laufzeit (Ableitungsbaum, Klassennamen u.a.), welches in vielen anderen objektorientierten Sprachen zur Verfügung steht, schmerzlichst vermißt. Es zeigte sich, daß eine Programmierung ohne diese Informationen nahezu unmöglich war. Um dieses Wissen verfügbar zu haben (Stroustrup schlägt hier selbst Techniken vor /36/), wurde eine umfangreiche Menge von Macros eingeführt, welche diese Information automatisch in Form von C++ statements generieren. Als Macro-Prozessor wird bisher der Standard-Macro-Prozessor der UNIX-Welt, m4, eingesetzt.

Weiter mußten umfangreiche Basisklassen gebaut werden, um Grundprobleme wie z.B. "dangling pointers" zu lösen. Diese Lösungen konnten durch Vererbung auf die beschriebenen Anwendungsklassen übertragen werden, doch wurde hierdurch der Ableitungsbaum wesentlich komplexer. Allerdings wurde das Fehlen solcher Mechanismen erst während der Implementierung bemerkt, nachdem mehrmals aufwendig Fehler gesucht werden mußten, die auf dieses Problem zurückgingen. Aus heutiger Sicht stellt sich die Frage, inwieweit eine "Industriestandard"-Sprache hier nicht eine wesentlich bessere Unterstützung anbieten sollte.

Das Klassensystem besteht in seiner derzeitigen Implementierung aus ca. 300 Klassen. Incl. der Dokumentation sind diese in ca. 300.000 loc niedergeschrieben, der Gesamtumfang beträgt ca. 3 MB Source-Code.

5.3. Organisation, Dokumentation und Management des Klassensystems

Das Management mittlerer und großer Klassensysteme erfordert einigen Aufwand, zumal hier die aus dem CASE-Bereich bekannten Methoden für konventionelle Programmierung nur bedingt anwendbar sind (/12/, /17/). Alleine die Frage, wie die verschiedenen Klassen dargestellt werden, so daß leicht eine Übersicht gewonnen werden kann bzw. die Definition einzelner Klassen wiedergefunden werden kann, ist für das Management und die Nutzung solcher Klassensysteme von nicht zu unterschätzender Bedeutung. Cox (/9/) führt hierzu den Begriff der "packaging technology" ein.

Für die Implementierung wurde der von Gibbs et al. (/12/) aufgezeigte typische Weg zur Implementierung in C++ unter Unix gewählt: Die Darstellung einer Klasse erfolgt in zwei Teilen, die sich auch in zwei unterschiedlichen Dateien befinden: In einer Header-Datei, gekennzeichnet durch die Endung ".h. wird die Definition der Klasse sowie die Definition aller inline-Funktionen (zur Erläuterung der Begriffe Definition, Deklaration und inline siehe Beschreibungen von C++, z.B. Ellis/Stroustrup /11/, Lippman /20/, Bause/Tölle /3/, Stroustrup /36/, Wiener/Pinson /39/) gehalten, während in der Sourcedatei, gekennzeichnet durch die

Endung .C, die Definition alle anderen Methoden der betreffenden Klasse aufgeführt sind.

Weiter wurden genaue Richtlinien erarbeitet, wie die Dokumentation der betreffenden Klassen gestaltet sein muß (/24/) und eine genaue Konvention zur Vergabe von Namen in den betreffenden Klassen beschrieben (/25/).

Durch eine zusätzliche Einführung in das Klassensystem (/26/) ist es möglich, nach dem Studium von etwa 20 Seiten einen ersten Überblick über die vorhandenen Klassen zu erhalten. Hierdurch ist die Einarbeitung in das vorhandene System erleichtert. Das Problem, eine solche Einführung möglichst automatisch auf dem neuesten Stand zu halten, ist damit nicht gelöst.

Hierzu werden in der Literatur (vgl. z.B. /33/) verschiedene alternative Lösungsansätze wie z.B. die Verwendung von Class-Browsern, Versionskontrollsystemen etc. empfohlen. Gibbs et al. (/12/) stellen eine Menge von Eigenschaften zusammen, und erste Werkzeuge hierzu sind vorhanden (z.B. ObjectWorks von ParkPlaceSystems oder Softbench von HP (/13/)), eine vollständige Darstellung aller wichtiger Eigenschaften eines Klassensystems und seiner einzelnen Klassen konnte hier jedoch nicht vorgefunden werden. Auf einen Einsatz wurde deshalb verzichtet.

Für die Arbeit an den verschiedenen Klassen wurde das Werkzeug SCCS (vgl. /34/) verwendet, welches Bestandteil von UNIX ist. Hierdurch war es möglich, eine Versionskontrolle durchzuführen und Mitarbeitern, welche diese Klassen benutzten, eine automatische Einbindung mittels Make-Files (vgl. /22/) zu geben. Die Verwendung von SCCS hat sich insbesondere deshalb bewährt, weil nahezu alle Klassen nicht nach der ersten Implementierung fertig waren, sondern erst nach und nach zu dem Format heranwuchsen, welches sie heute haben. Dies hat die in der Literatur vorhandenen Aussagen, daß die Erstellung von Klassen ein evolutionärer Vorgang sei (/1/, /12/), voll bestätigt.

Trotz der umfangreichen Dokumentation stellt die Einarbeitung neuer Mitarbeiter in das Klassensystem ein sehr großes Problem dar. Aufgrund des Umfangs des Codes fehlt eine geeignete Hilfestellung, die das Suchen von Klassen erleichtert. Hier wurde bisher keine Lösung gefunden. Ein Gesamtüberblick über den entstandenen Klassenbaum ist im Anhang wiedergegeben.

5 Zusammenfassung und Ausblick

Aufgrund der Nutzung der objektorientierten Methode ist es gelungen, ein System zu bauen welches als Referenzmodell und Kernsystem für anpassungsfähige Leitstände dienen kann. Dieses System befindet sich gerade in der Evaluation durch Anwendung auf Fallbeispiele.

Durch Objektorientierung konnten somit die Ziele Anpaßbarkeit und Änderbarkeit sehr gut erreicht werden. Insbesondere die Übereinstimmung der menschlichen Vorstellung mit dem implementierten Code und das daraus resultierende fachübergreifende gemeinsame Verständnis der Anwendung bieten eine hervorragende Basis für effizientere Software-Entwicklung auch in anderen Bereichen. Objektorientierung sollte deshalb bereits in der Analyse- und Designphase von Projekten angewandt werden.

Im Bereich der Werkzeuge ist eine größere und breitere Unterstützung der objektorientierten Methodik wünschenswert, insbesondere hätte eine bessere Unterstützung der Dokumentation des Codes zu noch besseren Resultaten geführt.

Abschließend kann, trotz einiger Detailprobleme, nur empfohlen werden, die objektorientierte Methode in neuen Software-Projekten, wenn immer möglich, anzuwenden.

6. Literaturverzeichnis

/1/ Barth, Gerhard; Welsch, Christoph: Objektorientierte Programmierung. Informationstechnik it 30 (1988) 6. München: Oldenbourg Verlag 1988.

/2/ Bader, W.: In der Übertragung liegt die Lücke. Computerwoche FOCUS 3, 28. Juni 1991, S. 26-27.

/3/ Bause, Falko; Tölle, Wolfgang: Einführung in die Programmiersprache C++. Braunschweig, Wiesbaden: Vieweg, 1989.

/4/ Boehm, Barry W.: A Spiral Model of Software Development and Enhancement. IEEE Computer May 1988

/5/ Booch, Grady; Vilot, Michael: Object oriented analysis and design. The C++ Report 3 (1991), Nr. 8, S. 7-10.

/6/ Booch, Grady: Object oriented design. Redwood City, California; Fort Collins, Colorado; Menlo Park, California; Reading, Masschusetts; New York; Don Mills, Ontario; Wokingham, U.K.; Amsterdam; Bonn; Sydney; Singapore; Tokyo; Madrid; San Juan: The Benjamin/Cummings Publishing Company, Inc.1991

/7/ Curth, M.A.; Giebel, M.L.: Management der Softwarewartung. Stuttgart: B.G. Teubner, 1989

/8/ Coad, Peter; Yourdon, Edward: Object-Oriented Analysis. Englewood Cliffs: Yourdon Press Computing Service published by Prentice-Hall, 1990.

/9/ Cox, B.J.: Object-Oriented Programming: An Evolutionary Approach. Addison Wesley, Reading, Mass., 1986.

/10/ Dahl, O.J.;Nygaard, K.: SIMULA - an ALGOL-based simulation language. Communications of the ACM, September 1966.

/11/ Ellis, Margaret A.; Stroustrup, Bjarne: The Annotated C++ Reference Manual. Reading, Mass.; Menlo Park, Calif.; New York; Don Mills, Ontario; Wokingham, England; Amsterdam; Bonn; Sydney; Singapore; Tokyo; Madrid; San Juan: Addison Wesley, 1990.

/12/ Gibbs, Simon; Casais, Eduardo; Nierstrasz, Oscar; Pintado, Xavier; Tsichritzis, Dennis: Class Management for Software Communities. Communications of the ACM Vol. 33, No. 9, September 1990.

/13/ Goos, Anke: Tour d'Objectworks, OWC++: eine Entwicklungsumgebung zur Programmierung in C++. In: UNIX Magazin, Ausgabe 3, März 1991, S. 102-109.

/14/ Henderson-Sellers, Brian; Edwards, Julian M.: Oriented Systems Life Cycle. Communications of the ACM 33 (1990), Nr. 9, S. 143-159.

/15/ Jeffcoate, Judith;Hales, Keith; Downes, Valerie: Object Oriented Systems: The commercial benefits. ISBN 0-903969-42-4, London: Ovum, 1989.

/16/ Kernler, H.: PPS-Ziele mit dem elektronischen Leitstand erreichen. In: ZWF 86 (1991) 2. München: Carl Hanser Verlag, 1991.

/17/ Korson, Tim; McGregor, John D.: Understanding objectoriented: A unifying paradigma. Communications of the ACM Vol. 33, No. 9, September 1990.

/18/ Kreutzer, W.: Grundkonzepte und Werkzeugsysteme objektorientierter Systementwicklung - Stand der Forschung und Anwendung. Wirtschaftsinformatik 32 (1990), Nr. 3, S. 211-227.

/19/ Kurbel, K.; Pietsch, W.: Expertensystem-Projekte: Entwicklungsmethodik, Organisation und Management. Informatik-Spektrum 12 (1989), Nr. 3, S. 133-146.

/20/ Lippman, Stanley B.: C++ Einführung und Leitfaden. Bonn; München; Reading, Mass.; Menlo Park, Calif.; New York; Don Mills, Ontario; Wokingham, England; Amsterdam; Sydney; Singapore; Tokyo; Madrid; San Juan: Addison Wesley, 1990.

/21/ Lippold, J.; Schulz, K.: Steuern der Fertigung mit wissensbasierten Beratungssystemen. In: ZWF 86 (1991) 2. München: Carl Hanser Verlag, 1991.

/22/ MAKE. Sun OS 4.0 Doku - 10: Programming Utilities and Libraries, Chapter 8. Rev. A, Part Number 800-1774-15, 9 May 1988.

/23/ Meyer, Bertrand: Objektorientierte Software-Entwicklung. Wien: Verlag Carl Hanser 1990.

/24/ N.N.: Dokumentationsrichtlinien für die Klassen des FIKS-Projektes. IAO Stuttgart 1991.

/25/ N.N.: Namenskonventionen im FIKS-Projekt. IAO Stuttgart 1991.

/26/ N.N.: Einführung in das Klassensystem des FIKS-Projektes. IAO Stuttgart 1991.

/27/ Nagl, Manfred: Softwaretechnik: Methodisches Programmieren im Großen. Berlin, Heidelberg, New York, London, Paris, Tokyo, HongKong, Barcelona: Springer Verlag 1990.

/28/ Nicolai, Ulrich: Leitstände im Echtzeit-System zwischen PPS, Lager- und Materialwirtschaft zur Werkstattsteuerung. In: Leitstandsorganisation für die Fertigungssteuerung, V. Fachtagung 12. - 13.06.91. München: Techno Congress, 1991.

/29/ Otterbein, Thomas: Objektorientiertes Datenmodell als Basis für den Fertigungsleitstand der nächsten Generation. In: Congressband VIII zur Online 91 in Hamburg. Velbert: Online GmbH 1991.

/30/ Parnas, D. L.: On the Criteria to Be Used in Decomposing Systems into Modules. Communications of the ACM, vol 5, no. 12, pp. 1053-1058, Dec. 1972

/31/ Pomberger, G.; Bischofberger, W.; Kolb, D.; Pree, W.; Schlemm, H.:Prototyping - Oriented Software Development - Concepts and Tools. Structured Programming 12 (1991), S. 43 - 60.

/32/ Reisch, S.; Lutze, F.W.; Mertins, K.; Albrecht, R.: Industrielle Softwareproduktion für die Fertigungsleittechnik. In: ZWF 86 (1991) 2. München: Carl Hanser Verlag, 1991.

/33/ Sandermann, Heinz: Grundlagen der objektorientierten Programmierung. In Seminarunterlagen zu: Objektorientiertes Programmieren. Köln: Infodas, 1991.

/34/ SCCS. Sun OS 4.0 Doku - 10: Programming Utilities and Libraries, Chapter 7. Rev. A, Part Number 800-1774-15, 9 May 1988.

/35/ Strack, Marei: Optimale Produktionssteuerung. Köln: Verlag TÜV Rheinland, 1986.

/36/ Stroustrup, Bjarne: The C++ Programming Language Second Edition. Bonn; Reading, Mass.; Menlo Park, Calif.; New York; Don Mills, Ontario; Wokingham, England; Amsterdam; Sydney; Singapore; Tokyo; Madrid; Bogota; Santiago; San Juan: Addison Wesley, 1991.

/37/ Tello, Ernest R.: Object-Oriented Programming for Artificial Intelligence. Addison Wesley, 1989.

/38/ Wallmüller, Ernest: Software-Qualitätssicherung in der Praxis. München, Wien: Carl Hanser Verlag, 1990.

/39/ Wiener, Richard S.; Pinson, Lewis J.: An introduction to Object-Oriented Programming and C++. Reading, Mass.; Menlo Park, Calif.; New York; Don Mills, Ontario; Wokingham, England; Amsterdam; Bonn; Sydney; Singapore; Tokyo; Madrid; San Juan: Addison Wesley, 1988.

/40/ Boehm, B.: Software Engineering. In: IEEE Transactions on Computers, Vol. C-25, No. 12, Dec. 1976, S. 1226-1241.

/41/ Lippe, J. von: Bringt die nächste Leitstand-Generation die Integration? ZWF 85 (1990), Nr. 12.

/42/ Ruffing, Thomas: Integrierte Auftragsabwicklung bei Fertigungsinseln. In: Scheer, August Wilhelm (Herausgeber): Fertigungssteuerung - Expertenwissen für die Praxis. München: Oldenbourg Verlag, 1991.

/43/ N.N.: Parallelen zu CIM-Konzepten. Die CZ. 26/88, S. 21.

/44/ DIN Deutsches Institut für Normung e.V. (Herausgeber): Schnittstellen der rechnerintegrierten Produktion (CIM) - Fertigungssteuerung und Auftragsabwicklung. Kommission Computer Integrated Manufacturing (KCIM). Berlin, Köln: Beuth Verlag, 1989.

/45/ Dangelmaier, W.: Auftragssteuerung in einem CIM-Konzept. In: Fertigungstechnisches Kolloquium (FTK). Stuttgart: 1988, S. 37-44.

/46/ Scheer, August Wilhelm: Wirtschaftsinformatik. 3. Auflage. Berlin, Heidelberg: Springer Verlag 1988.

/47/ Bauer, R.; Bowden, J.; Browne, J.; Duggan, J.; Lyons, G.: Shop Floor Control Systems. London, New York, Tokyo, Melbourne, Madras: Chapman & Hall, 1991

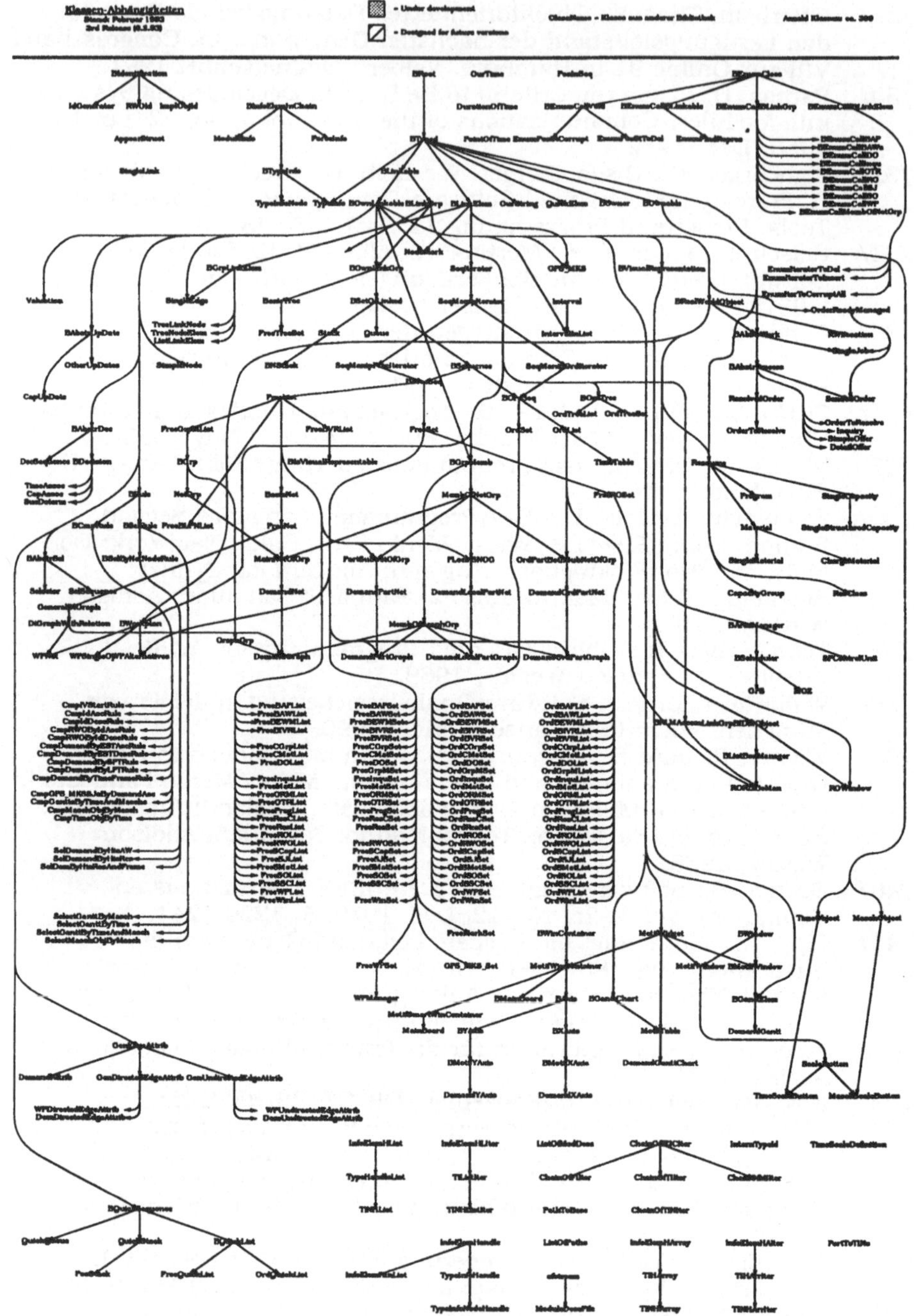
Klassen-Abhängigkeiten
- Under development
- Designed for future versions